Planning Programs for Adult Learners

Planning Programs for Adult Learners

THIRD EDITION

A Practical Guide

Rosemary S. Caffarella and Sandra Ratcliff Daffron

JOSSEY-BASS
A Wiley Imprint
www.josseybass.com

The Jossey-Bass Higher and Adult Education Series

Cover design: Michael Cook

Published by Jossey-Bass

A Wiley Imprint

One Montgomery Street, Suite 1200, San Francisco, CA 94104-4594—www.josseybass.com

Jossey-Bass books and products are available through most bookstores. To contact Jossey-Bass directly call our Customer Care Department within the U.S. at 800-956-7739, outside the U.S. at 317-572-3986, or fax 317-572-4002.

Wiley publishes in a variety of print and electronic formats and by print-on-demand. Some material included with standard print versions of this book may not be included in e-books or in print-on-demand. If this book refers to media such as a CD or DVD that is not included in the version you purchased, you may download this material at http://booksupport.wiley.com. For more information about Wiley products, visit www.wiley.com.

Library of Congress Cataloging-in-Publication Data
Caffarella, Rosemary S. (Rosemary Shelly), 1946-
    Planning programs for adult learners : a practical guide / Rosemary S. Caffarella and Sandra Ratcliff Daffron. —Third edition.
        pages cm.
    Includes bibliographical references and index.
    ISBN 978-0-470-77037-5 (pbk.), ISBN 978-1-118-41824-6 (ebk),
    ISBN 978-1-118-41543-6 (ebk), ISBN 978-1-118-52531-9 (ebk)
        1. Adult education—United States—Administration. 2. Adult education—United States—Planning. I. Daffron, Sandra Ratcliff. II. Title.
LC5225.A34C34 2013
374—dc23

2012045974

Printed in the United States of America

FIRST EDITION

PB Printing   V V10016396_121719

We are dedicating this book to our husbands, Ed Caffarella and John Daffron, and our children, Christy Zaidi, Sarah, Sally, and Casey Ratcliff and their families for their continued support and encouragement in the writing of this book, and the love, laughter, and happiness they bring to our lives.

Our very special thanks to Erin Smith as this book is much richer thanks to her tireless energy and the many hours she gave to us. Erin received her undergraduate degree at Cornell University in Human Development in 2011, and her master's degree in Educational Psychology in May 2012 from the State University of New York at Buffalo, and she is employed by the Human Resources Research Organization (HumRRO). We appreciate her library skills, computer expertise in setting up the many exhibits and applications exercises, her continuous feedback throughout the editing on the content of the book as a newcomer to program planning, and the final copyediting of the book.

Contents

Figures, Exhibits, and Exercises

Figures

Exhibits

Exercises

Figures, Exhibits, and Exercises Available Online

FREE
Premium Content

JOSSEY-BASS™
An Imprint of
⊛WILEY

This book includes premium content that can be
accessed from our Web site when you register at
www.josseybass.com/go/Caffarella
using the password **josseybasshighereducation.**

Figures

Exhibits

Exercises

Foreword

PLANNING EDUCATIONAL PROGRAMS is a pervasive and critical activity in adult education. Being effective in this task is thus a core competency for adult educators regardless of the social and organizational context in which educational programs are offered. These contexts are incredibly diverse as adult educators serve in a variety of roles that include, but are not limited to, leaders and continuing educators in community colleges and higher education; human resource and organizational development specialists in business and government; labor and union educators; social movement educators; instructional developers for distance education; adult literacy educators; community educators and developers at the local, national, and international level; and educators in professional associations. For well over fifty years, adult education scholars have published books and articles to characterize the key elements of the program planning process in order to offer guidance to practitioners engaged in this core professional activity. Among this tremendous array of publications, the Third Edition of *Program Planning for Adult Learners* offers one of the most comprehensive and useful approaches for practitioners who plan educational programs for adults.

Although this book is being published as the third edition, it is the fourth book that Rosemary Caffarella has contributed to the program planning literature. I have been teaching the program planning course in graduate programs since 1980 and first assigned students to read Caffarella's original text, *Program Development and Evaluation Resource Book for Trainers* (Wiley, 1988), in the late 1980s. I have used that book as well as the first edition of *Program Planning for Adult Learners* (1994) and the second edition (2002) with hundreds of students and practitioners in workshops throughout the world over the past twenty-five years. The Interactive Model of Program Planning that forms the backbone of the books has been greatly valued by adult educators in these courses and workshops. As Malcolm Knowles said in the Foreword to the 1994 edition, "Rosemary Caffarella, one of the most effective scholar-practitioners of our era, explores the existing program planning models (which are mostly based on a linear, step-by-step process), extracts the best features of each, and incorporates these features into an essentially new model. This new model transforms program planning from a fundamentally mechanistic operation of following the steps to a creative operation of designing adventures in learning." Sandra Daffron is an outstanding scholar-practitioner who has extensive experience across many social and organizational contexts for adult education. Her scholarship and experience in areas as diverse as adult literacy, judicial education, and community development in global contexts significantly enrich the third edition.

Without a doubt, the special contribution of *Program Planning for Adult Learners* is how the Interactive Model continues to evolve and adapt to new theories and realities. The second and third editions, for example, incorporated the new work on the political and social analyses that Cervero and Wilson offered in our books through the planning table metaphor. This third edition has integrated the relevant literature from the past decade on globalization, culture, and technology, which have so influenced the world in which adult educators now practice. The book is filled with examples and scenarios that illustrate the precepts and advice from the Interactive Model. The checklists in each chapter summarize and remind practitioners what to focus on in their practice. Practitioners and students alike have found these scenarios and checklists to be effective features of the book. It is striking that the Interactive Model continues to grow and develop so that it is clearly relevant to the demands of practice. Thus, it should be useful for practitioners in many diverse planning contexts and should continue to serve as a required text in program planning courses in graduate programs in adult education and related fields.

Finally, we have to be clear about what a program planning model can contribute to strengthening the practice of adult education and related fields. Practitioners will tell you that models do not plan programs, people do. This statement is correct. Forester agrees, but reminds us, "Nevertheless, good theory is what we need when we get stuck. Theories can help alert us to problems, point us toward strategies of response, remind us of what we care about, or prompt our practical insights into the particular cases we confront" (Forester, 1989, p. 12). With the Interactive Model of Program Planning, Caffarella and Daffron provide adult educators and practitioners in related fields a set of intellectual and practical tools to plan effective educational programs for adults.

Ronald M. Cervero
Professor and Associate Dean for Outreach and Engagement
College of Education, The University of Georgia

Preface

PLANNING AND EVALUATING education and training programs for adults is like trying to put together a puzzle. Sometimes we manage to get through the puzzle quickly and feel a real sense of satisfaction that we can do it with such ease. Other times we just cannot figure out how some pieces of the puzzle fit together or we think we are close to finishing but we discover that there seems to be a missing piece, a frustrating yet challenging obstacle. So it is with program planning. Some programs run smoothly from beginning to end. Other programs have minor but fixable glitches, such as presenters being sick or equipment not working. Still other programs seem to wander all over the place, with lots of revisions and changes along the way, and some even stall before they get off the ground. Often, when the norm is an evolving and changing planning process, many of the alternative avenues that must be explored cannot be anticipated. Rather, we find ourselves turning differing pieces various ways to make them fit or having to change the pieces previously matched by what had first appeared to be the same color or pattern, and move them to other parts of the puzzle to see where they might fit better. For example, imagine it is the night before a conference you are organizing and the keynote speaker is stuck at the airport. She had been there most of the day and has just learned that she cannot get a flight out until early tomorrow morning. Unfortunately her presentation was scheduled in the morning. It's time to grab the pieces and reorganize! Gather the program committee, reschedule the keynote speaker to the afternoon, shift some of the afternoon presenters to the morning, track down the presenters to notify them of the changes, and rearrange some room assignments. The keynote speaker arrives the next morning, and a number of program participants comment on their program evaluations that they really appreciated how well the unavoidable dilemma was handled. Even when these seemingly unmanageable issues spring up, programs do have successful endings, and we feel a real sense of accomplishment and satisfaction with our work when this happens. We wrote this book to assist people who take on this challenge of putting together the many "puzzle pieces" that are a normal part of planning programs for adults, whether the puzzle is simple or complex.

Numerous models of planning education and training programs for adult learners exist, ranging from conceptual and data-based studies on program planning to how-to handbooks, guides, and workbooks. Some of these planning models are considered seminal works, such as R. W. Tyler's *Basic Principles of Curriculum and Instruction* (1949), Cyril Houle's *The Design of Education* (1972, 1996), Malcolm Knowles's *The Modern Practice of Adult Education* (1970), and Ron Cervero and Arthur Wilson's *Planning Responsibly for Adult Education: A Guide to Negotiating Power and Interests* (1994). Other authors have provided very useful, but often brief or incomplete descriptions of the planning process. And many of the models have limited application as they are targeted at planners who work in very specific contexts, such as corporate settings, health care organizations, and governmental agencies.

Planning Programs for Adult Learners is distinctive for two major reasons. First, the Interactive Model of Program Planning presented in this third edition both captures and reconfigures classical and current descriptions of the program planning process. The result is a comprehensive eleven-component model, the Interactive Model of Program Planning, which draws on the best conceptual, empirical, and practice knowledge from across a variety of contexts—the corporate sector, continuing education for the professions, public schools, colleges and universities, health care, international development projects, social agencies, nonprofit organizations, governmental agencies, community action programs, religious institutions, and other less formal programs. In addition, the Interactive Model takes into account three key factors that make this model a viable resource for educational planners: the practicality and usefulness as a technical description of the planning process, the emphasis on people being the heart of the process, and the recognition that we live in a globalized world where the diverse culture of the audiences attending education and training programs has become the norm.

Second, *Planning Programs for Adult Learners* provides a concrete framework for program planning and a how-to guide and resource book for practitioners. This eleven-component framework can be applied in many ways, as there is no one best way of planning education and training programs.

Program planners are asked, for example, to select which components of the model to use and when and how to apply these components based on their professional judgment. Smart and effective planners make these decisions in collaboration with other key stakeholders. Planners also may start the process at varying points, focus on only one component at a time, or work on a number of components simultaneously, depending on their specific planning situation. In addition, they also may choose to give some tasks more emphasis than others and may need to revisit components or tasks more than once during the planning process. Therefore, program planning for adults, working within this framework, is an interactive and action-oriented process in which decisions and choices are made about learning opportunities for adults; thus, flexibility is a fundamental norm of the planning process.

The how-to part of *Planning Programs for Adult Learners* serves as a practical guide and provides hands-on resources for staff members who are constantly in the middle of planning one program or another. The many exhibits, figures, and lists presented throughout the text give readers substantial information in a concise and easily usable format. Many of these materials could be used by planning staff to assist them in completing the different tasks required for successful programs. In addition, there are application exercises at the end of each chapter to help readers apply the material addressed within the chapter to their own program planning situations.

This book is intended for novice and experienced people who plan education and training programs for adults in a variety of settings. It is targeted primarily at people who either have or aspire to obtain full- or part-time positions as program planners. These people already have (or will have) major responsibilities related to planning and evaluating education and training programs as all or part of their jobs. Their work settings are diverse, with multiple responsibilities. In addition, there are two other audiences for whom *Planning Programs for Adult Learners* can be helpful. The first is paid staff members who plan education and training programs as only a small but important part of what they do, whether or not planning is a part of their official position descriptions. For example, many staff members who are not identified as program planners, such as managers, supervisors, and subject matter specialists, are expected to plan education and training opportunities for their staff members. The second audience is the legion of volunteers who develop programs for adult learners—from committee and board members of social service agencies to community action groups. The commonality among all the many audiences for this book is that they are all responsible in some way for planning and evaluating programs for adult learners, whether these learners are colleagues, other staff members, customers, external audiences, or the general community.

Overview of the Contents

Planning Programs for Adult Learners is organized into two major parts, followed by a closing chapter that allows readers to revisit the Interactive Model of Program Planning and receive a brief glimpse of the future of program planning. The first three chapters of the book, which constitute the first part of the book, lay the groundwork for the rest of the volume by introducing what program planning is all about—in other words, the Interactive Model that provides the framework for the remainder of the book, and the basic knowledge bases on which the model is grounded. More specifically, Chapter One describes those who plan and sponsor education and training programs, how these programs are planned, the purposes of these programs, and the two major sources that were used in constructing the Interactive Model—the classic and current descriptions of program planning models and approaches; and the practical experiences of program planners. Chapter Two provides an overview of the components and tasks associated with the Interactive Model of Program Planning, the basic assumptions on which this model is grounded, how to determine which parts of the model to use where and when, who finds the model useful, and the importance of ethics in program planning. Chapter Three presents five areas of fundamental knowledge that are especially important in understanding how to design and carry through programs for adults—adult learning, cultural differences, building relationships, power and interests, and technology.

The second part makes the Interactive Model of Program Planning come alive—this framework becomes a working guide for practice. Each of the eleven components of the framework is explained, and practical tips and ideas related to concrete tasks within each of the components are given. The next eight chapters of the book focus on the components that program planners use in designing and evaluating the educational and training programs. Unless program planners pay careful attention to each of these components that are appropriate for the programs they are planning, the chance of meeting the goals and objectives of these programs are slim to none. The topics of these chapters are:

Chapter Four: Discerning the Context

Chapter Five: Building a Solid Base of Support

Chapter Six: Identifying and Prioritizing Program Needs and Ideas

Chapter Seven: Developing Program Goals and Objectives

Chapter Eight: Designing Instruction

Chapter Nine: Devising Transfer of Learning Plans

Chapter Ten: Formulating Program Evaluation Plans

Chapter Eleven: Selecting Formats, Scheduling, and Staffing Programs

The next three chapters center on those components that stress the administrative tasks that are critical to any education and training program being planned. When these components are needed and viewed as secondary or do not receive the consideration they deserve, usually one of two outcomes emerge—programs will be cancelled before the day of the event or program participants will not be happy with the program. The topics of these chapters are:

Chapter Twelve: Preparing and Managing Budgets

Chapter Thirteen: Organizing Marketing Campaigns

Chapter Fourteen: Details, Details, Details

The book closes, as noted earlier, with a chapter that allows readers to revisit the Interactive Model of Program Planning and receive a brief glimpse into what the future might hold for program planners. Highlighted is how the model has changed since its first introduction in 1994. A review of the current model and tasks that make this model a useful and viable resource for practitioners is then provided, followed by a snapshot of what the future might hold for program planners. The chapter concludes with a short personal reflection from the authors on the writing of the third edition of Planning Programs for Adult Learners.

How the Contents of the Book Are Provided

This book is available both in print and e-book formats, with supplementary materials available online at www.josseybass.com/go/Caffarella using the password josseybasshighereducation. The supplementary content includes numerous exhibits, scenarios (or stories) of practice, figures, and application exercises related to all but Chapter Fifteen of the book. These supplementary materials are integral to the content of the book in that they give readers numerous opportunities to expand further their knowledge of the program planning process for adults. These materials may be used simultaneously, which the authors recommend that readers do, or can be accessed when readers want to delve more into specific content areas.

Acknowledgments

WE ARE PLEASED to present this third edition of *Planning Programs for Adult Learners.* The initial edition of this book, which was published in 1994, was inspired by practitioners, students, and colleagues who wanted a sound conceptual model—but one that was grounded in practice, while at the same time usable and practical. We recognize the progression of work in the field since the initial and second editions that has helped to shape and form the concepts presented in this book. In particular, we recognize the issue of globalization and crossing of borders that has made our world smaller and much richer. Although technology advances have provided tools to ease some of the program planning work, much remains the same in using adult education principles and assumptions to plan successful programs. Program planners still recognize the need to establish the right context and environment for learning but can use the results of recent research and apply them to transfer learning to practice.

We wish to thank our graduate students in the College of Education at Cornell University and Western Washington University, and other universities we have been affiliated with over the years, as well as the many practitioners we have worked with throughout our careers. They have inspired us and helped us to write the scenarios and exhibits by example and with conviction. Many insights into the realities of planning programs to bring about change, and the dedication to save lives as a result, were found in Malaysia with breast cancer survivors who tirelessly volunteered.

We appreciate the help and patience of our editor, David Brightman at Jossey-Bass, and the outside reviewers who provided feedback on the 2002 edition, and suggested useful changes for this edition. Fred DiAddezzio, Ed Webster, and Erin Smith gave great insights into the world of marketing programs and using technology. We also appreciate the friendship and encouragement of Sharan Merriam.

The Authors

Rosemary S. Caffarella, Ph.D., is a Professor Emerita of Adult Education and an International Professor in Education. Her Ph.D. is in Adult and Continuing Education from Michigan State University. Her research and writing activities have focused on adult learning, program planning, and designing culturally sensitive programs for adults. Caffarella teaches in three major areas: learning in adulthood, education and community development in international settings, and non-Western and Indigenous ways of learning, knowing, and teaching. In addition, she is a partner in a private consulting firm, Caffarella and Caffarella.

Caffarella's current major research and development project, in collaboration with Universiti Putra Malaysia, Cornell University, and a number of other organizations and individuals from Malaysia, the United States, Australia, and the Netherlands, is in educating Malaysian cancer patients, their families and friends, health care professionals, and the general public about the early detection, treatment, and survivorship for those diagnosed with cancer. As the cofounder and codirector of the Cancer Resource and Education (CaRE) Program in 2003, she provided leadership for the program for seven years, after which leadership was successfully transitioned to the Malaysian staff. The initial major goal of this project was achieved in May 2012—that CaRE would become a sustainable program for and by Malaysians—as a Center of Excellence at University Putra Malaysia. Caffarella continues to work with this program as an advisor and consultant.

Caffarella has authored or coauthored fourteen books, two of which have been translated into Chinese and one into Japanese, and numerous book chapters and articles in refereed journals. Caffarella received the prestigious Cyril O. Houle World Award for Literature in Adult Education for

Learning in Adulthood: A Comprehensive Guide (2nd Ed.) (1999), coauthored with Sharan Merriam in 2000, and then again in 2007 for the third edition (2007) of *Learning in Adulthood,* coauthored by Sharan Merriam, Rosemary Caffarella, and Lisa Baumgartner. In addition, she is the author of *Planning Programs for Adult Learners* (2nd ed., 2002). Caffarella was inducted into the International Adult and Continuing Education Hall of Fame in November 2009; was awarded a Fulbright Specialist Award in 2010; and honored by Springfield College, her undergraduate alma mater, with the Distinguished Alumni Award in 2011.

Caffarella also enjoys her teaching and advising of graduate students, and has been awarded a number of teaching and research awards throughout her career. Outside of Caffarella's educational pursuits she takes pleasure in being with her family and friends, traveling, reading, and advocating for cancer survivors and research.

• • •

Sandra Ratcliff Daffron, Ed.D., is an associate professor of Adult and Continuing Education in Woodring College of Education, Western Washington University, in Bellingham, Washington. Daffron's Ed.D. in Adult and Continuing Education is from Northern Illinois University. Her research and writing activities have focused on program planning, transfer of learning, and e-learning. Daffron teaches in the major areas of leadership, continuing professional education and training, and program planning. She also has a focus on educational policy development in the Middle East and North Africa. In addition, she is the president and chief executive officer of the international consulting firm The Institute for Professional Training and Education (IPT&E).

Daffron divides her time between three areas of research and projects. She collaborates with Rosemary Caffarella and faculty and staff at the Universiti Putra Malaysia in the Cancer Resource and Education program (CaRE) in Malaysia. Daffron also continues to work in developing curriculum, special programs, projects, and assessment of programs for the state courts in the United Sates, and has extensive work and experience with the Administrative Offices of the Courts in the states of Hawaii, Illinois, New York, Utah, and Kentucky. Daffron's third research and developmental project is with policy and model creation for education of the youth of the Middle East and North Africa (MENA) region. Daffron is a frequent lecturer on the experiences of working for the United States Agency for International Development (USAID) for two years on a Rule of

Law project in the West Bank and Gaza (Palestine). She and her husband, John, lived in the West Bank for two years and worked closely with the Palestinian universities and the courts.

Sandra Ratcliff Daffron has over thirty years of experience as a program planner, continuing professional educator, project and program director, administrator, and organizational executive in the United States and the Middle East. She has worked extensively as a trainer and continuing professional educator with lawyers, judges, teachers of adult education, correctional educators, physicians, and United States Army trainers. She has eight years of experience with a court education and reform organization, The American Judicature Society, where she served as executive director, vice president, and assistant executive director. Daffron served as assistant dean for IIT Kent College of Law and assistant director for the Illinois Institute for Continuing Legal Education. She has planned and presented at hundreds of conferences and workshops for the courts and several universities.

This book is Daffron's second; she is the coauthor of *Successful Transfer of Learning,* published in 2011 with Mary North.

Planning Programs
for Adult Learners

Chapter 1

Planning Programs for Adults
What It's All About

PLANNING PROGRAMS FOR adults is like swimming in the ocean. Some days the ocean is calm and welcomes people with open arms. It beckons people, even nonswimmers, to splash and play, jump the waves, float comfortably on their backs, and just enjoy the sun. On calm days like these, program planners, even those who are new at the business, feel like they are on top of the process—all is going smoothly and everyone just seems to agree on what to do, when, and how.

On other days, when the surf is somewhat rough and the waves higher, the ocean provides challenges for even the best of swimmers. On these days nonswimmers may just wade, while more experienced ocean adventurers eagerly dive through crashing waves and ride the surf. Experienced program planners on these rough days find their work especially exciting as they maneuver through the many tasks that just keep coming at them and negotiate with people holding vastly different ideas and agendas. Conversely, novice planners may back away and just let the planning process take its course, unless more experienced planners willingly give them direction and support.

Then there are those stormy days when the ocean is dark and gray and the giant waves grab for anything they can find, toss it around with ease, and pull it every which way. Few people even want to be on the beach, let alone in the water. Both experienced and novice program planners on stormy days would prefer to sit tight, away from the fray, and let whatever develops run its course. But staying on the fringes and not tackling the issues head-on often means disastrous consequences for the planning process; the participants, planners, and other stakeholders; and the program itself. Thinking on their feet and acting in the moment are what usually get planners through these turbulent and unpredictable times.

Playing and swimming in the ocean, even on the calmest days, also offer many surprises, some delightful and some downright frightening. On a chance day, dolphins might be seen leaping up and down close to shore, and for the very lucky swimmers the dolphins may come to swim with them. On another day, dangerous undertows and currents may suddenly grab swimmers and pull them away from where they want to be. So it is with planning programs for adults—some days planners find themselves with unexpected resources and support. Then there are those days when nothing seems to go right no matter what they do, and staying afloat and on track seems hopeless. Program planners can find themselves constantly being pulled in one direction or another, struggling to maintain a course toward their original destinations.

The purpose of this first chapter is to give people who plan programs for adults a glimpse of the what, who, where, why, and how of program planning for adults. To this end, we first describe what education and training programs look like. Next we explore the many roles of people who plan programs, and the variety of settings where these programs are held, followed by an examination of the purposes and primary outcomes of programs for adults. We then discuss how programs are planned, and why planning models are a useful tool in the planning process. We conclude the chapter with an exploration of the two sources on which the model presented in this book, the Interactive Model of Program Planning, is grounded: the classic and current descriptions of program planning approaches and models, and the practical experiences of program planning.

What Programs for Adults Look Like

Education and training programs for adults come in all shapes, sizes, and formats. They vary from highly formal to informal programs. from information or skill sessions lasting only an hour or two to daylong workshops. and from conferences to highly intensive residential study at corporate training centers, universities, and wilderness experiential learning programs. Organizations and groups who sponsor these programs may offer one or more of these kinds of options. For example, a local book club meets once every other week for an hour and a half. They primarily use an open discussion format, with no set parameters. Members like this open-ended way of learning and have resisted efforts by some to make the meetings more formal with moderators and structured questions. They have also chosen not to engage as a group in any other educational activities, such as attending lectures or events hosted by the local bookstore. In contrast, most training programs in corporate settings offer a wide variety of education and training, including courses, workshops, seminars, retreats, and activities like job shadowing and peer coaching. Although employees may choose to attend some of these programs, many are mandatory, such as orientation sessions for new employees and skill updates.

Programs for adults are also planned by or for individual learners, designed for small or large groups of learners, including community-wide programs, and developed at regional, national, and international levels. Methods like individual learning plans and portfolios are used to tailor programs for learners. For group learning experiences, such as workshops and national or international conferences hosted by professional associations, participants come to one location, or they may take a course from work sites, libraries, or from their homes through distance learning.

Finally, some programs are planned for a small, select group of people, such as senior managers from a given organization or cross-country leaders of international programs. Other programs, such as classes and activities sponsored by community recreation programs or senior centers, are open to whoever signs up. Still others are planned for the general public, such as voter forums and civic and community educational activities.

Planners of Education and Training Programs

Education and training programs for adults are planned and coordinated by people in numerous roles who have varied backgrounds and experiences. Chen-Seng, for example, a relatively new training specialist in the international division of a global corporation for Central Asia, is responsible for planning programs for new midlevel managers who have little or no experiences working in this part of the world, and for the most part limited experience working outside of the "Western world." Although he has extensive experience as a manager throughout the Asian region and attended and even assisted as a member of the planning committees for a number of workshops and conferences, Chen-Seng has no formal background in developing education and training programs in the Western world.

Dave, an elementary school principal, does have a bachelor's and master's degree in education, but little experience in planning programs for his adult staff. Yet Dave is expected to respond to a number of state and federal mandates that require his staff to take on new instructional practices. One of the ways he responds to these mandates is through planning and organizing, mostly by trial and error, in-house and districtwide staff development programs. Malcolm, a local volunteer coordinator of a statewide group advocating social justice, also finds himself, like Dave, planning numerous programs, such as community-wide forums and action-oriented events, by "just doing it." Although he and his volunteer staff are highly committed to their work, all of their planning expertise has come from earlier volunteer activities and a few training sessions hosted by the state organization. Unlike the people already described, Katrina, an assistant director of continuing education at a small private college, does have a graduate degree in adult and continuing education and five years of experience as a program specialist in that unit. Still, she finds that the program planning and delivery processes continue to change in many ways, driven mostly by technology and the changing nature of the clientele that her program serves.

Although some staff, like Chen-Seng and Katrina, have clearly defined roles and responsibilities as trainers and program planners and carry official titles such as director of continuing professional education, training specialist, and assistant director of continuing education, many people who plan educational programs for adults do not (Chan, 2010; Kasworm, Rose, & Ross-Gordon, 2010; Shipp, 1998; Winston & Creamer, 1998). For example, supervisors and line administrators, like Dave, are often expected to serve as staff developers and trainers through such mechanisms as coaching, the supervisory process, and even planning formal educational and training programs. Yet their job descriptions may or may not reflect these responsibilities and tasks, and some supervisors are not rewarded or even recognized for their efforts. In addition, many people also give countless hours as volunteer program planners for community groups, professional associations, and nonprofit organizations, as do Malcolm and his volunteer staff. In essence, the centrality of responsibility for the people who plan education and training programs is defined differently depending on their level of responsibility.[1]

Those who have primary roles as program planners spend the majority of their time developing, implementing, and evaluating programs, often with support from other people. In addition, they may take on other tasks, such as organizational development and facilitating change activities (Chan, 2010; Milano & Ullius, 1998; and Rothwell & Cookson, 1997). Others are responsible for program planning tasks as one of their many duties for which they are accountable. Examples of roles that include numerous other responsibilities, in addition to planning programs, are managers of human resource development and volunteer planners. Still others plan programs for adults as more of a tertiary activity, a smaller but often important part of their roles.[2]

Sponsors and Purposes of Education and Training Programs

Many types of organizations sponsor education and training programs for adults (Kasworm, Rose, & Ross-Gordon, 2010; Wilson & Hayes, 2000). As in staff roles, the centrality of these programs to these organizations varies by the mission and goals of the sponsors. For example, providing education and training programs for adults may be the primary mission, such as at continuing education divisions or conference centers, whereas for others, such as professional organizations or cultural institutions, it is a secondary or tertiary mission. In addition, these programs may be sponsored by non-educational organizations (i.e., business and industry, military).[3]

In addition to formal organizations, a number of more informal groups, such as hobby clubs, support groups, book clubs, and community action committees, also provide educational programs for their members.

Education and training programs for adults are conducted for five primary purposes and, as noted earlier, for a variety of audiences (Chan, 2010; Kasworm, Rose, & Ross-Gordon, 2010; Merriam, Caffarella, & Baumgartner, 2007; Wilson & Hayes, 2000):

- Encouraging continuous growth and development of individuals
- Assisting people in responding to practical problems and issues of adult life
- Preparing people for current and future work opportunities
- Assisting organizations in achieving desired results and adapting to change
- Providing opportunities to examine community and societal issues, foster change for the common good, and promote a civil society[4]

Education and training programs often serve more than one purpose. For example, workplace literacy programs are usually designed to assist individuals in developing their language and computation skills while at the same time meeting organizational and societal needs for competent workers.

Change as a Primary Outcome of Education and Training Programs

Implicit in each of these five purposes for conducting education and training programs is the expectation of change as an outcome or result (Hall & Hord, 2011; Ewert & Grace, 2000; Rogers, 2003; Rothwell & Kazanas, 2008; Tennant, 2000). Education and training programs foster three kinds of change: individual, organizational, and community and societal change. Individual change relates to the acquisition of new knowledge, building of skills, and examination of personal values and beliefs. Organizational change leads to new or revised policies, procedures, and ways of working. Community and societal change provides ways for differing segments of society (e.g., members of lower socioeconomic classes, women, ethnic populations, governments, and business enterprises) to respond to the world around them in alternative ways, which can result in positive changes like the civil rights movement in the United States, or other situations where program planning aids in overturn of oppressive governments, for example, during the "Arab Spring." Sample program outcomes in all three categories are outlined in the following subsections.

Sample Outcomes: Individual Change

Older adults who are attending a series of classes on how to use social media are pleased that that they are learning new ways to communicate with their children and grandchildren, which was the major reason they joined these classes. As part of the practice sessions they were asked to communicate with each other using the new systems they were learning, and bring a list of issues they were having in applying what they have learned. The majority of the participants were surprised to find they were enjoying this new form of communication and even making some new friends with members of the class, which they attributed to the practice sessions they had with each other, both in and outside of class. In reflecting on what they learned from this experience, all the participants agreed they were now competent in using the forms of social media they had focused on in the class, and were also eager to keep up with the "latest developments" in this arena. In addition, most were also overjoyed to report that they now were in at least weekly contact, and some daily, with their grandchildren, and with some of their class members, plus they had even begun to contact old friends with whom they had not been in touch for quite a while.

• • •

Sandy is taking an individual spiritual journey to discover what she really believes and how she wants to live her life. This journey was precipitated by the death of her husband and her entrance into middle age. The resources she uses are books, seminars, quiet retreats, friends, and a spiritual guide. She also is committed to being in residence at a spiritual community for a three-month period. After the first six months of her journey she has already decided that she will change her place of residence and the kind of work she does.

Sample Outcomes: Organizational Change

All budget managers of state-level departments in New York State are being asked to adopt a new budgetary system that will be implemented by the state three months from now. In preparation to effectively manage their budgets through this new system, the provider of this system is holding three hour-long training sessions over the next two months, each of which will address a different aspect of this new system. In addition, online tutorials will be available after each training session to assist participants in actually trying out various components of the new system. Supervisors of these budget managers have agreed to provide on-the-job time to actually practice using the system components. Once the two-month training program is completed, the provider will administer a test of each manager's competencies to use the new system. Those who do not pass this test will be required to attend additional training activities related to the specific competencies they are lacking.

• • •

Except for staff members who can demonstrate proficiency in Spanish, all new and current staff members who are responsible for providing information, medical care, and services to patients and their families are required to enroll in an intensive Spanish language program, most of which is web-based. The reason for this requirement is that the patient population has changed drastically in the past three years and now is primarily Hispanic. The end result of the program will be that staff will be able to effectively communicate verbally with customers in both English and Spanish. As part of this organization-wide training initiative, the personnel system will be modified to provide incentives for current staff members who are able to demonstrate or achieve language proficiency.

Sample Outcomes: Community and Societal Change

A nationwide cancer organization will sponsor action workshops on a regional level on how to affect state and national policies related to cancer prevention, treatment, and education. One of the major goals of the workshop is to develop regional and statewide networks of people who will lobby for legislative action in their geographical areas.

• • •

A group of medical personnel has agreed to undergo training, funded by an international nongovernmental organization, for providing medical assistance in low-income countries. They will participate in an online training program, a regional workshop, and a national meeting focused on a wide range of issues related to delivering medical services in low-income countries. In addition, they have agreed to partner with a medical specialist in their area who has given service in these types of settings to learn and practice new techniques that have been shown to work in the countries where they will be practicing. In return for this training they have agreed to spend four to six weeks in a low-income country on a voluntary basis, and provide coaching for other medical personnel in their area who join the program.

● ● ●

Although change of some form is an assumption of most, if not all, education and training programs, the reality of these programs is that planning for change, that is, preparing concrete and workable transfer of learning plans, is often overlooked (see Chapter Nine). Contextual factors that affect the change process, such as organizational constraints and political and economic realities, are also not routinely taken into account (see Chapter Four). Rather, people responsible for planning and implementing education and training programs have assumed that those attending these programs will be able to apply what they have learned, without planned assistance and support being an integral part of the programs they deliver. In addition, those who are responsible for ensuring that the desired changes actually take place rarely allocate enough time for the changes to be integrated into the daily lives of those affected, especially when these changes are major. As Hall and Hord (2011) so astutely observe: "Change is a process and not an event. In other words, change is not accomplished by having a one-time announcement by an executive leader [other people, or even oneself], a two-day workshop . . . , and/or the delivery of the [most up-to-date technology or other resources]. Instead change is a process through which people and organizations move as they gradually come to understand, and become skilled and competent in the use of new ways" (p. 4).

How Education and Training Programs Are Planned

Some education and training programs are carefully planned, others are literally thrown together, and still others are thoughtfully planned in an organized matter.[5] Although the second process may appear to be fairly logical and orderly, progressing from discerning the context to identifying ideas to program design and implementation to transfer and evaluation activities, it often is not.[6] For most people who develop and coordinate education and training programs, the progression seems to be more a mass of decisions, political maneuverings, negotiations, details, and deadlines than precise and clear steps of what should be done, when, where, by whom, and how.

Careful planning of education and training programs also does not guarantee their success, nor does it mean that all tasks will run smoothly and people-related problems will not arise. Instead a lot can and does go wrong, some of which is in the planner's control, some of which is not. This lack of certainty in the planning process can be overwhelming, especially to novice planners, but also to more experienced ones. One avenue that helps many planners get through this maze of tasks, people issues, and political agendas is to have a guide or road map of the planning process to assist them in getting from start to finish. A program planning model is one way to provide this needed guide. Program planning models consist of ideas of one or more persons about how programs should be put together and what ingredients are necessary to ensure successful outcomes. These models come in all shapes and sizes. Program planning models may be simplistic in their orientation—with steps one through five, for example— or very complex, using highly developed flowcharts or in-depth qualitative descriptions to depict a comprehensive array of issues and decision points (e.g., Cervero & Wilson, 2006; Green & Keuter, 2005; Knowles, 1980; Sork, 2010).

Sources for the Model

The Interactive Model of Program Planning, the model presented in this book, is derived from two major sources. These include: (1) the classic and current descriptions of program planning approaches and models, and the concepts and ideas related to each approach; and (2) the practical experiences of program planners. The authors share this foundational knowledge as well as the voices of practitioners to help provide an understanding of how the Interactive Model was constructed and has since evolved, and to credit the many individuals that have assisted with this process along the way (Caffarella, 1994, 2002). Discussed first are three approaches to program planning, followed by a description of practitioners who have assisted in reformulating the model.

Approaches to Planning Programs

Three of the most often used approaches to planning programs are: the conventional or traditional approach; the pragmatic or practical approach; and the radical approach. The revision of the Interactive Model of Program Planning presented in this book is drawn from each of these ways of thinking about program planning as illustrated by the following approaches. Linkages are made to each of these approaches with both the revised model as well as the first two renditions of the model (Caffarella, 1994, 2002).

Conventional or Traditional Approach

The conventional or traditional approach as described by Sork (2010) "labels those ways of thinking about planning that are still largely grounded in the technical rational tradition" (p. 7), which in essence means planning programs primarily in a stepwise progression, where you move logically through the planning process. The majority of writers, at least in education and related fields, have constructed their frameworks for planning within this conventional approach. Major voices have developed models using this approach and include the seminal work of Tyler (1949), Houle (1972), and Knowles (1970). Other models framed primarily in the conventional approach have been developed in a number of fields and settings, such as health care (Green & Kreuter, 2005), human resource development (Allen, 2006), residential wilderness programs (Day & Petrick, 2006), human service programs (Kettner, Moroney, & Martin, 2008), adult education (Boone, Safrit, & Jones, 2002), social work (Netting, O'Connor, & Fauri, 2008), and student affairs administration (Claar & Cuyjet, 2000). Manuel, in Scenario 1.1, illustrates the conventional or traditional approach to program planning.

 SCENARIO 1.1:   KNOWING WHAT TO DO

Manuel, who is director of Training and Human Resource Development at a major corporation, has been asked by his manager to put together a one-day training program for key administrative support staff to be held in two days. Because a recall of one of their hottest selling products would be announced at week's end, Manuel's task is to conduct a fast-tracked training program so that staff members can respond effectively to their supervisors, and put themselves in a crisis-response mode. Manuel was caught by surprise, but knowing the importance of the task, he attacks it with a fury. Thank goodness he has a step-by-step playbook that he uses when he finds himself in need of putting a program together with little, if any lead time, and he has found it for the most part to be foolproof. Manuel also knows that his training program will be the model that other trainers will use, both within the organization and in other locations where the company is located.

Planners who act out of this approach believe the best way to get a program done right is to follow a systematic path from needs assessment through evaluation. Once the program is planned there is little if any change in how it is carried out, and the program objectives should match how the program is carried through, which in turn should match the program outcomes. In addition, others should be able to use the same program in similar settings, with few modifications, no matter whether they are in the United States, Nigeria, or Australia.

The Interactive Models of Program Planning, presented in editions one and two of this book, have primarily been categorized as conventional models, although these authors would argue that they have never viewed the model as a stepwise progression, but rather as one that could be entered at any point in the model; the second edition (Caffarella, 2002; Daffron, 2005) also included other approaches to program planning, as is noted later in this section. However, most of the components of these models, except for transfer of learning, are included in the majority of conventional models, and many authors from this approach have informed our work.

Pragmatic or Practical Approach

The pragmatic or practical approach, or adopting planning to what Friedmann (2008) has termed "real-world constraints," takes into consideration the continuing changing conditions and the complexity of practice. Rather than planning in a stepwise fashion, which assumes you can end up with the results you initially state up front, this approach recognizes that changes will be made throughout the process, and at times planners may not even be sure where they are going as they run into novel or surprising situations. A health care worker in Bangladesh demonstrates this approach.

 SCENARIO 1.2: THE COMPLEXITY OF PRACTICE

Fatima, a health care worker in Bangladesh working with an international nongovernment organization and a major research hospital from the United States, knows that she is working in a complex and difficult situation in developing a breast cancer education program in her home country. Breast cancer, although a deadly cancer for women, is just not talked about among women and often not even in families when a woman has been diagnosed with the disease. In essence, breast cancer is a taboo subject, and one of her main tasks will be to make it an acceptable conversation among women, and also in the public sphere, especially by policymakers and governmental and nongovernmental agencies committed to women's health. But for this change to happen, which could lead to more women surviving the disease, Fatima is well aware that ways of thinking about breast cancer, and especially early diagnosis of the disease, must be changed. She is intrigued by what she has been learning from a more experienced program planner about alternative approaches to program planning, and decides, in consultation with her colleagues and survivors of the disease, to choose the practical approach, which acknowledges cultural norms, the complexity of the problem to be addressed, the willingness to confront tough issues, and flexibility in the planning process.

In more recent years, a number of scholars and practitioners have worked hard at making their colleagues believe the situations in which planners find themselves do have a major influence in how they respond to the many voices clamoring to be heard. Among those who have made a difference in merging the reality of the specific and wider contexts in which planners find themselves with the process of planning are Cervero and Wilson (1994, 2006), Forester (1999, 2009), and Netting, O'Connor, and Fauri (2008). The authors find the issues they raise, through the "telling of stories" by practitioners or via theoretical and conceptual frames, very helpful, perplexing, and challenging.

In addition, within the practical approach, two additional sources have addressed other aspects that speak to the everyday experiences of practitioners. Sork (2010) has again reminded planners of the "artistic nature of planning." He uses the image of improvisational theatre where as "the story unfolds the characters come and go, the best and worst of human nature is on display, surprises occur, dilemmas arise, decisions are made, and relationships are forced and strained" (p. 19).

Gboku and Lekoko (2007) have brought to the forefront planning in different parts of the world. Specifically, they have developed a program planning model from an African perspective which, even though it consists of many of the same components as displayed in conventional models, is to be interpreted through the different lens of African knowledge and experience. Gboku and Lekoko (p. 45) ask planners to adhere to a set of critical practices, a sampling of which includes:

- Appreciation and understanding of African indigenous knowledge and experience and have the capacity to integrate the two into program development

- Gearing content toward integration of the individuals into their communities and the wider African society

- Stakeholder commitment to ensure African solutions to meeting the needs of adult learners

These authors encourage planners to think differently about practicing in nations other than their own, and to explore how the realities of these countries make a major difference in their practice as planners.

More recently, Bracken (2011) and Ryu and Cervero (2011) have also brought to the forefront, although in very different ways, the importance that context and culture play in program planning. Bracken (2011), drawing from "a critical ethnographic study of a Latin American feminist community-based organization," discusses "the centrality of feminist identity to understanding and analyzing day-to-day program-planning process issues within" these types of organizations (p. 121). One of her findings focuses on the theme of leveraging power in the community as one of the core competences women in such organizations need to demonstrate to effectively negotiate in the community when representing a feminist organization. Among the strategies described within this theme are using contextual-based methods, assessing and managing risk, and building alliances with nonfeminist groups. Ryu and Cervero (2011), through in-depth interviews of planners in Korea, illuminated how Confucian values "shape the way in which program planners construct educational programs" (p. 156) and influence the exercise of power and negotiations of power and interests. More specifically, they found that the following values "were mentioned throughout the course of this study: (a) group harmony, (b) respect of hierarchy, (c) propriety, (d) face, (e) bond of affection; and (f) distinctive gender roles" (p. 146).

Practitioners in the pragmatic approach are willing to confront tough issues; facilitate difficult meetings; are flexible; and openly address issues of power and control, often in creative ways. In addition, they carefully access the context and culture in which they are working, which they view as an important determinate of what direction a program should take. They adopt strategies such as negotiation, listening, willingness to learn, respecting differences, dialogue, and debate to address these types of issues.

In addition, they ask planners to think of the planning process in different images as well as through different ways of knowing, thinking, and acting in the reality of the everyday life of those with whom they plan. Although the experiences of practitioners were included as part of the sources used to develop the original Interactive Model of Program Planning (Caffarella, 1994), the model has taken more fully into account these experiences in the second edition, and in the revised model (Caffarella, 2002).

Radical Planning

The radical approach to program planning, with its focus on social activism, democratic principles, and transformation, has a long history, dating back to the eighteenth century (Beard, 2003). Many social movements come to mind when thinking of the radical approach to planning—Gandhi's commitment to peaceful societal reform; the workers' and civil rights movements; and the uprisings in the Arab world and in countries in Africa. Although not often discussed in the adult education literature in these terms, societal change—whether social, economic, or political—as a goal of program planning has had many advocates over the years (Alinsky, 1969; Brookfield & Holst, 2011; Freire, 1970; Newman, 1995, 2006; Beard, 2003; Cervero & Wilson, 2006; Forester, 2009; Holst & Brookfield, 2009). There are very few "models" of program planning that have emanated from this approach. Rather, concepts and ideas about important aspects to consider in working within this framework—such as power, conflict, negotiation, democratic ideals, cooperative and participatory planning, and social learning—are the major contributions from these practitioners and scholars. The radical approach to program planning is illustrated in Scenario 1.3, through the way Mustafa, a community developer and educator, works.

SCENARIO 1.3: FACING SEVERE SOCIAL, ECONOMIC, AND POLITICAL PROBLEMS

Mustafa is employed as a community developer and educator for an international nongovernmental agency (NGO) based in Australia that is known for its ability to work in low-income countries and has a focus on effectively assisting grassroots movements related to pressing social and economic issues. He has just relocated to serve as the director of Development and Training at a new branch of this NGO in South Sudan, the newest nation and poorest country in Africa. Mustafa is well aware how difficult this assignment will be from choosing which needs to target to meaningfully involving local participation and activism toward common goals and objectives. In addition, South Sudan is still a country with an uncertain future, where insecurity, hunger, and ethnic and tribal conflict abound (Gettleman, 2011). Mustafa knows that his only real choice is making a difference in one small, but important area of need for the people of Sudan, which calls for radical change. However, he must move slowly and deliberately at first, and listen closely to the voices of key stakeholder groups like government officials, other NGOs, and, most important, to those who will be most directly affected by the organization's interventions. Therefore, his first six months will be spent in gaining a clearer understanding of the context in which he is working and the major problems, as well as building relationships with those in power and "grassroots" leaders.

The image of the planning table, as explored by Cervero and Wilson (2006), is especially potent from this approach when asking such questions as: Who is allowed at the table? Who is being listened to and who is being ignored? Which voices constantly get in the way of the planning process? There is some overlap between the pragmatic and radical approach as viewed through the lens of both approaches; however, the major difference between these two approaches is the willingness of those from the radical approach to confront and work through pressing social, economic, and political issues, such as environmental concerns, repressive leaders of communities and nations, and abject poverty. In addition, a hallmark of this approach is the participation of those most affected by these issues from the initial design of the program plan through evaluation and transfer of learning.

Practitioners using the radical approach spend quite a bit of time up front in gaining a clear understanding of the nature of the problems they will address. They listen well to those most affected by the issues and conflicts presented by these problems. A major portion of this up-front time is spent building relationships with potential program participants, which requires them to welcome new ways of thinking and being in the world. This entry process often requires them either to modify plans they had in mind or abandon them completely and start from scratch to create even a chance of making any kind of lasting change related to the workings of the current social, political, or economic systems. They also are very aware of the factor of time as part of the process, as are those who plan primarily through the pragmatic approach. They embrace the fact that these kinds of changes at the community or societal level can take many years, and therefore must focus on program capacity building and sustainability, developed in partnerships with local leadership (Caffarella, 2009). Major ideas from this approach have been incorporated in constructing the redesigned Integrative Model of Program Planning.

Practitioners' Voices

As noted earlier in this chapter, the second source used in developing the Interactive Model is the practical experience of program planners. This bank of experiences is generated by scholars who ground their work in the stories and context of actual planning situations, the authors' own experiences, and other professionals whose daily work is planning programs in a wide variety of settings.

Authentic Planning Experiences Captured by Scholars

Scholars who have provided fascinating glimpses of the program process include Pennington and Green (1976); Cervero and Wilson (1994, 2006), Gboku and Lekoko (2007); and Forester (1999, 2009). Pennington and Green (1976) were among the early scholars to challenge the assumption that program planners always follow specific models of planning and include all the steps in those models. Although they found that planners could identify a clear set of tasks and decision points, they saw major discrepancies between what planners did and what popular models of program planning said they should do. For example, comprehensive needs assessments were rarely conducted as the basis for program development, and often those designing the actual instructional activities did not take into account the background, characteristics, and experiences of the particular group of learners who were to attend the program.

Three of these scholars have used the stories of authentic planning situations that they observed as well as conducted extensive interviews of the planners to capture what they actually were doing (Cervero & Wilson, 2006, 1994; Forester, 1999, 2009). Cervero and Wilson, both of whom have many years of experience as planners, chose three narratives, which they use throughout their work, to illustrate the rich ideas that they discuss, both in terms of the practice itself as well as in confirming new ways to think about planning. They found that power, personal interests, ethical commitment, and negotiation "are central to the planners' everyday work" (2006, p. vii). They became very aware that, yes, planners do influence the planning process, but the other players in the process and the context of where this process is taking place influence these planners' decisions and actions. In other words, program planning is an interactive and action-oriented process in which decisions and choices are made that do not follow the conventional approach to planning, even though the authors link their stories to specific components of planning, such as needs assessment, instructional design and implementation, and the administrative aspects of programs (Cervero & Wilson, 2006).

Forester (1999, 2009) developed what he terms "practitioner profiles," which are highly descriptive of the specific everyday practice of planners. He uses profiles, captured from a wide variety of places (e.g., the desperately poor cities in the United States, cities in Israel, rural Venezuela, and the native homeland of the Hawaiians). Narrative accounts of planners came from environmental specialists, planning consultants, community developers, architect-planners, and university-based planners. Forester tackles many topics such as cultivating surprises, exploring values-based disputes, envisioning possibilities, recognizing opportunities in the face of conflicts, and encouraging transformational learning experiences. As Forester observes: "These stories illuminate complex and messy situations of real life no less than they portray the tragic choices citizens face in a world of deep conflict" (1999, p. 15). Therefore to promote a useful interaction and dialogue to address this messiness, program planners "must *facilitate* conversation . . . , must *moderate* an argument, . . . and to promote successful negotiations . . . must *mediate* proposals for action" (2009, p. 7, italics in the original).

An international perspective has been added by Gboku and Lekoko (2007) about the importance of culture and place, in this case Africa, to the planning process. They point out how the "experiences of slavery, imperialism, colonialism and apartheid have contributed much to changing African attitudes, values, ways of thinking and, ultimately ways of acting" (p. 10). However, they also stress the traditional ways and principles on which many of the African societies were based, such as "acting in a co-operative and collaborative manner, . . . and connectedness as opposed to individualism" (p. 10). Therefore "programmes that are well negotiated with their perspective learners in association with local authorities and leaders are likely to be more effective than programs that are simply put to offer" (Oxenham, et al., 2002, p. 3, as cited by Gboku and Lekoko, 2007, p. 11).

Experiences of Those Immersed in Planning Programs

The experiences that practitioners themselves bring to the planning table were also very useful in constructing the Interactive Model, and especially the vignettes used throughout the book to illustrate ways of thinking and acting within planning situations. The authors of this book have both lived through many a harried planning process, observed others in these roles, and have gathered stories over the years from students and colleagues.

One of the authors remembers well a two-day conference she was planning in Maine. Unfortunately, a winter storm was predicted for the day before this conference was to open, which had the potential to disrupt travel both for the participants coming from all over the state of Maine as well as four of the major speakers, who were coming from out of state. The planning team breathed a sigh of relief when on the day before the conference there was only rain in Maine. What a surprise to learn later that day that Boston had gotten a great deal of snow, which is surprising as it is south of Maine, and all of the presenters, one of whom was the opening speaker, were stuck in the Boston airport and could not get a plane out to where the conference was being held until the next afternoon. By that time the planners knew that the majority of the participants, who were coming fairly long distances, were on their way or already in Orono. So the planning committee quickly met and reframed all of the activities for the first day of the conference; within three hours they had all the resources in order, including confirmation from the out-of-state presenters of their flights for the next day. Though they needed to do a bit of explaining at the opening session that the "conference order" had changed, the meetings all went well, despite what could have been a last-minute disaster.

Both authors also have learned and continue to learn about what works and doesn't work in their roles as program planners and program participants. "Fond memories" of workshops and conferences abound where the planners and facilitators did an excellent job. Both of these authors remember well a research conference they attended that went off without a hitch. Were they ever proud of the planning committee, consisting mainly of students, who pulled it off so well. These students had worked long hours, and paid close attention to "the big picture," such as matching the theme of the conference to the call for papers, and ensuring the venue included a taste of the local foods and a boat trip that highlighted the beautiful site where the meeting was held. In addition, the planning committee considered all of the detail work that can make or break a conference, such as travel arrangements among different physical spaces where conference activities were housed, special meals that met the needs of conference participants, and hosts being provided to the speakers and VIPs to help them with their needs at the conference.

The authors are in awe of models of program planning through technical efforts such as that of Wael Ghonim, head of marketing for Google in the Middle East and North Africa. Ghonim is credited for energizing the protests and demonstrations in Egypt in January 2011 that led to the revolution in Egypt that is still not at rest. He created one of the most visited web sites in the Arab World and brought Egyptians together for the revolution through blogs, Twitter, Facebook, and LinkedIn—a model of program planning with social networks. His social network model has spread throughout the world and is credited with uprisings in many more countries.

Colleagues and students of the authors are always ready to share their experiences, both formally in class and informally over coffee or dinner. One young man from Africa, who had worked in poor rural India for a summer putting programs together for mothers related to the health of their children, found the experience to be fascinating and frustrating at the same time. Although he spoke his native language and English well, he did not speak Hindi, the language of the people with whom he was working. The mothers kept wondering what he was saying and always wanted to hear him talk, though they could not understand him, even when he was talking with his colleagues. Although he was stumped at times as to how he could best be part of the team, he found ways to work around the language difficulty (e.g., using hand signals, pictures, and a translator to assist with any discussions and conversations he had with them). Another of his colleagues on this venture was Anu, a woman from Nepal. Unlike Joseph, Anu could speak Hindi as she lived close to the India border, and she found the experience to be fulfilling in terms of what she could bring to these mothers, and a great learning experience. Knowing Joseph from previous programs prior to going into this experience, she was especially helpful to him in communicating with the mothers.

E-mail is another way the authors have received feedback on the book. One of the authors received an e-mail from a student, Cecilia Hutchinson, who just completed a class in program planning at the University of Alberta in Canada. Cecilia provided feedback related to an assignment she was asked to do in class, a series of two-page reflection papers on topics of their choice (personal correspondence, March 2009). Among the topics she chose was one of the assumptions on which the Interactive Model was grounded in the second edition of the program planning book (Caffarella, 2002). This assumption, focused on diversity and cultural differences, stated that "People who plan programs for adults are sensitive to diversity and cultural differences in many forms" (p. 27). Cecelia rightly observed that this assumption, for some, if not perhaps many people who are involved in program planning, "is dangerous because it gives the learner the impression that anyone interested in program planning is automatically knowledgeable about and interested in diversity and cultural difference. In fact, the majority of individuals, including myself, know little about cultural differences and how to prepare for or react to situations in which we experience diversity and difference. In my opinion, the assumption that Caffarella makes about program planners' depth of knowledge glosses over the complexity of the subject and makes light of a very weighty social issue" (personal communication, December 2009).

Her timely critique, coupled with the authors' and colleagues' similar experiences as program planners in diverse cultures, has been taken into account in this edition of the book, resulting in reframing the wording of this assumption (see Chapter Two). In addition, as a result of these observations, more information on cultural differences and how to address these differences has been added as one of the foundational elements in using the model (see Chapter Three). Moreover, integrated throughout the book are the ways planners can apply this knowledge to their work as well as examples from practice.

In essence, these authors have learned through years of experience, as both scholars and practitioners of program planning, that in building models of this practice it is important to understand the theory and research on which program planning is based, but also the reality of what it takes to plan an effective and workable program. There is no one "right way" to plan programs for adults. Rather, program planning is a continuous journey consisting of twists and turns, wide expansive views, and an ever-changing landscape, meaning that what has worked today may or may not work tomorrow.

Chapter Highlights

Variety and difference are key words that characterize the what, who, where, why, and how of planning education and training programs for adults. These programs take on many forms, including formal and informal learning situations, and use many different formats (e.g., half-day workshops, three-day conferences, informal study groups, and support networks). As such there are a number of areas that are important for program planners to know:

- People who plan programs, including paid staff and volunteers, have diverse backgrounds and experiences. In addition, for some (i.e., training specialists, continuing professional educators) program planning is central to their work, whereas for others it is not considered a major or even secondary part of what they do (i.e., supervisors, content specialists).

- A variety of organizations sponsor programs for adults, and the centrality of these programs to these organizations varies according to the mission and goals of the sponsoring groups.

- Education and training programs for adults are conducted for five primary purposes: (1) encouraging ongoing growth and development of individuals; (2) assisting people in responding to practical problems and issues of adult life; (3) preparing people for current and future work opportunities; (4) assisting organizations in achieving desired results and adapting to change; and (5) providing opportunities to examine and foster community and societal change.

- Changes in individuals, organizations, and the wider community are the driving force and one of the underlying themes that link together all types of education and training programs for adults.

- Some education and training programs are carefully planned, while others just seem to be thrown together. In addition, although on the surface program planning seems like a very rational and orderly endeavor, those involved know that it is often chaotic and unsystematic in nature.

- The Interactive Model of Program Planning, the focus of this book, is derived from two major sources. These include: (1) the classic and current descriptions of program planning approaches and models; and (2) the practical experiences of program planners.

- Three program approaches, which originated from the examination of the classic and current descriptions of program planning, are: the conventional or traditional, the pragmatic or practical, and the radical. Each of these approaches has informed how the Interactive Model is constructed and use.

- The practical experiences of program planners are brought into this version of the Interactive Model of Program Planning through the voices of scholars who have captured authentic planning situations by listening to and observing the planners involved; and stories of practice situations the authors have experienced over their careers.

The next chapter explores the components and tasks that make up the Interactive Model of Program Planning and the assumptions upon which this model is grounded. The chapter also addresses which components of the model to use and when, who has found the model useful, and the ethical issues planners face in their daily work.

Notes for Additional Online Resources

1. See Figure 1.A: Centrality of Responsibility for Education Programs and Training.

2. For illustrations of each of these roles, see Scenarios 1.A: Program Planning as a Primary Responsibility; 1.B: Program Planning as One of Multiple Responsibilities; and 1.C: Program Planning as a Tertiary Responsibility.

3. See Exhibit 1.A: Examples of Education and Training Programs for Adults.

4. For specific examples of each of these purposes, see Exhibit 1.B: Examples of Program Purposes.

5. See Scenarios 1.D: Throwing Together a Program and 1.E: Planning Thoughtfully.

6. See Scenario 1.F: Despite Perfect Planning.

Application Exercises

This chapter's first application exercise helps you understand your role as a program planner in your organizational setting. The final two exercises assist you in defining the purpose of your education and training programs, and reflect on the approach or approaches to use as a program planner.

EXERCISE 1.1

Understanding the Roles of Program Planners
in Organizational Settings

1. List your present title and give a brief job description.

_____

_____

_____

_____

2. Is the role of program planner a formal part of your job description?

_____Yes _____No

   If no, what roles, if any, do you play as a program planner?

_____

_____

_____

_____

3. Outline, on the following chart, the personnel in your organization (or a specific subunit of your organization) who are responsible for planning and conducting educational programs. Indicate whether this responsibility is a formal or informal part of their job. Then outline the tasks each person does as part of this work.

Position, Name, and Program	Formal or Informal Responsibility	Tasks Related to Educational Programming
_____	_____	_____
_____	_____	_____
_____	_____	_____
_____	_____	_____
_____	_____	_____
_____	_____	_____

4. How might those who do program planning in your unit and/or organization be supportive of each other's efforts? List specific suggestions below.

_____

_____

_____

_____

EXERCISE 1.2

Defining the Purpose of Education and Training Programs

1.   Within the framework outlined below, list examples of education and training programs you have participated in or planned within the last two to three years.

To encourage continuous growth and development of individuals

_____

_____

_____

_____

To assist people in responding to practical problems and issues of adult life

_____

_____

_____

_____

To prepare people for current and future work opportunities

_____

_____

_____

_____

To assist in achieving desired results and adapting to change

_____

_____

_____

_____

To provide opportunities to examine and foster change related to societal and global issues

_____

_____

_____

_____

2.   Highlight the positive points of these experiences as either participant or planner and indicate what problems or disappointments you encountered.

_____

_____

_____

_____

_____

EXERCISE 1.3

Approaches to Program Planning

1.   For those with experience as program planners, reflect on your own ways of working and thinking as a program planner, and select one or more of the approaches to planning that you use or have used in planning programs for adults. Explain why you chose to use either one or more of these approaches, and why you believe this approach or these approaches work for you.

_____

_____

_____

_____

_____

_____

_____

_____

_____

_____

2.   For those with little or no experience as program planners choose which approach or approaches you might use in planning programs for adults. Explain why you might use either one or more of these approaches, and why you believe this approach or these approaches could work for you.

_____

_____

_____

_____

_____

_____

_____

_____

_____

_____

Chapter 2

Introducing the Interactive Model of Program Planning

MANY TYPES OF people, as described in Chapter One, are called upon to plan educational programs for adults. Some have advanced degrees in adult education or related fields whereas others have no formal education or experience in this arena, nor do they necessarily have the knowledge, skills, or abilities to become program planners. Program planning is challenging with its many components that must be addressed, such as knowing well the situations in which planners work, conducting needs assessments, and acting in multiple roles from instructor to grant writer. In addition, program planners find themselves handling what seems like thousands of details, which if not addressed well can go horribly wrong and ruin a program. People who are new to program planning may find some or even all of their new roles a bit daunting, as illustrated in Scenario 2.1.

 SCENARIO 2.1:   FEELING CONFIDENCE: YES, BUT ALSO NO

Ashley, an experienced nurse, has just been appointed the director of education for a medium-size hospital. As director she will be responsible for planning all of the educational programs and related services that the center offers to patients and their families, health care professionals, and the general public. Ashley feels confident about the administrative aspects of the job as she has worked as a manager of nurses in two different settings. She also has had quite a bit of experience teaching through her roles as a "bedside educator" and an instructor in many different kinds of programs, such as continuing education workshops for nurses and outreach programs for targeted groups, such as caregivers, and the general public. However, Ashley feels less competent about her ability to take on the planning of the wide variety of programs for which she will be responsible. As Ashley takes on her new role as director she is especially concerned about three major programs, which she is expected to plan all during the same time frame, and she is not sure where to start.

Even experienced program planners find themselves mired in a complex maze of the tasks and numerous details that must be done "right now" for a program to function, and wonder how they might change their practice to be more effective and efficient in their jobs (see Scenario 2.2).

 SCENARIO 2.2:   CHANGING WAYS OF PLANNING

Due to recent budget cuts, the staff positions in the Office of Continuing Education at a community college have been reduced from five to two, including the director. Joe, who is an experienced program planner, is miffed about the decision to cut staff because the program has been a moneymaker for the college and has served the community well. Joe has primarily been responsible for the numerous connections that the office has with the businesses in the area, and has designed many programs in cooperation with those organizations by meeting their specific needs. Needless to say, this type of planning has taken a great deal of time through face-to-face meetings, which Joe has not minded, but now he has also been asked to take on other major programming responsibilities, and is unsure of how he will ever get it all done. One of his close colleagues has just begun to plan the majority of her programs via technology and speculates whether this strategy might help him in this dilemma to save time and money. The more Joe thinks about it he could hold some of these planning meetings, especially the second and third meetings, by Skype calls without losing the relational aspects of planning that he knows are important to get the job done well.

It is these kinds of common situations in which program planners realize that it would be very helpful to have a program planning model to guide them through what goes into planning effective and enjoyable learning programs. Having a practical set of materials on their shelves, stored in their computer files, and access to online resources can save countless hours of trying to figure out what to do.

In this chapter we first provide a description of the Interactive Model of Program Planning, including the major components of the model and the tasks that need to be addressed within each component of the model. We follow this description with an outline of the assumptions upon which the model is grounded, and then an exploration of how to determine which components of the model to use and when, and who finds this model useful. We close the chapter with an examination of the importance of ethics in program planning.

Description of the Interactive Model of Program Planning

The Interactive Model of Program Planning for adults, which is shown in Figure 2.1, displays the eleven components that compose this model. In addition, depicted in this figure are the five areas of foundational knowledge that are especially important for program planners to understand in both designing and carrying through programs for adults—adult learning,

FIGURE 2.1

The Interactive Model of Program Planning

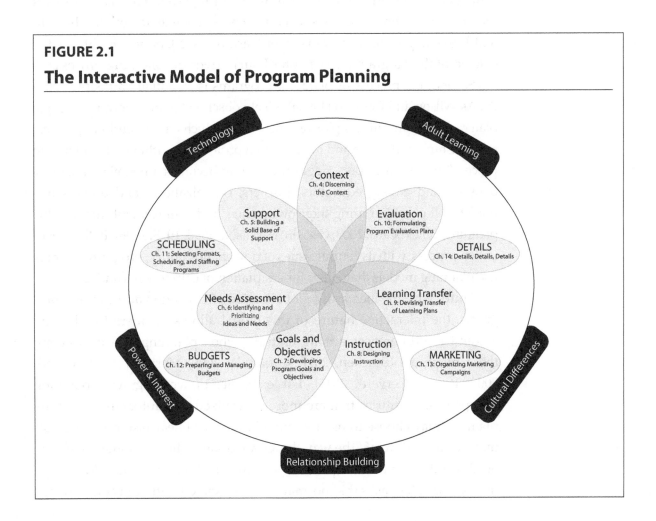

cultural differences, power and interests, relationship building, and technology (see Chapter Three). This model is presented as a guide, not a blueprint for practice, and represents a way of thinking about program planning that is interactive in nature.

There are four major differences between this model and other models of program planning, which tend to be more linear. First, the model has no real beginnings or endings. In other words, planning programs is rarely, if ever, a linear step-by-step process (Houle, 1996; Morell, 2010; Netting, Connor, & Fauri, 2008; Sloane-Seale, 2001). Rather, persons responsible for planning programs for adults may find all of the components are applicable or they may use the relevant parts of the model in any order and combination based on the planning situation (see Chapter Four). In addition, program planners often work with a number of planning components and tasks at the same time and not necessarily in any standard order. For example, in planning a large national conference, the logistics of the meeting (such as place, date, and time) often have to be handled before the theme or objectives of the conference are determined. In planning other programs, a needs assessment may be the starting point (see Chapter Five), whereas for others the content (see Chapter Seven), transfer of learning (see Chapter Eight), or the context of the program (see Chapter Four) drives the planning process.

Second, the process of planning programs is essentially a people activity. As Wilson and Cervero (1996a) wisely observe: "in our view, real people plan real programs in complex organizations, which have traditions, political relationships, and needs and interests that profoundly influence the planning process" (p. 6). Therefore, program planning becomes a negotiated activity between and among educators, learners, organizations, and other stakeholders, all of whom bring their own beliefs and contexts with them to the planning table (Beard, 2003; Cervero & Wilson, 1996, 1998, 2006). In this negotiation process, with its central issues of power and control, program planners use planning models that allow for adaptation of components and tasks.

Third, with the increasing globalization of education and training programs, the interactive nature of this model allows planners to take into account the differences among cultures when planning and conducting these programs (Bracken, 2011; Caffarella, 2009; Merriam & Mohamad, 2000; Ryu & Cervero, 2011). For example, in working with planning groups from countries that are more centralized and autocratic in nature, planners may choose to use the model in a very linear fashion that better matches the nature of "the way things are done." These planners may also need to interpret the components somewhat differently and add or subtract some of the tasks that normally are associated with that component.

Finally, program planners find the Interactive Model of Program Planning a useful and practical tool. These program planners have made three major observations about its use in practice.

- The model is one of the few among a multiplicity of models that describes what needs to be done and provides specific practical suggestions for how to tackle each component.

- The interactive nature of the model actually mirrors how program planners practice, and therefore confirms for many that they are using good principles in planning programs, and for others expands their thinking about what goes into the planning process.

- The model assists experienced practitioners in framing education and training sessions for their own staff and other planning groups. Both new and experienced practitioners from a variety of sociocultural backgrounds have been able to use the model and adapt it to their specific contexts.

In essence, the key to using the Interactive Model of Program Planning is flexibility. Therefore, the model should be tailored to respond, for example, to the issues presented by learners, planners, and the stakeholder groups, and to the demands that specific situations place on the nature of the program to be developed (Daffron, 2005) (also see Chapters Four and Five).

Tasks Within Each Component of the Model

Each program component of the model includes a set of specific tasks and decision points. A complete outline of these tasks and decision points is provided in Exhibit 15.1 in Chapter Fifteen. As noted previously, not all of the components—and therefore not all of the tasks—are addressed in developing every program, and often need to be altered depending on the people and the context.

Program planners use the list of tasks differently, depending primarily on the context and on their level of experience with planning education and training programs for adults. Novice planners are often overwhelmed by all of the tasks within each component of the model and wonder where they should start and how many of these tasks they can realistically take on with their limited experience and knowledge base. One strategy that novice planners find helpful in addressing the needed tasks is to work collaboratively, either in actually planning programs with more experienced planners, or in a mentoring or coaching relationship with them. These experienced planners help novice planners select which components and tasks to direct their attention to why and how the program context plays a part in this section.

A second strategy that novice planners find useful is to start by addressing each component, and the tasks within those components, in an almost linear fashion. They begin with the first component and work their way through the Interactive Model, again only using those appropriate components and tasks that they can handle and appear to be essential to their specific situation. Finally, novice planners use the application exercises to help them frame and reflect on their practice.

More experienced planners address these tasks by thinking of them as a planning tool. For example, some planners construct job aids for themselves or their planning teams to keep track of which tasks are important for a particular planning process. In using these processes with planning groups, members collectively decide on which tasks are essential, who will do each task, and when that task has to be completed to keep the process running as smoothly as possible.

Another strategy that experienced planners employ is to make sure they capture, while in the throes of the planning process, the components and tasks that are new to them and thus not a routine part of their practice. Using the many exhibits and examples provided in this book that describe what these tasks look like in practice is another way these planners gain knowledge and skills.

Finally, experienced planners use the model to educate others new to or unfamiliar with planning education and training programs about the complexities of this process. For example, they may refer to the task checklist, or provide copies of it, when working with stakeholders who have a commitment to educating adults about specific topics, but have no idea how much time and effort this process actually entails, especially for endeavors that require major changes in individuals, organizations, or the wider community (see Exhibit 15.1).

Each of the tasks is discussed more fully in Chapters Four through Fourteen, with one chapter devoted to each component of the model. In using both the Interactive Model of Program Planning and the tasks associated with the model, it is important to understand the authors' thinking in terms of the assumptions that they hold about planning programs for adults, which are provided in the next section.

Assumptions on Which the Model Is Grounded

The Interactive Model of Program Planning rests on nine major assumptions. Through these assumptions the authors are conveying their personal belief systems about the planning process, and the foundational principles of the

Interactive Model of Program Planning. In order to use the Interactive Model effectively and in an ethical manner, these assumptions are taken into account by program planners as they work their way through each planning process.

Assumption 1: Focusing on Learning and Change

Educational programs focus on what the participants actually learn and how this learning results in changes in participants, organizations, or societal issues and norms (Hall & Hord, 2011). Program planners possess a clear understanding of why they are doing what they are doing. They are able to articulate what change will or could come about as a result of the educational program. In addition, planners are aware that unintended changes, both good and bad, might occur. These changes may be work-related or focused on other practical issues and problems of adult life, on organizational adaptation, or on alterations in societal norms and practices. Some of these changes can be demonstrated almost immediately, such as learning a specific job skill, whereas other changes, such as abolishing discriminatory practices, may take years of continuous effort on the part of educators.

Assumption 2: Applying What Is Known About Adults as Learners

Having a clear understanding about adult learning and the factors that affect their learning is fundamental to planning programs for adults. This knowledge base has increased tremendously over the past twenty years, as more research has been completed and new questions are being asked and debated about the many ways that adults learn (Merriam, Caffarella, & Baumgartner, 2007; Boucouvalas & Lawrence, 2010). Program planners take into account the fundamental knowledge that we have about learning in adulthood (e.g., the focus of learning is change in behavior, skills, and values and beliefs; learning from experience is one of the major ways that adults learn). In addition, planners acknowledge and incorporate into their programs other ways of learning (e.g., transformative learning; the impact of culture on ways of knowing and learning).

Assumption 3: Honoring and Taking into Account Cultural Differences

People who plan programs for adults need to be sensitive to cultural differences in their many forms (Reagan, 2005; Merriam & Associates, 2007). "Gender, race, ethnicity, and class remain the central concerns" (Sork, 1997, p. 7), but other cultural factors such as language, religious affiliation and spiritual practices, values, and family and kinship patterns represent differences that must be considered in the planning process. Planners are aware of how people from different cultures communicate, take part in the educational process, regard instructors, and "relate to people from other cultures . . . It is not enough to recognize and respect these differences; educational planners must be able to design workshops [and other program formats] that fully engage people in learning who might have very different cultural traditions and expectations" (Sork, 1997, pp. 10–11).

Assumption 4: Discerning the Importance of Power and Interests

Program planning is contextual in nature; that is, people plan programs within a social, economic, cultural, and political climate (Forester, 2009). Planning then becomes "an integration of . . . planners' actions and the . . . context within which they work" (Wilson & Cervero, 1996b, p. 8). As a result of the varying interests and needs of those involved in the planning process, the final program is often a negotiated product, meaning a blending of the interests of those involved in the planning process. These stakeholder groups include people who are at the planning table, or people who influence those sitting at the table. Planners therefore give consideration to the power relationships among the parties involved, both those at the planning table and those who are behind the scenes, and negotiate in responsible and ethical ways. This acknowledgment of power gives program planners a mandate to ensure that those who should be heard become a part of the planning process. In essence, in taking into account the program context, program planners are technically competent, politically savvy, and ethically grounded.

Assumption 5: Building Relationships

The importance of building working relationships throughout the process of program planning and implementation has been highlighted by program planners as a key part of the process (Cervero & Wilson, 1999; Sork, 2010). Establishing these types of relationships may be relatively easy when planning partners think alike, but if there are differences in how they approach planning and what they believe to be important in the planning process it can be a formidable undertaking. In addition, program planners acknowledge that other factors come into play, such as ethnicity, gender, race, class, and social norms, when making decisions about building relationships as a central focus throughout the planning process.

Assumption 6: Making Use of Technology

Knowledge and familiarity with the technological tools and programs available, as well as their potential uses, are fundamental to program planning practice. Program planners use technology in all aspects of program planning, such as when making the best decisions regarding the learning needs of their program participants, assisting program participants in learning new knowledge and skills, and reaching broader audiences. In addition, knowledge about technology equips planners with the power to make the most efficient use of their time, spend their funds wisely, and handle all of the many details they cope with during the planning process. Although technology is not always accessible or practical in every context and setting, program planners are familiar with the options and know when to utilize this resource.

Assumption 7: Being Ethical Is Fundamental

It is critical that program planners act ethically in their practice (Cervero & Wilson, 2006). In essence, what acting ethically means is that planners are willing to address issues of "right and wrong," but not in a legal sense. Rather planners work through a complex array of personal, organizational, and wider environmental values and beliefs seeking solutions to issues that are ethical in nature. For example, ethical issues arise when planners are confronted with (1) being asked by upper level management to plan next year's training program based on employee needs, but then being told the topics to be addressed; and (2) learning that an instructor who has always done an excellent job has a drinking problem that is affecting his teaching.

Assumption 8: Accepting That Program Planners Work in Different Ways

Designing educational programs is anything but an exacting practice as there is no single method of planning educational programs that ensures success. Rather, program planners are very much like orchestra conductors. They are able to bring together diverse players and pieces in a harmonious and balanced effort, most of the time. This task may not be easy: some of the pieces may be much more difficult than anticipated, and some of the players may not be as adept at their parts as was hoped. Each orchestra conductor has his or her own way of making sure the orchestra is ready to play on opening night.

Assumption 9: Understanding That Program Planners Are Learners

Individuals, using one or more planning models as guides, can learn to be more effective program planners through practice. Effective program planners are not born that way and not everyone is suited to be a program planner. Through trial and error, they become more skilled at balancing the various components and tasks of the process, taking into account integrating technology, accommodating the many different ways that adults learn, building relationships, traversing cultural borders, and negotiating among planning parties. It is important for planners to reflect upon and evaluate their planning efforts to see where they have been effective and where they can improve.

A question the authors are often asked is whether or not it is necessary to use all of the program components in the planning education and training programs. Our response is a qualified "No!" as explored in the next section.

Determining Which Components of the Model to Use and When

There is no exact method for determining which components of the model to use. Selecting the components that apply to a specific planning situation is based on professional judgment, and smart planners make these decisions in collaboration with other stakeholders. Even though there is no specific formula for applying the model, program planners have found four considerations, each of which is discussed in greater detail in this section, useful in making these judgments:

1. All of the components are commonly used in developing and revising comprehensive programs.

2. Depending on each planning situation, there are times when only selected components need to be used in the planning process.

3. There are essential components that need to be addressed at some point related to the program under consideration.

4. Unforeseen changes in planning circumstances often force planners to revisit some or all of the components of the Interactive Model.

Program planners developing and revising comprehensive programs for adults generally use all of the components of the model. Examples of such programs include:

• National and international professional and trade conferences

• Adult degree programs in colleges and universities

• Training programs mandated for all employees of an organization

• Social action initiatives

Even if program planners determine that they need to use all of the components of the model, they may apply the model in different ways, even for programs that are similar in nature. They may, for example, start the program planning process at any one of a variety of different points;

focus on only one component at a time or work on a number of components simultaneously; choose to give some tasks more emphasis than others in the planning process; or revisit a component more than once during the planning process.[1]

Depending on the specific planning situation, often program planners use only selected parts of the Interactive Model. The planning context, for example, might demand that programs be developed in a very short amount of time. In this case, program planners must make quick decisions about which components are absolutely necessary to complete and which can be ignored or put on hold. In other cases, such as when mandated content and formats, staff, and locations are predetermined, the model helps planners dictate what actions and tasks still need to be considered.[2]

Although planners choose to use only selected components of the Interactive Model of Program Planning, there are some components that are essential to most planning processes. These critical components are: discerning the context, identifying program ideas, developing clear program goals and objectives, designing instructional plans, devising transfer-of-learning plans, and formulating evaluation plans.

To put these essential components in another light, it is not that the administrative components, such as budgeting, marketing, scheduling programs and staff, and taking care of details, are less important. Instead, what matters to learners and most sponsors is that the substance of the program is matched to the context in which the learning is to be applied, and that the program is instructionally sound. For example, glitzy marketing with content that is inadequate or irrelevant, or the use of the "latest and greatest technology tool," with little thought as to whether integrating this tool makes for good instructional practice, is neither a cogent nor an ethical way for program planners to act. On the other hand, inadequate planning for the budget, a poor hotel choice, or even late marketing can ruin a program, even one that has excellent speakers, clear goals and objectives, and learning transfer as a part of the program.

Contextual or other outside forces, whether positive or negative, may dictate that planners revisit some or all of the components of the Interactive Model to get a program up and running or keep it functioning as they respond to these unexpected changes. Two examples of these program planning "interruptions" are highlighted:

> A major new program initiative was announced on the assumption that start-up funds were available to get the new program up and moving forward (after which it would be self-sufficient). Now, however, unanticipated budget cuts have

eliminated that start-up funding. The question is whether alternative funds can be found or the program should be canceled.

A very popular program for volunteers of an organization has been oversubscribed. The instructors know that if all of the people who have registered in advance actually come, what they have planned in terms of format and teaching methods will not work. The organizers do not want to tell some of the participants not to come, because they are afraid they would lose some good volunteers. The questions are: (1) can they redesign the instructional part of the program and find additional instructors so a larger number of people are accommodated, or (2) should they offer the program a second time and give people the opportunity to choose one of the two times?

In summary, what is readily apparent in choosing which components to use and when, as stressed earlier in this chapter, is the need for flexibility on the part of all involved in the program planning process.

Who Finds the Interactive Model Useful?

As touched on briefly at the beginning of this chapter, novice and experienced planners alike find the Interactive Model of Program Planning useful. The Interactive Model assists novice planners to better use their planning resources of people, time, and money. For example, this model can help clarify the broad picture of what planning teams need to do to get a program up and running. Planning teams can save time by not having to figure out all the essential ingredients by themselves and not having to go back and do or redo parts they had forgotten or did not realize were important.

In addition, the daily work of novice program planners is made easier with the Interactive Model, because the model provides a list of specific tasks that they may need to address. Because the model helps novice planners choose and lay out needed tasks beforehand, they need not haphazardly limp along and then play catch-up at the last minute. Being on top of needed tasks is particularly feasible for those program elements that can realistically be preplanned, such as developing program goals and objectives, preparing instructional and transfer of learning plans, and selecting satisfactory facilities. When essential tasks are not done, holes are left in the planning process itself and in the final product of that process. For example, checking facilities and equipment for an upcoming program is of prime importance. Failure to complete this task before the program can lead to disastrous results.[3]

Experienced planners often use the Interactive Model to revisit and expand their knowledge and skill base in planning programs for adults. They then adapt the materials to apply to their own planning situations. For example, experienced planners may find that the ideas of discerning the context and working within the framework of power and negotiations (see Chapter Five) or preparing transfer of learning plans (see Chapter Ten) may be new. These concepts also may be ones that program planners have to sell to both their organizations and staff members. They may choose to use selected exhibits or figures from this book to illustrate what each of these planning components includes to help their supervisors and other key players better understand the process.

Experienced planners also arrange training sessions for those involved in the process who are unfamiliar with part or all of the program planning process. Putting everyone on the same page helps foster teamwork within the group and gives them a concrete guide for action. The model provides a means for clarifying roles and responsibilities for all involved, which can lead to a better spirit of team cooperation and less confusion over who is supposed to do what. The following scenarios, which include two possible descriptions of the same situation, illustrate this benefit. The scene is a planning session via a teleconference of a meeting of a regional conference committee. The chair has asked each person to review his or her assignments for the upcoming conference to be hosted by the association in three months.

 ### SCENARIO 2.3:   NOT FOLLOWING THROUGH

Sue, one of the committee members, responds to the chair's request by asking if the chair can review again what each of the committee members was to do. She does not remember the specifics, nor does a colleague of hers who is not present and whom Sue has been asked to represent. The chair fumbles through his notes of the last meeting trying to figure out just what was said. Meanwhile, two other members fume—they have already completed their tasks and are ready to get this part of the process moving.

 ### SCENARIO 2.4:   PLANNING COMMITTEE FUNCTIONS WELL

Each person at the session describes what he or she has accomplished. The chair provides a summary of the work that has been completed by the two missing members. The group reviews the next set of tasks as described on the conference planning check-list they developed three months earlier. Due to some last-minute changes, some minor modifications need to be made to their work plan, but all agree they are right on target in their planning of the conference. They agree to meet again via a conference call in one month to ensure that all the final arrangements are completed.

Needless to say, we would not have wanted to be a member of the plan-ning group in Scenario 2.3. These types of meetings usually are a waste of time, and often create more issues for the chair of the committee than she is ready for or even wants to address. It can be especially problematic if a continual lack of organization is the norm, for even in the most organized program planning efforts unexpected problems and changes of direction are the norm. Members of a disorganized team quickly lose interest and figure they do not need to meet deadlines themselves.

Making Ethical Decisions in Program Planning

Using an ethical approach in making decisions about education and train-ing programs for adults should be of concern to all parties involved in the process of planning such programs. "To overlook ethical concerns is a blatant disregard for the value of human beings" (Apps, 1991, p. 113). However, having a strong belief that being ethical in one's practice and act-ing on that belief are two separate things. "Ethical quandaries are complex and their resolution often are nuanced [and] fluid, demand considerable flexibility on the part of [program planners], and [call] for a continuous process [to provide responses versus] merely right answers" (Johnson & Ridley, 2008, p. xvii, as cited in Burge, 2009a, p. 2). These same authors also stress that program planners often encounter coworkers with compet-ing interests and other stakeholders who are fighting for similar resources and participants. Pressures abound as program planners try to meet deadlines, produce programs that will work, or (for some) simply stay in business—while at the same time balancing their home and personal life. These pressures sometimes lead planners into situations where ethical questions could easily be raised. In addition, unfortunately there are plan-ners who are willing to do almost anything to ensure that their programs are successful and they, too, may find themselves embroiled in ethical dilemmas[4] (Aragon & Hatcher, 2001; Burge, 2009b; Brockett & Hiemstra, 2004; Gordon & Sork, 2001; Sork, 2000, 2009; Wilson & Cervero, 1996b).

Framework for Ethical Decision Making

Having a framework for responding to ethical dilemmas that occur in the process of planning programs for adults can be very helpful in assisting program planners to analyze the issues related to a situation of this nature and map out alternative ways of addressing the dilemma(s) they are facing (Brockett, 1988; Brockett & Hiemstra, 2004; Burge, 2009b; Cooper, 2012; Lawler, 2000; Johnson & Ridley, 2008; Lewis & Gilman, 2012; Rowson, 2006; Sork, 2009).

There are multiple factors that need to be considered in making and acting on program decisions that have ethical dimensions. These ethical factors are: (1) personal values of program planners; (2) professional principles of practice or codes of conduct; (3) organizational values; and (4) the values and beliefs of the wider environment, which manifest themselves in such areas as types of political systems, and acceptance of different cultures.[5] In most cases when a program is comprehensive in scope a greater number of these factors will come into play (e.g., a program being developed with a large number of stakeholders or at a national or international level). This increase in the number of factors, whether in a comprehensive program or not, makes it more likely that planners will find it difficult to negotiate workable solutions agreeable to all parties involved. For example, responding to ethical dilemmas internal to an organization that stem from the beliefs or actions of one or two people is easier than coping with ethical dilemmas resulting from major differences among program planners, funding agencies, and powerful community or business groups.

In using this framework, program planners must first have a clear understanding of and commitment to their own personal values (Brockett & Hiemstra, 2004). Affirming their own values in resolving ethical dilemmas may be the only part of the equation over which planners are able to exercise any control, and if not thought through carefully may result in dire consequences, such as being fired or demoted. For example, if a planner publicly accuses his boss of some questionable behavior related to reporting the results of a recent program, and yet has little hard data to back up that accusation (whether true or not), there is a good chance that this planner will be looking for another job. Of course there are times when an employee winds up in the same situation when in fact he did have solid materials to support his claim. These instances are sure to happen in the life of program planners, who take seriously the task of building solid support systems and bases of power to obtain backing in the difficult times (see Chapters Four and Five).

Connected to this first factor, program planners must also have this same understanding and commitment to a set of basic principles, or code of ethics, of the professional group to which they belong, which constitutes the second factor of the framework (Cooper, 2012; Lawler, 2000; Lewis & Gilman, 2012; Rowson, 2006). However, even though most program planners are considered to be professionals, there are planners who are members of fields where neither a set of principles nor a code of ethics has been adopted (for example, adult education). This lack of either of these mechanisms may make it difficult for planners to make sound ethical judgments.

The third factor, organizational values, pertains to the values of the organizations in which program planners work as well as the partner organizations involved in the planning process. These values are usually not stated in terms of education and training, unless of course the core business of that organization is focused in that area (e.g., professional continuing education organizations, professional associations related to adult and continuing education and human resource development). A sampling of these value statements includes:

- Ethical practice is expected of all employees and volunteers. Validated knowledge and active inquiry form the basis of professional practice.

- Discrimination, based on gender, race, ethnicity, religion, social class, or sexual orientation, is not tolerated.

The final factor, the values and beliefs of the wider community, are often difficult for program planners to identify, especially in the fast-paced and ever-changing world in which the majority of program planners live and work. Locating materials that contain information on community or societal values and beliefs, although still not easy, has become less difficult with the advent of online searches on the web. Planners are careful about which sources of information they rely on. Even when this kind of information is found there are other snags in making sense out of all the data, given the often competing values and belief systems in areas in which they are practicing. However, there are some planning situations where it is vital to gain as much information as possible in planning and initiating programs for adults. Examples of such situations include planning educational programs on major social concerns (for example, environmental issues or health care for those without insurance) or for large numbers of people (for example, all state or federal employees, and participants in national and international forums). Being able to find this information is especially critical when program planners find themselves in unfamiliar territory, in touchy situations, or in environments where subterfuge is the norm. Again, if program planners have established their professional support systems, and are in regular contact with mentors and other colleagues in the field, they will have many more avenues for gaining ideas on how to handle these challenging situations.

Ethical Decision Making in Practice

Although ethical frameworks are useful in initially thinking through ethical dilemmas, when program planners are confronted with such dilemmas they also need practical strategies they can use to move through what can be, as noted earlier, messy and emotionally charged situations. As wisely observed by Lewis & Gilman (2005), ethical decision making is "not menu-driven, like computer software: if this, then that—then hit the key. There is no mechanical procedure, no automatic scheme, no standardized bubble sheets of correct responses to ethical dilemmas" (p. 145). Rather, planners have to first filter what they know about the situation in terms of the actual facts that have been documented, versus people's opinions on what they think they saw or heard. This filtering process probably will be done a number of times to separate as much as planners can between what really happened and what people thought happened to clearly define the situation as accurately as they can. Through this first step planners should have a good idea of the following: the facts; the probable causes; the people or organizations involved; and any statements of principles or codes of ethics that are relevant to the parties included (Lewis & Gilman, 2012).

The second step is for program planners to consider alternative options for action and possible consequences of those options for the parties involved. Examples of these alternative options and possible consequences is provided in Exhibit 2.1 (Brockett & Hiemstra, 2004; Cooper, 2012; Lewis & Gilman, 2012).

In the final step, program planners make decisions about what option or combination of options they will take to resolve the situation at hand and then let the parties involved know of their decisions. In making this final step planners need to answer the following questions (Cooper, 2012; Lewis & Gilman, 2012; Lawler, 2000):

1. Am I willing and likely to follow through with the decision I have made?

2. Have I chosen the best option, and can I justify to myself and others the decision I have made?

3. Am I treating the parties justly and fairly?

4. Can I live with the action or actions I will take?

5. Am I prepared, if necessary, to make this decision public, if this decision is in the public interest?

EXHIBIT 2.1

Options for Actions and Possible Consequences

Options for Actions	Possible Consequences
Do nothing, say nothing	The parties involved will be relieved.
	If no one else in the groups or organizations involved is aware of this problem, then actions of other staff members will continue, including those that are unethical in nature.
	Word may leak out throughout the various networks that exist in all organizations of this decision, which could lead to anger and distrust among the ranks of the people who chose this course of action, and to others not wanting to work with the involved parties.
Encourage active participation of all parties involved in the decision-making process in reaching a final course of action	Both parties will accept this decision as a fair and realistic solution to solve the problem.
	The party or parties involved are not satisfied with the decision and take steps, which again could either make the situation worse or even impossible to solve within the confines of current organizational policy and operating procedures.
	One or more of the parties included could take legal action against the planner and the organization.
Make a decision about the action(s) to be taken and let the parties know what that decision is (e.g., give the person who created the ethical dilemma a second chance if she agrees to rectify the problem with all of the parties involved; or fire the person or persons involved)	Negotiate a specific course of action between or among the parties involved to which all agree (e.g., a change in the policies and the operating procedures of the organizations to ensure this type of situation will not happen again).
	This decision-making process exacerbates the problem to the point that the "injured" party or parties decide to go public with the issue, thus making the situation more difficult to resolve and could lead to legal action.

6. Have I taken the proper precautions for my staff and myself if the reaction warrants legal consequences or safety concerns?

Although there are both researchers and practitioners who believe that the basic premise of this decision-making process is rational in nature, others view this process very differently. Rather, they view the process as coming from both the mind and heart, which means taking into account that this process often evokes strong emotional responses as well as logical thinking. It is not unusual for program planners to find they feel confused, conflicted, or just plain frustrated. These feelings happen to the most rational of people, especially when presented with an ethical issue they never thought they would have to address.[6] Making ethical decisions, as noted earlier, is often complicated and messy, with no simple or easy answers to the many questions that such decisions raise.

There are times when planners choose to leave an organization or group as there is no meeting of the minds on ethical issues, or the sponsoring organization or other parties involved have stepped "over the line" in terms of the planners' values and beliefs. This decision to leave is not an easy process and is often a lonely one as there are few, if any, people that program planners can confide in, except perhaps their spouses or trusted colleagues who will keep their discussions about this situation confidential. Thoughtful program planners think through how they will leave the organization as illustrated in Scenario 2.5.

 ### SCENARIO 2.5:   TIME TO LEAVE

Ramone has decided to leave his position as the director of the African-American Cultural Center, as the center is not receiving the promised financial support from the local city council, which is composed primarily of white and Hispanic middle-class men and women. The city council has continually cut the funding to the center over the past three years, despite the fact that full funding was promised for the center's operations for at least five years. The reason given by council members for the funding cuts is that center staff members should be generating even more of their own funding than they currently are.

Ramone's decision to leave has been difficult as he is very committed to the center and its programs, and he believes the center has provided a positive place for gatherings and learning opportunities for people of all ages and ethnic groups. Ramone also thinks, as do his staff and those who use the center, that he has been an effective director. In addition, he is also a well-respected leader in the black community. Ramone is fraught with all kinds of feelings and thoughts, from anger at the city council to self-doubt about the way he has handled the funding situation. Now that Ramone's decision to leave is final, he needs to decide how he will make his exit—whether in silence, telling a chosen few about why he decided to leave, or by making a public announcement.

When a public announcement is the chosen path, this statement must be crafted with both head and heart. Good questions to ask in deciding when and what to say are: What is the worst thing that can happen if I make public my reasons for leaving? Who might be helped by my statement, and who might be hurt? When and where will my announcement have the most impact? How will my future employment be affected by my statement? And what might the legal ramifications be, if any, if a public announcement is chosen?

Returning to Ramone's situation, he made a public statement, as he believed it was both an ethical and practical obligation for him to do so. From the ethical side, he wanted the general community to be aware of how city council members had reneged on their funding commitment, especially as the center has been successful in all of their programming endeavors. On the practical side, he hoped that his public announcement would generate support for restored funding from the city, as well as additional support from private foundations and individuals. Ramone truly wants the center to both survive and thrive, and he believes his resignation and a public statement of his departure are the only ways this outcome might happen.

 **Chapter Highlights**

The Interactive Model of Program Planning is presented as a guide, not a blueprint for practice and represents a way of thinking about program planning that is interactive in nature. There are four major differences between this model and other models of program planning: the model has no real beginnings or endings; the process of planning programs is essentially a people activity; the interactive nature of this model allows planners to take into account the differences among cultures in the way these programs are planned; and program planners find the model to be a useful and practical tool. The Interactive Model consists of eleven components, with each component containing a series of tasks and decision points:

- Discerning the context for planning
- Building a solid base of support
- Identifying and prioritizing program ideas and needs
- Constructing program goals and objectives
- Designing instruction
- Devising transfer of learning plans

- Formulating evaluation plans
- Determining formats, schedules, and staff
- Preparing and managing budgets
- Organizing marketing campaigns
- Details, details, details

Program planners often work with a number of components and tasks at the same time and apply the model in different ways. In addition, they are required to continually negotiate and renegotiate both the processes and products of their work as they function within varying social, political, economic and cultural environments. Therefore, the key to using the Interactive Model is remaining flexible in its application throughout the planning process.

The Interactive Model is grounded in nine assumptions. Examples of these assumptions include:

- Educational programs focus on what the participants actually learn and how this learning results in changes in participants, organizations, or societal issues and norms.

- Having a clear understanding about adult learning and the factors that affect their learning is fundamental to planning programs for adults.

- People who plan programs for adults need to be sensitive to cultural differences in their many forms.

The importance of building working relationships throughout the process of program planning and implementation has been highlighted by program planners as a key part of the process.

Knowledge and familiarity with the technological tools and programs available, as well as their potential uses, are fundamental to program planning practice.

Although there is no specific formula for applying the model, program planners have found three considerations useful in making these judgments:

1. All of the components are commonly used in developing and revising comprehensive programs.

2. There are essential components that need to be addressed at some point in the planning process related to the program being planned.

3. Unforeseen changes in planning circumstances often force planners to revisit some or all of the components of the Interactive Model.

Both novice and experienced planners find the Interactive Model helpful in their practice. Novice planners discover that using the model makes their daily work easier as it provides a list of specific tasks that they may need to consider, depending on the planning situation. Experienced planners observe that the Interactive Model assists them in reviewing and expanding their own knowledge of program planning and in framing education and training sessions for their own staff and other planning groups. In addition, both new and experienced planners from a variety of sociocultural backgrounds and settings have been able to use the model and adapt it to their specific contexts.

Whether program planners are novices or experts it is important for them to have a working knowledge base related to learning in adulthood, cultural differences, building relationships, power and negotiations, and technology. Each of these areas is discussed in Chapter Three.

Notes for Additional Online Resources

1. See Exhibit 2.A: Examples of Program Situations and Components to Be Addressed.

2. See Exhibit 2.A for additional examples.

3. See Scenario 2.A Overlooking the Details.

4. Examples of decisions that illustrate ethical dilemmas in relationship to selected components of the Interactive Model of Program Planning are provided in Exhibit 2.B: Ethical Dilemmas.

5. See Figure 2.A: Sample Framework for Ethical Decisions in Program Planning.

6. See Scenario 2.B Enduring a Tough Board Meeting.

 ## Application Exercises

The application exercises assist you in thinking more about the Interactive Model of Program Planning, the assumptions upon which this model is grounded, and the ethical issues related to using the model.

Examining Components of the Interactive Model to Use

1. Describe briefly an educational program you are or have been involved with as part of the planning effort.

   _____

   _____

   _____

   _____

   _____

   _____

   _____

2. Indicate with a check mark those components of the Interactive Model of Program Planning that you believe have to be or were addressed. Place a second check by those that are receiving or did receive special emphasis for this program. Using Figure 2.1 and Exhibit 2.A will assist you in completing this exercise (see web site).

Components to Address	Components to Emphasize	Interactive Model Components
❑	❑	Discerning the context for planning
❑	❑	Building a solid base of support
❑	❑	Identifying and prioritizing program ideas and needs
❑	❑	Constructing program goals and objectives
❑	❑	Designing instruction
❑	❑	Devising transfer of learning plans
❑	❑	Formulating program evaluation plans
❑	❑	Determining formats, schedules, and staff
❑	❑	Preparing and managing budgets
❑	❑	Organizing marketing campaigns
❑	❑	Taking care of details

3.   List those components that needed special emphasis and briefly note why.

_____

_____

_____

_____

_____

_____

_____

EXERCISE 2.2

Making Ethical Decisions in Program Planning

1. Describe two ethical dilemmas that you faced or two that you think could happen to you. Be as specific as possible in this description.

    _____

    _____

    _____

    _____

    _____

    _____

    _____

    _____

2. Using the following chart, explain for each of the dilemmas described in number 1 what you chose to do or what you might do in the situation. Then describe why you made or could make that decision and what were or could be the possible consequences of your actions.

What You Did or Might Do	Why You Made or Might Make the Decision?	What Were or Could Be the Possible Consequences?

Chapter 3

Exploring Foundation Knowledge of Program Planning

COMPLEXITY, UNCERTAINTY, AND resistance to change are not uncommon to program planners in most settings. Sure, planners develop programs that appear to run without a hitch—programs that were probably fairly simple to put together. But most planners work within situations that are messy and often downright uncomfortable during some or all phases of the program progress.[1]

To assist program planners in using the Interactive Model in all kinds of situations, we explore five areas of foundational knowledge especially important to understand in both designing and implementing programs for adults—adult learning, cultural differences, relationship building, power and interests, and technology—are drawn from the literature and practice of program planners (Forester, 2009; Merriam, Caffarella, & Baumgartner, 2007; Reagan, 2005; Sork, 2010; Wang, 2010). We connect each topic to components of the Interactive Model of Program Planning through the examples and scenarios in this chapter and throughout the book.

Adult Learning

Fundamental to planning programs for adults is having a clear picture of how adults learn and how this in turn affects the program planning process. The knowledge base on adult learning is constructed from a number of fields and disciplines such as adult and continuing education, psychology, sociology, anthropology, neurosciences, and cultural studies (Merriam, Caffarella, & Baumgartner, 2007). As the number of sources for material on adult learning has grown, so has the topic areas that are now addressed, ranging from experiential learning to intelligence to narrative learning. Current in-depth descriptions, conceptual frameworks, and models of adult learning that are especially helpful can be found in Illeris (2004); Merriam (2008); Merriam, Caffarella, and Baumgartner (2007); Jarvis (2006); Reagan (2005); and Tennant (2006, 2012). From the many ways of thinking about learning in adulthood, researchers have highlighted three content areas to illustrate the connections between adult learning and planning education and training programs for adults: experiential learning, transformational learning, and non-Western and Indigenous ways of knowing and learning.

Experiential Learning

Experience as a foundation for learning in adulthood has been around since the dawn of humankind, and been discussed in the literature for a number of years (for example, Bergsteiner, Avery, & Neumann, 2010; Dewey, 1938; Fenwick, 2003; Jarvis, 1987, 2006; Kolb, 1984; Knowles, 1980; Silberman, 2007). As observed by Knowles (1980): "adults derive their self-identity from their experience [and] . . . define who they are in terms of the accumulation of their unique sets of experiences" (p. 44). In other words, to not take into account the learning that adults have acquired through their experiences is essentially a denial of who they are, where they have come from, and their differences and similarities. Therefore, it is important to bear in mind the prior and current experiences of potential participants in the program planning process (Gravani, 2012). For example, Joyce, an instructor teaching a series of classes on child rearing to parents, did not take into consideration what they had already learned from their experiences as parents. She learned the hard way that not acknowledging the parents' experiences made her teaching much more difficult, as the participants kept challenging many of her assertions, based on their own experiences as parents, and both Joyce and the learners became very frustrated with their never-ending arguments. Taking into account learners' experiences does not mean that everything they know about a specific topic or issue is right, but rather that allowing them to voice their observations and experiences, both the good and the bad, provides motivation for these learners and also often adds new insights into the discussion.

Program planners gather this information in a number of ways, such as formal needs assessments (see Chapter Five) and target audience analyses (see Chapter Thirteen). However, generating a clear picture of the experiences participants may bring to a specific program is not always an easy task, and sometimes the information received is not correct.[2] In addition, program planners and instructors sometimes make assumptions about learners that turn out to be incorrect.

Experiential learning happens in formal settings, such as universities and places of business; in informal locations, such as in people's homes and during walks in the woods; and on one's own. It may come through a planned activity that focuses on learning from experience, through discussions of topics in areas where learners do have experiences, or through happenstance. Some techniques, such as storytelling, fit well into all these types of learning experiences, whereas others fit better into one of the settings, such as a group simulation, whether in-person or online (see Chapter Eight).

A number of authors view reflective practice as a critical aspect of learning from experience. This form of practice also underlies another theory of adult learning that is discussed in this section, transformational learning. One of the most useful frameworks of reflective practice that researchers have found was constructed by Schön (1983), a seminal scholar in this area, through his study of professional practice. He views reflective practice through two different lenses: "reflection-on-action" and "reflection-in-action." Reflection-on-action is the most typical way program planners have used reflective practice, as discussed in the writing of many different scholars, including Boud, Keogh, and Walter (1996); Fenwick (2003); and Kolb and Kolb (2008). In essence, learners using this form of reflection examine what they have learned through a specific experience after it has happened. Keeping reflective journals and exploring a specific situation with a group, colleagues, or friends are two ways in which reflection-on-action happens (see Cain, Cummings, & Stanchfield, 2005, for a helpful guide for facilitators of reflective practice). In contrast, reflection-in-action, which program planners and instructors find more difficult to do, usually involves changing one's actions or ways of thinking as they are happening. Instructors often use this type of reflection when they somehow just know that participants do not understand the content they are addressing or that the techniques they have chosen for learning just are not working. One critical thing to remember in using reflective practice is that it is not just a rational analysis, but that emotions also play an important role in examining our actions and ways of thinking (Dirkx, 2008).

Transformational Learning

Transformational learning is a process in which adult learners question the basic values, beliefs, and perspectives that they hold about their own lives and how they interact with the wider world in which they live. This learning process, first explained by Mezirow (1978), has become one of the most widely studied theories of adult learning (English & Peters, 2012; Mezirow, Taylor, & Associates, 2009; Newman, 2012; Taylor, 2007; Taylor, Cranton, & Associates, 2012; Tennant, 2006). It is also one of the few theories that has been explored outside of Western culture, as discussed in the next subsection on non-Western and Indigenous ways of learning (Chang, Chen, & Huang, 2012; Easton, Monkmann, & Miles, 2009; Merriam & Ntseane, 2008; Ntseane, 2011, 2012). Transformational learning is most often triggered by an event that holds a special meaning for individuals and groups, including personal experiences and local or national occurrences. What is a life-changing event for some is viewed by others as a part of their everyday experiences, such as the birth of a child, the death of a loved one, or living through or being deeply affected by a natural disaster. What makes these events transformative in nature for some and not others? Although researchers have guesses, all they really know is that there is something in a specific event or series of events that makes adults begin to think differently about their lives, what they hold dear, and the way they act. Scenario 3.1 illustrates a life-changing event that led Mazalan to specific action he had never even thought of previously.

 SCENARIO 3.1:   A LIFE-CHANGING EVENT

Mazalan, a postdoctoral student from Malaysia, was deeply affected when a close friend and neighbor, also from Southeast Asia, lost almost all of his family members in a devastating tsunami that "roared into" Indonesia. As Mazalan was leaving on business that was taking him to that part of the world, this event spurred him to immediate action. He, his family, and his friends began to solicit donations of much-needed medical supplies and the like that could be used by survivors who were from his friend's home area. Mazalan personally delivered these items and assessed further how he and others might provide assistance in rebuilding the village during a trip he had already planned to that part of Indonesia. This initial effort grew into a nonprofit organization that has helped to rebuild schools, mosques, and housing in the area, which was literally flattened by the waves, and Mazalan continues to make regular trips to help in this area, as the destruction was massive and it will still take many years to rebuild.

There is no doubt that this event led to a transformational learning experience for Mazalan. When discussing the situation, he observed that he had fundamentally changed his beliefs and actions related to providing aid to those experiencing natural disasters. He related that he had always been willing to donate money to the victims of such disasters, but now he had transformed into a person who became fully involved in actually helping to rebuild the social structures of communities. So it is with other experiences that adults encounter, such as serious illness, death of a child, or becoming unemployed, that lead them to perceive their worlds differently and act accordingly. But these events are not always negative; there are many transformative events that are happy events, such as the birth of a child, earning a GED, or working overseas.

As noted earlier, reflective practice and, more specifically, critical reflection, are key aspects of the transformational learning process. Mezirow (1991) provides a concise and helpful way of thinking about the basic elements of reflective practice that form the foundation of transformational learning—content, process, and premise reflection. "Content and process reflection are the dynamics by which [people's] beliefs . . . are changed" (p. 11), whether the outcome is reinforcing, elaborating, creating, negating, or identifying problems related to those changes. These two forms of thinking allow people to reflect "on what [they] perceive, think, feel, and act . . . [and] how [they] perform the functions of perceiving" (Taylor, 2009, p. 7). Getting to the essence of who the individuals are and how they perceive the world is the heart of reflective practice, promoting an awareness of why they have changed their perspectives. "Premise reflection, the least common of the three and the basis for critical reflection, refers to examining the presuppositions underlying [people's] knowledge of the world" (Taylor, 2009, pp. 7–8). In other words, "to reflect critically [they] must . . . examine the underlying beliefs and assumptions that affect how [they] make sense of the experience(s)" that lead to transformational learning (Merriam, Caffarella, & Baumgartner, 2007, p. 145).

Hoggan, Simpson, and Stuckey (2009) and Mezirow, Taylor, and Associates (2009) provide excellent descriptions of ways that instructors and facilitators can foster and provide assistance to adults as they move through the process of transformational learning. The authors discuss techniques that are well known to educators, such as storytelling, creative and reflective writing, conversations, and coaching, as well as some that call for different ways of thinking about the learning process. These books are not only useful to educators, but learners could also benefit from reviewing the techniques, which can be used individually and in informal groups. One major theme found in both of these resources, the power of intuitive knowing and imagination, is especially intriguing. Using the body as a way of exploring people's basic assumptions about life through meditation and movement is an example of a technique not often used, in addition to music, action projects, and collaborative inquiry.

Non-Western and Indigenous Ways of Knowing and Learning

Although the focus of this subsection is on examining ways of knowing and learning from a non-Western and Indigenous framework, researchers acknowledge there are no clear demarcations between non-Western and Indigenous ways of thinking about what constitutes knowledge and ways of learning (Merriam & Associates, 2007; Reagan, 2005). They cannot even say that there are systems that describe all Western cultures, as those who have traveled extensively in these nations can attest, even though many people tend to lump them all together. The same statement is also true of ways of knowing and learning among non-Western and Indigenous peoples (also termed "local knowledge" by some). However, what program planners learn from people who represent these differing ways of knowing and learning is very important, and enriches their practice across geographic borders and within their own countries, especially as much of what is known about adult learning is driven by Western ways of knowing and learning.

How do program planners learn about these non-Western and Indigenous ways of knowing and learning? There are a fair number of recent publications that provide very useful overviews of these different forms knowing and learning (Bracken, 2011; Dei, Hall, & Rosenberg, 2000; Hensley, 2009; Iseke, 2010; Merriam & Associates, 2007; Reagan, 2005; Ryu & Cervero, 2011; Semali & Kincheloe, 1999). What is interesting about these publications is that they all include descriptions of specific ways of knowing and learning across a wide variety of peoples from different parts of the globe, such as Malaysia, sub-Saharan Africa, India, New Zealand, Botswana, Hawaii, and China. The cultural differences, discussed in the next section, are very apparent in these writings and provide us valuable insight into how culture affects learning. Other types of print- and technology-based resources are also highly effective in gaining a deeper understanding of how people from other cultures learn and act on their learning. Although the central topic of many of these resources is not specifically learning in adulthood, but how adults learn and grow is interwoven in both nonfiction and fictional sources. Especially enlightening examples include: *Fifty Miles from Tomorrow: A Memoir of Alaska and the Real People* (Hensley, 2009); *Namesake* (Lahiri, 2003), and *Grandmothers Counsel the World* (Schaefer, 2006). Another major resource is experienced practitioners who have worked across borders and have incorporated into their practice non-Western and Indigenous ways of knowing and learning as they work with groups from varying populations representing different cultural groups.

One of the major questions arising from gaining knowledge about non-Western and Indigenous ways of knowing and learning that is extremely important to the practice of program planners is regarding whose definition of knowledge counts (Dei, Hall, & Rosenberg, 2000; Gboku & Lekoko, 2007; Reagan, 2005). People must be willing to invite and listen to multiple voices and move beyond their own perspectives and strong options about what is legitimate knowledge, as opposed to what many have termed folklore, outdated traditions, or hearsay. For example, "evidence-based" evaluation has entered our language of practice as not only the best, but for many the only way projects will be judged. Evidence-based evaluation means that planners can demonstrate in a rational and unbiased manner the outcomes of an educational program. It is a very manageable way to evaluate programs that are technical in nature, such as teaching a specific skill or knowledge base. However, the system breaks down when other forms of knowledge are the norm, such as spiritual ways of knowing; viewing one's self, and thus one's knowledge, as intimately tied to the natural world; and the importance of emotions in learning. For example, Walter (2007) demonstrated through his study of activist Buddhist monks in rural Thailand how these three latter forms of knowledge worked together in "a popular movement to protect local forest, land, and water resources" (p. 329).

Although there is not a system for categorizing non-Western and Indigenous ways of knowing and learning, themes have begun to emerge from the literature that appear to be similar among these populations (Abrokwaa, 1999, Castellano, 2000; Gboku & Lekoko, 2007; Merriam & Kim, 2008; Merriam, Caffarella, & Baumgartner, 2007; Viergever, 1999). Among these themes, four are most often cited: the communal nature of learning, the oneness of learners with their natural world, the oral tradition of learning, and knowledge as holistic and grounded in the experience of daily living and culture. For example, the connectedness among learners and the importance of taking into account relationships among learners cannot be overlooked by program planners. One method of allowing this connectedness is the oral tradition of learning, such as storytelling, use of proverbs and metaphorical language, or wise sayings. This method can be incorporated into a number of different components of the program planning process, including needs assessment, instruction, transfer of learning, and evaluation. The oral tradition of learning is also important in the other two topic areas we have discussed in this section (experiential learning and transformational learning).

Cultural Differences

For far too long, taking into account cultural differences has not been a serious concern of many program planners when designing educational programs.

The majority of the literature in this arena has focused on the United States and other Western nations, and when culture is taken into account in this literature it often addresses the needs of people of color. The exception to this body of literature has been the more recent interest in understanding non-Western and Indigenous ways of knowing and learning, as discussed earlier. For example, many program planners have attended professional meetings which generally seem to take a very similar format: general sessions, fifty-minute breakout sessions, roundtable discussions, and poster sessions. These formats do not necessarily fit well with diverse audiences who come with many different preferences for and ways of knowing and learning. Some learners prefer more informal methods of learning, from hall conversations to learning groups consisting of people with similar cultural backgrounds. Others would like space set aside for sessions designed for diverse groups of people, and allow time for the groups to spend more than the traditional fifty-minute session together. An example of this type of session would be to have members of the group learn about unique aspects of the different cultures they represent. Another type of session would be content oriented, where presenters would use alternate techniques of teaching that demonstrate different ways of knowing and learning, such as art, music, and meditation.

When acknowledging and honoring cultural differences, program planners need to have a basic understanding of how culture is defined, how to build relationships across cultural borders, and how cultural differences affect communication. Each of these topics is discussed in the following subsections.

How Culture Is Defined

Rothman (2007) "defines culture as a set of values, beliefs, and practices grounded in common history and experiences shared by a group, which is viewed as distinct and different from that of other groups" (p. 8). Cultural differences that manifest themselves in programs for adults are fostered by a number of cultural factors that span from organizations and communities to regions and nations (Smith & Sadler-Smith, 2006). Examples of these factors include ethnicity, social class, gender, language, and spirituality. These factors must be taken into consideration in planning programs, depending on the specific planning situation and content[3] (Merriam & Associates, 2007; Merriam & Ntseane, 2008; Netting, O'Connor, & Fauri, 2008; Reagan, 2005; Tisdell, 2003). One factor is that many descriptions abound, and those given are the most useful in the program planning process.

"To have a culture, there must be something significant that links individuals together. Knowing and understanding what links people to one another or bonds the whole community is necessary" to the practice of program planning (Netting, O'Connor, & Fauri, 2008, p. 217). For instance, a community may identify itself by ethnic background, religion, and family and kinship networks. Adults can all think of communities of this nature, such as Irish Catholics in the United States, or the Indian or Chinese communities in Singapore.

To explore how these factors affect program planning, we will examine one of these factors, spirituality and religion, to see the connections between how learning is viewed and the planning process. We chose this factor because it has had an enormous impact on program planners working "across borders" and yet it is not often recognized, let alone discussed (Tisdell, 2003). The importance of this factor cannot be overlooked in today's world, as religion and spirituality are driving forces for formal and informal educational programs and social action (Merriam & Associates, 2007; Merriam & Ntseane, 2008; Tisdell, 2003; Walter, 2007). Unfortunately, spirituality and religion also cause grave divisions between and among groups that may be "hidden" at one end of a continuum, with the other end leading to outright war and violence, such as the continued conflict between Israel and Palestine.

Tisdell (2003) has written an especially useful volume that explores the connections between spirituality and culture. Through stories of real people she brings to life these connections and highlights themes that capture the essence of spirituality, such as spiritual development over time, the intersection of "gender and culture in relationship to spiritual development . . ., the process of claiming a sacred space, and [the] role of spirituality in claiming a positive spiritual identity" (p. xv). She weaves into these stories implications for the practice of educators, and includes a more in-depth discussion of these practices in Part Three of the book. Tisdell focuses on approaches that instructors in formal settings can use to bring spiritually grounded and culturally relevant pedagogy into their instructional processes. More specifically, she outlines seven elements of this form of pedagogy, which include: an emphasis on authenticity (both spiritual and cultural); an environment that allows for the exploration of the cognitive, affective and relational, and symbolic aspects of learning; and collaborative work that envisions and presents manifestations of multiple dimensions for learning and change. Tisdell does stress, however, that culturally relevant teaching is not easy; instructors need to be highly committed to mastering all of the intricacies that are demanded when choosing to address subject matter in this way.

Merriam and Associates (2007) provide examples of spiritual and religious practice that connect to education, including those of Indigenous peoples, Islam, Hinduism, and Buddhism. Islam, for example, calls for a lifelong learning mandate that has two major purposes. The first is to obtain knowledge that leads one to God, the source of all knowledge. The second purpose requires that this knowledge be used for the good of society, which dictates their actions with humankind (Kamis & Muhammad, 2007). Hinduism also stresses two types of learning: "gaining knowledge from the world, so it is outer directed," and "self-understanding, the source being the person's own spirit . . . through meditation" (Thaker, 2007). The first form of knowledge comes through life experiences and formal study, which are viewed as important processes of learning.

Cultural factors naturally lead to cultural differences, which are important to take into account in program planning. Ginsberg and Wlodkowski (2009) speak about the current enrollment in colleges and universities in the United States, and how the U.S. population has dramatically changed in the past thirty years. As they observe: "If [people] look only from the perspective of ethnicity and language, [they] realize . . . that every one in four people speak a language other than English in their home" (p. 5), and that ethnic backgrounds of the population are quite diverse. These population changes have led to major changes in the ethnic mix at many colleges and universities, and also have affected students' ability to use well what is termed "college-level English." In addition, "73% of all college students today can be identified as 'nontraditional learners'" (p. 5). Nontraditional learners are most often categorized as twenty-five years of age and older, with the majority of these students being adult women. Serving these students' cultural differences, as program planners and instructors, calls for much more than respecting "similarities and differences among human beings," but even more important, "to move beyond simply developing sensitivity to active and effective responsiveness" (p. 11). This same sentiment holds true for working as planners and instructors in a variety of formal and informal settings with learners who display cultural differences. More specifically, building relationships and communicating well with these learners and other stakeholders in the educational enterprise are major ways that program planners can act responsibly where diversity in cultural backgrounds is most often the norm, which is the focus of the next section.

Relationship Building

Building relationships means that planners are able to interact well with the various individuals and stakeholder groups they work with as part of the planning process. These stakeholder groups vary from program to program, and may include learners; instructors; other program planners; organizational personnel; partners; people from funding agencies; and individuals and groups from the wider community. Having knowledge of the people with whom planners work, including their ways of knowing and learning, interests, ethnic identity, and cultural backgrounds, is critical to understanding the various stakeholder groups (Indabawa & Mpofu, 2006; Merriam & Associates, 2007; Reagan, 2005; Sheared, Johnson-Bailey, Colin, Peterson, 2010, & Brookfield, 2010).

What is interesting is that there have been only a handful of scholars who have spoken about the importance of relationship building as central to the work of program planners (Bracken, 2011; Sork, 2010; Terry, 2006), although this has been implied by a number of other writers. Only discussion surrounding one component of the model—designing instruction—has incorporated relationship building as a major theme for a number of years (e.g., Terry, 2006; Ray, 2010; Tisdell, 2003; Wlodkowski, 2008). Regardless of these trends in the literature, practitioners frequently discuss this topic as critical to their work as planners.

Building Relationships That Have Different Meanings

Relationships that planners build are both formal and informal in nature, and between and among individuals, groups, and organizations (Cervero & Wilson, 2006). Formal relationships come in many forms (e.g., work supervisors and subordinates; legally constituted boards and advisory committees; community groups; and partnerships with other organizations; see Chapter Five). The nature of these relationships often takes on different qualities and thus different meanings for those involved. Supervisors, for example, may view their subordinates as colleagues, which mean they primarily interact as equals: high trust exists between them; communication is open and free flowing; and they work collaboratively as a team. At the other extreme, supervisors treat their subordinates as staff that work for them, giving them specific tasks to do and expecting that they will do those tasks as instructed.

This second kind of relationship often engenders competition among staff members to do the best job for the learners and other stakeholders, but also to please their supervisor. For example, program planners may make power plays among staff, or among staff and supervisors, to try to block others' actions. In addition, poor communication patterns may emerge that create problems in getting the work done. Needless to say, program planners need to think very carefully about how their actions in building and maintaining relationships will affect both the process and outcomes of their programs (Netting, O'Connor, & Fauri, 2008; Rothman, 2007).

Informal relationships tend to be more flexible and open-ended, meaning that the boundaries of such relationships are more flexible and fluid. However, there are important lessons in relationships for program planners as illustrated by Scenario 3.2.

SCENARIO 3.2:   ALWAYS THERE FOR EACH OTHER

Julie and Latasha have been colleagues and friends over many years. They first became acquainted at a national association conference in human resource development and were introduced by mutual colleagues. Julie worked as a trainer for a large corporation, while Latasha was employed by the state government in the same role. They hit it off right away, as they both had similar experiences as trainers, even though they worked for very different kinds of organizations, and were delighted to find they lived only an hour away from each other. In addition, both Julie and Latasha had children, and also found themselves discussing how they each handled the demands of their jobs as well as their child-rearing responsibilities, and how they often found themselves "pulled apart" in terms of mixing these two roles. Over time, they started getting together every month or two, which sometimes included either observation or taking part in each other's programs as well as family outings. Even though Julie eventually took a new position many miles away, this move did not dampen their interactions as colleagues and friends. Latasha and Julie often talked about the importance of what they learned from each other and how their mutual support had gotten them through a number of difficult times both on the job and in their personal lives. They each knew the other was just an e-mail or a call away.

Although some of these informal relationships also include friendships, the majority do not. Rather, they take many forms, examples of which include mentoring relationships and making contacts with key community leaders and colleagues from similar organizations. Mentoring relationships involve senior or experienced persons who provide assistance and guidance to newcomers to a field. These relationships are formed in a number of ways, such as introductions by other senior colleagues to newcomers with the same interests, junior staff members seeking out specific people they would like to have as a mentor, and relationships between two people that evolve over time. Building relationships with key community leaders and colleagues from similar organizations provides opportunities for people to get a better sense of the context in which they work and who and where to go to in garnering support for their activities. For example, having good working relationships with key community leaders allows program planners to know who could be helpful in fundraising campaigns or when controversial programs are being launched.

Influence of Culture on Building Relationships

As Ryu and Cervero (2011) have wisely observed, "program planning activities are not culturally neutral but are replete with various cultural values and affected by them" (p. 139). They assert that "although the social and political aspects of program planning emphasize the importance of contexts that are embedded in society, culture as a context variable has not received much attention from researchers and practitioners" (p. 156). As noted earlier in this chapter, culture is grounded in the values, beliefs, and practices that are shared by groups of people and make them distinct from other groups, and it is manifested by such factors as ethnicity, social class, language, and religion and spirituality. Cultural differences are found in all nations of the world, and therefore planners need to be aware of how they affect program planning whether they are working in their own country or internationally. For example, Maruatona (2005) learned through a study focused on gender and diversity issues that "in spite of being a multiethnic society, literacy education in Botswana has ignored gender and cultural diversity . . . [This study demonstrated] how planners endorsed a technocratic view of planning, emphasizing their curriculum expertise instead of the learners' realities" (p. 149).

As can be seen in Maruatona's study (2005), building relationships is definitely influenced by culture, and effective program planners know that in order to develop positive relationships they must approach people differently depending on with whom and where they are working (Netting, O'Connor, & Fauri, 2008; Rothman, 2007; Ziegahn, 2000). Hayden, a Peace Corps volunteer in Malaysia, is an example of a planner who found these differences played a major role in her work and whether or not she should even continue her work.[4]

Although Hayden did have difficulties during her entry into the rural village where she was assigned, she decided to stay and was highly effective in her role as well as happily accepted by the villagers. She followed the elder's advice and met a number of times with the three women he had suggested, and she grew to be close friends with two of them. The lessons she learned from these women were invaluable and without their practical advice and counsel she probably would have left. A sampling of their observations included the following:

- Being a woman matters in how you approach and interact with people

- Having white skin is an asset

- Approaching elders without a formal introduction is not the norm

- Getting to know a person is more important than conducting "business" when first meeting

- Acknowledging the communal nature of their decision making is a necessity

- Telling stories is a very useful way to get messages across

What Hayden learned from these women was that in order for her to build working relationships she needed to do two things: understand how she is perceived by those in a different culture from her own; and change the ways she interacted with people, adopting their ways of communicating and making decisions. The most important lesson for her was to realize she was the guest in another country and she was the one who needed to adapt to the Malaysian culture.

Cultural Competence in Building Relationships

In recent years, there has been more attention to the topic of "cultural competence" in building and maintaining relationships. Chang (2007) defines "cultural competence as a process composed through experience of internal discovery and external adjustment. Faced with a new culture, adults discover cross-cultural similarities, differences, novelties, and difficulties, and therefore they adjust their actions, behaviors, interpreting perspectives, or even their mindsets to help them work more effectively, and comfortably" (p. 190). Some of these writings are rather shallow, in that the messages they provide are overly generalized—most especially "the rule books" that focus on what to do and not to do in a specific culture. However, there are other resources that provide helpful observations related to building relationships when program planners first enter into different cultural settings. These are key areas to remember as planners continue their work (Chang, 2007; Forester, 1999, 2009; Netting, O'Connor, & Fauri, 2008; Rothman, 2007; Ziegahn, 2000).[5]

In addition, Netting, O'Connor, and Fauri (2008) have provided useful material on organizational values that support cultural competence, which is quite important for program planners to effectively work in different cultural settings. Examples of these values are:

- Respect for the unique, culturally defined needs of diverse [audiences]

- Acknowledgment of culture as a prevailing factor in shaping . . . [audience] behaviors and values

- Understanding when values of cultural groups may come into conflict with societal or organizational values

- Respect for cultural preferences that value process rather than product and emphasize harmony or balance in one's life over achievement (p. 232)

Without this type of support, planners often find themselves "running into brick walls" as they may be blocked by their own organizations and other organizational partners from successfully establishing much-needed programs. It is especially difficult for planners who work with organizations that espouse these values, but whose policies, procedures, and ways of working do not align with or match the local customs or practices. Program planners often follow a fine line of working with the pace and customs of the host country but having to follow the pace and rules of those sponsoring and paying for the program they represent. Also closely related to building relationships are the power grabs between and among individuals, groups, organizations, and other stakeholders that are a normal part of most planning processes, as discussed in the next section.

Power and Interests

"Power to the people" was a cry often heard during the civil rights movement of the 1960s and '70s. In this case, "the people" meant African Americans whose voices were basically silenced in the majority of mainstream society. Both individuals and organizations took up this slogan, and pictures of protest marches, Freedom Rides, Martin Luther King's "I Have a Dream" speech, and burning cities framed this movement. Education and community development strategies were often ways that were used to bring this movement alive, and the heritage of this era optimized the need for program planners to address power and interests when planning these types of programs.

Power is a concept that comes with many meanings. For the purpose of this discussion, power is defined as the ability to influence others through position, reputation, expertise, persuasion, negotiation, and coercion, including armed force (Cervero & Wilson, 2006; Forester, 1989; French &

Raven, 1959). For example, program planners are sometimes overruled by their supervisors or someone higher in the organization regarding the content of the programs they are planning.[6]

Some program planners are caught by surprise by this behavior, either because they really have not been in this situation before or are totally naive about the power dynamics within organizational settings. Others take this change in plans as normal and, depending on the situation, may try to negotiate a solution that meets the expectations of agency staff and the director. Program participants, on the other hand, may be put off by the supposed "experts" who participants feel have never been in the trenches in terms of what they need to do in their daily work lives. For example, half of the people attending a training session that they found totally useless took off right after lunch, mumbling under their breath that this program had been a complete waste of their time.

Negative and Positive Uses of Power

One key idea that is important to grasp is that power can be used either in negative or positive ways. Program planners often think first of the negative ways that power is used in our world. Negative power is having "control over," meaning that our options are limited in what we are able to think or do. In addition, negative power can lead to oppression of different cultural groups to the point where they have very few if any rights. Negative power has exhibited itself throughout history from the Apartheid in South Africa to the shunning of people who practice different religious traditions from those in power. The dynamics of power are a reality of life, whether in personal situations, in our work lives, or in the society at large. On the one hand, program planners are all familiar with situations of positive power where power sharing is the norm, such as parents making decisions about their children. On the other hand, planners also have all experienced negative power in one form or another, such as an abusive supervisor or legislators that just will not agree on anything to the point that government comes almost to a standstill.

Less discussed both in the literature and everyday life is using power in a positive way. Positive power gives us the opportunity to use our influence to assist others to achieve their goals, to give voice to those who have been silenced, to cross boundaries where deep divides exist, and to build relationships for the good of all involved. Program planners view this kind of power in people who are highly committed to racial equality and social justice (Forester, 1999, 2009; Sheared et al., 2010). It is displayed in many walks of life. For example, Nelson Mandela and Jimmy Carter are world leaders who, in their formal positions of power and after they retired from official public life, have been willing and able to share their power with others. This willingness to share power has been demonstrated through their incredible ability to develop working alliances and negotiate solutions to some of the world's toughest problems.

The Centrality of Power in Program Planning

Umble, Cervero, and Langone (2001) observe that program planners construct some form of power structure (whether simple like a designated planner or complex like an inter-agency committee) that allows some parties to influence the plans (see Chapter 5). This structure, in concert with the players involved, allows for some interests to surface (and usually there is a need to prioritize among those interests), while others are ignored or suppressed. Although there is no way that program planners can address all of the interests raised by the various stakeholders in the process, there have been patterns where it becomes obvious that certain topic areas are rarely, if ever, put on the table for open discussion or even allowed to be a part of the planning process. An example of this phenomenon is why funding for some programs is never questioned, whereas other programs raise many concerns and continuous queries even when they have been funded.

Cervero and Wilson (1994, 1999, 2006) are credited with "foregrounding . . . power and interests as fundamental social processes of planning" (Sork, 2010, p. 161) in adult education. Using data from three different case studies of planning situations in very different settings with varied populations—adult literacy teachers, professionals in a continuing education program, and an educational program for managers—Cervero and Wilson observed that the primary role of educators is twofold. The first role is to use these power relations to provide top-quality and accessible programs, and the second is to challenge the status quo in terms of the "distribution of knowledge and power in society" (1999, p. 27). Therefore in developing programs. planners continually need to ask: Are the best products being prepared? Who benefits from taking these programs? Who has been excluded or overlooked?

One image that Cervero and Wilson (2006) have used to illustrate the power dynamics in program planning is "the planning table." This image has caught the attention of both practitioners and scholars in thinking through the issues of who benefits from these programs, and who has been excluded and overlooked. Who sits at or is missing from that planning table, what roles are played by those who sit at the table, and how they influence the planning process can tell us a great deal about the dynamics of power within a specific situation. For example, in many planning situations there are usually silent members and those who talk too much. On the one hand, people who are silent may just be shy or perhaps new to the group or to planning programs. On the other hand, they may be the lone person in the group representing an underserved population, and as a result find it difficult to express their ideas; or perhaps from past experiences they have learned that to speak up may actually be dangerous to their cause. People who talk a lot may just be that way, meaning that in any group they are almost always the most vocal, which to some is highly annoying. Or they may view themselves as having more power than most, if not all, members of the planning group, and thus believe what they have to say is critical. What is really difficult for a program leader or group facilitator to handle is when in reality a highly talkative person actually does wield a great deal of power, which usually means she also knows how to control the direction of the planning process. These two characterizations are just the tip of the iceberg related to the power dynamics that operate within program planning situations. Clearly, learning how to cope with these dynamics is a critical part of being a skilled program planner. Cervero and Wilson offer a set of skills that planners need to possess, such as knowing how to decide whose interests matter, using power relation to facilitate outcomes, and negotiating democratically at every step in the process (see Chapter Five for further discussion of these skills).

In retrospect, program planners have found power and interests to be a difficult topic to explore as there has been a limited amount of useful material on alternative ways of understanding how planners can address the power dynamics in real planning situations (Cervero and Wilson, 2006). The majority of the work that has been useful has focused on negotiation and influencing tactics used by educators when confronted with issues of power in planning situations (Forester, 1989, 2009; Newman, 2006; Yang, 1999). In addition, planners have observed that practitioners learn best about this issue through the telling of stories, whether their own or their colleagues', found in in-depth case studies and in Internet sources.

When planners explore the concept of power in workshops and classes on program planning, participants can readily identify situations in which they have felt they were in the middle of a tug-of-war with other stakeholders. However, many felt powerless to change what was happening, especially when there were ethical questions involved, as is illustrated in Scenario 3.3.

 SCENARIO 3.3:   POWER FROM ABOVE

The story of Rehema, a workshop participant from Rwanda, really resonated with the other participants. As director of a staff development program for teachers, Rehema knew she had one of the biggest challenges of her career ahead of her. Recently Rwanda had adopted English as the official language of the country, although it was only spoken by a minority of people. As a result, in 2008 the Rwandan Ministry of Education mandated that beginning in January 2009, which was only nine months away, all classes would no longer be taught in three languages, but in English only. This ruling created a very difficult situation for Rehema, as she knew it would be impossible to provide adequate programs to allow these teachers to become proficient enough to provide their instruction in English, for most of her district's teachers had either little or no knowledge of the English language, and of course they still had to teach full time. However, Rehema was also fully aware that it was not only useless, but perhaps even dangerous, to voice her thoughts to the district supervisor, and so all she could do was move ahead to assist these teachers in responding to the mandate as well as they could.

Other participants also told stories of when they had at least tried to confront issues of power they had encountered in their work as program planners and instructors, some of which resulted in positive outcomes, and others where they either were able to have at least some influence over the process or just gave up trying.

As is seen in the following section, technology has given many planners more power in the planning process.

Technology

Technology is continuously changing and becoming more accessible and easier to use. In the early 1990s it was rare to see computers, projectors, or wireless devices (e.g., phones, cameras, video recorders) in conference rooms, offices, or classrooms. Now, laptops, built-in overhead projectors, and Internet-capable wireless devices (e.g., cell phones, iPads, tablets, etc.) are the norm. These tools and the many applications, including social media and other types of programs they introduce, can be skillfully and creatively utilized by program planners to improve practice (Joosten, 2012).

For the past few decades, program planners have focused heavily on integrating technology into education (Moore, 2012; Palloff & Pratt, 2007; Rocco, 2007). Stipulations for technology use have been attached to grants, universities have committed to technology initiatives (e.g., the National

Science Foundation's Internet2 project), conferences have been created (e.g., the Instructional Technology & Strategies Conference presented by the Organization for Educational Technology and Curriculum), and newsletters have surfaced to address this issue. Despite all these efforts, technology is still not used to its fullest potential in program planning practice. King (2003) and King and Lawler (2003) have proposed a number of reasons to explain this trend:

- Lack of funding or resources
- Lack of educators training on tools
- Educators' apprehension or misunderstanding of tools
- A continually changing field of technology

Though these deterrents may be difficult to overcome, they all can be! Grants for technology can be sought and planners can attend workshops, read books, and consult with other planners on the use of technology in their trade. Program planners do not need to be experts in technology use, but they should be familiar with the possibilities and up to date with relevant technological developments. This knowledge and familiarity will serve to increase the efficiency of a planner's daily routine and provide a crucial resource throughout the program planning process.

The Planning Process

Effective use of technology in the program planning process is like oiling the gears on your bicycle: oil will make your bike shift gears more easily, reduce the noise, and make the overall ride a more enjoyable experience. In program planning, use of technology can improve planner efficiency, increase accessibility of resources, and reduce human error throughout the planning process. At times, it may also liven up the entire process or make it run more smoothly. Thus, program planners can use the tools that are available through technology in all components of the Interactive Model of Program Planning.[7]

Program planners use technical tools to make their work more efficient. One of the real difficulties for program planners and most educators is in keeping up with the latest technical tools and then finding time to use the new tools and integrate them into their work. Just as program planners need to take time to keep up with the research in the field of adult education, they need time to keep up with the technology, not only to make their jobs easier but also because their clients and stakeholders will be using the newest technology and will expect the same for the program planner.

Available Technology Tools

From small uses, such as file organization, file management, and quick communication (e.g., e-mail), to large uses, such as data storage and learning management systems, program planners have to learn to manage all the tools. In addition, planners need to retrieve information in databases, handle video conferencing, and web page maintenance. Four general types of tools are utilized in the planning process: physical tools, supportive computer programs, educational programs delivered by various kinds of software, and interactive platforms.

1. *Physical Tools:* The physical tools used in the planning process are the pieces of equipment often used for a singular purpose. Examples of the physical tools are cameras, video recorders, scanners, clickers, Smart Boards, overhead projectors, telephones, and computers. They assist with specific details throughout the planning process and may even introduce more creativity into the process and learning itself.

2. *Supportive Computer Programs:* Familiarity with supportive computer programs can greatly improve the overall efficiency and flow of the program planner. General computer programs include the software and applications used for specific organizational and communication purposes. Examples of these supportive computers programs are: word processing programs for writing, spreadsheet programs for information storage and data analysis, or other graphic programs for creation of visual presentations, e-mail clients (e.g., Yahoo!, Hotmail, Outlook, Thunderbird or Gmail) for quick and timely communication, online meeting polls, and calendar-sharing software (e.g., Doodle Easy Scheduling, online video live chatting (e.g., Skype, Google Chat, Elluminate) for more interactive communication, and cloud computing (e.g., Google Documents, Dropbox) for real-time file collaboration and virtual storage and access. These tools, along with the majority of the tools discussed next, can be accessed through "open source" or no-cost versions found online.

3. *Educational Programs:* Another type of tool, educational software, is used most frequently in the instructional phase. Educational software incorporates two distinct types of tools: software specifically designed as an instructional and knowledge building tool (e.g., Rosetta Stone), and software that was built for a general purpose but utilized by the instructor to meet a learning goal or objective (e.g., databases, concept mapping tools programs, spreadsheets, system modeling tools, visualization tools, hypermedia, and simulations) (Jonassen, Strobel, & Gottdenker, 2005). The latter type may include programs that are also

discussed as supportive computer programs; however, they are used as a tool for learning in this category, as opposed to a tool for organization and communication. According to Jonassen, Strobel, and Gottdenker (2005), use of educational programs and software for programs can promote conceptual change and meaningful learning among participants through "model building." Participants start with "mental models," or ideas and perceptions about the content, problems, and external relationships pertaining to a specific domain. Through learner-centered use of these programs, individuals work to shape and restructure their knowledge—and their "mental models" change.

4. *Interactive Platforms:* Interactive platforms are the last type of general tool used by program planners. Interactive platforms are the online tools that promote communication, collaboration, discussion, and idea sharing across time and space. They include online social media tools (e.g., blogs, Facebook, YouTube, discussion boards, wikis), online resource centers (e.g., course or conference webpages with materials, course management systems), and group communication tools (e.g., live chats, online presentations/workshops, Skype, Elluminate). These tools are also being used to deliver a new type of completely technology-based program: online courses. According to Bonk and Zhang (2008) and Palloff and Pratt (2009, 2011) online courses are the major way in which program planners have integrated technology into practice.

According to King and Lawler (2003) "technology certainly facilitates communication, but it is also a cause for reflection and dialogue to encourage and empower educators to capture its greatest potential" (p. 13). Knowledge of the different options allows planners to pick the one that is best for their task and their audience. Clarke (2011), Joosten (2012), Wang (2010), and Warschauer and Liaw (2010) provide helpful reviews of the specific tools that are currently available.

Observations on Technology in Practice

Technology probably will not replace traditional ways of communicating and interacting with people, but it can assist, as noted earlier, in speeding up the process of program planning and to reach people outside of the program planner's office. On a daily basis, using appropriate technology can maximize program planners' efficiency and provide them with a larger toolkit with which to meet the demands of their trade.

Although technology is a practical and necessary resource for today's program planners, the use of certain tools is done only with careful thought and reason. For example, the introduction of online learning environments into a program or workshop, the use of cloud computing for conference organization, and the integration of online software into individualized learning transfer plans should be carefully considered before they are put into action. A new technology tool should not be used just because it is the latest and greatest thing but because it is the best way to achieve the learning process—that is, the physical, cognitive, and emotional learning process.

Herrmann, Fox, and Boyd (2000) also caution that the introduction of certain technological tools into a program changes the learning environment. There are many unintended consequences that ought to be recognized and, if necessary, managed. For example, if face-to-face meetings were replaced with videoconferencing, participants could lose some of their personal connections with one another as they no longer have the individual time before and after the meeting to chat among themselves. However, through videoconferencing, more people could participate in the program, and the savings in time and gas might outweigh the advantages of the face-to-face meeting. These kinds of situations require more thought about benefits versus limitations.

Program planners owe learners many and varied ways to experience technology's value in the learning process and use it to take charge of their own learning. Technology introduces new ways of knowing and learning that can strengthen the learning outcomes (Joosten, 2012). Furthermore, familiarity with these tools is becoming a "gatekeeper" to success for adults (King, 2003; Warschauer & Liaw, 2010); knowledge and experience with these tools can make or break whether or not an individual lands a job or earns a promotion. Planners should therefore consider their audience and incorporate the technologies that fit the needs and skill levels of their participants.

Finally, the context of the program may determine what technological tools can be used. For example, many developing countries, especially in rural areas and even in some cities, do not currently have the same technology-based infrastructure as Westernized societies (Jhurree, 2005). Even when the infrastructure is in place, the systems may go down, often due to the lack of sufficient training programs and resultant lower skill levels of the workforce. Other problems include:

- Lack of technical "know-how" if the equipment or tools stop working

- Equipment and tools are available, but no one has the necessary knowledge to set them up, so they just sit idle

- "End users," such as program planners, instructors, and learners, have limited or no skills to use the available tools, due to the lack of training

- Equipment and tools are still often not available to those who work in poverty-stricken places

The one tool that is available in most parts of the world are cell phones (also called mobiles), again except in areas when reception is not accessible or spotty at best, or steeped in poverty. Though this situation continues to change, as technology becomes more mainstream and developing countries begin to invest in equipment and training, the context of the program environment and the needs of the participants should always be analyzed to decide if a specific technical tool is practical.

Chapter Highlights

- Five areas of foundational knowledge that are especially important to understand in both designing and implementing programs for adults include: adult learning, cultural differences, relationship building, power and interests, and technology. What is known about each of these areas is drawn from the literature as well as the practical knowledge that program planners possess.

- The knowledge based on adult learning is constructed from a number of fields and disciplines such as adult and continuing education, psychology, sociology, anthropology, neurosciences, and cultural studies. Three content areas that are especially helpful to program planners are experiential learning, transformational learning, and non-Western and Indigenous ways of knowing and learning.

- Experiential learning results from the occurrences that adults encounter throughout their lives that happen both formally (e.g., attending college and training programs, workshops, conferences) and informally (e.g., by talking with colleagues and friends, trying out a new skill such as dancing or skiing, or acting in a parental role).

- Transformational learning is a process in which adults question the basic values, beliefs, and worldviews that they hold about their own lives, and how they interact with the wider world. This type of learning is triggered by an event that holds a special meaning to individuals or groups, and is a process that happens over time and varies for each person or group.

- Non-Western and Indigenous ways of knowing and learning lead program planners to question the definition of what constitutes knowledge, and enriches their repertoire of teaching techniques.

- Cultural differences encompass a number of factors including ethnicity, social class, gender, language, spirituality and religion, geographic borders, family and kinship patterns, political ideologies, and ways of knowing and learning.

- Building relationships means that planners are able to interact well with various individuals and stakeholder groups, and although it is an important aspect of planning effective programs there is only a limited literature base that addresses this area in program planning.

- Relationships that program planners foster are both formal and informal in nature and take on many different meanings and qualities depending on, for example, the people involved, the settings, and cultural differences.

- Possessing cultural competence means that planners have the knowledge and skills to enter into and maintain relationships with cultures that are different from their own, whether they are working in their own countries or internationally. These kinds of competences consist of knowing how people communicate depending on one or more cultural factors; planners' attitudes towards cultural differences; and possessing specific skills, such as how to tailor programs to fit the needs of different cultural groups being served.

- Power is defined as the ability to influence others through position, reputation, expertise, persuasion, negotiation, and coercion, including armed force. A key idea to grasp is that power can be used in either negative or positive ways.

- In most planning situations power dynamics are a way of life for program planners, and having the skills to work within these situations is central to these planners' effectiveness and ability to take positive action.

- Technology is continually changing and becoming more accessible and easier to use. Therefore, obtaining a strong knowledge base and skills in the various technological tools that are available (with new ones arriving seemingly every day) is a necessary part of how program planners conduct their daily activities.

- Four general types of tools are utilized in the planning process: physical tools, supportive computer programs, educational programs delivered by various kinds of software, and interactive platforms.

- The context of program planning may determine what technological tools can be used. For example, many developing nations often do not have the same sophisticated technology-based infrastructure as those in wealthier nations; they lack trained people who can install and troubleshoot technical equipment and tools; or their program planners, instructors, and participants have limited or no skills needed to use the available tools, due to lack of training. However, the one tool that is available in most parts of the world is the cell phone or mobile.

Having a solid grounding in each of the knowledge areas discussed in this chapter assists program planners to be more effective and efficient in their work, which readers will see as they review each of the eleven components of the Interactive Model of Program Planning, beginning with the following chapter, which addresses how to discern the context of planning.

Notes for Additional Online Resources

1. See Scenario 3.A: Program Planning Is Messy.

2. See Scenario 3.B: A Keynote Speaker's Disaster.

3. See Exhibit 3.A: Cultural Factors and Descriptions.

4. See Scenario 3.C: Fostering Relationships in Malaysia.

5. See Exhibit 3.B: Skills Related to Being Culturally Competent for example of skills that are useful to program planners who work in cultures different from their own.

6. See Scenario 3.D: A Useless Needs Assessment.

7. See Scenario 3.E: Improvement in the Daily Grind.

 ## Application Exercises

The first two application exercises assist you in exploring further the five basic knowledge bases related to program planning, and in learning more about culture differences. The third exercise focuses on the power dynamics within the planning process.

EXERCISE 3.1

Becoming More Familiar with Foundational Knowledge

1. Choose two of the following areas of knowledge that you are especially interested in to either become familiar with or increase your knowledge in these areas: adult learning, relationship building, and technology.

2. Read three to five sources in each of these areas.

3. Outline for each source the key points in these materials made by the author(s), and questions or observations you have related to these key points.

4. Discuss, with two or three other current or aspiring program planners, what you have learned from reviewing these materials and why you believe each of these knowledge areas is important for program planners to learn about.

EXERCISE 3.2

Learning About Cultural Differences

1. Choose a person who is from a culture different from yours to interview. Develop questions using Exhibit 3.A (see web site) that reflect the cultural factors that pertain to each of the areas appropriate to the person being interviewed. Either tape-record or take notes of the key ideas and observations that are made by the interviewee.

2. Share and discuss this interview with one or two of your colleagues who are either current or aspiring program planners.

EXERCISE 3.3

Power Dynamics in the Planning Process

1. Talk with one or two experienced program planners and ask them to share a story regarding a planning situation they experienced where power dynamics came into play and affected the planning process and the outcomes of the program. Either tape-record or take notes related to the story or stories told.

2. Share and discuss these stories with one or two of your colleagues who are current or aspiring program planners.

Chapter 4
Discerning the Context

PROGRAM PLANNERS DO not work in a vacuum and need to understand the context for the programs they carry out. They can no longer ignore the context in which they practice, as demonstrated by the following scenarios. Their organizations are constantly changing. The political and economic climates in which they operate are ever fluctuating, and sometimes are even volatile. There is also a growing diversity among people who plan and attend education and training programs.

SCENARIO 4.1:   A PROGRAM FAILURE

Jon is program planner for a continuing legal education organization, whose target market are attorneys in a highly populated state in the United States. The majority of his responsibilities for the organization surround planning educational programs and sometimes serving as the instructor for certain continuing legal education programs. He has worked for this organization for six years and is comfortable with his role. He is well respected by his supervisor and the lawyers with whom he works. Jon's tried-and-true program on law firm management has always been successful over the years and attracted a large group; however, it has failed miserably during two recent presentations. Jon is feeling perplexed, but also frustrated and angry about the whole thing. More specifically, the participants' feedback was that they did not like what was said, nor did they appreciate how the materials were presented.

SCENARIO 4.2:   NEW DIRECTIONS

Nadia, who works for a competing legal education organization, is serving as the lead program planner and is one of the course instructors for the law firm management program. She worked previously as the continuing legal educator for her law school for three years, is very familiar with the law firms in her state, and has been following the changes in law practice and management for some time. Nadia has a strong reputation with this group of law firm managers as a professional educator and one who knows what the lawyers in her state need. Over the past five years, Nadia has found firms becoming more "global" in their operations and beginning to form partnerships with law firms in other countries. Nadia has sought out and studied these changes and has found several examples of the new directions from their mission and belief statements:

- Diversity in thought, action, background, and experience are viewed as strengths.

- Collaborative planning and assisting clients to negotiate among planning partners are operating norms.

- Multicultural understanding is foundational to how staff members work internally and with clients.

Nadia concludes that law firm management practices are forming a new context with a need for programming that helps managers cope with new external environments, other cultures, different practices, and how to thrive with a very diverse staff and clientele.

Discerning the context, which is both a skill and an art, is a major component that program planners address as they design educational programs. In this chapter we first describe the facets of the planning context that are explored by planning personnel, and follow with a discussion of the issues program planners consider when using this contextual knowledge—the human element, the organization, and the wider environment. Next, we provide information on sources planners use to obtain knowledge about the planning context, and close the chapter with an exploration of two common issues program planners consider when using this contextual knowledge: power and negotiation. Having the ability to work within power relations and successfully negotiate difficulties allows planners to move forward with the planning process.

Facets of the Planning Context

Program planners need to be aware of the context in which the program they are planning exists. The context, consisting of human, organizational, and environmental facets, affects the decisions planners make throughout the program planning process (Bates & Khasawneh, 2005; Bolman & Deal,

2008; Daffron & North, 2011; Daley, 2001, 2002; Daley & Mott, 2000; Dwyer, 2001; Forester, 2009; Hendricks, 2001; Taylor, Marienau, & Fiddler, 2000). For example, it is important to consider all of the players involved in the planning process when devising transfer of learning plans. The people in the setting where the learning is to be applied (i.e., a community organization, the workplace, a person's home) should be receptive to providing the time and support necessary for successful transfer of learning. These factors are not unconnected in how they affect the planning process, and they often merge into major issues that educational planners address as they navigate through their planning tasks.

The Human Element

Program planners are responsible for organizing the planning process and ensuring that it goes well. Daily decisions made by these planners form the context of the program, such as who should be invited to the planning table, which persons should do what tasks and when, whose e-mail or telephone calls should be responded to first, and who really holds the power over which programs actually get constructed and why they hold this power. Therefore, planners must have finely tuned social and communication skills, and the ability, in many planning situations, to negotiate among all involved parties (Daffron & North, 2011; Daley, 2001; Forester, 2009; Sork, 2010; Wilson & Cervero, 1996b; Yang & Cervero, 2001).

Different planning situations call for different groups of people to be involved. Some programs, such as an Attention Deficit Disorder (ADD) adult support group, only require learners and facilitators, whereas others, such as workplace learning programs, include a number of key stakeholders—learners, program planners, work supervisors, instructors, and senior-level management. Still other programs, such as welfare-to-work programs or community development projects, also involve governmental bodies and the general public. The more stakeholders involved, the more complex the interactions become among the various groups. As today's program planners increasingly find themselves working in culturally diverse settings within the global marketplace, knowledge of the context of the planning situation is critical to managing and directing the planning process.

In an effort to demonstrate how complex these issues are and how different players in the planning process might react to the same planning situation, "the voices" of those related to the two opening scenarios are presented. These stakeholders' reflections on each planning situation illuminate how important it is to consider who the program is planned for and where they are coming from in the planning situation.

Reflections on *A Program Failure*

Jon, the program planner in the first scenario: I know there are some new materials that I should have included for the law management program, but it was easier to move forward without changes. I had recently been charged with the planning of several more programs and was expected to make a tidy profit from all. It was difficult to make a profit with the turn in the economy and the competition in the state from professional law associations and law schools presenting programs that competed directly with our programs. With all of these pressures, I believed I could use this "canned program" for several more years without any major changes, and still serve our clientele well.

. . .

Juan, a new member of the advisory committee: I was highly skeptical of the written material Jon sent the committee related to the law management training workshop to review prior to their first planning meeting. I thought I had gotten my point across in the initial meeting about how the training program should be changed to address the needs of supervisors who are now managing a very different workforce than the mostly Caucasian staff of three or four years ago. I also tried, to no avail, to describe to Jon the changing backgrounds and experiences of the supervisors from my firm and other firms as well those who are also from various ethnic backgrounds.

. . .

Jennifer, a human resource development director who serves as the liaison on Jon's advisory committee, representing a major law firm in the city: I know I should have had more meetings with Jon and his assistant as they finalized the plans for the program, but from my perspective further sessions would have been unproductive. Jon has done very little listening to the need for the content to be revised, nor to how our organization has changed since we bought out two major Asian law firms. I even tried bringing in some staff who have recently moved to international assignments, but Jon kept stressing that "supervision is supervision" no matter where you are working. Jon also made all of us aware of how well he knew our managing partner, how often he had worked with our firm, and the successful track record his company had with the various training programs they have conducted for us.

. . .

Hamilton, a program participant: I was really looking forward to the law firm management program, hoping to learn new ways of supervising employees within the law firm's new structure, especially employees from different cultural backgrounds, but was I ever disappointed. I know that other participants, even before the program started, resented the fact they had to take two days out of their overbooked schedules as the program appeared to cover basically the same content as the previous year.

Reflection on *New Directions*

Nadia, the program planner in the second scenario: I have been pleased with the new direction the program has taken in response to the changing needs of the firms that our organization has worked with over the years. Reading the mission statements from a number of these organizations confirmed what I had been reading and hearing at professional conferences and from my colleagues about the movement toward the globalization of law firms.

• • •

Levi, a senior level manager of a local law firm, serving on the advisory committee: As a member of the advisory committee, I am delighted to have a chance to work with Nadia again. Although Nadia is not a lawyer, she is an adult educator, and has done her homework on what the law firms in the city are about and how they operate, identifying their needs and their problems. Our committee does not mind meeting with Nadia because she is always prepared, conducts the meeting with skill, and makes sure that everyone on the committee has a chance to express their ideas and opinions. She is also aware of our time limitations, so she keeps the meetings to the two-hour limit and holds the meetings at either lunch time or later in the day so we can stop by the meeting before we head home at the end of the day. For those serving on the committee in other countries, she has Skype calls with them on a regular basis to make sure their voices are heard.

• • •

Shawna, a human resources representative from a smaller law firm serving on the advisory committee: As one of the younger women on the committee, I have been made to feel comfortable enough to speak up to alert the committee of the change my firm has in personnel. I have asked for the program to address the needs of supervisors who are now managing a very different workforce than they did three or four years ago—more non-English speakers, a high percentage of first-generation immigrants, and more women.

One of our lawyers who was sent to Asia, who is on the Skype committee calls, told the committee how our firm prepared him with lessons on the cultural issues he would face when he arrived in Asia. The firm gave him language lessons. He thinks the consultant brought in to prepare him for the transition in managing his staff in Asia would be a good addition to this program. The advisory committee accepted this idea and added it to the plans for the program.

• • •

Several program participants: We just recently joined the law firm management teams in the city, and have been sent by our law firms to take this two-day training workshop. Some of us really wanted to participate, while others did not want to attend as they already had acquired management content and skills through previous training and supervisory experience, albeit with the organization in Scenario 4.1. Once the workshop began, it became clear to all of us that this workshop was well planned, reflected the real issues we now face as managers, and that the information will help us do our jobs better. The workshop evaluations and reports back to our law firm supervisors were very positive.

• • •

As can been seen through the thoughts of the different people involved in these two planning processes, what these people were thinking about the planning process, the content of the programs, and their roles in the planning were often very diverse. Although Jon might have been a good planner and instructor, his people skills and his ability to facilitate communication among the planners are not evident in his actions. One thing that Jon's actions did was to allow him to keep control of the planning process and the final product. This control led to program failures, whereas if he had been willing and had had the skills to facilitate an open dialogue and negotiate the end product, he may have experienced very different outcomes—useful and successful programs. Nadia, on the other hand, did her homework and preparation for the planning process. The advisory committee praised Nadia for knowing what the city's law firms needed, for conducting the committee meetings with skill and a professional attitude, and for keeping everything under control. Nadia knew that if she could prepare her advisory committee chair and get support, she was likely to be able to produce a program that was relevant and met the needs of those in attendance. It was a win-win situation!

The Organization

Inherent contextual factors that are embedded within organizations are broadly categorized under three headings: structural, political, and cultural (Bolman & Deal, 2008; Forester, 1989, 2009; Mills, Cervero, Langone, & Wilson, 1995). Each category of contextual factors is further defined and explored below. Specific examples of practices, policies, events, and conditions that fit into each category are also presented.

Structural Factors

Structural factors include the mission, goals, and objectives of an organization; administrative hierarchy; standard operating policies and procedures (e.g., how staff are selected, supervised, and trained); the system of formal organizational authority; information systems; organizational decision-making patterns; financial and other resources; and physical facilities.

Examples:

Standard Operating Procedures

- Staff members at all levels are given the opportunity to attend the equivalent of three days of educational programs per year at the organization's expense.

- Before participating in an educational program, a person must receive permission from a specified person (such as work supervisor or executive director).

Organizational Decision Making

- Decisions about educational programs within the organization are made primarily through a formal, hierarchical chain of command.

- Decisions about educational programs are made in a collaborative and democratic manner, with each staff member having an equal voice.

Political Factors

Political factors comprise coalition building; bargaining and jockeying for position; power relations among individuals and groups; and the politics of funding and providing other resources.

Examples:

Coalition Building

- Planning staff and clients from community-based and governmental agencies meet monthly to strategize how to best meet the educational needs of new immigrant populations coming into their community.

- Coalitions of special interest groups internal to a large multicampus university have a long history of jockeying for power over sparse resources for educational programs.

Power Relations Among Individuals and Groups

- A networking system, which includes key program sponsors, sympathetic legislators, and public figures (such as the president of the local community college and the governor's wife), has a good track record for increasing public funding for literacy programs.

- A small but powerful group of people, none of whom hold formal positions of authority, manage to continually thwart efforts by staff members to change the program planning practices of the organization.

Cultural Factors

Cultural factors incorporate the history and traditions of the organization; organizational beliefs and values; and organizational rituals, stories, symbols, and heroes.

Examples:

History and Traditions of the Organization

- Offering educational programs for adults has a long history at this institution, with an emphasis on quality and service to the participants.

- This organization has a strong tradition of viewing education for job advancement as the responsibility of the individual worker.

Organizational Symbols

- The organizational logo includes the words "learning for life," visualized in the symbol of a continuous circle.

- Persons who complete the Senior Management Institute are given pewter mugs engraved with the organization's symbol; they are expected to display these mugs in their offices.

- When taking into consideration contextual factors related to organizations, program planners are cognizant of those factors internal to their own organizations, such as those portrayed in the scenarios and examples. In addition, they are aware of these same factors operating within the external groups with whom they plan and sometimes compete. Of particular concern to educators and trainers are the structural, political, and cultural aspects and learning climates of:

- Organizations and groups (e.g., professional associations, regulatory bodies, governmental and quasigovernmental agencies, private nonprofit entities, and grassroots community groups) that have major influence or control, including regulatory or funding responsibilities, over the programs being planned.

- "Official" planning partners for a specific program event (e.g., a consortium of colleges and universities in cooperation with local businesses).

- Sponsoring organizations, whether or not they have a role in the planning process.

- Other providers of similar education and training programs

The Wider Environment

The more the economic, political, and social climate within which program planners work becomes important, the more complicated this environment will be, especially as planners work across numerous types of borders, from geographic to cultural to ideological (Boone, Safrit, & Jones, 2002; Daley, 2001; Daley & Mott, 2000; Green & Kreuter, 2005; Indabawa & Mpofu, 2006; Sork, 2000; Weissner, Sheared, Pooneh, Kucharczyk, & Flowers, 2010). This importance is seen in specific program topics (for example, getting help with funding problems), hosting a conference for administrators besieged with political influences, or planning a program in one country to be carried out by planners and instructors from countries that are culturally different from that of the program planners).[1]

The wider environmental context in which a program planner works influences programs both negatively and positively. The economic downturn and proposed funding cuts jolt an organization, in collaboration with a group of stakeholders, into action to prevent funds being cut. The political environment leads to programs being canceled. Overall, addressing the challenges in their wider environmental context leads program planners to filter the work they do through a variety of groups and organizations, within the framework of the larger community, and the societal sphere in which they practiced.

Questions that program planners ask when they consider the wider environment include:

- What are the economic conditions that may affect their work? Are these conditions thought to be transitory or of a long-term nature, and who may be negatively affected?

- What political agenda does the organization in which the planner works have, either openly or implied, and how might it affect the decisions made about the programs to be offered?

- When programs are focused on social issues, are these issues ones that the wider community embraces and will support? Or does a very vocal group within that community try to block the program's social agendas?

- Is the work of the organization for the "common good," or does it serve the needs of a limited few?

In general, the wider environmental facets of a program can give rise to some common issues and concerns spanning one or all of these arenas, but they also make up a richer context that assists planners in meeting goals and objectives of the programs. The question that then remains is: how do program planners new to an organization obtain as clear a picture as possible of the environmental context, or how do those familiar with the context make sense out of changing political, economic, or social aspects of those environments, all of which often change unexpectedly and quickly?

Obtaining Knowledge About the Planning Context

Where is information about the planning context found? Five basic sources are accessible to program planners: written documents, people, group meetings and gatherings, professional and trade associations, and technology-based resources.[2]

Informal sources of information are also invaluable in gaining knowledge about the context in which you are or will be working. The authors both know from personal experience how important these informal networks are in gaining both initial insights and in-depth knowledge about the planning context. It pays to listen well to those around you, and to observe closely and ask questions of respected program planners. It is also helpful to make connections with people who are key decision makers related to the programs for which planners are responsible. These connections can be fostered over coffee, volunteering to serve on committees which they chair, in casual office conversations, and introductions from colleagues. It is helpful to become a part of informal networks that include people who always seem to be "in the know." These types of networks could be face-to-face, such as noontime walking partners, or via social networks online.

It is also helpful for planners to have access to people who are sources of power in their fields; they should be "seen" by those who are the leaders in their field. For example, program planners may be invited to eat in the executive dining room, or may find a way to appear there; asked to attend meetings with senior management personnel as supporters; go to a ball game or play golf with a group of people "in the know"; or shop and have dinner with colleagues. In a recent program for women professionals, some good advice was to use lunch breaks to the best advantage, not to run errands or eat at their desk, but to have luncheons with people who can help them with professional growth and becoming known in their fields. At the same program, it was also suggested that women can expand their network by participating in receptions and dinners given in the field and by joining or becoming active in local professional association activities rather than going directly home after work. Program planners, especially women, often find this way of informally meeting colleagues difficult if they are supporting a family, but necessary to help climb the ladder in their field.

In addition, the level and depth of the information that people need to have about the context for planning varies. For example, depending on the roles of planners, their background and experience in this context, the education and training programs being planned, and the nature of the organization and the wider environment in which these planners work often determines the type of information they need to have.[3]

Common Issues When Using Contextual Knowledge

Using contextual knowledge is neither an easy nor a "surefire" answer to ensure program success and, even for the most experienced planners, can be complex and challenging. Planners' knowledge about context, especially when all three types are considered (knowledge about the people, the organizations, and the wider environment), is often contradictory and sometimes even paradoxical. For example, when governments at all levels are mandating school reform, devising an educational program for the public about these reforms can be a nightmare. Whose stance do planners take when there is conflict between the views of different stakeholders, which can include national or local governments, teachers and administrators, school board members, parents, unions, and the general public? Should planners attempt to present all sides, or might that be impossible in the current political climate in which they practice? What about the fallout affecting organizations for which these planners work? Will the program help or hinder the reputations of these organizations? What about meeting certification requirements that leave little or no time to discuss issues or allow for the application of adult education principles that support retention of information?

Running through these questions and concerns are primary issues that planners using contextual knowledge of any kind must consider: issues of power and the ability to negotiate (Cervero & Wilson, 1996, 1998, 2006; Cervero, Wilson, & Associates, 2001; Forester, 1999, 2009; Greene, 2000; Newman, 2006). As Wilson and Cervero (1996a) observe: "Planners must learn to negotiate power and interests responsibly, because their actions (that is, their planning tasks) validate whose interests matter . . . Planners must know who they are responsible to (that is, whose interests matter, both politically and ethically)" (pp. 98–99). These major issues—power and negotiation—are explored next in greater depth.

Power Is Central

In responding to contextual clues, power is a central issue to address in the planning process. Program planners have the opportunity to empower themselves and those with whom they work. "Learning the game of power requires a certain way of looking at the world, a shifting of perspective" (Greene, 2000, p. xix). Learning how to gain and use power effectively may feel objectionable, because in today's world program planners are expected to appear civilized and fair, to treat everyone with respect, and to be above feeling like we need to control the situation.

In addition, planners want to ensure that other parties, such as program participants and other stakeholders involved in the planning, also have a say. However, if planners lack power or the will to use it, they can be quickly crushed by others who want to run the programs. Outwardly, program planners must appear to be professional and highly capable, but inwardly, they should follow the advice of Napoleon: "Place your iron hand inside a velvet glove" (Greene, 2000, xviii). If planners believe they can opt out of the power game, they will appear weak and incompetent, and will lack the power needed to serve participants and their stakeholders well. Others, either directly or indirectly, will quickly step up to seize the power, and no matter how talented or capable the planners, they will lose their ability to manage the planning process and to ensure that others involved in the planning process are not excluded. Once the program planners' power is lost, it is no longer an option for planners to guide the planning to a successful program.[4]

How Power Influences the Planning Process

There are a number of ways that power is used to influence what happens in the planning process. The most common tasks are: shaping "felt" needs, setting program agendas, determining populations to be served, making decisions, allocating types and amounts of resources, and choosing who benefits from the program (Cervero, Wilson, & Associates, 2001; Forester, 1999; Greene, 2000).[5]

Using information as a source of power is often how people involved with the planning process, whether directly or indirectly, make their influences known. How to and by whom this information is communicated, examined, and debated is critical. The actual language that program planners use is an important variable in this communications process (Cervero & Wilson, 2006; Rees, Cervero, Moshi, & Wilson, 1997). Planners must carefully choose their words to get their message across so it can be heard in a world of competing interests. This information-sharing process is made even easier as technology allows for instant communication; however, at the same time it can be more difficult as information, good or bad, is delivered instantly, whether or not that information is even complete or useful to the planning situation. In addition, Forester (1989) also observes that "misinformation of several distinct types—some inevitable, some avoidable, some systematic, and some ad hoc—can be anticipated and counteracted by astute planners" (p. 28). For example, planners should always review important and sensitive messages before they hit the "Send" button and need to remember that e-mail messages are not private and can come up years later to do damage. Therefore, as stressed earlier, it is critical for program planners to have excellent communication and interaction skills. One communication skill in particular that is essential for program planners when addressing issues of power is being willing and able to negotiate between and among the various stakeholders involved in the planning process. This skill, which is both an art and a science, is discussed later in this section.

A Practical Way to Measure Planners' Power and Influence

Yang (1999) has developed a valid and reliable instrument to assess what kinds of tactics educators and trainers use when confronted with issues of power in a planning situation (also see Yang & Cervero, 2001). This instrument, the Power and Influence Tactics Scale (POINTS), measures seven different behavioral patterns associated with negotiating organizational political processes. These tactics range from planners using logic and evidence (Reasoning) to taking willful actions that cancel the efforts of the other co-planners (Counteracting). Other types of tactics described by Yang (1999), with specific examples provided for each action, are provided in Figure 4.1.

The POINTS instrument is used by planners "to reflect on their planning practice and to identify effective planning strategies" (Yang, 1999, p. 1).

FIGURE 4.1

Power and Influence Tactics Used with Co-Planners

Tactics	Description	Examples of Action
Consulting	Planners seek ideas and direction from co-planners	Using group and individual interviews with different co-planners to gather their ideas to share at the next planning meeting
Networking	Planners pursue the support of others who can influence the co-planners	Meeting with key influencers from select organizations of co-planners to request that they encourage co-planners to work cooperatively in this planning process
Bargaining	Planners offer to change or substitute parts of the program that co-planners believe are important	Demonstrating a willingness to incorporate some of the ideas proposed by the co-planners in exchange for the program to go ahead
Pressuring	Planners make direct requests or take coercive actions against co-planners	Making direct demands on co-planners related to specific activities of the program, or threating to pull their funding from the program

In interpreting these data, it is crucial that the tactics planners employ be situation specific. Two variables, which are also measured by the instrument, are key for determining which tactics planners use: the amount of conflict among the various stakeholders in the planning process, and the power base of the planner in relation to the planning situation. For example, if there are no serious conflicts of interests and the planner holds no less power base than the target person or groups, "the effective tactics are *reasoning* and *consulting*. However, if your power base is limited by the situation, you might want to use the tactics of *appealing* and *networking*. When the conflicts of interest are significant and your power base is limited, such tactics as *pressuring, counteracting,* and *reasoning* are more plausible" (Yang, 1999, p. 7). In other words, "an effective planner should be a tactical agent who understands the planning situation well and is able to use a variety of power and influence tactics according to the situation" (Yang, Cervero, Valentine, & Benson, 1998, p. 242). Although she views the POINTS instrument as reliable and useful, Hendricks (2001) cautions that this "instrument should be refined with the purpose of increasing the reliability of the influencing subscales" (p. 233), which are related to the choice and nature of the most appropriate tactics to be used.

Good Laws of Power to Follow

Greene (2000) has forty-eight laws of power that are helpful to program planners no matter what programs they plan. Several examples of these laws are given below.

- Law of Power #9: "Win Through Your Actions, Never Through Argument"

   An able program planner can always argue a point and win, but the winning may cause resentment and ill will that in the long run brings about retribution. *"It is much more powerful to get others to agree with you through your actions, without saying a word. Demonstrate, do not explain"* (Greene, 2000, p. 69).

- Law of Power #18: "Do Not Build Fortresses to Protect Yourself—Isolation is Dangerous"

   Program planners work with a wide variety of people, some of them bent on controlling or overriding the program planner's decisions. Power games prevail when it comes to determining topics, getting money for programs, or looking for ways to advance in the job. It is tempting to close the door, do your job, and stay out of the way of these power-hungry people. *"It is better to circulate among people, find allies, mingle. You are shielded from your enemies by the crowd"* (Greene, 2000, p. 130).

- Law of Power #23: "Concentrate Your Forces"

   Learn to identify those who can help you with your programs and your work. Rather than flitting around gathering support from many, dig deeper for those you can trust and count on. *"When looking for sources of power to elevate you, find the one key patron, the fat cow who will give you milk for a long time to come"* (Greene, 2000, p. 171).

- Law of Power #45: Preach the Need for Change, But Never Reform Too Much at Once

   Too many new ideas at once are threatening to those involved in the day to day operation of a program. *"If you are new to a position of power, or an outsider trying to build a power base, make a show of respecting the old way of doing things. If change is necessary, make it feel like a gentle improvement on the past"* (Greene, 2000, p. 392).[6]

Closing Observations on Power as Central to Planning

Cervero and Wilson (1999, 2006) and Cervero, Wilson, and Associates (2001) argue that people who plan programs for adults are always operating in "socially organized relations of power [which] define both the possibilities for action as well as the meaning of the learning for all stakeholders" (1999, p. 34). The primary role of educators and trainers then is twofold: to use these power relations to provide top-quality and highly accessible programs, and to challenge the status quo in terms of "the distribution of knowledge and power in society" (1999, p. 27).

But all too often, when a situation is challenging, planners think they should accept the situation to keep the peace. Patterson, Grenny, Maxfield, McMillan, and Switzler (2008, p. 4) say that accepting a situation is a major problem and a worldwide problem. "We've come to believe that when we face enormous challenges that can be solved only by influencing intractable behaviors, we might attempt a couple of change strategies. When they fail miserably, we surrender." They tell us to seek wisdom and take action. All problems we face in this world can be solved and will be solved if people act differently and use the power they can garner. Therefore, in developing programs the planners should continually ask, "Are these the best products I can deliver?" Sork (2000) cautions program planners not to invent power relations in situations where perhaps they do not exist. Rather, Sork challenges planners to take each planning situation as it comes, and to use their analytical, experiential, and intuitive knowledge in determining their plans of action.

Being Willing and Able to Negotiate Is Essential

When planners acknowledge that discerning contextual factors is a crucial part of the planning process, then being willing and able to negotiate is an accepted and essential task. Negotiation, as defined by Newman (2006), "is a process of trying to reach a 'nonconsensual agreement'" (p. 118), meaning that the stakeholders involved have differing and often conflicting views and opinions related to the planning process and outcomes. In addition, Newman observes that "negotiation can only take place when all parties have some kind of power" (p. 118). Negotiation requires that planners have finely tuned communication skills, listen to multiple voices, are good analytical thinkers, and are willing to take unpopular stands. More specifically, program planners need to be able to communicate effectively through a variety of means, have excellent group process skills, understand what taking risks really means, and have the ability to operate effectively within relationships of power (Forester, 2009). Negotiating begins early in the program planning process by determining who is invited to the "planning table" (Cervero & Wilson, 1998).

When Negotiations Happen

Negotiations usually continue throughout the planning process and address various components and tasks of that process depending on the specific planning situation. Selected components from the Interactive Model of Program Planning that are dependent upon the negotiation process and samples of the negotiated tasks associated with each of these components are highlighted in Exhibit 4.1.

Cervero and Wilson (1998, 2006) and Umble, Cervero, and Langone (2001) alert planners that they are usually operating simultaneously on two levels when they are acting as negotiators in the planning process: substantive negotiations and meta-negotiations. On the one hand, most program planners are aware that they are acting at the substantive negotiation level, that is, "negotiating about the important features of educational programs" (Cervero & Wilson, 1998, p. 20), and often even gladly

---

EXHIBIT 4.1

Sampling of Negotiated Tasks and Items

Components of Interactive Program Planning Model	Sample Negotiated Tasks
Building a solid base of support	• Who becomes a part of the support base and why? • Will a specific group that holds political clout be excluded from the support base if this group's agenda is to change the fundamental mission of the sponsoring organization?
Sorting and prioritizing program needs and ideas	• Who decides which organizations or people will prioritize which programs to be offered? • Who will have control over choosing which criteria are used in the process?
Preparing transfer of learning plans	• Can the information that is applied from a workplace learning program be negotiated and, if so, who decides when and how? • Will there be recognition for learning transfer to practice, and if so, what forms will it take?
Formulating evaluation plans	• Who has control over what will be evaluated and the criteria for success? • Will the evaluation data be shared, and if so, with whom (e.g., learners, work supervisors, general public)?
Preparing budgets and marketing plans	• Who will have primary control over the budget when multiple organizations are sponsoring a program? • What will be the primary purpose for marketing (e.g., to give useful information about the program or to provide a "slick" brochure that will make the sponsoring organizations look good)?

take on the challenge. On the other hand, many planners are not cognizant they are also operating at the meta-negotiations level, that is, negotiations "about the social and political relationships of those who are included and excluded" (Cervero & Wilson, 1998, p. 20) while at the planning table. The task of the planner at the meta-negotiations level is quite different. Rather than bargaining about specific aspects of the program being planned, program planners may find themselves negotiating between and among angry stakeholders, all of whom want a place at the planning table.[7]

Planning at the intersection of these two kinds of negotiations also brings with it ethical dilemmas and questions (See Chapter Two). For example, in doing a credible job in serving one population, do planners need to exclude other groups who also have the same need? Do planners serve the "greater good" by delivering programs they know are not a major priority yet make a huge profit, so they can then use those profits to sponsor programs they believe are really needed but for which funding is not available? Do planners "call an organization" on its shoddy practices in a desperately needed program, such as workplace literacy, and run the risk of losing the program entirely? Cervero and Wilson (1998) assert that resolving these types of situations is "the fundamental political problem of our work as . . . educators [and trainers]" (p. 20).

Negotiations in Values-Based Situations

One of the most difficult situations program planners face in the negotiation process is when there are fundamental differences in values and beliefs of the various people involved, whether those differences are between or among individuals, groups, or organizations. "Crucial themes that characterize values-based disputes [are] those of history and identity, loss and grief, respect and recognition" (Forester, 2009, p. 59). Often these types of disputes are connected to such areas as culture, environmental issues, religious traditions, ethnic membership, and gender. (See Scenario 4.3.)

 SCENARIO 4.3:   ADVISORY COMMITTEE PLANNING PROCESS ENDS UP IN A STALEMATE

Geoff, a cooperative extension professional who works with three different counties in the northeastern United States, found himself in the middle of a very messy negotiations process related to a program he was planning consisting of a series of community forums on hydraulic fracturing, or "hydrofracking" as it is popularly called. For those unfamiliar with hydrofracking, it is a process of extracting natural gas and other energy sources (such as petroleum) through rock layers using highly pressurized fluid, such as water mixed with chemicals (Charlez, 1997). As Geoff well knows, hydrofracking is a very controversial and highly charged emotional issue, and what he hoped to do in these forums is to provide a program that considered all of the issues that are swirling around in the communities where he works. These issues range from the benefits of the potential economic gains for individual landowners and increased tax revenues for local and state government to what are viewed by some as very serious environmental issues (e.g., water quality, storage, and treatment and disposal of toxic wastes that are a by-product of the process). Geoff thought he had put together a program advisory committee that would work together in the planning of a well-balanced program. At first, the planning meetings went well, or at least everyone was cordial, but by halfway through the process some committee members were in shouting matches. Geoff is a skilled facilitator, but trying to handle this situation had him totally stumped. Even though he knew this program was needed and important, he wondered if he should just cancel it. In addition, Geoff was also aware that the Cooperative Extension program statewide could be affected, either positively or negatively, by whatever he chose to do at this point.

There is no easy answer to Geoff's question about whether he should continue with the planning process or just call off the program and hope for the best in terms of a possible public relations nightmare, especially as the program had already been advertised through a number of venues (e.g., on the Cooperative Extension web page, through a series of articles in the local newspaper, and on posters placed throughout the two counties). He finally decided to seek assistance from the university where the statewide Cooperative Extension program was based. In essence, Geoff learned from the consultations two things that really helped him make the decision to go forward with the planned program: (1) how value-based conflicts that erupt in a planning process differ from those disputes that are based primarily on the interests of the parties involved; and (2) some alternative ways to move forward in a positive way with the planning process itself.

Fundamentally, "when *values conflict* [in a planning process], *assume the need for all parties to learn:* about each other, about the issues at stake, about the practical options that lie before them. *Recognize that indeed their values differences might be irreconcilable*" (Forester, 2009, p. 90, italics in original). However, finding a workable way to move past these differences is possible and mutual agreements can be reached, rather than just giving up on the process, often based on the belief that in this type of situation nothing worthwhile can happen and that the disputes will just get louder and also more personal. In other words, planners must believe they can work with these kinds of deep-seated conflicts and be familiar with the strategies they can use to assist planning group members in being helpful and productive while retaining their pride and dignity. Many of these strategies would be more useful if they were incorporated into the planning process at the beginning rather than after the process goes awry; however, they are also useful when major conflicts do arise.[8] Being willing to literally stop the current interactions and bluntly say from your perspective, "what we are doing now just is not working and we need to take a break from the meeting to rethink what each of us is saying."

In addition to using general strategies, such as working informally with leaders of the planning group and setting "major ground rules" for group dialogue, there are other ways to enable productive program planning processes in values-based conflict situations that focus on using creative group approaches that change the way that planning group members interact with each other. Grounded in case studies of planning practitioners, Forester (2009) provides two different examples of these approaches, one that is used to initiate group planning meetings and another that could be effective after the conflict has erupted.

Revisiting Geoff's situation, because he knew this issue was a "charged" issue, rather than having the advisory committee's first meeting be a group discussion on which topics were the most important to include and who the speakers should be, which actually turned into a heated debate, Geoff could have asked the group members to first just brainstorm what topics they thought would be important to include. Brainstorming involves having each group member first write down their choices, and then share their ideas until all ideas are out on the table. Then, rather than prioritizing these ideas, Geoff could ask the members to think of these ideas as fitting into a book about hydrofracking, and then spend the remainder of the meeting putting this book together, chapter by chapter. He could have filled one wall of the meeting room with newsprint, and asked group members to spend the rest of the meeting playing around with the book, seeing which topics fit where, and rearranging the newsprint as the chapter order changed or some topics were deleted and others added. Geoff could end such a meeting by asking the group to think about the chapters and whether what was still included would fit into the format. He hoped that the end result would be a surprise that the group was able to come up with a reasonable plan for the content of the program. Rather than ending up debating which topics should and should not be included, the dialogue could be both productive and even fun at times. Geoff would then ask group members to jot down ideas for speakers that could provide useful and understandable information about each topic and bring them to the next meetings.

If conflicting opinions surface later in the planning process, there are other alternative strategies to use. For example, in Geoff's case, once the values that drove the group members' thinking about hydrofracking (e.g., beliefs in preserving natural environments and the nature of living in rural communities versus the economic gains that would result) surfaced in an unproductive way, Geoff could have focused on making major alterations to the way the group members interacted. He could choose to limit the interaction to three people at a time to gain a clear and less biased perspective on the major arguments that had been thrown out at the previous meeting. This process would allow the group to discuss the issues in a more manageable way that could help bring the standstill to a close and permit the group to move on with the planning process itself. In addition, he could post where everyone could see them the major arguments that had previously put a stop to any useful dialogue. Geoff could set the stage for using this approach by acknowledging, "We all know the last meeting didn't work very well in terms of this facilitation thing. So here it is. We're going to try something absolutely different . . . If you have something to say [related to each of the arguments that were made at the last meeting, three of you take center stage and talk with one another] . . . When you are done or . . . if you see someone waiting, [move from the front] and make room for him" (Forester, 2009, p. 96).

In this way, Geoff could turn over the facilitation of the meeting to the advisory committee members and then step in again to wind down "to some kind of conclusion." He hoped that the advisory committee members would then become a part of an active dialogue that would allow them to learn more about the reasons these arguments were being made, and thus gain a clearer understanding of why the opinions of some of the group members so sharply differed. It would be his role at this point to actually discuss with the group members how the process could help them to gain new knowledge and insights about their often conflicting arguments so that they could move on with the planning process.

 **Chapter Highlights**

A major skill and an art, discerning the context is an essential component that planners continually explore as they design education and training programs for adults. The context, consisting of the human, organizational, and environmental facets, affects the decisions planners make throughout the process. People plan programs, and thus program planners are constantly bombarded with issues related to the people with whom they work. Planners must have finely tuned social and communication skills, and the ability to negotiate among all involved parties—other individuals, groups, organizations, and the wider community. Major factors that are rooted within organizations are broadly categorized under three headings: structural, political, and cultural. When taking into account these contextual organizational factors, planners must be cognizant of those internal to their own organization, as well as those of external groups with whom they plan or compete in the programming arena. In the context of the wider environment, the factors that planners need to take into account include the general economic, political, and social climates. This "macro-picture" of planning has increasingly become more important as people cross numerous borders in their work as educational planners, from geographic to cultural to ideological.

In discerning the context for planning it is important to address the following tasks:

- Become knowledgeable about the human, organizational, and wider environmental contextual facets that affect decisions made throughout the planning process.

- Know and be able to access sources of information about the context of the planning situation (e.g., written documents, technology-based sources, professional and trade associations, group meetings and gatherings, and interactions with individuals).

- Be well informed about the issue of power that is present in most planning situations and the influences that power relationships have in the planning process.

- Cultivate and enhance negotiation skills required to navigate situations in which power is a central issue. Negotiation requires that planners have finely tuned people skills, are able to listen to multiple voices, are good analytical thinkers, are willing to communicate effectively through a variety of means, have excellent group facilitation skills, understand what taking risks really means, and have the ability to operate effectively within relationships of power.

- Gathering, reflecting on, and using contextual knowledge as a program planner is challenging, even to the most experienced planners, as this knowledge is often contradictory and sometimes even paradoxical.

The importance of having sound knowledge about the contexts in which planners work will become apparent in subsequent discussions of the other components and corresponding tasks included in the Interactive Model of Program Planning. Without having credible contextual knowledge, it is difficult, if not impossible, to complete the other parts of the planning process.

In addition, as discussed in the next chapter, program planners need to have a strong support base, including key people with whom they work, their organizational setting(s), and the wider community in which they work.

Notes for Additional Online Resources

1. For illustrations of these wider environmental issues, see Scenario 4.A: Economic Realities Move a Group to Action and 4.B: Political Climate Rules a Program Planning Initiative.

2. See Exhibit 4.A: Examples of Sources of Data About the Planning Content for examples of each of these sources and what planners do in practice related to each type of source.

3. See Scenario 4.C: From Insider to Trainer and 4.D: From Outsider to Insider.

4. See Scenario 4.E: Shandra Caught in the Middle, for an example of those who did not understand the importance of using power in the planning process.

5. See Exhibit 4.B: How Power Influences the Program Planning Process for specific examples of positive and negative influences on each of these common tasks of the planning process.

6. Examples that illustrate how these laws of power have been used successfully in the planning process are provided in Exhibit 4.C: Examples of Laws of Power.

7. See Scenario 4.F: Fireworks over the Fourth of July Celebration.

8. See Exhibit 4.D: Strategies Planners Can Use When Major Conflicts Arise for examples of these specific strategies.

 ## Application Exercises

The first application exercise helps you analyze the planning context of an organization, while the second allows you to reflect on your beliefs, actions, and negotiation skills in power-based situations. The third exercise focuses on negotiating in situations that are grounded in deeply held values.

EXERCISE 4.1

Analyzing the Context for Planning

1. Describe briefly an organizational setting—either your present one or one in which you worked previously—where part of your role is or was to plan education or training programs for adults.

    _____

    _____

    _____

    _____

2. Identify, within the framework outlined below, key contextual facets that have or could influence the program planning process in the organization that you described above.

    People Issues

    _____

    _____

    _____

    _____

    Organizational Factors

    Structural

    _____

    _____

    _____

    _____

    Political

    _____

    _____

    _____

    _____

    Cultural

    _____

    _____

    _____

    _____

3. Identify critical aspects of the wider economic, political, and social environment in which the organization is situated that has or could affect how programs are planned within the organization you described above.

   _____

   _____

   _____

   _____

4. Using the chart provided here, list sources you could use to investigate further the contextual environment in which you have or do work. Using the categories listed, be as specific as you can in highlighting what sources you would seek out.

Written Documents	People	Group Meetings and Other Gatherings	Trade and Professional Associations	Technology-Based Tools
_____	_____	_____	_____	_____
_____	_____	_____	_____	_____
_____	_____	_____	_____	_____
_____	_____	_____	_____	_____
_____	_____	_____	_____	_____

5. Review this material with a colleague and add additional ideas as needed.

Reflecting on Your Beliefs, Actions, and Negotiation Skills in Power-Based Interactions

Understanding that using contextual knowledge in planning programs is complex and challenging, this exercise gives you an opportunity to reflect on: (1) your beliefs and actions as a program planner when faced with situations where the power that stakeholders have will affect both the planning process and outcomes; and (2) what negotiation skills you have that you would want to revise or add to your repertoire of such skills.

1. How do you react when confronted with power issues when planning education and training programs? What might you change about your current beliefs and actions when acting within power relations as a planner?

    _____

    _____

    _____

    _____

    _____

    _____

    _____

    _____

    _____

    _____

2. What negotiation skills do you possess that you use or could use well in planning education and training programs? What negotiations skills would you want to revise or add to your repertoire of skills?

    _____

    _____

    _____

    _____

    _____

    _____

    _____

    _____

    _____

    _____

EXERCISE 4.3

Negotiating in Situations That Are Grounded in Deeply Held Values That Differ Among Stakeholders

Negotiating in situations that are grounded in deeply held values that differ among those responsible for planning programs are difficult at best; with this understanding, respond to the following questions.

1. Do you feel comfortable and have the skills to facilitate a program planning process, either before or during the process?

    _____

    _____

    _____

    _____

    _____

    _____

2. If you believe you are competent in working in such environments, what beliefs do you hold and what skills do you have that allow you to act in these often difficult situations?

    _____

    _____

    _____

    _____

    _____

    _____

3. If you do not feel you are comfortable or do not have the skills needed, what resources (including people) would be helpful in building your confidence or your skills?

    _____

    _____

    _____

    _____

    _____

    _____

Chapter 5

Building a Solid Base of Support

 SCENARIO 5.1: THE BEST DECISION IS TO BIDE ONE'S TIME

Robert begins his new position as a program planner for a professional organization for dentists, the American College of Dentists (ACD), where his major role is to plan continuing education programs for dentists. The director of the ACD is excited to have someone with Robert's educational background and experience in adult education join his team, but he encourages Robert to meet and get to know the various types of dentists to become more familiar with the field of dentistry. Although Robert's schedule is already very full, he finds the time to meet fourteen dentistry professionals in the first two weeks of his appointment. He goes to their workplaces, in large and small offices, meeting those in sports dentistry, operative and laser dentistry, orthodontists, endodontic practices, and others with general practices. He also meets with several members of his organization's board. Robert quickly learns that these people are dedicated to their field and to continuing education activities, both face-to-face and online. Robert is able to gain a perspective he would not have gotten from simply reading about the specialties of a dentistry practice.

Establishing a firm base of support for planning and conducting education and training programs is critical for program planners to embrace. As evidenced in the opening scenario, Robert took the lead from his supervisor to get to know the field of dentistry by interviewing a variety of different kinds of dentists at their convenience and seeking their opinions on matters of importance. Interviewing these dentists was a smart move that both empowered the dentists as knowledgeable individuals in the field and set the tone for their relationship with Robert as one in which they would help

106

to advise and mentor this person new to the field of dentistry. If Robert had met the individuals for lunch in a restaurant or asked them to come to his office, a different tone would have been set and the results would have been very different. As Greene observed, "Half of your mastery of power comes from what you do *not* do, what you do not allow yourself to get dragged into. For this skill you must learn to judge all things by what they cost you" (Greene, 2000, p. xxi).

In this chapter we first address strategies for ensuring support for program planners from a variety of people and groups, including potential and past program participants, supervisors, middle- and top-level managers, and other stakeholders. Next we explore building organizational support, which includes taking into account the centrality of the education and training function and promoting an organizational culture that supports continuous learning and development. We then address the importance of obtaining and maintaining the support of the wider community within which the organization resides, focusing on two strategies: the use of advisory committees and professional boards. Next we look at designating tasks, selecting members, and conducting meetings for these two groups, followed by a discussion of the importance of building support through the use of partnerships. The chapter closes with an exploration of the importance of gaining support through the Internet and social media.

Ensuring People Support

In many organizations, there are certain key people who continually are tapped for support, especially when planning education and training programs is part of a centralized unit or the major mission of the organization. For example, in securing stakeholder support for an education program for adults wanting to earn their Graduate Equivalency Diploma (GED) housed within a community college, it is important to gain support from the college president, the director of continuing education, representatives of the various organizations and community groups that the program will affect (such as specific businesses and industries or other literacy programs), and the potential participants themselves.

Although there will be, in all likelihood, a fairly set group of people who support education and training programming for an organization, the supporters may need to change for different programs, depending on the context in which the program will be held, goals and objectives of new programs, needs and backgrounds of potential audiences, and organizational sponsors. For example, if this same community college were asked to extend its operations to deliver, in cooperation with a local literacy volunteer organization, a new program for adults to learn English as a second language, an expanded network of stakeholder support would be needed. This network of support would again need to include the president and director of continuing education as well as the director and volunteers of the local literacy organization and leaders of groups that have regular contact with the potential learners for this program (such as local churches, migrant worker associations, local Native American tribes, and local businesses).

There are numerous ways to gain support from the key stakeholders for planning education and training programs. In building stakeholder support for programs like this, one or more of the following types of people are included in the planning process:

- Potential, current, and former participants of programs

- Senior and mid-level managers and administrators in work situations

- Immediate supervisors in work situations

- Other stakeholders who have a vested interest in either the planning process or the results of education or training programs such as organizations for professionals, advisory boards, planning committees, community groups, and funding agencies

There are numerous ways to gain support from key people for planning education and training programs. Outlined next are ideas for obtaining support from potential and past participants, immediate supervisors in work situations, mid- and senior-level managers, and other stakeholders. Some of the ideas presented are also used to respond to needs of potential participants and sponsors (see Chapter Six), in choosing instructional techniques and formats (see Chapters Eight and Eleven), as transfer strategies and techniques (see Chapter Nine), and as sources of data for evaluating instructional activities and programs (see Chapters Eight and Ten).

Support from Potential, Current, and Former Participants

A good strategy for getting support for a program is to ensure that the program is successful and that participants are able to take this information back to their work and personal situations (see Chapter Nine). Many former participants of programs will spread the word if a program is well presented and useful to them. And if they perceive an education or training program as poor or ineffective, they will probably be even more vocal about it. Therefore, program attendance, especially for those programs where participation is voluntary, is definitely influenced by former participants. But even in programs where participation is mandatory, former participants can and do affect attendance. For example, if the word is passed around in a work situation that a particular mandatory program is a waste of time, the next group of participants attending the program are more apt not to pay attention, to bring other tasks to do during the sessions, or to come late and leave early. This kind of behavior is especially prevalent when the immediate supervisors of the participants also believe that the program is pointless.

A second strategy for building learner support is to actively involve participants before, during, and after the formal program is completed (see Exhibit 5.1).

By using the strategy of keeping in touch with participants after the program, program planners follow up to see if transfer of learning has taken place in terms of knowledge, skills, and abilities. This strategy keeps the former participants engaged, ensures the usefulness of the learning activity, and builds support for programs, program planners, and organizations (see Chapter Nine for strategies to make transfer happen). Using this strategy becomes a win/win situation and if problems arise or the program meets with criticism, planners have actual feedback about how well

---

EXHIBIT 5.1

Activities for Participants Before, During, and After Programs

Time frame	Activities
Before	• Assist in planning the program (e.g., providing input on how they could apply what is being learned into work roles or other life situations)
	• Help recruit new participants
During	• Serve as instructors or resource people
	• Ask the experienced practitioners to serve as mentors to novice program planners
	• Provide feedback on how the sessions are going and make changes, as appropriate, based on their suggestions
	• Reflect on what they have learned and develop specific application plans
After	• Provide feedback on the transfer of learning strategies and techniques they are using in terms of whether they are actually assisting them in applying what they learned on the job
	• Serve as peer coaches or mentors to each other in applying what they have learned
	• Assist in collecting and reviewing evaluation data
	• Develop small teams to give support to each other as they engage in the transfer of learning process

the program was received after the program is over. They can then take steps to make corrections for the next program.

Support from Immediate Supervisors

Support from participants' immediate supervisors is crucial at all points in the educational cycle, from assessing needs to learning transfer and evaluation.[1] Supervisors exert considerable influence over staff attending education and training programs and play a critical role in whether what has been learned in these programs can actually be applied on the job. If supervisors understand and support the objectives of the education and training efforts, it is easier for staff to change their practice (and for supervisors to positively reinforce that change). As with participant support, immediate supervisors' support for education and training activities is necessary for the employee to use the new information on the job and to transfer the learning (see Chapter Nine).

Support before, during, and after education and training activities from immediate supervisors, as with participants, is best gained by providing worthwhile programs and involving the supervisors at various times in the programming cycle. The opportunities for supervisory involvement are many.[2]

Although supervisor support is crucial to all aspects of the educational process, it is especially important that planners seek the active involvement of supervisors before and after the programs. Supervisors might need assistance from program planners in order to help their staff members apply what they have learned in the actual work situation. Guiding staff through this application phase can be a time-consuming activity for supervisors, but can be very beneficial to all parties involved and the organization as a whole and can lead to transfer of learning on the job. One strategy for assisting supervisors in this phase is for program planners to provide, as needed, mentoring to supervisors.

Supervisors often provide differing levels of support throughout the educational process, from informal conversations to full support. When the level of support is primarily negative (e.g., from viewing education and training programs as a waste of time to sincerely doubting that what is being learned will be helpful back on the job), participants can find themselves caught between wanting to implement what they have learned and being either overtly or covertly blocked at every step by their supervisors (see Chapter Nine).

Although this blocking behavior by supervisors often causes frustration and even anger, there are strategies that learners can use with or, if necessary, around supervisory staff.[3] A word of caution: when, how, and by whom such strategies are undertaken depends a great deal on how the work group interacts (e.g., whether the groups are collaborative or prone to infighting) and the relationship supervisors have with their staff (e.g., open and receptive to staff ideas versus a top-down approach).

A final way for staff to respond to supervisors who block the application of their learning is to request or build upon the support already given by mid- and senior-level managers. Finding ways to ask for and use this support, especially for those with little job security, is difficult at best and at worst may result in being fired. Yet there are times when some staff members are willing to take that risk, usually when they know the changes being fostered will result in better products and services, working conditions, or personal well-being.

Support from Mid- and Senior-Level Managers

It is important to garner support from both middle- and senior-level managers. Although the assumption of having support from top management is often viewed as a given, less attention has been paid to middle managers. As Wiggenhorn (1996) has astutely observed: "Middle managers often have to mediate between what is and what should be, making them primary players in creating and managing change. This in no way is intended to dilute the power and influence of top management's commitment to change programs. But it is often middle managers who have the task of forging connections between reality and the vision" (pp. 30–31).

Support for educational programs from both middle- and senior-level managers is reflected in individuals' style and practice as leaders and managers, their budgetary commitment to these programs, and their public support of the educational function in organizational publications and key organizational meetings. Their support can be gained in a number of ways.[4]

At times it is easy to get discouraged trying to gain the support of key organizational leaders, an effort that can take a considerable investment of time, yet may offer few initial concrete results. However, time may be one of the keys in gaining managerial support. Because education and training programs for adults are not the primary focus of many organizations, it will, in most cases, take longer for senior executives to take note of such activities and offer more than nominal support. Therefore, it is important to develop a consistent track record of successful programs and communicate that record in effective ways.

Support from Other Stakeholders Who Have a Vested Interest

Program planners are skilled in encouraging representatives from professional organizations, advisory boards, planning committees, community groups, and funding agencies to be a part of the planning process. Interfacing with these representatives has two purposes, as observed by Boone, Safrit, and Jones (2002): "First, interfacing with and mobilizing these leaders is a key to building the element of trust that is essential to program planning. Next, from this trust and from our assumptions about the underlying community values these leaders represent, collaborative educational needs identification, assessment, and analysis can be conducted" (p. 139). Ideally this interface works well and the program becomes richer and is supported by some or all of these stakeholders, depending on the program being planned. In addition, Cervero and Wilson (2006) add that program planners also need to negotiate the program's educational, management, and political objectives. This negotiation "is one of the most critical activities that planners undertake, because these types of objectives serve as the pivot between the many needs that could be met and the ultimate priorities that guide instructional, administrative, and evaluation decisions" (Cervero & Wilson, 2006, p. 160).

Cervero and Wilson (2006) also urge planners to negotiate these objectives with appropriate stakeholders by considering these three points:

- Recognize that people who have a stake in the program have educational, management, and political objectives that they seek to achieve through the planning process

- [Realize] that negotiating objectives for a program has historical antecedents and that objectives will continue to be negotiated during the program and beyond

- Anticipate how power relations affect both who is at the table to negotiate the development of objectives as well as the power dynamics that occur at the table (p. 160)

Employing these strategies provides a way for program planners to understand that program planning involves being willing to change the way they view the educational, management, and political objectives throughout the planning process, which may in turn assist them in being more successful in the negotiations process.

Building Organizational Support

In building organizational support two major facets are considered. The first facet is structural in nature and focuses on how the education and training function is positioned within the organization. Is education and training the central "job" or "product" of the organization or are these activities a secondary or even a random occurrence? The culture of the organization is the second major aspect. Does the organization view continued learning as a basic tenet of that organization's way of doing business? Is continuing professional education mandated? Is learning a planned part of what goes on in the life of the organization, or is the importance of learning and development just giving "lip service"?[5]

This support takes the form of both commitment and action. *Commitment* is viewed as a recurrent promise, which usually comes in the form of written or verbal statements. For example, one chief executive officer emphasizes in his annual "state of the union" address that continuing learning is foundational to the mission of the organization. *Action* involves having people at all levels of an organization respond to that commitment in the form of budgetary and other resource allocations and actual involvement in the education and training function. The planner in this situation sees *actions* in the variety of education and training activities embedded as a part of the job as well as in the activities available in formal programs, both internal and external, for all staff and volunteers. In addition, there are resources allocated to these activities, transfer of learning activities are the norm, and one of the major goals of supervisory personnel is to promote both individual and organizational learning. When advocating for education and training programs, program planners pay attention to how to garner people and organizational support, including assistance from the wider environment and from the stakeholders in which their organizations reside.

Structural Support

Establishing the type of structural support that program planners need depends primarily on how central the education and training function is to the organization. Therefore, planners carefully and realistically evaluate their position and function within their own organizations. The ways in which education and training programs are incorporated into organizations vary widely, but most organizations fall into three general categories.[6]

1. Organizations that sponsor education and training programs for adults as their primary mission (e.g., consulting firms that provide only education and training services, continuing professional education organizations, and adult literacy programs).

2. Organizations that have as a major function of their operations a centralized division or unit charged with managing education and training programs (e.g., colleges of continuing education in universities, staff development units in public schools, and human resource divisions in business and industry).

3. Organizations that provide education and training programs as one of their services but do not have separate units charged with managing or coordinating functions (e.g., organizations offering programs in which nurses teach patients in primary-care settings, principals plan staff-development programs, chiefs of firefighters and police officers set up training for a local station, and managers become mentors and coaches for selected staff).

Promoting an organizational culture or climate that supports continuous learning and educational programming is often a priority in the good times but forgotten in the bad times. Unfortunately, some or even all of the formal training and education programs are often the first things to go during budget cuts, no matter what the institution's mission or goals. The exception to this statement is of course organizations whose central mission and goals are education related. The organizations that maintain education and training, even at a reduced rate during the tough times, are often the very organizations that grow and thrive. It does not seem to matter whether the organization is a for-profit or nonprofit; having a climate that fosters learning and development comes from the top down and drives the organization to be innovative and grow. This culture of support for education and training takes work and the program planner can help lead the way.

Despite such difficulties and frustrations, there are ways to build a favorable organizational culture for learning and for planning education and training programs. Apps (1988) and Schein (1999) suggest a specific process of renewal for education and training programs through which organizations can build a more supportive organizational culture for training and education programs for adults. The center of this process focuses on questioning the basic assumptions and values about how the organization perceives these programs.[7]

In organizations whose primary purpose is to deliver education and training programs for adults or where program delivery is decentralized, one result of the previously described renewal process could be a revision of both the mission of the organization and the policies and procedures related to the education and training programs. In organizations where a centralized division for managing education and training programs exists, in addition to changes in the overall mission and policies, that division itself can also revise its mission or, if none exists, draft one. A new or revised mission or policy statement should be approved by senior management prior to its circulation among organizational personnel. Once it is approved, care should be taken to see that all appropriate individuals (e.g., division directors, supervisory personnel, external stakeholders) receive a copy. This distribution ensures that key players have at least some basic information about the overall scope and responsibilities of the education and training unit.

Obtaining and Maintaining Support of the Wider Community

As discussed in Chapter Four, the wider community and forces within that community (such as the economic, political, and social climate) are critical considerations in planning programs for adults. Four specific strategies are discussed for gaining wide community support: (1) constructing advisory committees; (2) putting together strong legally constituted boards; (3) forming learning partnerships; and (4) using technology-based formats.

Support Through Advisory Committees

The most common type of group that program planners work with is an advisory committee. Such committees are given a variety of informal titles, such as advisory councils, steering committees, coordinating committees, and ad hoc planning boards. Although these committees are advisory and therefore not empowered to make decisions that must be followed, members can nonetheless influence how planners work, the direction and outcomes of the planning process, and the focus of the education and training function in organizations. Program planners appreciate the impact that advisory committees can have, and therefore spend time building relationships between and among members and staff so these committees can work well together and provide useful suggestions and ideas (Wilbur, Smith, Bucklin, & Associates, 2000).

Advisory groups and committees may be permanent, or put together on an ad hoc basis. For example, a vocationally oriented program for low-income adults, funded through federal and state dollars and currently housed in a local community college, may ask for representatives from a number of different groups to serve on a program advisory council (e.g., the faculty, representatives of the business sector, community activist groups, funding agencies, and learners). This council's functions range from offering guidance and counsel for planning specific programs to wider environmental scanning and intervention activities. Council members could provide, for example, assistance in understanding general economic conditions and trends; recommendations for new markets where employees are needed; information on funding options; political clout to help ensure that funding continues; and assistance in designing programs to fit the diverse populations being served.

It is often program planners' responsibility to constitute advisory committees to assist in accurately depicting what is needed in programming to serve the adults in the organization and in providing advice throughout the planning process. Using the metaphor of the "planning table," Cervero and Wilson (2006) provide four basic reasons why it is important to form these groups. Those who sit at the planning table:

1. Determine the specific features of an educational program such as its purpose, content, audience, and format . . .

2. Draw attention to when judgments are made that determine the features of an educational organization . . .

3. Draw attention to the fundamental social and political character of educational planning . . .

4. Connect the technical, political and ethical domains of planning. (pp. 80–83)

The purpose, function, authority, and operating procedures of advisory committees should be understood by all involved, including group members, staff, and top-level leadership. Guidelines for achieving these principles and ways of operating and fostering successful advisory committees include making sure that members clearly understand what they are supposed to do, have a working knowledge of the program, and have real tasks to do (Birkenholz, 1999; Knowles, 1980).[8]

A number of time-consuming tasks and problems for program planners come from dealing with advisory committees; however, the assistance these committee members provide cannot be understated. Advisory committees, whether they are permanent or ad hoc, should not outlive their usefulness. When members believe they are wasting their time—or even worse, know that they are nothing more than names on a piece of paper—it is time to refocus or disband the group. This notion of refocusing includes both advisory and legally constituted entities, the latter of which is discussed in the following section.

Support Through Legally Constituted Boards

 SCENARIO 5.2:   AN UNWANTED SURPRISE

Roberta was excited to win the election to serve on the board of directors of the American Association of Adult and Continuing Education (AAACE). Roberta had worked her way up the ladder from a member of the Adult Basic Education (ABE) section of her state organization to serving as president of the Illinois Adult and Continuing Education Association (IACEA). Through her work with these groups and in her professional role she knew how to work with committees, plan conferences and workshops with volunteers, and, most important of all, work with Illinois legislators, adult education directors, teachers and adult students in furthering the work of adult education in her state. Roberta believed she could take her experience up a notch by helping with these same types of activities on a national basis. She went to her first AAACE board meeting in Washington D.C. and was told that the guidelines for travel expenses had changed, that all board members had to fund their own travel to the four meetings each year, and that there were tax issues to settle with the nonprofit status of the organization. The AAACE president let all board members know that they may have to contribute $1,500 each to handle the tax penalties because it was their fiduciary responsibility as board members. Roberta was shocked to know that she may have to contribute funds to the IRS as part of her legal responsibility as a board member and that her travel expenses would not be covered.

Roberta was not the only board member who was stunned by this turn of events. Roberta had believed serving on this board was an honor because she had been elected, and it was a natural progression of her service to her field. She had never considered her legal and fiduciary responsibilities in serving on a board of directors.

The roles and responsibilities of board members are often extensive, reach beyond participation in meetings, and are significantly different from serving on advisory committees (Epstein & McFarlan, 2011; Ingram, 1999; Walker & Heard, 2011). For example, as noted earlier, decisions that advisory committees make are not binding, whereas members of legally constituted boards are held accountable for all actions that are taken through a formal voting process, like Roberta learning that she may need to contribute funds to ensure that AAACE could pay its tax penalties. People who are asked to serve on legally constituted boards related to program planning should be fully apprised of what their roles and responsibilities are prior to accepting either an invitation or being elected to this type of board.

BoardSource (2012), DeWitt (2011), Epstein and McFarland (2011), Wilbur et al. (2000), and Walker and Heard (2011) provide examples of the responsibilities that these board members have such as ensuring that the mission of the organization is carried out; selecting, supporting, and evaluating the chief executive officer; and carrying out fiduciary responsibilities.[9] These responsibilities help to clarify duties of legally constituted boards; however, program planners may not be as clear on their own duties and responsibilities in terms of how they interact with the board, depending on their roles and position descriptions (e.g., chief executive officer (CEO), director of programs, or a member of the planning staff). Whatever position program planners hold, it is important to clarify their roles and responsibilities with the board. For example, directors of planning only attend board meetings in which issues related to their areas are being discussed. In contrast, CEOs normally attend all board meetings, although they are only ex-officio members, which mean they have no voting rights. However, because they are expected to provide leadership, guidance, and management to the organization and the board and staff, this type of planner interacts with individual board members and groups of members. CEOs especially must establish excellent working relationship with the board chair, the person on the board with whom they work most often (Epstein & McFarlan, 2011). In addition, under "normal circumstances, the board chair turns over more rapidly than the CEO position. This [rapid turnover] means the CEO not only has a deeper grasp . . . of the operational nuances [of the organization] but also often a much longer insight into how issues are playing out in their context" (Epstein & McFarlan, 2011, p. 19).

There are a number of problems that can come from legally constituted board members when their roles and responsibilities are not clear, or when the accepted operating procedures for the board are not followed and the balance of power becomes a problem among members of the board, the executives of an organization, and staff members.[10] As discussed in Chapter Four, when not handled properly, these kinds of power issues can make everyone uncomfortable, ruin careers, and raise havoc in organizations. By having a clear picture of the organization's mission and functions, as well as the roles and responsibilities of board members, CEOs and sometimes other staff members help with selecting board members. This premise is similar in choosing advisory committee members, except that staff members take the lead role in the selection process.

Designating Tasks and Selecting Members of Advisory Committees and Legally Constituted Boards

It is essential that members of advisory committees and legally constituted boards have real tasks to do, know what their tasks are, and understand what is expected of them related to these tasks. Keeping in mind that advisory committees only give advice, but boards set policy and make judgments in the best interest of the organization, examples of tasks appropriate for both types of groups include assisting with environmental scans, using existing power bases, and ensuring that the voices of all constituents are heard (Birkenholz, 1999; Epstein & McFarlan, 2011; and Wilbur et al., 2000).[11]

Selecting members for advisory committees and boards requires careful deliberation (BoardSource, 2012; DeWitt, 2011; Houle, 1989; Walker & Heard, 2011). Six major factors to consider are:

1. Diversity (e.g., age, gender, class, ethnic background)

2. Community connections with various kinds of people and organizations (e.g., community leaders, funders, partner organizations, and business)

3. Individual qualities (e.g., leadership skills, political and economic clout, willingness to work, knowledge of the industry and the subject matter, excellent people skills)

4. Personal style (e.g., consensus builder, good communicator, visionary)

5. Areas of expertise (e.g., management, fundraising, entrepreneurship)

6. Geographic location, especially for regional, national, and international programs

One way to ensure that these specific factors are taken into account when choosing members is to be clear about the criteria for making these choices. It is helpful to use a board matrix for selecting and recruiting board members.[12]

In addition to these six major factors, planners consider other criteria as well. For example, Birkenholz (1999) emphasizes that care must be taken to select individuals who "are respected among their peers; reflect the diversity of the target audience; are sincere, dedicated, conscientious, credible, [and] principled; speak their own mind, but can compromise; and are available [and] willing to meet and serve" (p. 60). BoardSource (2012) and Wilbur et al. (2000) have also suggested useful criteria for selecting current members of legally constituted boards for the various board positions such as chairperson, vice president, secretary, treasurer, and other at-large positions.

When being asked to serve on either advisory committees or legally constituted boards, potential members must ask themselves some key questions before agreeing to join. Epstein and McFarlan (2011) have provided a series of helpful questions to assist in making this decision. Although these questions are designed for those considering membership on a legally constituted board, they are equally useful for potential advisory committee members. Examples of these questions include:

- Do I believe in the mission of the organization? . . .

- Do I have the time available to do this work and [do their meeting times] work for me? . . .

- Are there potential conflicts of interest between this organization's board [or advisory committee] and other activities [with which I am involved]?

- Do I have the background and skills that are appropriate to the needs of the organization?

- Do I understand the real reasons that I have been chosen?

- Will my [family] be supportive of this relationship or will [serving on this board or committee] be intrusive? (pp. 165–166)

In addition, Epstein and McFarlan (2011) suggest a number of things that new advisory committee and board members do once they have committed to being a part of these groups (e.g., obtaining the dates and times for meeting, meeting with the chair of the board or advisory committee to gain insights into the past organizational decisions and organizational operating style).

Conducting Advisory Committee and Legally Constituted Board Meetings

Program planners often find that part of their responsibility is to plan and sometimes chair the meetings of their advisory committees. However, when CEOs also have planning responsibilities, they usually do not chair or plan advisory committees, for their major responsibility is working with the board chair and staff members in planning the agenda for board meetings. These committee and board meetings serve as important tools where information is introduced and shared, ideas are generated, and plans are made for present and future programs. We have all attended pro forma meetings where there is little, if any, chance for participation, and other meetings that are exciting, where the ideas and thoughts presented by members mattered and made a difference. The actions of a program planner can make this difference.

Committee members appreciate receiving via e-mail agendas and whatever reports and material are to be reviewed (which is required for board meetings) with enough time to read them before the meeting so that they can come prepared (Mancuso, 2011). Having the information needed prior to meetings, including a well-structured agenda, allows committee and board members to focus their discussions on generating new ideas, handling problems, developing strategies, and planning for the future. In addition, in face-to-face meetings, smart planners have coffee, tea, and cold drinks available, and ensure that meeting rooms are both functional and comfortable.

People today seem much busier and have less time to spend in face-to-face meetings. Fortunately, program planners have the option of bringing together members of these advisory committees and boards through virtual means, such as hosting a web conference that allows everyone to listen and see the person initiating the meeting on camera, or via a conference call. The trend for these groups is to have people come together sometimes through virtual meetings and other times for face-to-face meetings to achieve the objectives and intended results in an organized and concise manner. Well-run meetings have less reporting (e.g., reading of past minutes to the members) and more summarizing to limit the time spent on an unproductive fact review. For example, as noted above, it is not unusual to expect board and committee members to read reports and other materials prior to the meeting and to generate questions for those who summarize the report, so that their discussion can be richer and to the point.

The importance of running meetings efficiently cannot be overstated because so much of the program planners' time is spent in meetings that take a great deal of time and effort on the part of planners and participants. Therefore, the more efficiently meetings are run, the better the quality of the results for programs and organizations (Whetten & Cameron, 2007). A sampling of very useful ideas for preparing and conducting meetings provided by Whetten and Cameron (2007) include knowing the purpose of the meeting, understanding the different perspectives of how to run a meeting, and planning and conducting meetings effectively.[13] Additional useful resources for preparing and conducting productive board and committee meetings include Epstein and McFarlan (2011), Jay (2009), Mancuso (2011), Shepard (2003), Wilbur et al. (2000).

Support Through Partnerships

"In basic terms, partnerships imply that the organizations [involved] benefit from [this form] of . . . relationship" [whether between or among organizations] (Calley, 2011, p. 211). Partnerships for planning programs for adults, according to Donaldson and Kozoll (1999) and Highum and Lund (2000), come in all shapes and sizes. More specifically, Donaldson and Kozoll (1999) assert that although there are many forms of partnerships, the most highly developed and complex are those grounded in collaboration. Collaborative partnerships are characterized by being "organizations [unto] themselves [although often of a short duration], . . . employ unconventional kinds of governance, and rely more on informal mechanisms" (p. 3). In addition, the leadership functions differ for planners who operate in partnerships versus those who work from one organizational base. These planners span boundaries of culture, space, and ways of operating as they move between and among the organizational partners. Other forms of partnership arrangements include cooperation (that is, providing mutual assistance on an ad hoc basis) and coordination, where institutions consistently take into account what types of programs for adults are being offered by similar groups, and find their own market niches rather than being in direct competition (Kanter & Fine, 2010).

Building and Maintaining Partnerships

In addition to how partnerships are defined, the relationship between or among partners may be informal or formal, voluntary or involuntary, and result in a variety of interactions. In addition, these partnerships among organizations can be characterized as amicable to openly hostile. A number of authors describe fundamental principles or ways of operating to ensure that the partnerships are truly collaborative in nature (Brabham, 2009; Donaldson & Kozoll, 1999; Kanter & Fine, 2010; Kouzes & Posner, 2007; McCullum, 2000; Sparks, 2000; Wilbur et al., 2000). Although people are good and intend to be helpful, not all partnerships stay on track to be meaningful and productive. Partnerships need to be carefully monitored. More specifically, there are nine critical operating principles or norms for building and maintaining partnerships.[14]

Putting these principles into practice, however, is not an easy task; more often than not, it is messy and can feel like an endless process as partnerships evolve. Put in more positive terms, one of the challenges that members of successful partnerships gladly embrace is educating members on these critical principles or norms, and continuous feedback to each of the partners on their interactions and actions.[15]

An excellent source of questions to assist planning partners in assessing the strength and intensity of their work has been developed by Donaldson and Kozell (1999). These questions focus on program complexity and scope, leadership and vision, tension, strategies, and fragile relationships. In addition, Kouzes and Posner (2007) provide strategies for addressing many of the factors cited by Donaldson and Kozell (1999); Kanter and Fine (2010) discuss making these same connections and partnerships through online interactions.

In addition to thinking about building and sustaining partnerships, those in partnership arrangements also need to acknowledge that there is a time for many of these groups to end (Donaldson & Kozoll, 1999). This disbanding of partnerships may be on friendly terms—for example, the goals of the partnerships have been successfully met and therefore their task is done. These endings may also be due to continued inaction or even hostile relationships between or among partners. Whatever the reason, the partners need to assess the partnership or collaborative effort and decide if it can be mended or whether they should let it go.

For those partnerships that are ending and have had great working relationships, there may be feelings of sadness and even loss, as well as celebrations of accomplishments, all of which needs to be acknowledged. Where lack of activity is the major issue, someone just has to take the initiative to end the relationship, which is fairly easy for informal partnerships, but more complex for groups that have legal ties. If open conflict and purposeful noncooperation are the problems, steps have to be taken to dissolve the partnership as amicably as possible, which can be a difficult but important undertaking, as the aftermath of open hostility can last for long periods, resulting in continuing squabbles and lack of cooperation between and among these groups. A disheartening consequence is when these hostile partnerships serve as a major component in further change processes. The groups may refuse to work with each other or even sabotage each others' best efforts. Examples of these destructive types of endings include planning such events as parades that honor one's ethnic or cultural group, but are opposed by other groups; professional development programs on procedures that are mandated by law or administrative fiat, but are diametrically opposed by program participants; and community action activities that are for the "common good" of the whole community, but are attacked by a few powerful interest groups with political clout.

Gaining Support Through the Internet and Social Media

Organizations can connect people, build relationships, and lead groups to support their causes, all online without face-to-face interactions (Kanter & Fine, 2010). The communication tools available through the Internet along with the networking tools available through social media (see Chapter Thirteen) have introduced new ways for planners to reach and gain support from the wider community as well as with other members and stakeholders in the planning process. These tools foster the quick spread of ideas and rapid communication across great distances, bringing the world together.

New methods of communication and collaboration between planners and other key players in the planning process have arisen from advances in tools and applications available via the Internet. Though few would disagree with the preference for gathering an advisory committee or a board together face-to-face, use of the Web to bring these groups together and build successful planning relationships has become an acceptable alternative for face-to-face meetings. New communication tools (e.g., video conferencing, "cloud computing," document sharing, online scheduling tools), and selective social media networking tools (e.g., LinkedIn Group pages, Blogs, Facebook Group pages) permit planners to develop an ongoing dialogue and have "face-to-face" live chats with key players across great distances (see Chapter Thirteen). These tools permit planners to build relationships with prominent figures in the field, not just the individuals who are in proximity.

An example of the advantages of these tools for the planning process can be seen in the planning of the Western Region Research Conference on the Education of Adults (WRRCEA) Conference in 2007 (Scenario 5.3). The WRRCEA conference has continued to be presented two more times, with the same support system, collegial interactions, and successful online participation as the original 2007 conference.

SCENARIO 5.3:   BUILDING RELATIONSHIPS FOR CONFERENCE PLANNING

The planning for this conference began with a face-to-face meeting and was followed by an online needs assessment of the target audience. After the needs assessment indicated an interest and commitment to form the conference, an advisory committee of nine prominent professors in the field of adult education was formed. Over the course of eighteen months, the professors met nine times through live audio connections on the web. Students enrolled in a class on program planning at Western Washington University were also invited to assist in the planning process. The students collaborated with one another and with the advisory committee through discussions on a course management system (CMS) as well as through audio conferencing online. Fresh ideas were brought to the planning table by the inclusion of students, the students were able to gain real-life planning experience, and the advisory committee was able to effectively design and develop a conference without needing to take the time to travel great distances and meet face-to-face.

On the first day of the conference, many students and professors who had come to know each other well through the course of the planning process greeted each other in person for the first time. A collegial spirit and a successful conference were developed on the Internet, without physical, in-person interactions.

The Internet and social media also present a number of opportunities to build relationships and gather support from the larger community. As seen in recent upheavals around the world, social media can provide program planners with a means to reach a larger audience and gather support (both financial and social) in a quick manner. According to recent research on the social networks that have evolved from the social media tools, Stanley Milgram's "six degrees of separation" have been shortened to about four degrees of separation (Kwak, Lee, Park, & Moon, 2010), which means that one person can be connected to any other person in the world through four other people, on average. For example, Becky in Berkeley, California, is connected to Aleksei in Moscow, Russia, through her friend Jason in Canada, who is friends with Finn in Ireland, who is friends with Emily in England, who is friends with Aleksei. Social media tools are effectively working to shrink the global community and help planners reach a larger audience.

Today's connections span the world. Although online communities are not a substitute for face-to-face connections, they do serve an important role in staying connected. "Indeed, these networks are more than random gatherings of people online. Social networks have specific structures and patterns to them. In order to engage them well, organizations need to understand the fundamental building blocks of social networks" (Kanter & Fine, 2010, p. 27). One method for organizing support groups online is to form "crowdsourcing."

Brabham (2009) introduces the term of "crowdsourcing" to describe a method for "harnessing collective intellect and creative solutions from networks of citizens in organized ways that serve the needs of planners" (p. 257). Crowdsourcing is a model of online collaboration, with problem solving to get the groups of people or the public to comment on planning projects. Brabham (2009) acknowledges the benefits of participation for program planning and outlines "the theories of collective intelligence and crowd wisdom, arguing for the medium of the Web as an appropriate technology for harnessing such far-flung genius" (p. 243). Fiskaa (2005) agrees that collaboration on projects is beneficial and says "the purpose of . . . participation is of course to obtain better plans, meaning that they are well accepted by most, and therefore easier to carry out" (pp. 160–161). Another point in the wisdom of using crowdsourcing is discussed by Surowiecki (2004):

> After all, think about what happens if you ask a hundred people to run a 100-meter race, and then average their times. The average time will not be better than the time of the fastest runners. It will be worse. It will be a mediocre time. But ask a hundred people to answer a question or solve a problem, and the average answer will often be at least as good as the answer of the smartest member. With most things, the average is mediocrity. With decision making, it's often excellence. You could say it's as if we've been programmed to be collectively smart. (p. 22)

Program planners can use social networks and crowdsourcing to structure communications, build relationships, and garner support from the larger community. Though these tasks primarily serve to promote program support and the development of relationships, they may also be accompanied by some challenges. Planners may need to figure out when to include or exclude individuals and how to handle resistance. Therefore, thinking through strategies for obtaining support from the wider community with social media and the Internet is essential in the planning process. Depending on the nature of the program, a wider community can enhance the value of the program with support coming from not only localized groups (such as cities and regions) but also those at national and international levels. Social media can be used in an effective manner to gather support and build relationships with the larger community, but you must first decide who should be targeted and what message should be conveyed (see Chapter Thirteen for a discussion on identifying a program audience and developing a marketing message).

Chapter Highlights

Establishing a firm base of support for planning and conducting education and training programs is central to ensuring that effective and useful programs are developed and successfully implemented. As Keith Sonberg states: "What really drives performance is not metrics. It's passion plus pride equals performance. I call it the three P's . . . The [program planner's] job is to create an environment where people are passionate about what they're doing and take pride in what they're doing. The end result will always be performance" (Sonberg (2002) as cited by Kouzes & Posner, 2007, p. 130). To reach "performance," planners enlist others to support them. The support comes from staff members, professional colleagues, program participants, people willing to serve on their boards and committees, and other stakeholders.

In building a solid base of support for program planning, program planners concentrate on six major tasks:

- Ensure support from key constituent groups, including current and potential participants, all levels of organizational personnel, and other stakeholders through such mechanisms as participating in planning and conducting education and training activities, supporting transfer of learning strategies, and serving on advisory committees or legally constituted boards.

- Cultivate continuous organizational support through establishing appropriate structural mechanisms (e.g., mission and goals statements, standard operating procedures and policies, what formal authority the unit has over programs), the choice of which depends primarily on the centrality of the education or training function.

- Promote an organizational culture in which continuous learning and education and training programs for all staff are valued.

- Obtain and maintain support from the wider community through formal and ad hoc groups and boards, with key underlying assumptions that ideas and observations from members are heard and used, democratic planning is fostered, and collaborative interaction is the operative norm.

- Build and sustain collaborative partnerships with other organizations and groups that provide different vehicles for program planning and delivery that are in the best interests of all involved parties.

- Connect to people, build relationships, and lead groups to support all aspects of the planning process through a variety of online tools.

These tasks, if viewed as an ongoing and integral part of the planning process, often are revisited in a more formal way only at the start of major new program initiatives, when people take on new positions or additional planning responsibilities, or on a scheduled periodic basis. As in discerning the context for planning, establishing a solid basis of support for education and training programs is vital in carrying through the other components and corresponding tasks of the Interactive Model of Program Planning. In the following chapter we discuss identifying and prioritizing needs and ideas for programs, a component in which planners often involve people, organizations, or the community in providing the base of support for their programs.

Notes for Additional Online Resources

1. See Scenario 5.A: Influence from Supervisors.

2. See Exhibit 5.A: Activities for Supervisors to Support Education and Training Programs Before, During, and After Programs.

3. See Exhibit 5.B: Strategies Staff Can Use to Work with or "Around" Supervisory Personnel.

4. See Exhibit 5.C: Ways Planners Gain Support for Middle- and Senior-Level Managers.

5. See Scenario 5.B: Commitment to Collaborate.

6. A sampling of specific ways to build structural organizational support—organizational mission and goals, standard operating procedures, and organizational authority—within each of the three organizational frameworks are provided in Exhibit 5.D: Ways to Build Structural Organizational Support.

7. See Exhibit 5.E: Process to Build a Supportive Organizational Culture.

8. See Exhibit 5.F: Guidelines for Fostering Successful Advisory Committees.

9. See Exhibit 5.G: Sample Responsibilities of Legally Constituted Boards for a description of these and additional board member responsibilities.

10. See Scenario 5.C: Managing the Power and Support of Board Members.

11. See Exhibit 5.H: Examples of Tasks Appropriate for Legally Constituted Boards and Advisory Committees.

12. See Exhibit 5.I: Board Matrix Worksheet.

13. See Exhibit 5.J: Useful Ideas for Preparing and Conducting Meetings.

14. See Scenarios 5.D: Voluntary Joint Planning and 5.E: Mandated Joint Planning.

15. See Exhibit 5.K: Critical Operating Principles for Building and Maintaining Partnerships.

16. See Exhibit 5.L: Strategies for Building and Sustaining Partnerships for sample strategies planners use for building and sustaining partnerships that relate to these critical principles and norms.

Application Exercises

The first two application exercises help you establish a solid base of support for program planning by first gaining support from key stakeholders and building organizational structural support. The third addresses obtaining and maintaining support from people in the wider community, and the fourth focuses on specific strategies that are used in building and maintaining partnerships.

EXERCISE 5.1

Ensuring Support for Education and Training Programs

1. Complete the chart with ideas for how you have or could have involved learners, supervisors, and mid- and upper-level managers in an organization's education and training activities. Be as specific as possible in naming the persons or types of personnel you would like to or have included.

	Before the Program	During the Program	After the Program
What Current or Past Participants Can Do			
What Supervisors Can Do			
What Mid- and Upper-Level Managers Can Do			

2. Review your ideas with a colleague or your planning committee and revise as needed.

_____

_____

_____

_____

_____

_____

_____

_____

_____

_____

_____

_____

_____

_____

_____

_____

_____

_____

_____

EXERCISE 5.2

Building Structural Support for Education and Training Programs

1. Describe briefly your current organizational setting or one that has as all or part of its function planning education and training programs for adults.

_____

_____

_____

_____

_____

2. Indicate whether planning these programs is:

   a. The primary mission of the organization

   b. One of the functions of the organization, with a centralized unit to manage that function

   c. One of the functions of the organization, but with no centralized unit to manage that function

3. Identify, within the organizational framework you have indicated above, how you would build structural support for planning education and training programs within that organization.

Structural Factors	Specific Examples of Ways to Build Support
Mission Statements	
Policies and Standard Operating Procedures	
System of Formal Organizational Authority	
Organizational Decision Making	
Financial Resources	
Physical Facilities	

EXERCISE 5.3

Obtaining and Maintaining People Support from the Wider Community

1. Briefly describe an education or training program that you are currently planning or have planned in the past two years in which an advisory committee or a legally constituted board was involved in the planning process.

    _____

    _____

    _____

    _____

2. Using the chart provided below, list a sampling of people from one or more of these groups who were involved in the planning and/or implementation process. What roles and/or actions did these members play in this process? Was their involvement helpful, and if so why, and if not why not?

Name of Person	Roles Played and/or Actions Taken	Results

EXERCISE 5.4

Strategies for Building and Sustaining Partnerships

1. Briefly describe a situation in which your organization either is or has been involved with one or more partners for the purpose of planning educating and training programs.

2. Following the instructions in either 2.a. or 2.b., use Exhibit 5.K to complete the chart given below (see web site).

   a. For a partnership arrangement that your organization currently has, outline a sampling of the strategies that have been or are being used in both building and sustaining this partnership. For each of the strategies, provide reasons why the strategy did or did not work.

   b. For a partnership arrangement that your organization was involved in, outline a sampling of the strategies that were used in both building and sustaining this partnership. For each of these strategies, provide reasons why each strategy did or did not work.

Strategies	Reasons Did or Did Not Work
Building Partnerships	
Sustaining Partnerships	

3. Discuss with colleagues from your organization or others with whom you work your analysis of why the strategies used by your organization for either building or sustaining partnerships did or did not work.

Chapter 6
Identifying and Prioritizing Ideas and Needs

IDENTIFYING RELEVANT IDEAS and needs—the program content—is one of the major tasks of people involved in planning education and training programs (Altschuld & Kumar, 2010; Barbazette, 2006; Gupta, Sleezer, & Russ-Eft, 2007; Houle, 1996; Sork, 2001). Although some prepackaged educational programs are appropriate to use across organizations, when choosing program content planners cannot assume that the participants in different organizations have the same needs. Rather, participants' needs as well as their situations, even when the organizations seem similar, may be different (see Chapter Four). Program planners thus have to be knowledgeable about the various available sources and how to assess needs and gather ideas for programs.

In most program planning models, this component of identifying ideas is called a needs assessment, needs analysis, or performance analysis. Although each process is somewhat different, they are all conceived as a highly structured process, sometimes rather lengthy, with a series of steps and specific procedures. "Although (a formally structured) needs assessment can be a powerful tool to justify and focus the planning effort" (Sork, 1990, p. 78), conducting this form of needs assessment is only one of many ways ideas are generated for education and training programs. This same sentiment is echoed by Grant (2002) as she observes that a formal "needs assessment has a fundamental role in education and training, but care is needed to prevent it from becoming a straightjacket" (p. 56). In actual practice, a highly structured needs assessment may not be necessary or even useful in identifying program ideas, either in terms of time or money spent (Altschuld & Kumar, 2010; Gboku & Lekoko, 2007; Grant, 2002; Sork, 2000, 2001). For example, when an educational program is mandated as part of federal or state regulations, to see whether either the organization or the staff desires such a program, using a formally structured mechanism to identify ideas for programs that address this mandate is a waste of time. Likewise, program participants may, while attending a current program, recognize and let the program sponsors know that there are additional knowledge and skills they need to learn before taking on an upcoming new assignment in another country.

We address first in this chapter what planners are looking for in this phase of the planning process, and then describe the most often used sources from which program ideas and needs are derived and examples of settings from which these are generated. We next explore the multiple techniques for identifying these ideas and needs. These techniques are appropriate for all forms of generating program ideas and needs, from informal to structured needs assessments. We then examine reasons program planners choose to conduct structured needs assessments, and describe one such model. An exploration of contextual issues in identifying program ideas and needs is then discussed, followed by an overview of how to prioritize these needs and ideas. As not all of the prioritized ideas and needs can be solved through education and training programs, we conclude the chapter with a brief look at alternative ways to address these issues.

Knowing What You Want to Accomplish

A number of concepts or descriptors have been used to define what program planners are looking for in generating ideas and needs for education and training programs—educational needs, performance problems, new opportunities, changing conditions, problems, concerns, areas for improvement, data-driven practice, societal issues, customer demands, resource availability, and images of ideal practice (Dick, Carey, & Carey, 2009; Green & Kreuter, 2005; Gupta, Sleezer, & Russ-Eft, 2007). No matter what term is used, program planners are seeking to respond to what they and the people, organizations, or communities they work with perceive as important topics, skills, and belief or value systems that adults should examine or know more about. Is it important to have these kinds of data? "Given that there is a risk in not meeting a need [or an idea], it is [important]—especially since needs [and ideas] guide so many of our collective activities" as program planners (Altschuld & Kumar, 2010, p. 13).

The term *educational need* is by far the most common descriptor in the literature and rhetoric of practice as the focal point for identifying ideas for education and training programs. An educational need is most often defined as a discrepancy or gap between what presently is and what should be (Dick et al., 2009; Leigh, Watkins, Platt, & Kaufman, 2000; Rothwell &

Kazanas, 2008; Sork, 2001). This "what should be" is described in a number of ways—as desired results, future states or conditions, changes in performance, or expected outcomes. The discrepancy or gap can appear in many forms. For example, an unemployed individual may enroll in a class on job-seeking skills because he wants to get another job yet cannot seem to find one. An organization might offer "outplacement" seminars for employees being laid off in hopes that these employees can learn to sell themselves elsewhere. Or a local activist group may approach the director of continuing education at a community college to lobby for additional job training programs to alleviate the continuing high rate of unemployment in the community.

Although defining educational needs as "gaps" is common and can be helpful in identifying ideas for education and training programs, it can also be limiting. This limitation stems primarily from the negative connotation inherent in seeing the "need" as a discrepancy or gap—the perception that something is missing or wrong with a person, an organization, or society and has to be fixed. For example, the implementation of an efficiency management program (which is mandated by senior management) is sometimes interpreted by staff members and customers as an administrative statement that services or products are less than acceptable, and that only with new training will staff members perform in ways that are truly cost-effective, and provide excellent products and service. If staff members believe they are already performing at high efficiency levels, they may resent the implication that their operations are not up to standard and the intrusion on their currently successful way of doing business. Likewise, previously satisfied clients may be frustrated that staff members are not as available as they were before (because they always seem to be in training sessions) and that procedures they liked and trusted are changing, and the clients may also fear that their costs will escalate.

Responding to needs as a way to justify program planning also implies that developing education and training programs is primarily a reactive versus a proactive process. Trainers and educators may be viewed as people who come in to put out organizational or community fires rather than proactively initiating innovative changes based on assets and strategies of the group or organization (Altschuld & Kumar, 2010). For example, some colleges and universities in the United States continue to sponsor required faculty development programs on diversity, which usually run only an hour or two. The expectation for these programs is that the campus will be more welcoming to faculty, staff, and students of color, or those with disabilities, and the like, with the end result that minority groups will be fully integrated into the college community. In reality, one often hears comments by many faculty members that these sessions are boring and just a waste of their time, whereas others are just plain angry, as they believe such programs do not address in depth the problems of discrimination that still exist on their campuses.

To further complicate the planning process, individual, organization, or community ideas of what is needed are not always in sync. This lack of agreement comes from many sources, such as practical arguments for and against proposed changes, strong disparities in beliefs and values, as well as ethnic and cultural differences (Forester, 1999; 2009; Indabawa & Mpofu, 2006; Newman, 2006). For example, antiabortion groups may demand that Planned Parenthood programs not be allowed to continue educational activities that contain information on abortion. Instead, they want staff to counsel young women only on certain options, such as adoption and raising the child themselves. On the other hand, other external groups believe providing information on all alternatives, including abortion, is critical. As demonstrated by this example, there is often an added dynamic to these messages sent by external groups, which are often contradictory and even diametrically opposed. Such a situation can result in either overt or covert conflict, which can then create difficult questions and issues for planners (Forester, 1989; 2009; Newman, 2006). For example, can program planners realistically respond in a way that will satisfy all of the conflicting parties? If not, which group or groups should be listened to, and why? How do staff members respond to those groups whose ideas were rejected?

Sources of Ideas and Needs for Education and Training Programs

Ideas for education and training programs surface in a number of ways, as described in the previous section, from identified needs to specific problems and opportunities. These ideas are gathered through informal to highly structured processes and stem from four primary sources: people, responsibilities and tasks of adult life, organizations, and communities and society in general. Examples of specific sources are drawn primarily from the work of Grant (2002); Gloku and Lekoko (2007); Green and Kreuter (2005); Knowles (1980); and Pearce (1998).[1]

Often the first sign that education and training programs are warranted is a specific idea, need, problem, or opportunity that surfaces from one of these four primary sources:

People

- Physicians from rural hospitals are finding that having direct access to a large medical center in their region is very helpful in both the diagnoses and treatment plans for their patients. However, they are also having difficultly using the technology, which is highly complex.

- Program participants are very vocal about how difficult it is to register for programs and how unhelpful staff members are when answering questions.

Responsibilities and Tasks of Adult Life

- Balancing work and family is problematic for a number of women and men, especially those who are committed to both their families and to time-consuming jobs and careers.

- Coping effectively with life events (such as the illness of a parent, job changes, returning to school, parenting teenagers, retirement) is a major challenge for many adults.

Organizations

- The Peace Corps has discovered a rich source of knowledge and skills among the new directors of regional programs worldwide that should be used in redesigning the training for these directors and for Peace Corps volunteers.

- Community organizations that depend on volunteers are having a difficult time recruiting and maintaining volunteer staff for their programs.

Communities and Society

- Recent massive cuts for public school education, stemming from large reductions in local, state, and national funding, has raised the concern of a variety of stakeholders (e.g., state and local boards of education, administrators, teachers, and parents). These different constituencies are demanding educational programs that clearly explain how these cuts will affect them in the short and long term.

- Issues related to culture (e.g., race, ethnicity, religion, gender, sexual orientation, and social class) continue to surface at the local, national, and international levels.

At this point, the job of educators and trainers is to explore the problems, ideas, needs, and opportunities in more depth. This process of problem clarification and analysis, which can be done in a number of ways, often occurs when gathering, analyzing, and prioritizing program ideas and needs.

Generating New Program Ideas and Needs

Ideas for education and training activities are identified in a number of ways, as illustrated in Scenarios 6.1 and 6.2.[2]

SCENARIO 6.1:   NEW IDEAS FROM A CONFERENCE

Matt, a staff member in the College of Continuing Education, attended a teleconference on new systems for the delivery of online programs. Because he believed the ideas presented would be very helpful to his unit's staff and to faculty members, he revisited the materials he had downloaded and those that were suggested as other sources for training (e.g., two videos he had not previously seen). He then discussed the idea over a luncheon meeting with two key staff members, the associate dean for the college, and three faculty members who had extensive experience with online delivery of courses. All were enthusiastic about creating a staff and faculty development program that would allow the participants to explore these alternative systems.

SCENARIO 6.2:   CHANGES IN HEALTH CARE POLICY

The director of continuing education for a national health care organization has been asked to conduct a nationwide needs assessment related to planning a three-day conference on how the recent government reorganization of the health care system will affect the way they currently practice. Juanita convenes a committee of five people to assist her in planning and conducting this effort. The committee is charged with outlining the specific purposes for this assessment, what data collection and analysis methods will be used, and how and to whom the results will be reported and used. As the members of this committee are all very busy people with tight schedules, she plans to hold e-meetings for committee members rather than face-to-face meetings.

These two scenarios illustrate the broad range of ways to collect ideas for programs, from observations and conversations based on personal experiences to less formal or highly structured needs assessments. Key techniques used by program planners to get a sense of what potential program participants might want or have to know are described in the next section.

Key Techniques

Ten of the most widely used techniques for generating ideas and needs for education and training programs are given in Exhibit 6.1. A description of each technique is provided, along with basic operational guidelines.

Many of these same techniques are also used to collect data for instructional and program evaluations (see Chapter Ten). In addition, data collected about program ideas and needs can be gleaned from what is learned about the context (see Chapter Four), formulating transfer of learning plans (see Chapter Nine), and program and instructional evaluations (see Chapters Eight and Ten).

In addition to the techniques described in Exhibit 6.1, there are numerous other methods for eliciting program ideas. Some of these methods, such as social network and trend analysis, are quite technical in nature and are primarily used by the corporate sector and selected government agencies (Scott, 2000). Other techniques, such as reviewing prepackaged education and training programs and bringing back ideas from various conferences and trade shows, are employed by a variety of organizations. Especially helpful resources that include more in-depth descriptions of techniques for generating program ideas and needs are contained in materials by Altschuld and Kumar (2010); Gboku and Lekoko (2007); Gupta, Sleezer, & Russ-Eft (2007); Lee and Owens (2000); McCawley (2009); Piskurich (2006); Rothwell and Kazanas (2008); and Silberman (2010).

No one technique for generating ideas and needs for programs is better than another. Each technique has its own strengths and weaknesses, depending on the context and the data required. How, then, do program planners determine which technique or combination of techniques is best for their situation? The following five criteria, extracted primarily from the work of Newstrom and Lilyquist (1979) and Rothwell and Kazanas (2008), are helpful to those selecting techniques:

- Consider characteristics of the target group(s) for the potential program(s).

- Determine how much involvement is reasonable in collecting data from potential respondents.

- Estimate time, cost, and other constraints.

- Ascertain type and depth of data required.

- Consider ability of planning staff members to use the technique(s).

EXHIBIT 6.1

Techniques for Generating Ideas for Education and Training Programs

Technique	Description	Operational Guidelines
Questionnaires	Gathering opinions, attitudes, preferences, perceptions, knowledge, practices, and other desired information through a question and answer format. Distributed via hard copy or electronic format.	Acceptable level of validity and reliability of the instrument for the target population should be established through previous research (your work or others) or a pretest of the instrument. If a pretest is done, the instrument format and content should be revised based on the findings.
Observations	Watching people individually or in groups doing actual or simulated tasks and activities.	Can use observations that are open-ended or structured (with specific variables to investigate). Examples of specific types of observations include time-motion studies, task listings, behavioral frequency counts, the recording of critical activities or events, and unstructured observations.
Interviews	Conversing with people individually or in groups, in person, by phone, or online.	Can use interviews that are open-ended, nondirected, or formally structured (with specific questions to ask). Should pretest and review interview questions unless they have been successfully used before with a similar population. Interview respondents can be chosen randomly, consist of a convenience sample, or be key informants (people who are highly respected and knowledgeable about the areas being addressed).
Group Sessions	Identifying and analyzing ideas, problems, and issues. Start with an idea, problem, or issue known to be of concern to those in the group. May be conducted face-to-face, via a conference call, or online.	Use one or more group facilitating techniques such as brainstorming, nominal group techniques, focus groups, consensus ranking, or large- and small-group (or a combination of the two) facilitated discussions. Ensure there are competent group facilitators to lead the process and group members who are both knowledgeable and willing to participate.

Technique	Description	Operational Guidelines
Job and Task Analysis	Collecting, tabulating, grouping, analyzing, interpreting, and reporting on the duties, tasks, and activities that make up a job. Tasks may be cognitive or skill-based.	Be sure the analysis is of a current job and performance. Provide for data collection from all knowledgeable parties (e.g., job incumbents, supervisors, managers, human resource personnel, volunteers, and clients or customers). Use a variety of techniques to collect data, such as questionnaires, task checklists, individual and group interviews, observations, a jury of experts, work records, and analysis of relevant technical publications.
Tests	Using paper-and-pencil or computer-based tests to measure a person's knowledge, skill, problem-finding and -solving capabilities, or attitudes and values.	Know what the test measures (knowledge, skills, problem finding and solving, attitudes, and values) and use it as a diagnostic tool for only those areas. Choose a specific test carefully. Be sure that what the test measures is relevant and important to the particular situation (e.g., do not use a test for knowledge if you are really interested in a hands-on skill). Make sure the test is both reliable and valid.
Documents and Artifacts	A variety of forms of these materials exist: strategic planning reports, web sites, computer files, policies and procedures manuals, historical records, photos, maps, calendars (specific events, religious holidays, etc.), performance evaluations, minutes of meetings, employee records, job efficiency indexes, monthly and annual reports, research and evaluation studies, curriculum reviews, statements of professional standards and competencies, books, professional and trade journals, and legislation.	Maintain up-to-date, active files that pertain to your current and future educational activities. Materials related to past programs may be useful, but should be culled on a regular cycle.

(Continued)

EXHIBIT 6.1 *(Continued)*

Techniques for Generating Ideas for Education and Training Programs

Technique	Description	Operational Guidelines
Performance and Product Reviews	Review of specific skills, procedures, actual performance, or tangible items that potential participants are currently doing or have produced.	Choose carefully what to review to ensure the performance or product is relevant to what needs to be analyzed. Determine what tool will be used in the review process (e.g., checklists, expert judgments, rating scales).
Social Indicators	Variables representing important characteristics of a group or social situation that are kept over a number of years by government, education, and social service organizations. These data, usually quantitative in nature, describe such areas as level of education, economic status, and demographic information.	Choose carefully the sources to ensure the data are up to date and accurate. Determine whether these data are pertinent to the target audience or local situation.
Informal Interactions with Colleagues, Friends, Family, and Acquaintances	Interacting informally with people about ideas for educational programs. These conversations take place over coffee, at lunch, in the hallways, in meetings, at professional conferences, and so on in person, over the phone, through e-mail, and via social networking sites.	Record and file ideas for current and future reference. Use a variety of ways to check out these ideas (e.g., check them once a month, make a file of priority or innovative ideas).

Observations, for example, normally require a low level of involvement by those being observed, whereas interviews and group sessions require a higher level of involvement. Costs and time requirements for well-designed questionnaires and job analyses are usually high; in contrast, costs and time requirements for conversations with colleagues and friends, and for reviewing print and computer-based materials, are generally low or moderate.

The techniques described in this section for generating program ideas and needs, as noted earlier in the chapter, are appropriate for all forms of identifying program ideas, ranging from highly structured to informal methods. Explored next are reasons why program planners choose to conduct structured needs assessments; included is one model for carrying out this process.

Conducting a Structured Needs Assessment

A structured needs assessment is defined as a systematic method, usually involving a rather lengthy process and based on formal needs assessment models or analyses, for identifying education and training problems, needs, issues, and the like. The focus of the assessment is not to find solutions for specific problems but to clarify and define the problems. Conducting a highly structured needs assessment, as noted earlier, is one of many ways that ideas and needs are identified for education and training programs. Although program planners often do not use them, nor are they a necessity, the myth still prevails that conducting this form of needs assessment is one of the major components of the program planning process. As Pearce (1998) has observed: "Much to the dismay of authors extolling the many virtues of [highly structured] needs assessment, programmers are not exhibiting poor professional judgment if they choose not to use them. Many highly successful programs have no needs assessment component" (p. 267), let alone those that are structured in nature.

Because conducting a highly structured needs assessment is not the way many planners identify ideas and issues, how do planners decide that using this method of generating program ideas is appropriate? Although there is no single definitive method to determine whether a highly structured needs assessment is warranted, there are some general guidelines when they should be done:

- When little is known about an idea, issue, or problem and more depth analysis is justified, because planners and other stakeholders deem the idea worthwhile and important.

- When more in-depth knowledge is required about the characteristics of the target audience and their perceptions about the idea, issue, or problem (e.g., Who is really interested in this idea? Who would be interested in planning an education or training program based on this idea? What does this idea mean to them?).

- When the expected results of responding to the idea, problem, or issue require major in-depth changes in people, organizations, or communities.

In addition, Pearce (1998) has provided a useful four-stage process for thinking about whether this form of needs assessment is warranted. The process begins with voicing program ideas and then moves to doing the initial assessment. Planners' reasons for presenting the program are then considered, followed by asking whether a more in-depth structured needs assessment is necessary; Pearce provides focused questions that planners can ask themselves as they complete this fourth stage.

There are three specific programming situations that stand out as usually necessitating and in some cases even mandating a highly structured needs assessment. First, many funding agencies, both governmental and private, require that a highly structured needs assessment be completed as part of the justification for funding a grant. Second, planners may choose to use a highly structured needs assessment in tandem with a marketing thrust to provide needed visibility for a new, and often risky, program prior to its formal planning. Finally, conducting a structured needs assessment may be a way planners can contend with power issues that arise (see Chapter Four). For example, through this process planners can empower those who are disenfranchised by asking them to be members of a needs assessment planning committee, or by making sure they are a part of the respondent group. Giving these groups a legitimate vehicle for expressing their opinions and needs can be a useful way to ensure their insights have a chance of being heard.

A number of models or descriptions of procedures have been developed for conducting systematic needs assessments (Altschuld & Kumar, 2010; Gupta, Sleezer, & Russ-Eft, 2007; McCawley, 2009; Morrison, Ross, Kalman, & Kemp, 2011; Pearce, 1998; Rothwell & Kazanas, 2008; Sork, 2001).[3] Although a structured needs assessment may occur in logical order or in a step-by-step fashion, most often, as with the Interactive Model of Program Planning, the various elements overlap, need to be revisited, or have already been addressed through other planning activities. As observed by Altschuld and Kumar (2010) some planners, especially those who are new to the planning field, believe that "the steps prescribed are exactly how to go about the process and if followed you will sail right through it with a good breeze and no major whitecaps. Nothing could be further from the truth . . . [as] the steps provide guidance but are not a straightjacket" (p. 29). For example, planners may already have made a conscious decision to conduct a formally structured needs assessment as part of an initial overall planning session and may also have appointed an ad hoc task force. In addition, even as data are being collected, the process may have to be revised, as the initial findings may not be realistic due to contextual factors or budgetary concerns.

One of the most important outcomes of a structured needs assessment may be a commitment by those involved in the process to ensure that the ideas from the needs assessment are actually used in the program planning process. According to Bradley, Kallick, and Regan (1991), "This [statement] may seem self-evident, but we would be wealthy if we had one dollar for every [highly structured] needs-assessment process that was undertaken and the data not used. Don't raise false hopes in those who contribute to [this form of] needs assessment" (p. 168). Ensuring this use of the data for planning means making sure at the outset that those in authority are willing to listen to the voices of those who respond, and that they will actually implement programs based on the assessment's findings. One helpful way to let respondents know that they have been heard is to inform them (through e-mail, web sites, newsletters, meetings, follow-up, and so on) how the results have been translated into upcoming programs and why some of the ideas have not yet been or will not be implemented.

Contextual Issues in Identifying Program Ideas and Needs

Human, organizational, and wider environmental factors (see Chapter Four) are often interwoven with the process of identifying ideas and needs for programs, whatever form that process takes. The initial phase of a need-generating process to set new program directions for a community-based Latino center is described in Scenario 6.3 to illustrate how these contextual variables come into play.

 SCENARIO 6.3:   A COMMUNITY CULTURAL CENTER

The board of directors charged Manuel, the new director of the Latino Community Center, and selected individuals who were very involved in the center's activities to collect ideas for new education and community action programs, with a main goal of assisting the board in setting new directions for the center. Manuel and his team of volunteers collected a wide variety of suggestions, impressions, and opinions from various sources, including groups who meet regularly at the center, Latino community leaders, and agencies in the community who primarily serve Latino families. Manuel's next steps in the process involved bringing these ideas back to the board of directors for their reactions, and gauging the wider community's reactions to the ideas presented.

The executive committee of the board and many of the Latino community leaders interviewed conveyed to Manuel that the center had often come under attack by the wider community for raising unpopular issues, such as school dropout rates of Latino children and the underemployment of a large percentage of the Latino population. These attacks had often been instrumental in blocking any programs the center wanted to initiate. As Manuel was not a "local" and had only been on the job for three months, this past history was new information and a bit disconcerting, especially with his personal commitment to social action and change.

Manuel had expected board members to discuss the information that had been collected and summarized and make at least preliminary recommendations for what directions the center should take. Rather, there was quite a bit of heated discussion about these data and it became very apparent during the board meeting that the members were split on the direction the center should take. Although Manuel was aware of this split, he was under the impression he had been hired because a majority of the board was committed to more community action programs, which were his forte and passion. In fact, more than half of the board was highly vocal at the meeting against many of the ideas that were community action–oriented, and they appeared unwilling to entertain these ideas further. One person in particular, who continually spoke loud and clear about moving away from a community action focus, seemed to be using her position on the board to advance her own political career in the community.

As the board meetings are always open to the public, a number of community leaders, neighborhood groups, and a local reporter were in attendance. The resulting newspaper articles, talk among local leaders, and neighborhood gossip created additional obstacles to moving the process toward actually making recommendations for action. A number of letters to the editor also appeared in support or rejection of the different options for changes in the center's direction.

As demonstrated in this scenario, this needs assessment process definitely did not work, but rather was stopped dead in its tracks. Before conducting the interviews neither Manuel nor the board had considered the various contextual factors that would affect how these data would be reviewed and used in setting the new directions for the center. A sampling of these factors included Manuel's lack of experience in the community; who the key stakeholders were; how to construct a workable decision-making process; who was needed to build coalitions around ideas judged to be worthwhile; and who had the political clout to make this process work for both the Latino and wider community.

A different outcome might have occurred if Manuel and the board had considered these factors beforehand and chosen a different process for reviewing the data and making recommendations about the center's future directions. For example, the director could have formed a special committee made up of board members, influential community leaders, and active participants of the center to analyze the data that were collected and make preliminary recommendations that they first discussed with the executive committee of the board. Then, if the executive committee believed that the recommendations would not be well received by the board or the community, rather than discussing them at the board meeting, individual and small-group meetings could have been held with key people to determine the best process for discussing the differences and moving the process forward in a positive way. As noted in Chapter Four, using contextual knowledge is neither an easy nor "surefire" way to ensure that the information gathered would be used to set new directions for the center. Rather, using this knowledge requires that Manuel and others be willing to address issues of power and to negotiate differences that have already and would continue to emerge if the process tried to move forward after the disastrous board meeting (see Chapter Four).

Prioritization of Ideas and Needs

No matter what kind of process is used for generating ideas and needs, and whether or not it goes smoothly, there are no magic formulas for deciding which program ideas are the best. There is no formula because often there are too many good ideas and needs that surface and "must" be addressed, or problems that "must" be solved. For example, "many African countries are faced with too many problems to work on, too much content to teach, and too many groups of learners to reach within the limited time and resources available" (Gboku & Lekoko, 2007, p. 77). The ideas, needs, and problems for programs may contradict each other, be unclear, or be unrealistic in terms of time, staff expertise, and cost. So even with enormous amounts of data or long lists of good ideas, program planners must figure out ways to make decisions about what ideas and needs are important, affordable, necessary, and so on. This prioritizing process is normally an element in most structured models of needs assessments, but also may need to be a part of an informal process. In addition, developing an education or training program also may not be the best way or even a viable way to respond to the ideas and problems that have been identified (Gupta, Sleezer, & Russ-Eft, 2007) as illustrated in Scenario 6.4.

SCENARIO 6.4:   WHERE TO START?

Christy has just been appointed the statewide director of staff development for the Cooperative Extension Service. She has been with Cooperative Extension for twelve years, eight of those years as a county agent and four as an extension specialist. Because the position has been vacant for six months, there is already a pile of requests for staff development activities sitting on her desk. In addition, her predecessor had conducted a statewide needs assessment, but none of the recommendations have been implemented. Christy decides she should get some programs up and running fast.

In reviewing all the program requests and the needs assessment data, she comes to two major conclusions: there are too many good program ideas to start up all at once, and some of the items appear to be problems that cannot be addressed by an educational program (e.g., the problem of staff being repeatedly asked to take on too many assignments). After consulting with her staff, Christy puts aside those items for which an educational intervention is clearly not appropriate. She plans to talk with the assistant director about what alternative ways she should recommend to tackle those issues. Next, she decides to plan, with a quickly constructed ad hoc committee, a series of workshops on volunteer leadership development. She knows this topic of improving volunteer leadership addresses one of the major goals of the statewide strategic plan, was cited as a major problem in the needs assessment report, and is viewed by county boards as a critical issue. In addition, Christy decides to respond to three of the many requests she has on her desk that seem amenable to an educational intervention. It just so happens that these three requests are from colleagues whom she knows she can count on to get people to the programs, and the programs deal with issues that county and federal government officials have asked the Extension Service to show they are doing something about.

As seen in this scenario, identifying ideas for education and training programs is usually not enough. People involved with program planning also have to sort through ideas to determine which of them make sense in terms of planning an education or training program, and which call for alternative interventions. Then, from the pool of ideas considered appropriate for educational activities, they decide which ideas should have priority. These two tasks, sorting ideas into categories and prioritizing needs and ideas, are often not considered by program planners, at least not in any systematic way. Rather, some planners just assume they are supposed to do everything, while others may prioritize ideas and needs, but in a haphazard manner with little thought to interventions other than education and training programs.

Defining Priority Ideas and Needs

What constitutes a priority idea in the context of program planning? Priority ideas are often thought of as the most important or the most feasible to address. Depending on the specific planning situation, however, other factors are considered, such as the number of people affected and availability of resources (Altschuld & Kumar, 2010; Gboku & Lekoko, 2007). As Sork states (2001), "priority setting involves deciding which needs [and ideas] will be addressed in what order" (p. 108).

Which program ideas become priorities is also tied to the context within which the decisions are being made (see Chapter Four). For example, do those responsible for planning programs have the power to make decisions about priorities, or must all such decisions be cleared with someone higher up? Are planners expected to use a collaborative style of making decisions? If so, is collaboration a genuine operational norm or one that senior staff just parrot, with the real expectation being quick results or an ever-increasing number of program participants? Can the planners make decisions within the confines of their own organizations, or must they form decision-making networks with outside groups, such as funders, regulatory agencies, or other outside agencies? Do the current economic, political, or social situations block or enhance ideas that may be viewed as priorities? Again, flexibility is the key, because the context for planning programs can change overnight. For example, major budget cuts, changes in leadership, and unanticipated conflicts could drastically change how decisions are made about future programs.

Selecting People for the Prioritizing Process

People who are involved in the actual priority-setting process may be the same individuals or groups who did the analyzing and sorting, or a combination of these people and additional individuals or groups. Yet, even at this stage, some planners often ignore the importance of having others be a part of the decision-making process. Rather, they tend to think that the most urgent issues and ideas will be obvious to everyone involved (and thus will be handled first). Even worse, some program planners simply accept the fact that part of the program planning business is their being "overwhelmed," and they use that as an excuse for not being responsive to why ideas and needs have or have not been translated into education and training activities.

Depending on the planning context, any combination of the following people could be involved in setting program priorities: past and current participants, representatives of professional organizations and funding organizations, content experts, and staff members.[4] Those responsible for planning programs may consult with these people on an individual basis or involve them in group discussions. Group meetings may be of an informal nature, or they may be formally organized committees (such as formally constituted education or training committees) that meet face-to-face, by phone, or online.

Procedures for Determining Priorities

"While there are many criteria and methods for prioritizing [needs and ideas], keep the procedure simple" (Althschuld & Kumar, 2010, p. 109). There are two primary approaches for prioritizing ideas for education and training programs: quantitative and qualitative (Althschuld & Kumar, 2010). Quantitative methods are based on numerical measures and usually involve some sort of rating charts. Qualitative strategies are more descriptive in nature, with choices being made primarily through open-ended group or one-on-one methods. Planners can choose to use both of these approaches in a priority-setting process or just one, depending on the nature of the ideas and needs identified, the time frame allotted to the process, and the preferences of the decision-making group. Each approach to priority setting is described later in this section. Whatever approach is used, a key element of the priority-setting process is to select or develop criteria.

Selecting and Developing Criteria

Criteria provide the basis on which priorities are judged, and also serve as the justification for the eventual choices. Althschuld and Kumar (2010), Gboku and Lekoko (2007), and Sork (1998) have offered a variety of criteria for making priority judgments. These criteria generally fall under two major categories: those dealing with importance and those dealing with feasibility (Althschuld & Kumar, 2010; Gboku & Lekoko, 2007; Rothwell & Kazanas, 2008; Sork, 1998). An overall judgment about an idea or need can be made only by its relative importance or feasibility, or on both importance and feasibility.[5]

These sample criteria are only a partial set of guidelines on which decisions about priorities are made. Not all the criteria under each category may be useful, and other criteria not outlined might be more appropriate, depending on the planning context. As Sork (1998) has observed: "No single set of criteria is suitable for all adult education settings . . . It is likely that most priority decisions are based on a few criteria considered important by decision makers" (p. 281).

Quantitative Approach

There are a number of quantitative approaches that can be used in determining programs that can help planners, in a timely and organized manner, to choose priorities among identified ideas and needs for programs (Althschuld & Kumar, 2010; Green & Keuter, 2005). Priority rating charts, using numerical data, are especially helpful when priorities are determined by a number of individuals or groups. The charts can be completed individually and the results then compiled, or a group as a whole may complete them. The size and complexity of these charts depends on how many criteria have been chosen and whether the criteria are rated equally or whether some criteria should have greater impact on the decision than others. For example, when applying criteria that are weighted equally, people are asked to give a ranking on each idea using a range of 10 (highest) to 1 (lowest). The rankings are then totaled, and the idea receiving the highest number is considered the top priority.[6] When the decision makers believe that some of the criteria should have more impact than others, weighting factors are assigned to each criterion. To carry out this task, assign the criteria weights, starting with criteria that should carry the most weight. Those criteria that carry the most weight are assigned the highest numbers, while those that carry the least are given the lowest. These numbers, on a scale of 10 to 1, are decided by those who are responsible for coordinating the prioritizing process. When program planners use a priority system in which the criteria are not equally weighted, the process is more complex than when each criterion is equally weighted.

Qualitative Approach

Qualitative approaches to setting priorities are also used, as noted earlier, either in concert with a quantitative approach or by themselves. Rather than being based on individuals or groups rating the ideas numerically, the ideas and needs that have been identified are most often discussed in small or large groups, or in a series of one-on-one interactions. These discussions may be face-to-face, via conference calls, or through e-conferencing. The criteria used in these deliberations are usually more fluid and open to the interpretation of the parties included in the dialogues than those that are quantitatively based.[7]

Others have suggested using a set of descriptors when initiating discussions of prioritizing needs and ideas via this approach (Kaufmann, Rojas, & Mayer, 1993). Examples of two types of descriptive word sets are given below.

Set One

- This need/idea is very critical
- This need/idea is moderately critical.
- This need/idea is not critical (therefore, ignore it).
- This is not a need.

Set Two

- High/High (address in 30 days)
- High (address in three to six months)
- Medium (address in six months to a year)
- Low (address in one to two years)
- Not a need or idea (do not consider)

Having participants in either group or individual discussions first sort the needs and ideas using these types of descriptors can be very helpful, especially when you have defined a large number of areas to be addressed. For example, going back to the community action program scenario (6.5), an alternative way that Manuel may have initiated the priority-setting process would have been to have committee members use one of the systems noted above to narrow down the most important areas to discuss more in depth.

Alternatives to Education and Training Programs

As noted earlier, there are a number of needs, ideas, issues, and problems that often surface when identifying ideas and needs for programs that require solutions other than education or training programs (Altschuld & Kumar, 2010; Green & Keuter, 2005, Rothwell & Kazanas, 2008). Some of these include:

- Lack of willingness to change

- Poor quality or lack of physical facilities or resources

- Inadequate or lack of communication systems

- Lack of support for transfer of learning activities

- Organizational norms and expectations that are in conflict with the proposed ideas

- Political, cultural, and other outside environmental pressures

A sample of these issues and problems are illustrated in Scenarios 6.5 and 6.6.

SCENARIO 6.5:   INTRODUCTION OF A NEW STRAIN OF RICE IN AFRICA

Extension educators in Guinea had assumed that rural farmers would welcome a training program to assist them in the planting and production of a new strain of rice that has been proven to produce a higher yield. This assumption was grounded in the fact that the majority of these farmers barely could feed their families, let alone be able to market this product to others. Though some of these farmers did attend the training program and plant the new crop (at least for a while), the majority of them chose not to do so. It really puzzled the extension educators and the developers of this new strain of rice, as the benefits of changing to the new strain appeared to be something that the farmers would want to do to secure a better livelihood for their families.

Because of the farmers' low participation rate, the extension educators assumed that the farmers were just not willing to change their current ways of doing things. What they later discovered was that these farmers were well aware that this new strain of rice was genetically altered and that the color and taste of the rice was different from what they currently ate. In other words, the extension educators had not done their homework related to how the people might respond to the introduction to a major change that went against their current beliefs and was in fact very different from their current diet. Had these extension agents included several farmers on the planning committee they probably would have known about these problems and thought differently about the content, design, and marketing of the training program.

SCENARIO 6.6:   I CAN'T HEAR AND I'M JUST PLAIN UNCOMFORTABLE

A group of senior citizens have been complaining for months that the installation of a new heat and air conditioning system in their center has been troublesome because they cannot hear when volunteers come to the center to conduct learning activities. They also are too cold or too hot much of the time because the new system has been difficult to regulate. This group has finally collectively said, "No more," and they have refused to attend any more programs until these problems are solved, even though most of them have found the programs to be informative and well presented.

The problem in this scenario is that although the ideas related to program content are addressed well, another need of the learners is not—poor physical facilities that interfere with their learning. Conducting education and training programs requires an environment that takes into account the physical needs of the participants. Older adults, as illustrated here, often require acoustical adjustments in learning environments, especially when changes are made in which extra background noise is added. In addition, many are also sensitive to the high and low temperatures, and if they are placed in uncomfortable physical facilities for too long, they will not return no matter how interested they are in the programs provided.

Frequently Used Interventions

Useful descriptions of the most frequently used interventions are those described by Barbazette (2006); Langdon, Whiteside & McKenna, 1999; Rossett, 1998; and Rothwell and Kazanas (1998).[8] In considering which alternative interventions might be the most useful, planners often find it helpful to focus on where the intervention is directed: toward individuals or groups, jobs or tasks, whole (or parts of) organizations, or entire communities.

For many organizations and community groups, the most frequently used alternatives to education and training programs are job aids and technology system support. Examples of such aids are flowcharts on how to operate equipment, online information sites, or lists of key contact people with their phone numbers and e-mail addresses. There is also a widespread use of organizational development processes and techniques, especially in for-profit organizations. For example, when organizations are presented with internal communications problems, they may look to redesign the communications system, rather than sponsor training programs for staff on how to communicate more effectively.

Although most program planners do not have the responsibility for selecting and implementing these alternative interventions, it is helpful for them to know who is responsible for these tasks, comprehend how these processes work, and understand what role, if any, they do or should play. Having this knowledge can help planners be more successful in the initial sorting process, have a better sense of who they need to talk with about possible alternative interventions, and give useful observations to those who have the responsibility for implementing different responses.

Chapter Highlights

Identifying and prioritizing relevant ideas for education and training programs ranges from informal hallway conversations to comprehensive structured needs and priority assessments. These ideas and needs take the form of problems of practice, new opportunities, changing conditions, societal issues, participant and stakeholder demands, images of ideal practice, and so on. Program ideas and needs surface from a number of sources—people, responsibilities and tasks of adult life, organizations, and communities and society in general—and are generated in numerous ways. As not all of the needs and ideas identified can be addressed, prioritizing them is an important part of ensuring that planners take a realistic look at what is critical and doable. The following tasks are central in identifying and prioritizing program needs and ideas:

- Decide what sources to use in identifying needs and ideas for education and training programs (e.g., current or potential program participants, employers, organizational and community leaders, personal issues, government regulations and legislative mandates, community and societal problems).

- Generate ideas through a variety of techniques. Example of the most often used techniques include questionnaires, interviews, observations, group sessions, job analyses, review of print and computer-based materials, social indicators, and conversations with colleagues. Remain open to gathering program ideas and needs using a wide variety of techniques that may not have been predetermined or even considered.

- Be aware that structured needs assessments are not the only way to identify ideas and needs for education and training programs. In reality, this way of generating program ideas is not often used; less formal and informal ways are more often employed.

- Ensure that you can defend why a structured needs assessment is warranted, and choose or develop a model for conducting this assessment that is appropriate to your situation.

- Consider contextual issues that might affect how ideas for programs are generated.

- Select people for the prioritizing process, such as past, current, or potential participants; context experts; staff and volunteers; representatives of funding organizations; community leaders; and other stakeholder groups.

- Develop criteria on which the priorities will be judged, and which will also serve as the justification for the eventual choices. Two major categories of criteria include importance and feasibility.

- Select an approach, quantitative, qualitative, or a combination of both, for how you will determine the program priorities, grounded in the criteria chosen.

- Determine as part of the prioritizing process whether the needs and ideas that have been identified are appropriate for an education or training program or whether alternative interventions are needed, such as changes in policies and procedures, modifications of facilities and resources, or designing organizational development activities.

It is helpful to identify and prioritize the ideas and needs prior to developing program objectives for a given program or set of programs, which is discussed in the next chapter. However, as often happens in the planning process, many of the components of the model are done simultaneously, and planners move back and forth among them, always checking to ensure there is a match among these components as much as is possible in any planning situation.

Notes for Additional Online Resources

1. See Exhibit 6.A: Sources of Ideas for Education and Training Programs.

2. See Scenarios 6.A: Problems with Efficiency and 6.B: Social Action for additional examples of ways to generate needs and new ideas.

3. See Exhibit 6.B: Elements of a Formally Structured Needs Assessment for a composite description of how to design a highly structured needs assessment, consisting of eleven elements; the exhibit includes specific examples of how to carry out each step for an organization-wide needs assessment.

4. See Exhibit 6.C: People Who Could Be Involved in Setting Priorities.

5. See Exhibit 6.D: Two Major Categories of Criteria with Examples and Descriptions.

6. See Exhibit 6.E: Sample Priority Rating Chart with Equally Weighted Criteria for a sample form.

7. See Scenario 6.C: Priority Setting for a Community Action Program.

8. See Exhibit 6.F: Alternative Interventions to Education and Training Programs.

Application Exercises

The first two applications exercises are designed to help you identify sources and choose specific techniques that could be used in generating ideas and needs for education and training programs. The third exercise addresses the selection and development of criteria and the approach that will be or was used for prioritizing the identified needs and ideas.

EXERCISE 6.1

Identifying Sources of Ideas and Needs for Education and Training Programs

1. Describe briefly an education or training program that you are currently planning or have recently planned.

    _____

    _____

    _____

    _____

2. Outline what sources of ideas you are using or did use for the program you described above. Be as specific as possible in naming those sources (e.g., names of individuals and groups; specific life problems and opportunities; political, economic, or social climate), and indicate where the sources are or can be located (See Exhibit 6.A on web site).

    People:

    _____

    _____

    Responsibilities and tasks of adult life:

    _____

    _____

    Communities and society:

    _____

    _____

3. Based on the material you outlined in response to the previous question, make a list of those sources you are using or did use. Are there any you did not or would not choose to use at this time?

    Sources you did use/are using:

    _____

    _____

    Sources you did use/are not choosing to use at this time, and why not:

    _____

    _____

EXERCISE 6.2

Choosing Techniques for Generating Ideas and Needs for Education and Training Programs

1. Using the same program that you described in Exercise 6.1, suggest different techniques this group or organization could or did use to generate ideas for specific education or training program and indicate why these might be or were useful (see Exhibit 6.1):

   _____
   _____
   _____
   _____
   _____
   _____
   _____
   _____
   _____

2. Might there be or were there any contextual factors (people, organizational, or environmental factors) that might or did influence why certain techniques might be or were chosen?

   _____
   _____
   _____
   _____
   _____
   _____
   _____
   _____
   _____

3. Of those techniques you listed in response to the previous question, which ones do you prefer to use, and why?

   _____
   _____
   _____
   _____
   _____
   _____
   _____
   _____

EXERCISE 6.3

Selecting and Developing Criteria and Choosing an Approach for Prioritizing Needs and Ideas for Training and Education Programs

1. Again using the same program as you described in Exercises 6.1 and 6.2, select or develop the criteria that could be or were used to judge which needs and ideas are the most important to address, and also those for which alternative training interventions are more appropriate (see Exhibit 6.D on web site).

    _____

    _____

    _____

    _____

    _____

    _____

    _____

    _____

    _____

    _____

    _____

    _____

    _____

2. Identify the approach(es) that the planning team could or did use to determine the priorities that could be or were addressed in past, current, or future programs. Please be specific as to why the approach(es) you used were chosen, and whether you would use the same approach(es) again in similar situations.

    _____

    _____

    _____

    _____

    _____

    _____

    _____

    _____

    _____

    _____

    _____

    _____

Chapter 7

Developing Program Goals and Objectives

DEVELOPING PROGRAM GOALS and objectives is a component of the planning process that must be thought through very carefully, as the goals and objectives help shape the major foci of the program for organizations, participants, and other stakeholders, such as funders. However, there are programs where this component may not be needed, such as a series of open-ended discussion groups or other educational activities that are social in nature. We first discuss how program goals are defined and constructed and follow with an overview of program objectives, how program objectives are constructed, and how planners judge the clarity of these objectives. In the final section of the chapter, we explore ways that program objectives are used to determine whether a program is internally consistent or doable.

Defining and Constructing Program Goals

The terms *program goals* and *program objectives* are sometimes used interchangeably in practice: what one organization calls a goal, another may call an objective. In addition, others use the term *program objectives*, when in fact they are referring to *learning objectives*, which are a part of the instructional design process (see Chapter Eight). Program goals refer to broad statements of purpose or intent for education and training programs, whereas program objectives identify the specific outcomes of the program.

More specifically, program goals answer the questions: Why are we doing this? (Milano & Ullius, 1998); What do we hope will change in the future? (Gboku & Lekoko, 2007); and Why is the program worth doing? (Rothwell & Cookson, 1997). For programs sponsored by organizations whose primary function is the education and training of adults (such as family literacy programs), the major program goals are usually a part of the organizational mission statement (see Chapter Five). This statement is also true for organizations that have centralized units charged with the education and training function, but in these organizations, the goals are usually a part of the unit's mission statement. No matter where the statement is located, program goals "provide an ideal future, but also should be realistic" (Gkoku & Lekoko, 2007, p. 89); this is a fine line that can make goals difficult to clarify and construct, and you may need to go through a number of drafts.

This process of setting goals for programs can be messy and time-consuming, related to the levels and number of stakeholders involved; the complexity of the problems, issues, and needs being addressed; and the situation at the time. For example, in the time that it took for a set of program goals to be in the "close to final" draft stage, leadership may have changed, funding sources may have dried up or changed priorities, and the political landscape may be different. Despite all of these possible changing contextual conditions, if in fact the program goals are agreed to by a majority of the stakeholders, it is time to move the program forward, with the understanding in most cases that some components of the program planning process, including the program goals, can and do change as the program is being developed.

As part of their Contingency-Based Program Planning (CBPP) model, Rothwell and Cookson (1997) provide three alternative ways to approach the task of constructing program goals: directive, collaborative, and non-directive. The first is directive in nature because program planners "do not seek very much [if any] input from stakeholders about the purposes of [the program]" (p. 153). Some if not many of you may be wondering aloud—but doesn't this contradict what we have been saying earlier about the importance of stakeholders, including the potential participants, in the planning process? In most situations, yes, but in a few cases there are issues and needs that must be addressed, no matter whether the recipients are even interested or want to learn more about the chosen topic areas (see Chapter Six). For example, education and training programs related to hospital security are required by many countries to become or remain accredited, and requirements for these programs are set by the accrediting associations. In this type of situation a directive approach makes the most sense.

In other cases, being directive in constructing program goals may not be the best or the most productive way to bring about change through the process of education. In such cases, which are often mandated from the top, the recipients and other stakeholders in the process may respond in a number of different ways—from actively challenging the programs to attending and seemingly making those changes a part of lives while quietly just going back to the ways things have been done before, even though they appear on the surface to have accepted the changes in practices.[1]

The collaborative approach is the one most often addressed in this volume. Working in conjunction with stakeholders is the hallmark of this approach, although the degree of collaboration depends on the people with whom planners work and the situation in which planners find themselves (Gboku & Lekoko, 2007; Rothwell & Cookson, 1997). In some cases all stakeholders play a major role in all phases of the goal-setting process, but in others they may have only minor roles or serve in an advisory capacity. For example, Gboku and Lekoko (2007), writing about developing programs for adult learners in Africa, observe that key stakeholders must be involved at all levels of the process. "At the national and sub-national levels, goal-setting might be the focus of early programme development and sessions involving representatives of the different groups who will implement, manage and support the programme at that level, together with the prospective learners" (p. 90). The central government policies related to the issues and problems to be addressed are especially important at this level of stakeholder involvement. "At local level, a community's goals for an adult education programme might be formulated through formal meetings and informal discussions with the perspective learners, community leaders, and with local government officials and NGOs" (p. 90). It is at this level that negotiation and mediation are often needed to bring the different parties to some agreement as to the major issues and needs upon which the goals are eventually formulated. This stage of the process often brings up the problem of power dynamics among the various groups and organizations, which brings to the forefront the skills of program planners to negotiate among the various stakeholder groups (Cervero & Wilson, 2006) (also see Chapter Four). Although most program planning situations do not require government involvement in setting goals and objectives for the program, this practice is the norm in most African countries, as few programs will be effective on a long-term basis if the national and local governments are not involved in this part of the process.

In the facilitative approach for constructing program goals, rather than taking on a leadership role "program planners [facilitate] decision making among participants and/or other stakeholders but make [few, if any] decisions themselves about [the] program... goals" (Rothwell & Cookson, 1997, p. 154). These decisions are instead made by program recipients or stakeholders through, for example, teams or committees put together by local community members. This type of goal setting is typical of what is often termed a "grassroots" effort, led by community leaders who do not associate themselves with any specific formal group or organization (Alinsky, 1969; Schaefer, 2006: Walter, 2007). Such leaders are people with a cause who are often committed to solving social problems at the local and regional level, and sometimes even nationally. It is important, however, that program planners be willing to step in and take a more active role in formulating program goals if they sincerely believe the group they are working with is floundering as demonstrated in Scenario 7.1.

 SCENARIO 7.1:   ORGANIZING A LOCAL COMMUNITY ACTION PROGRAM

Volunteers from churches located in a rural area who had just experienced floods that totally devastated three communities in their area decided that they wanted to provide flood relief for the affected families. This volunteer group consisted of flood victims whose losses were not great and other interested people from the community. Although they were well aware that major local branches of organizations, such as the American Red Cross, were sending teams of people in and collecting monetary donations to assist in this effort, they wanted to do their part. One of the members of this local group had a neighbor, Carla, who had extensive program planning experience and volunteered to assist with this effort. Carla set this program in motion by constituting an advisory committee that determined, based on information from relief agencies in the area and their own experiences in the community, what kinds of needs the flood victims had for goods and services that they could supply. In addition, she worked with this group to develop specific program goals that were realistic for this group to meet. The group's next step was to form teams, each of which would have coleaders, to take on certain responsibilities, such as collecting and delivering food, cleaning up homes and yards, and offering child-care services to families whose day-care facilities had been wiped out by the flood. As the teams moved into action, Carla was able to identify possible leaders for the group, and discussed her ideas with the advisory group that was formed. Once this leader was chosen, Carla stepped back from her leadership roles, although she continued to provide advice to the leader and the advisory group.

Unlike the scenario just presented, the facilitative approach to setting goals and moving into action is often tricky for program planners to navigate, especially in voluntary action groups. On the one hand, planners want to be helpful to the groups they are working with in assisting them to frame the direction they want to go. However, their professional judgment sometimes leads them to feel a need to step in and become more directive to ensure that the process does not become so unwieldy that very little related to the task at hand will actually be accomplished. In other words, program planners using this approach must remember that they are working with a "grassroots" effort, which means that the leadership for establishing the program goals and tasks lies with the local community group.

Defining Program Objectives

Program objectives provide clear statements of the specific results to be achieved through education and training programs in alignment with the program goals. Program planners may choose to develop these objectives separately or work on them simultaneously. In addition to giving a clear statement of the specific direction of a program, these objectives also serve as the foundation for instructional plans (see Chapter Eight), concrete guidelines for developing transfer of learning plans (see Chapter Nine), and benchmarks against which programs are evaluated (see Chapter Ten). Developing these objectives requires program developers "to think through [with the appropriate stakeholders] what is to be taught or done by participants, the resources required to achieve programme objectives, and the end product expected" (Gboku & Lekoko, 2007, p. 94).

There are two types of program objectives: educational and operational (Knowles, 1980). The *educational program objectives* reflect what participants are expected to learn as a result of attending a specific education or training program. This learning results in changes in individual participants, groups of learners, organizational practices and procedures, or in communities or segments of society. Program objectives that focus on change in individual participants are often translated into learning objectives (see Chapter Eight). Samples of program goals for different kinds of education programs for adults are displayed in Exhibit 7.1; here, these goals are matched with program objectives so the linkages between them can be seen.

The operational program objectives are not always directly linked to the program objective. However, in some situations they are, in terms of enabling participants to meet the program goals and objectives. This type of objective outlines how program staff will improve the quality and quantity of program resources and other basic operational aspects of the program. People who plan programs often overlook those program objectives

EXHIBIT 7.1

Sample Program Goals and Educational Program Objectives

Program Goals	Program Objectives
Community Literacy Program	
To develop a literacy program where participants from all walks of life and ethnic backgrounds feel welcomed, respected, their voices heard, and their messages responded to in a timely manner.	To offer formal classes, individual tutoring, and advisement in settings that are accessible to the participants, at times when they are able to attend, and with child care services available.
	To ensure that 70% of adults who are eligible and enroll in this program are able to read and write at a level sufficient to work in entry-level positions within a three-year time period.
To assist program participants who are currently applying for work or will apply within six months of completing the program to find employment.	To provide on-site employment counseling to all participants who request this service. To integrate into the formal instructional materials learning objectives that pertain to skills needed by job applicants (for example, filling out job applications, reading want ads).
	To set up a system for participants to interview for job openings through local employment agencies.
	To make sure that at least 40% of their program participants who apply for work either during or six months after the program are able to find employment.
Participatory Planning in Africa	
To provide rural women farmers in Nigeria the recognition that is warranted related to the major roles they play in the agricultural sector.	To gain the support of tribal elders from three rural villages in Nigeria to permit women from their village to both plan and participate in a two-week training program sponsored by an international nongovernmental agency and the local government. This program focuses on improving women's knowledge and skills in the production and marketing of wheat as an alternative crop for both family consumption and to sell in the local markets.
	To have tribal elders from these three villages identify five women from each village to be a part of the planning team.
	To guarantee these women will receive training in how to plan and evaluate a gender-sensitive program.

Program Goals	Program Objectives
To involve rural women in the planning of training programs geared to their needs and the realities of their circumstances.	To pilot test the program with fifteen women from each village, including members of the planning team.
	To revise the training program, with the original team who developed the pilot program, based on feedback received from the women who attended, the instructors, and representatives from other stakeholder groups such as government officials from the region and funding agencies.
	To provide open access to this program to all women from the three villages who have not had a chance to attend. The planning team is responsible for collecting the evaluation data and disseminating the results to the village elders, the women who participated in the program, and the stakeholders.*
Grassroots Education	
To respond to the needs expressed by adults with Attention Deficient Disorder (ADD) who have expressed an interest and willingness to assist others who have this condition.	To form a group of volunteers who have expressed an interest and willingness to plan and coordinate this initiative in their local community.
	To plan and initiate educational and support programs open to all adults with ADD and their families and friends who live in or near their community.
	To provide participants in the program with up-to-date and accurate information materials and strategies for locating their own materials.
	To facilitate educational programs on topics of interest to the participants and build a network of experts who can provide information and discussions on new developments in the knowledge and treatment of adults with ADD.
	To initiate opportunities for participants to share their thoughts and feelings about living with ADD and the coping strategies they use.

*Although rural women in Africa are very active participants in the agricultural sector in Africa, they are often either not offered participation in training programs related to improving their own skills and livelihoods or they are sadly underrepresented.

that are directed at improving the quality of the program operations. Yet, as appropriate, if developing these kinds of objectives is included as a regular part of the process of constructing the overall objectives, the overall quality and efficiency of programming will improve in many cases. In addition, although operational program objectives are probably more applicable to

---

EXHIBIT 7.2

Program Objectives Focused on Program Operations

Program Operations	Program Objectives
Adequate physical facilities	To provide adequate physical facilities that would accommodate disabled persons.
Equipment	To write a grant for changing a face-to-face program to an e-learning program that includes the computers, software, and the course management system needed to deliver the program.
Revenues	To set the registration fee for the program over costs by 10% with the proceeds used to create a new program.
Education program	To establish a training program for volunteers who could assist program staff in planning and carrying out educational programs and activities for low-income families.

---

programs housed in formal education and training organizations or units, these types of objectives are also useful to those who conduct educational activities as part of their other job responsibilities. Examples of operational program objectives are given Exhibit 7.2.

Constructing Program Objectives

Constructing program objectives, like constructing program goals, is a challenging activity. The challenges stem from three sources. First, at the heart of formulating program objectives is defining specific program outcomes. These outcomes can be elusive, especially at the beginning of the process. For example, those working in literacy programs know that one of the major objectives of these programs is that adults who lack literacy skills will be able to read and write. But what does being able to read and write mean? Does it mean reading at a specified grade level, having the reading and writing skills necessary to be a productive worker or member of society, or both of these outcomes and more? Second, in the actual writing of program objectives, the parameters are not always clear.

As with program goals, program planners do not usually develop program objectives in a vacuum. It would be relatively easy to sit in the office, carefully crafting program objectives, but the risk is very high for producing impractical or irrelevant projected outcomes. Instead, similar to the process of developing program goals, the other stakeholders such as program participants, work supervisors, and cooperating organization, should assist in developing and reviewing objectives. This involvement can be handled in a number of ways. For example, education and training staff could request that key supervisors of potential participants help draft or review program objectives for their people. They could also ask a sample of potential participants to help. Questions and comments from both of these groups could be solicited on the relevance and usefulness of the objectives and on their understandability (especially concerning practical application and usefulness). In addition, if a formal education or training committee exists, this committee may serve as a review board and work to give advice and counsel in the initial writing or the redrafting of the objectives (see Chapter Five).

Finally, when developing program objectives at a national or international level it is less likely, as noted earlier in this chapter, that others outside the sponsoring organization(s) will be involved in drafting these objectives. If other stakeholders are involved at this level, most often an advisory group is formed to provide feedback on program objectives to the planning group of the sponsoring organization(s). These advisory groups are carefully chosen by the sponsoring organizations, and normally involve those from stakeholders groups with political clout and national or international experts in the content of the program. These objectives may then be put out for public comment either through face-to-face public forums or via a web site set up for this purpose. However, for the most part, stakeholder involvement at this level is often very limited.

When writing program objectives, it is important for program planners to consider how the program will be evaluated (see Chapter Ten). One of the major aspects of the plan that evaluators examine is whether there is a match between the program objectives and program outcomes, and if not, why not. This process can be difficult as there are differences among program planners in their beliefs about whether program objectives should be stated in measurable terms (a common belief), or whether these objectives can also encompass outcomes that cannot be expressed in "seeable" performance (Chan, 2010; Gboku & Lekoko, 2007; Mehrens & Lehmann, 1991; Morell, 2010; Wholey, Hatry, & Newcomer, 2010). In addition, some program planners take the position that education and training programs have some outcomes that are measurable and some that are not. Likewise, outcomes can be either intended or unanticipated, because it is almost impossible to know beforehand all the benefits a program could produce. Therefore, in constructing program objectives, it is important to state both measurable and nonmeasurable objectives and to be flexible in renegotiating and reshaping those objectives so that unanticipated but important achievements and outcomes of the program are highlighted. This notion of measurable and nonmeasurable and intended and unanticipated results is illustrated in Exhibit 7.3 with examples of specific program objectives.

Program objectives, whether they are learning or operational, "should be stated clearly enough to indicate to all rational minds exactly what is intended" (Houle, 1996, p. 193). Houle goes on to describe a number of properties that characterize clearly articulated program objectives; three of them are highlighted below.

- *Program objectives are essentially rational and thus impose a logical pattern on the educational program.* This rationality does not mean that the objectives do or even could describe all the possible outcomes of education and training programs over a specified period of time. For example, in the case of large programs, program objectives that are learner and operational in scope are usually not comprehensive enough to speak to all aspects of the program. Nor do these objectives address the commonly accepted but often unstated motives, aspirations, and objectives of those persons who plan or participate in education and training activities.

- *Good program objectives are practical and concrete.* As practical guides for action, program objectives neither describe things as they ideally should be nor focus on esoteric problems that have no basis in reality. "The ultimate test of an objective is not validity but achievability" (Houle, 1996, p. 183).

- *Good program objectives are discriminating.* By stating one course of action, another is ruled out. For example, if resources for the next calendar year are targeted for new personnel, other staff members for the most part are excluded from education and training activities. Whether this course of action is appropriate depends on a number of factors. Was an education or training program for new staff viewed as a priority need? Does senior management support this decision? Do the supervisors of the new staff believe the programs being planned meet the needs of their people?

In addition, good program objectives, when the expectations of the sponsoring organization(s) are that program outcomes can be demonstrated, are written in measurable terms.

More specifically, people who plan programs ask themselves the following questions to help them judge the clarity of the program objectives they have developed for both those that focus on participant learning

EXHIBIT 7.3

Examples of Unintended and Intended Measurable and Nonmeasurable Program Objectives

Type of Objective		Intended Achievements *(stated before the program is carried out)*	Unanticipated Achievements *(stated during the program or after it has been carried out)*
Program Objectives Focused on Participant Outcomes	Measurable achievement	To provide an intensive educational program for new directors of Peace Corps for countries all over the world. These directors would be able to demonstrate through problems and situations presented to them that they are competent to: (1) address a range of difficult issues with which they would likely need to confront; (2) refer to any potential diplomatic matters they encountered to the embassy staff; and (3) manage personnel problems with individuals and groups of staff.	About 25% of the participants developed a strong network committed to sharing what was working for them, problems they were encountering, and ways they had addressed those problems. They also agreed to generally support each other through a secure Internet system.
	Nonmeasurable achievement	To assist new trainers to feel they have more control over their daily work lives.	A number of the trainers remarked on the program evaluation that they felt more confident in their ability to carry out their jobs.
Program Objectives Focused on Operational Outcomes	Measurable achievement	To generate funds through grant writing and program fees for a statewide HIV/AIDS awareness organization to develop a system for online instruction that could also be used for collaborative meetings with partner organizations.	In addition to the original funders, one additional organization that had provided grants for other activities at the center was so impressed with a demonstration of how the new system is being used that it pledged enough funding to develop a second model classroom.
	Nonmeasurable achievement	Through training programs for volunteers, funded with revenue-producing programs, these volunteers would feel they were an important part of the staff.	A number of the volunteers let the coordinator of their program know that this training program inspired them to recruit other volunteers to work with the organization.

and program operations, as applicable (Gboku & Lekoko, 2007; Milano & Ullius, 1998; Sork & Caffarella, 1989):

1. Is there a clear relationship between the objectives and the ideas, problems, and needs that have been identified as priority areas?

2. Do the objectives reflect the prior knowledge, experiences, and abilities of potential participants?

3. Do the objectives focus on a crucial part of the program?

4. Are the objectives practical and achievable?

5. Are the objectives attainable in the time frame proposed?

6. Do the objectives clearly communicate the proposed outcomes or accomplishments?

7. Are the objectives meaningful and will all interested parties understand them?

8. Are the objectives supposed to be measurable; and if so, are they?

9. Are the objectives congruent with each other?

Program objectives, again like program goals, may need to be negotiated and reworked at some point (or points) in the life of a program. Practically speaking, these changes in the program objectives mean program planners are willing to eliminate, revise, or add program objectives as the situation warrants (see Chapter Four). This updating of program objectives should be done in concert with key stakeholders and in a thoughtful manner. Negotiating these changes as a normal part of the process can come as a surprise, especially to novice planners and stakeholders who are unfamiliar with this type of approach to planning. Therefore, in some situations, those proposing the changes need to be well prepared to explain why these changes are needed, and be willing to compromise on what they are proposing. However, staff should not modify or eliminate certain objectives just because they do not want to provide the necessary programs; rather, staff have to have a strong rationale for revising or adding to initially agreed-upon program objectives.

Using Objectives as Checkpoints

Clearly stated program objectives, both learning and operational, provide one of the major checks for ensuring that a program has internal consistency and is doable. As noted earlier, use of program objectives as checkpoints does not mean these objectives are necessarily constructed prior to working on or completing planning tasks. However, once these objectives have been developed, other aspects of the plan (for example, the transfer of learning activities, budget, marketing, and staffing) or the planning process itself can be revisited to see if what is being proposed really addresses the expected outcomes and can be done. Scenarios 7.2 and 7.3 illustrate this point.

SCENARIO 7.2:   ENSURING OBJECTIVES ARE REALISTIC

In planning a continuing education program for family physicians on a new software program for patient record keeping, at its third meeting the planning team reviews a draft of the program objectives. One of the major expected outcomes is that participants will be able to integrate this new system as part of their practice within the next six months. Three of the planning team members caution the team that the potential participants are probably at many different stages in integrating this type of system into their current practices and question whether this objective is realistic. Based on these observations, team members then decide to reexamine the activities planned for the program itself to determine whether they can develop a transfer of learning plan that addresses this issue.

SCENARIO 7.3:   ENSURING OBJECTIVES ARE FEASIBLE

In writing the final draft of a revised training program for new teachers, Cassie, the director of the statewide literacy program, notices that what has been proposed is probably no longer feasible, given some recently projected funding cuts in the training budget. She decides to ask the ad hoc committee who assisted her in planning this program to meet and provide ideas for how this plan should be changed in light of these projected budget shortfalls. When Cassie meets with the committee members she asks them to share what they view as critical and not critical programming. Cassie then goes back to her funding agency and negotiates changes in the program objectives to eliminate those objectives that are not critical. Cassie might also seek additional funding elsewhere.

Using the program objectives as an internal consistency check is especially helpful in matching instructional, transfer of learning, and evaluation plans to what people want to see happen (see Chapters Eight, Nine, and Ten). For some programs, the connections between and among program objectives, transfer activities, and the evaluation process are readily apparent—the strategies and techniques for instruction, learning transfer, and evaluation may overlap or be one and the same. For example, selected supervisors might be asked to be part of the instructional team and require that participants, as part of the instructional process, develop learning applications or transfer plans. All supervisors could use the formal supervisory process as a strategy to ensure that participants use what they have learned on the job. In turn, the evaluation plan may include interviewing supervisors about the usefulness of the program as well as reviewing performance appraisal data. Therefore, checking to see that these components of the plan line up with one another and sufficiently target the proposed outcomes may be relatively easy. In other programs, syncing the program components may be more difficult; however, this process is still of upmost importance, especially when the sponsoring organizations or groups are not responsible for monitoring or evaluating the transfer of learning activities and outcomes.

Chapter Highlights

Program goals and objectives are an important component of the planning process as they provide differing levels of intent for education and training programs. Program goals are broad in scope and provide an almost ideal future, but they also need to be realistic, whereas program objectives provide clear statements of the proposed outcomes or anticipated results of a specific program. Although primarily centered on what participants learn, program objectives may also address the operational aspects of a program. Participants' learning may result in individual, organizational, community, or societal changes. Constructing program goals and objectives is a process of successive drafts until the final goals and objectives are established. When this process is complex and messy, having skilled negotiators on the team is a must.

In constructing program goals and objectives, program planners are cognizant of the following tasks:

- When developing the program, have a clear picture of the changes they hope to make in the future and why this program is worth doing.

- Choose the process or processes to be used in developing the program goals (directive, collaborative, or nondirective approach).

- Write program objectives that reflect what participants will learn, the resulting changes from that learning, and the operational aspects of the program.

- Ensure that both measurable and nonmeasurable program outcomes, as appropriate, are included.

- Check to see whether the program objectives are written clearly enough so they can be understood by all parties involved (for example, participants, sponsoring organizations).

- Use the program objectives as an internal consistency and achievability checkpoint (to determine, for example, whether the instructional, transfer of learning, and evaluation plans are in sync with these objectives).

- Negotiate changes in program goals and objectives, as appropriate, among the parties involved with the planning process.

The information provided through the program goals and objectives, as noted earlier, often serve as the point of departure for the instructional design process, which is discussed in the next chapter. In addition, these objectives are used when devising transfer of learning plans and in formulating program evaluations in Chapter Nine. In turn, the instructional, transfer of learning, and evaluation plans may inform changes that are needed in the initially drafted program goals and objectives.

Note for Additional Online Resource

1. See Scenario 7.A: Good Intentions with Little Understanding.

Application Exercises

The first two application exercises are designed to help you develop program goals and construct program objectives. The third exercise focuses on how to evaluate program objectives, and the final exercise looks at the process of revising program objectives.

EXERCISE 7.1

Developing Program Goals

1. Briefly describe a program planning situation you are currently planning or were involved in planning.

_____
_____
_____
_____
_____
_____

2. For those of you who are currently planning a program, choose one primary approach from the following three for how you would manage the process of writing each goal statement and why you would use that approach (the directive approach, the collaborative approach, or the nondirective approach). In addition, indicate why you would choose this particular approach. For those who wrote about a program that has already been planned, describe which approach or approaches you used in developing these goals, and why you made this choice.

_____
_____
_____
_____
_____
_____
_____

3. For the program that you are currently developing, construct three clearly written program goals. For a program that you were involved in planning, examine and critique the goals that were developed or, if goals were not a part of the plan, construct goals that could have been used.

Goal Statement One:

_____
_____
_____
_____

Goal Statement Two:

_____

_____

_____

_____

_____

_____

_____

Goal Statement Three:

_____

_____

_____

_____

_____

_____

_____

_____

EXERCISE 7.2

Constructing Program Objectives

Construct three clearly written program objectives for each of the program goals you developed in Exercise 7.1. For those programs you have already planned move to Exhibit 7.3 to evaluate those objectives. As appropriate, include objectives focused on participant learning and program operations.

Goal Statement One	Program Objectives
Goal Statement Two	**Program Objectives**
Goal Statement Three	**Program Objectives**

EXERCISE 7.3

Evaluating the Program Objectives

Using the questions provided below, ask one or two of your colleagues to help you critique the program objectives you developed (or had previously developed) for one of the goals in Exercise 7.2.

Questions To Ask	Objective	Objective	Objective
Is there a clear relationship between the objective and the goal identified?			
Does the objective focus on a crucial part of the program?			
Is the objective practical and achievable?			
Is the objective obtainable in the time frame you have proposed?			
Does the objective clearly communicate the proposed outcomes or accomplishments?			
Is the objective meaningful and can it be understood by all interested parties?			
Is the objective supposed to be measurable, and if so, is it?			
Does the objective reflect the prior knowledge, experiences, and abilities of the potential participants?			

EXERCISE 7.4

Revising the Program Objectives

Using the feedback from Exercise 7.3, rewrite program objectives that need revising in the space provided, and provide a rationale for why you made that change. (Please note that you may need or want to do this critiquing and revising process a number of times with the same or different colleagues.)

Original Program Objective	Revised Objective	Rationale for Revising

Chapter 8
Designing Instruction

DESIGNING INSTRUCTION INVOLVES planning the interaction between learners and instructors, or between learners. Those responsible for designing instruction may be paid staff, volunteers, or persons internal or external to an organization or community. The outcome of the instructional design process is an instructional plan, which serves as a guide for the presenters or facilitators of the learning activity being constructed (e.g., a class, a workshop, a community event, or an online format).[1] Depending on the nature of the program, more than one instructional plan may be needed. For a half-day workshop, usually only one plan is needed, whereas for a major conference, depending on the type of presentations, multiple plans are often put together by the persons who will be presenting.

Those who provide the instruction most often develop the various components that make up the instructional plan. Even if these individuals receive assistance in putting the plan together, the responsibility for the final product is theirs. There are times, though, when designing instruction needs to be a team effort, especially when the education and training activities are very complex and comprehensive (Smith & Ragan, 2005). The composition of these design teams varies, depending on the purpose, format, content, and scope of the education and training activity. Types of staff who may be needed on these teams include instructors, participants, instructional designers, subject-matter experts, technology specialists, managers of planning teams or projects, and persons representing the various stakeholder groups such as the program sponsors (Morrison, Ross, Kalman, & Kemp, 2011; Smith & Ragan, 2005). For example, the design team for a combination of a three-day intensive workshop delivered online for educators who want to incorporate online instruction into their teaching could be composed of a program planner, two instructors, a technology specialist, two participants, and a member of one of the sponsoring organizations.

In this chapter we first describe the learning objectives and how they are constructed, and then present suggestions for selecting and organizing the content to be taught. We next review choosing instructional techniques;

included in this section is a description of the key factors instructors take into consideration when choosing these techniques. One of these key factors is the focus of the learning objectives (e.g., acquiring knowledge, developing psychomotor skills, strengthening problem-solving and -finding capabilities), and we provide examples of specific techniques by learning outcomes, including the fast-growing number of technology-based techniques and tools. Next, we explore instructional assessment including why these types of assessment are important and the techniques that are used in assessing learning outcomes. The chapter concludes with examples of two instructional plans and a description of ways instructors make the plans work for them and their learners.

Developing Learning Objectives

Learning objectives, also known as performance objectives and learning outcomes, describe what participants will learn as a result of attending an education or training session (Bowman, 2009; Diamond, 2008; Dick, Carey, & Carey, 2009; Mager, 1990; Morrison et al., 2011; Smith & Ragan, 2005). These learning objectives are rooted in the context of the program objectives, so that there is continuity between the two sets of objectives. The major difference between learning and program objectives is that learning objectives center on individual participants and sessions within a larger program, while program objectives are focused on the education or training program as a whole. Illustrations of program goals and objectives, which are drawn from Chapter Seven, and how they are translated into learning objectives, are shown in Exhibit 8.1.

Categories of Learning Objectives

Learning objectives are selected carefully, because they set the tone and direction for what participants are expected to do and learn during the instructional activity. Therefore, in preparing learning objectives, the developer must have in mind a clear picture of the proposed learning outcomes for the instructional unit. There are five major categories of learning outcomes: acquiring new knowledge; enhancing cognitive skills; developing psychomotor skills; strengthening problem-solving and problem-finding capabilities; and changing feelings, beliefs, or values (Bloom, 1956; Rothwell & Cookson, 1997; Smith & Ragan, 2005).[2]

Learning objectives are useful for four major reasons (Smith & Ragan, 2005). They provide a focus and consistency in the overall design of instruction, guidelines for choosing course content and instructional strategies,

EXHIBIT 8.1

Translating Program Goals and Objectives into Learning Objectives

Program Goals and Objectives	Learning Objectives
Grassroots Education	The participants will:
Program Goal:	Identify new sources of accurate information about ADD (for example, from books, web sites, people).
The goal of the program, to be developed by an ad hoc group of people who have been affected by Attention Deficient Disorder (ADD), is to initiate educational and support activities for adults with ADD and their spouses or partners.	
	Discuss with experts current knowledge about ADD and how to use this knowledge in their everyday lives.
Program Objectives:	
To provide participants in the program with up-to-date and accurate information materials and strategies for locating their own materials.	Express and explore their feelings with group members about living with ADD.
	Share strategies of how they deal with ADD as part of their life as adults.
To give opportunities for participants to share their thoughts and feelings about living with ADD and the coping strategies they use.	Provide assistance to group members who ask for help in addressing specific life issues.
To facilitate educational programs on topics of interest to the participants and build a network of experts who can provide information and discussions on new developments in the knowledge and treatment of adults with ADD.	
Participatory Planning in Africa	The paraprofessionals will:
Program Goal	Explain why the planting and harvesting of rice as an alternative crop for both family consumption and to sell in local markets is important to improving the lives of rural farmers.
The goal of this program is to train village men and women, who will take on the role of paraprofessionals to be effective members of a planning and implementation team in the introduction of a new crop, that of rice production, into tribal villages in their local areas.	
	Describe and demonstrate the process for planting and harvesting rice, and how to market this rice in their local areas.
Program Objectives	
To engage men and women identified by tribal leaders in three rural villages to work as paraprofessionals with local government agricultural specialists in planning a gender-sensitive program for men and women on the planting and harvesting of rice as an alternative crop.	Demonstrate the skills and knowledge needed to work in collaboration with agricultural and training specialists in planning a program for men and women from their villages related to rice production and marketing.
To have these paraprofessionals be part of the pilot testing the program that is developed on rice production and marketing in three selected villages.	Exhibit the knowledge and skills needed to assist farmers in the planting and harvesting of rice in the villages where the program will be pilot-tested.
To revise the training program, with the original team of paraprofessionals and government officials who developed the pilot program, based on feedback received from the farmers who attended, the instructors, and representatives from other stakeholder groups such as government officials from the region and funding agencies.	Translate what they have learned during the pilot tests to make improvements in the program.

a basis for evaluating what participants have learned, and directions for learners to help them organize their own learning. As with program objectives, learning objectives should be "stated clearly enough to indicate to all rational minds exactly what is intended" (Houle, 1996, p. 193). Ways to ensure that you are communicating objectives clearly and correctly include: avoid unfamiliar words and language that is vague; be concise; seek simplicity; convey clearly to learners what they will be learning, and how this learning will be, in many situations, applied (Dick et al., 2009; Rothwell & Kazanas, 2008).

Developing Learning Objectives

In developing learning objectives, people sometimes have difficulty coming up with a variety of action words that fit each category of learning outcomes. To assist in this task, a sampling of such words is always helpful to have (Morrison et al., 2011; Rothwell & Cookson, 1997; Rothwell & Kazanas, 2008; Vella, 2000).[3]

Although the three essential elements of all learning objectives are a statement of who (the learner), how (the action verb), and what (the content), other authors have suggested additional components that may be useful in clarifying further what learners are able to know or do. More specifically, Dick et al. (2009), Mager (1990), and Rothwell and Kazanas (2008) have described two more elements of learning objectives: conditions under which the learning is to be demonstrated and the standards or criteria for acceptable performance. Sample wording describing the given conditions are:

- Given a problem of the following type . . .
- Given a list of . . .
- When provided with a specific set of tools . . .
- Without the use of any reference materials . . .
- By checking a flowchart next to the property equipment . . .
- When a client is angry or upset . . .

  Sample wording describing the criteria for acceptable performance are:

- . . . with 98 percent accuracy.
- . . . getting 16 out of 20 correct.
- . . . in a 20-minute time period.
- . . . by brief responses (fewer than five sentences).
- . . . with no mistakes.
- . . . with all irate clients.

The latter two elements are appropriate only for learning objectives that are measurable through quantitative means. There are certain kinds of learning outcomes, as stressed in Chapter Eleven, that do not lend themselves to precise behavioral or performance criteria (Knowles, 1980; Caffarella, 2002; Morrison et al., 2011). Using specific behavior or performance criteria is especially not applicable in most situations when creativity, confidence, sensitivity, feelings, beliefs, and values are the focus of the learning activity. For example, changes in deep-seated values and attitudes about race, gender, and cultural differences are learning outcomes that are extremely difficult, if not impossible, to express in any meaningful way in behavioral terms. However, as noted earlier, the learning objectives must be written and it is key that they have meaning for the participants and the instructors, are understandable, and provide a clear direction for the education or training activity.

Selecting and Organizing Content

Selecting the content—that is, choosing what will be learned during a learning activity—is a challenge because instructors can rarely include all the material they would like to teach. These limitations stem from the amount of time, types of delivery systems, backgrounds and experiences of the participants, materials available, and instructor capabilities (Alessi & Trollip, 2001; Wlodkowski, 2008).

The starting point for selecting content is the learning objectives. Milano and Ullius (1998) recommend "playing" with the proposed content until key topics and points are arrived at for each learning objective. What does happen as designers categorize and rethink what might be covered is that some of the learning objectives may need to be revised or even dropped. Some instructors, to arrive at what they believe to be important and essential to learn, construct visual tools, such as a concept or content map, to assist them in this process, while others prefer either just talking it through or using a combination of methods. For example, once instructors have made a draft of the content they believe will be the most useful for learners to know before they finalize that material, they ask the following questions:

- What content is essential for learners to know and does this content address one or more of the learning objectives?

- What is the content that learners should know, which supplements the essential material?

- What is the content that might be interesting and relevant to the essential materials, but only addressed as time allows?

- What is the content that learners really do not need to know (that is, it may be useful but does not pertain to the learning objectives)?

What instructors often find in asking these questions is what they thought was crucial material really is only supportive in nature, or does not address any of the learning objectives, and that some of the content they believed would fit in well does not make any sense to include, no matter how interesting it is. In addition, as Tracey (1992) cautions, instructors must avoid leaving out important points and ideas, overemphasizing topics that do not merit extensive attention, and repeating the material presented.

The organization (or sequence) in which the content is delivered is also important. There is no one way to organize content. For example, should the content flow from general to specific or vice versa? Should it emanate from abstract to concrete or concrete to abstract? The ordering of the content depends on the participants' knowledge and experience, the nature of the content itself, the required level of achievement, and the teaching and learning styles of those involved.[4]

There are three common pitfalls that designers stumble into when organizing instruction: they plan too much material for the time allowed; they want instructors to impart more than learners are motivated to absorb; and they discount the context in which the learning is to be applied (Milano & Ullius, 1998; Wlodkowski, 2008). Those designing instruction need to constantly remind themselves that planning instruction, like program planning, is an interactive process—objectives, organization contexts, and evaluation mechanisms may change during the planning and implementation phases.

Choosing Instructional Techniques

How does an instructor decide which instructional technique(s) might best fit a specific situation? In fact there is no one best way of assisting people to learn.[5] Rather, there are eleven major factors that instructors take into consideration when choosing instructional techniques (Conti & Kolody, 2004; Cranton, 2000; Ginsberg & Wlodkowski, 2009; Joosten, 2012; Smith & Ragan, 2005; Vella, 2000). These factors include: learning techniques, instructors, learners, context, social media, transfer of learning, content, technique characteristics, variety, logistical constraints, and time.[6]

Of these eleven factors, the first four—the focus of the learning objectives, the capability of the instructor to use the chosen technique, the

experiences and backgrounds of the learners, and the learning context—
are key in formulating the basic plan for the instructional portion of the
program. The remaining seven factors take shape once these four key
factors are in place. The four key factors are discussed in the following
subsections.

Learning Objectives

The focus of the learning objectives, the first factor, includes acquiring
knowledge, enhancing cognitive skills, developing psychomotor skills,
strengthening problem-solving and -finding capabilities, and changing
feelings or values.[7] It is important to match the instructional techniques
with the objectives because when there are mismatches the outcome that
instructors had planned usually will not happen. For example, one mistake
often seen in practice is when instructors use methods such as lectures and
group discussions when they are supposed to be doing skill development.

Although this categorization of techniques offers a good representation
of how each instructional technique fits with a type of learning outcome,
in reality the categories of techniques are not that clear-cut. One technique
may be appropriate for two or three categories of learning outcomes.
For example, as discussed earlier, many of the online techniques can be
used across most of the categories, while different forms of group discussion could be used to impart knowledge, teach cognitive skills, enhance
problem-solving abilities, or examine feelings, beliefs, and values.

More in-depth descriptions of these and other instructional techniques
can be found in Brookfield and Preskill (2005); Bonk and Zhang (2011);
Cain, Cummings, and Stanchfield (2005); Conrad and Donaldson (2011,
2012); Galbraith (2004); Garrison and Vaughan (2008); Hoggan et al., (2009);
Joosten, 2012; Lawson (2009); Palloff and Pratt, (2011); Silberman (2005,
2010); Silberman and Auerbach (2006); Smith and Ragan (2005); and Taylor,
Marienau, and Fiddler (2000).

Capability of Instructors

The second factor in choosing instructional techniques is the capability
of instructors. Does the instructor have the knowledge, skill, and confidence to handle a particular technique? Does he or she feel comfortable
using it? If not, the instructor's discomfort may be distracting. For example, instructors who employ new techniques that do not seem to work
may continually apologize to the participants. Or they may not be adept
at using online learning tools and can make the learning experience very
frustrating for participants. And even worse, instructors may embarrass

or even blame learners for being unable to use the techniques well, when in fact it is the instructor's problem. There are ways that instructors who choose to employ new or unfamiliar techniques can try them out. For example, instructors could request that participants in face-to-face sessions join them in experimenting with new techniques and ask for feedback on whether they worked, and if they did, how effective they were. This feedback could come in the form of written responses to open-ended questions or through group discussions where both the instructor and the participants could discuss what transpired in terms of the "positives" and "areas for improvement." For those using online tools several practice sessions may be necessary with backup material in case the techniques do not work. In the best-case scenario instructors will have technicians standing by to assist participants.

Capable instructors of adults also are aware of and use well the principle of active learner participation in choosing techniques (Bowman, 2009; Hoggan et al., 2009; Knowles, 1980; Silberman & Auerbach, 2006; Vella, 2000). As Silberman and Auerbach (2006) observe:

> I have modified and expanded the wisdom of Confucius into what I call the Active Learning Credo:
>
> - When I only **hear**, I forget.
> - When I **hear** and **see**, I remember a little.
> - When I **hear** and **see**, and **ask questions** and **discuss** with someone else, I begin to understand.
> - When I **hear, see, question, discuss,** and **do**, I acquire knowledge and skill.
> - When I **teach** someone, I master what I have learned. (p. 2)

Learner Characteristics

The third factor, diversity of learners, is primarily based in cultural differences, such as gender, race, ethnicity, religion, social class, and language, which are found in most learning situations with adults (Davis, 2009; Ginsberg & Wlodkowski, 2009; Reagan, 2005b; Wlodkowski, 2008). In addition, learners, especially from non-Western and Indigenous populations (as discussed in Chapter Three), have different ways of knowing and learning (Reagan, 2005; Merriam & Associates, 2007). In instructing adults, thoughtful instructors have always been challenged by the differences learners bring with them to learning activities and what these differences mean for choosing instructional techniques. Traditionally, instructors have recognized that adults bring rich but often divergent experiences to learning activities, are immersed in various life roles, have preferred ways of learning, and want practical solutions to problems and issues (Cranton, 2000; Knowles, 1980; Merriam, Caffarella, & Baumgartner, 2007; Smith & Ragan, 2005).

As Smith and Ragan (2005) have observed:

> A common error resulting from failure to analyze the characteristics of an audience is assuming that all learners are alike. An even more common error is assuming that the learners are like designers. This means that we tend to explain things the way we will understand them, use examples that are familiar to us, and use instructional techniques that work well for us. (p. 58)

It is incumbent on instructors to first acknowledge their own biases, both the obvious and the hidden, as a starting point for addressing issues of diversity when teaching adults (Davis, 2009: Ginsberg & Wlodkowski, 2009; Guy, 1999a, 1999b: Hayes, Flannery, & Associates, 2000). For example, it is obvious when the authors first walk into most teaching situations that they are White females. By their dress, learners also may easily judge that they are at least middle class and, through their language, that they are well educated and primary English speakers. When their reputation as scholars is known, they also carry into the learning situation an air of authority and power, which for some learners is daunting and intimidating. The less obvious factors (although readily apparent for some in the room) are their beliefs regarding people of color; religious, class, and gender differences; sexual orientation; learning disabilities; and varied ways of knowing and learning.

Ginsberg and Wlodkowski (2009), Guy (1999a), and Wlodowski (2008) also challenge instructors of adults to go beyond just acknowledging their biases in teaching. Their view is that instructors must be willing to change their views about learners, the way they teach, and even what content they choose to include. This task of making teaching situations more inclusive is not easy, either for instructors or participants. More specifically, Wlodkowski (2008) has observed:

> When we are teaching, exclusion is usually an indirect act, an omission of opportunity or of someone's voice. We're usually not mean-spirited but, more likely, unaware that a perspective is missing, that a biased myth has been perpetuated, or that we aren't covering topics of concern to certain adults…

"People who regularly cross borders, that is those who work with other cultural groups either within their own countries or in international settings are often faced with uncertainty in both face-to-face and online learning situations, especially when they have had limited or no prior experience with the cultural milieu" (Ginsberg & Wlodowski, 2009, p.125). "Therefore, teaching in a culturally responsive way may require considerable transformation [whether in their own country of origin or in international settings]. Being skilled, prepared, and willing to deal with some of the tensions and difficulties that accompany this [work] is an essential part of the experience" (p. 331).

For example, instructors may have people who speak a number of different languages, are not accustomed to active learning practices, and believe it is disrespectful to engage in a critical dialogue with their instructors or, at times, even with other participants.

Instructors who take into account the many differences among learners adopt three key norms for practice:

1. The multiplicity of ways people learn and respond to learning situations is a given.

2. Instructors have the responsibility for designing instruction so that these differences are acknowledged and used to enhance the what, when, where, and how of learning situations.

3. Proceed with care and be willing to be flexible in where, how, and when you provide the instruction.

Helpful resources that provide examples of learning techniques that acknowledge differences, and ways to create inclusive learning environments for adults, include: Brookfield (2006); Brookfield and Preskill (2005); Ginsberg and Wlodkowski (2009); Guy (1999b); Pratt, Kelly, and Wong (1999); and Wlodkowski (2008).

Learning Context

The learning context, the fourth key factor that influences the choice of learning techniques, is the setting where the learning takes place (Smith & Ragan, 2005; Vella, 2000). Adults learn in a variety of settings, from formal class and training rooms, to their homes and workplaces, to the great outdoors. Some learning situations are more conducive to using certain techniques than others. For example, solving problems of practice in the settings where participants actually work calls for using "real-life" case studies, observations, and problem-based learning. Other places, such as multiple learning sites in a number of countries, are better suited for a mobile phone or online instruction, providing the technology is available.

In turn, in some learning contexts certain kinds of learning techniques work well, while in other settings the same techniques would be inappropriate. For example, teaching in a residential setting on an island in Alaska lends itself to using learning techniques, such as reflective practice, storytelling, and listening circles, all of which take time and where participants have a chance to build a community of learners. In contrast, using these same techniques in a busy workplace is often frowned upon, as the expectations are that participants will be in and out of training quickly and will be able to immediately apply whatever they are learning to their specific job tasks.

Selecting Instructional Resources

In addition to choosing appropriate instructional techniques, it is important that staff members who design instruction also know how to select and use appropriately a variety of instructional resources, as illustrated by the following scenario.

 SCENARIO 8.1   A SURPRISE ON THE FIRST NIGHT OF CLASS

> Heather, a community college professor, was well known for being a highly innovative instructor, and for integrating technology into her classroom. Although her students were adults, the majority were under thirty-five and grew up with computers, digital cameras, and cell phones; thus they were often well acquainted with the technology in the classroom and willing to try anything they were unfamiliar with. For example, as soon as blogging became all the rage she immediately incorporated student blogging about relevant issues into all her classes, with a very favorable student response. Recently, Heather had been asked to teach in a new off-site location and was totally surprised when she discovered on her arrival on her first night of class that the majority of her students were fifty and over, with a number in their sixties and seventies. What she had not realized when she had agreed to go to this new site was that there was a rather large new retirement community very close by. Needless to say, her "normal way" of teaching class and many of the types of resources that she used were not well received by many of the class members in this new setting.

There are numerous guidelines that help instructors choose which resources to use in their classroom (Dick et al., 2009; Gboku & Lekoko, 2007; Moore & Kearsley, 2012; Morrison et al., 2011; Rothwell & Kazanas,

2008; Sugrue & Clark, 2000). These guidelines recommend that instructors select resources that:

- Fit the experiences, interests, and abilities of the learners
- Are culturally suitable for the participants
- Instructors are capable of using
- Explain and illustrate well what is being taught (e.g., knowledge versus problem-solving capabilities)
- Focus attention on the essence of the content
- Effectively take advantage of the context in which the learning is taking place
- Are adaptable to the local context
- Can successfully be used in the environment where the learning activity is held
- Are useful to them in applying what they learned
- Are affordable
- Will be available at the time they are needed

Heather violated at least two, if not more, of these basic guidelines—choosing resources that did not fit the learners' experiences and abilities, and were not useful in applying what they had learned. In addition, she could have also asked more questions about the group she would be teaching.

Another important issue when using already existing resources is that "copyright permissions must be secured [for these resources]… whenever a copyright notice appears on the title page, or on a footer, of instructional [resource and] materials. It is unethical for instructors to do otherwise" (Rothwell & Kazanas, 2008, p. 263) There are numerous resources that instructors may want to use from the public and private sectors. It is important to note that instructors should assume that private-sector materials, including online sources, are copyrighted, unless otherwise stated. Public-sector documents, such as government documents and material from web sites, are often not copyrighted; but it is essential that instructors and planners consult the copyright regulations for their own countries. Even if the resource material is not copyrighted it is a professional courtesy to provide the authors' names and the sources of those resources.

A wide variety of instructional resources can be used to enhance learning, such as "real resources" (e.g., people; objects and devices, computers), printed materials, audio and visual materials, online sources, and interactive technologies (Conrad & Donaldson, 2012; Cranton, 2000; Gboku & Lakoko, 2007; Joosten, 2012; Lawson, 2009; Mitchell, 1998; Rothwell & Kazanas, 2008; Taylor, 2009).[8] There are also other types of resources that are still used widely in resource-poor settings. Examples of these resources, which are often viewed as outdated in many settings, include overhead projectors, slide projectors, transparencies, audiotapes, storyboards, radios, film strips, and slides (Gboku & Lekoko, 2007).

Conducting Instructional Assessments

Instructional assessment or evaluation is done for five major reasons (Diamond, 2008; Lawson, 2009; McMillan, 2010; Morrison et al., 2011; Wiggins, 1998; Wlodkowski, 2008):

- To assess participants' background, experiences, and readiness for learning when they enter an activity or program

- To improve the instructional process and materials

- To assist participants to be more effective learners

- To ascertain whether what the participants have learned has actually produced the desired outcomes that are reflected in the learning objectives

- To provide data for the overall program evaluation (see Chapter Eleven)

Each of these purposes for doing instructional assessment is discussed in the following sections.

Assessment at Entry

Assessment done either prior to or at the start of a learning activity allows the instructors to know what the participants know and can do and how they feel about the content to be presented. This entry-level assessment activity may also be done as part of identifying program needs and ideas (see Chapter Six) or as a part of preparing marketing plans (see Chapter Thirteen). Evaluation methods at this stage range from asking participants to complete simple questionnaires (on who they are, what background knowledge and experiences they have related to the content, and the like) to administering comprehensive tests on prerequisite knowledge or skills (McMillan, 2010). These data can also be used, as discussed later in this section, as baseline information for assessing the results of the instructional activity and the program as a whole (see Chapter Eleven).

Assessment of the Instructional Processes and Resources

Using instructional assessment to improve the instructional process and resources is done prior to, during (formative evaluation), and after (summative evaluation) the instructional event (Davis, 2009; Dick et al., 2009; McMillan, 2010; Morrison et al., 2011; Smith & Ragan, 2005). This type of assessment is usually completed by the instructors themselves or by the participants. Instructors benefit greatly by checking and reflecting on the instructional process and the content before, during, and after the session is over. Especially for instructional activities that will be offered a number of times, such as courses and workshops, conducting such assessments is important as it allows instructors to catch major weaknesses prior to offering the activities (Dick et al., 2010; Smith & Ragan, 2005). Depending on the time and resources available, instructors could:

- Request a content expert to check whether the materials are accurate and up to date

- Ask an expert on assessment to determine whether the assessment techniques will provide the type of data needed to make sound judgments on whether participants have actually learned what will be presented

- Ask a couple of colleagues to review the processes they have chosen to use

- Invite members of the program advisory committee or the committee as a whole to provide feedback on whether the activity will meet the needs of potential participants

Based on this assessment, instructors then revise the processes and resources that will be used before initiating the instruction.

There are a number of ways that instructors assess the processes and resources being used both during and after the instructional activities are completed, including self-assessments, questionnaires, conversations with colleagues, and small- and large-group discussions (McMillan, 2010). For example, one way for instructors to use self-assessments is to keep an online teaching journal or log in which they jot down and reflect on what was done well, what could have been done better, and what could be done differently. Team-teaching with a colleague also encourages instructors to reflect on instructional activities, as long as both instructors agree that debriefing sessions will be a regular part of their team-teaching process (Buckley, 2000). And finally, informal chats that instructors have with their colleagues over coffee or lunch can also prove very helpful.

Participant assessment related to resources and process is also very useful, and in some situations even mandated (e.g., at colleges and universities after formal courses are completed or at the end of continuing mandatory education programs to receive the credit). Having participants evaluate these areas of instruction is also beneficial while the instructional activities are in progress, as well as after they have been completed. Davis (2009) provides a number of ways that learners can contribute to this process (e.g., schedule feedback at times appropriate to the learning activity; convene focus groups). However, having participants complete these types of assessments can have some very negative effects if instructors are not willing to make changes based on the feedback given to them (McMillan, 2010).[9] This type of assessment, "without the use of instructional change is not formative" (McMillan, 2007, p. 118), but rather a waste of the participants' time. There are a number of questions that instructors can ask participants as part of assessing the processes and resources used in instructional activities (McMillan, 2010).[10]

Assessment of the Learning Outcomes

Instructors know that the assessment of learning outcomes is vital, but they primarily think of this type of assessment as happening at the end of the instructional activities, and participants are used to filling out these assessments prior to leaving the activity. However there is a second type of learning outcomes assessment that looks at whether learners are able to transfer the new knowledge, meaning whether they can apply what they have learned back in the workplace, as volunteers, or in their personal lives (Daffron & North, 2011; Morrison et al., 2011; Regan & Smith, 2005) (see Chapter Nine).[11]

Another term also used for assessing learning transfer is "confirmative evaluation," meaning that repeated assessments of outcomes should be completed for some time, with the end goal of maintaining over time what has been learned (Morrison et al., 2011). The problem of why assessment of learning transfer is often not being used is twofold. Instructors are frequently not asked to be a part of developing evaluation strategies for learning transfer, or not involved in the process of determining whether these learning activities have any impact at all. And program planners also often do not even think that instructors should have a role in this process, unless they are offering refresher sessions, or involved with the participants in other ways during the transfer process.

The starting point for assessing the learning outcomes of instructional activities, whether at the end of the instructional activities or during the transfer phase, is the learning objectives. The assessment techniques chosen need to match the focus of those objectives—acquiring knowledge, enhancing cognitive skills, developing psychomotor skills, strengthening problem-solving and -finding capabilities, or changing attitudes, beliefs, values, or feelings. Useful resources that describe instructional techniques that are used most often include Guskey (2000); Lawson (2009); McMillan (2010); Morrison, et al. (2011); Smith and Regan (2005), and Wiggins (2008).[12] Most of the assessment techniques that address these five purposes are now constructed and administered online as well as through more traditional ways (Conrad & Donaldson, 2011, 2012; Dick et al., 2009; Palloff & Pratt, 2011).[13]

Although categorizing assessment techniques is helpful, instructors know that depending on how the techniques are designed, they may fit into more than one category of learning outcomes, similar to the categorization of instructional techniques. For example, tests and reflective journals, depending on how they are constructed, are used to assess knowledge, cognitive skills, problem-solving and fact-finding capabilities, and changes in attitudes, beliefs, values, or feelings, or all of the above. In addition, another instruction assessment tool—portfolios—have become even more popular in recent years. Depending on the purpose of why portfolios are constructed, they can address all of the different types of learning outcomes (McMillan, 2010; Michelson, Mandell, & Contributors, 2004: Morrison et al., 2011; Wiggins, 1998; Wlodkowski, 2008). Portfolios provide direct evidence of learning through a collection of carefully selected materials (e.g., written papers, memos, artistic materials, audio and video clips, online materials, published articles, honors and awards, work-related products), and are either presented in a notebook or online. Accompanying this evidence are descriptive and reflective entries that allow instructors and fellow participants to gain a clear understanding of what each artifact represents. Portfolios are powerful tools for both individual and group learning.

McMillan (2001, 2010), Wiggins (1998), and Wlodkowski, (2008) have outlined key ideas to consider when choosing assessment techniques. Samples of questions that instructors should ask themselves are:

- Are they of high quality? That is, "are they technically sound and provide results that demonstrate and improve" participant learning (McMillan, 2001, p. 52)?

- Are they appropriate for the targeted learning outcomes (e.g., acquiring knowledge, changing attitudes, beliefs, values, or feelings)?

- Are they practical and efficient to use?

- Are they fair and can they account for individual and cultural differences?

- Do they appeal to their professional judgment and intuition about its usefulness?

- Will they be seen as credible and user-friendly by the learners?

- Are they going to turn into a self-inflicted chore for instructors and the participants?

- Have instructors planned enough time to use them in an effective manner?

- Have instructors tried out the techniques themselves?

In managing the assessment process, instructors first need to understand that many adults are very anxious about any type of assessment related to what they have learned, especially when it makes a difference in such areas as whether they will get a job or receive a promotion. Educators and trainers have to respond to this anxiety with concern and respect for the participants' feelings. Second, instructors must provide clear and complete instructions about how the assessment will be conducted, including specifying the format and length and what the assessment requires participants to do. Third, assessment should take place in a comfortable environment. Fourth, all resources to complete the assessment process should be readily available and in working order (e.g., laptops, technical equipment for video- and audiotaping).

Assessment to Assist Learning

The next reason to do instructional assessments is to assist learning (Brookfield, 1992; McMillan, 2010; Wlodkowski, 2008; and Wiggins, 1998). As Wlodkowski (2008) notes:

> *Feedback* is information that learners receive about the quality of their work. Knowledge about the learning process and its results, comments about emerging skills, notes on [specific activities or products], and graphic records are forms of feedback that instructors…use. Feedback appears to enhance the motivation of learners because learners are able to evaluate their progress, locate their performance within a framework of understanding… self-assess correct their errors efficiently, self-adjust, and receive encouragement from their instructors and peers. (pp. 314–315, italics in the original)

Brookfield (1992), McMillan (2010), and Wiggins (1998) go on to describe nine indicators that help instructors judge whether their assessment processes are useful and significant to learners engaging in the learning process, including whether they are clear, specific, constructive, timely, and useful.[14] Of the nine indicators, the indicators related to being affirming and suggesting changes that can be made are the most challenging and helpful to both instructors and participants. In addition, "learner's *readiness to receive feedback* is also important. If people are resistant to feedback, they are not likely to learn or self-adjust. In such cases, it may be advisable to hold off on the feedback until a personal conference can be arranged or until learners are more comfortable with the learning situation" (Wlodkowski, 2008, p. 321, italics in the original).

Assessment to Provide Data for the Overall Program Evaluation

The final rationale for doing instructional assessments is to provide data for the overall program evaluation (see Chapter Ten). Yes, there are differences in the focus of instructional and program assessment; that is, a "program evaluation focuses on larger organization questions and social contexts of the program (macro level), [while] evaluation of learning focuses on what and how learners learn and how educators help or hinder the process of learning (micro level)" (Deshler, 1998, pp. 305–306). Despite these different foci, data from learning or instructional assessments are valuable sources of information to use in making judgments about the program as a whole. (Dick et al., 2009; Rothwell & Cookson, 1997). Examples of data that are useful include:

- Instructional assessment data from learning activities collected right after each session can be used to determine whether the instructional outcomes were an indicator that the program objectives for the overall program were met, and whether all of the program arrangements (such as facilities, online access, meeting rooms) were satisfactory.

- Transfer of learning assessment data, which were a part of the instructional process, can also be used as indicators of whether the program objectives were achieved.

- Instructional assessment data gathered both during and after a series of workshops on a major social issue facing a community (e.g., racial tensions, increases in assaults on women) can be used to make judgments on whether this material was helpful and in developing a workable plan to address the issue that was the major goal for this program.

Unfortunately, instructional assessment data are not used as often as they should be in program evaluations, although there is an obvious link between whether the instructional activities provided the intended results and the overall value and worth of the total program. For example, at professional conferences, participants are usually asked at the end of each session to provide an assessment of that session. Common questions include: Were the session objectives clear and did the presenter successfully address each objective? Were the instructional techniques and materials helpful? Did the session contribute to your knowledge or skill level? Was the coffee hot and the room cool? Was the facility comfortable? What happens to these data after they are collected is often mysterious. Sometimes these data go directly to the presenters and are definitely not used in evaluating the overall conference. At other times, planning teams use these data primarily to decide whether a person should present at future conferences, but this reason is often not shared beyond the planning team. In still other cases, the conference evaluators integrate these data into their program evaluation reports, but even then it is not always clear how this integration has been done. But most often, conferees and presenters are not sure what has happened to the data collected at each individual session. One way to make sure these data are used is to build into the program evaluation plan how instructional assessment data are being collected and utilized in terms of assessing the overall program.

Preparing Instructional Plans

One of the major outcomes of the instruction design process is developing the instructional plans. These plans serve as a guide for instructors or facilitators of the learning activities being constructed (Milano & Ullius, 1998; Mitchell, 1998; Van Kavelaar, 1998). Instructors find that well-designed plans enable them to judge whether they have a clear set of learning objectives, instructional techniques and resources that complement the focus of those objectives, and an assessment plan that tells them if the learners have met those objectives. In addition, learning plans estimate a realistic time frame for each of the learning activities included in the plan, and the type of facilities, set-ups, and tools needed to successfully execute the plans (e.g., available breakout rooms, round tables with comfortable chairs for the participants, computers, and projectors). Having well-designed learning plans helps instructors stay within the boundaries of what they have planned, but also allows instructors to know when they have wandered too far off the topic so they can get back on track.

There is no set form for an instructional plan; however, major components of the activity that should be covered are outlined below:[15]

- Session title
- Date and time frame
- Name and titles of presenter(s)
- Brief description of the learning activity

- Learning objectives
- Instructional techniques
- Assessment plan
- Estimated time for each major part of the learning activity or activities
- Instructor and participant resources
- Facilities needed

The instructional plan should be used as a guide for how the instructor and the participants spend their time in the session, not as a document that dictates precisely what each person must do and when. There must be room for flexibility and change in both the content and the learning process, depending on the learners and what happens in the learning situation.

Making the Instructional Plan Work

Whether they are leaders of individual sessions or keynote speakers, how instructors put their instructional plans into action can either foster or block a positive climate for learning. Instructors enhance learning by sharing their content mastery, being helpful facilitators, using instructional techniques and assessment strategies appropriately and well, and establishing good rapport with the participants. All these actions assume that instructors have knowledge about the participants and are well prepared for the instructional event.

Motivating participants up front is a very important part of making the instructional plan work (Ginsberg & Wlodkowski, 2009; Wlodkowski, 2008). One major way to capture participants' interest is to get them personally involved with the material. Starting with a question-and-answer period or breaking the group into dyads or small work teams can set the stage for learner engagement with the content. In very large groups, presenters can use human-interest stories or prepare participants by highlighting two or three new and exciting ideas at the outset. However participation and interest are fostered, the method should be well thought-out and applicable to the program content. There is nothing worse than starting a session in an unorganized and vague manner. Impressions of whether presenters are good or bad are made in the first four minutes and rarely change after.

A second way to motivate the group is by encouraging instructors to be enthusiastic and energetic. Instructors who are open to questions and comments, use humor, and interact with the participants spark to the interest of even the most reluctant participants. In assisting the participants to learn content, instructors have to present the material in an organized fashion.

EXHIBIT 8.2

Helpful Hints for Instructors

- Remove or lessen participants' anxieties.
- Create safe and inclusive learning environments.
- Spell out clearly and up front the expectations for participants.
- Set or develop group norms (e.g., let participants know that active participation is encouraged, divergent opinions are welcomed, and a question-and-answer period is a part of the presentation).
- Let learners know the role of the instructor is to help them learn.
- Use nondiscriminatory language that all participants can readily understand, and treat participants in an unbiased way.
- Develop professional and caring relationships between and among learners and instructors.
- Give participants advance "organizers" (such as five key points) to help them follow the ideas presented.
- Use the resources and expertise of the participants.
- Use an outline or notes rather than reading a formally prepared paper or script.
- Use active learning techniques that allow time for reflection.
- Restate important ideas.
- Be generous with examples.
- Listen carefully to all ideas presented by the participants and respond appropriately.
- Keep a good pace, and be aware of time.
- Provide feedback and positive reinforcement to participants throughout the session.
- Recognize that emotions play an important part in the learning process.
- Be flexible with the presentation, instructional plans, and techniques (e.g., build on the unexpected).
- Be caring and openly committed to the participants' learning.
- Be ethical in instructional practice.
- Use humor and laughter.
- Have fun.

A number of different instructional techniques, as described earlier in this chapter, can be used, with the emphasis placed on active learner participation whenever possible and appropriate. Some helpful hints for instructors as they move through the instructional plan are listed in Exhibit 8.2.

Useful resources that describe more fully what instructors can do to ensure a positive learning experience include: Apps (1996); Bonk and Zhang (2008); Brookfield and Preskill (2005); Ginsberg and Wlodkowski (2009); Palloff and Pratt (2011); Silberman (2010); Silberman and Auerbach (2006); Tisdell (1995); Vella (2000); and Wlodkowski (2008).

As appropriate, instructors assist participants in examining how the new knowledge, skills, problem-solving and problem-finding capabilities, beliefs, or feelings they have learned can be applicable to their lives (see Chapter Nine). Five key transfer of learning strategies are: (1) ask learners, prior to the education or training session, to select projects or other activities to complete that encompass what learning is expected to be transferred; (2) use active learning techniques that enhance learning transfer (e.g., case studies, live or computer simulations, applications exercises); (3) incorporate having learners try out their new skills in either their own or similar settings; (4) provide learners opportunities to develop individual action plans to apply what they have learned in their workplaces or in other roles they play in their adult lives; and (5) ensure that learners receive future assistance or learning transfer (e.g., follow-up sessions, refresher courses, mentoring) (see Chapter Nine).

When participants develop individual action plans during the program, where possible a draft of these plans should be prepared and reviewed during the program (Berger, Caffarella, & O'Donnell, 2004). To help participants complete these plans, instructors encourage participants to indicate specific individuals who could provide assistance or support, especially when they are committed to making major personal, work, or community changes. This assistance or support can be given by a variety of people, such as fellow participants, work colleagues and supervisors, family and friends, community members, and professional educators. A sample form for an individual action plan that readers can complete is provided in this chapter's Application Exercises.

Chapter Highlights

Designing instruction involves planning the interaction between learners and instructors or between individual learners or groups of learners. Those responsible for designing instruction may be paid staff, volunteers, or people internal or external to an organization or community. The outcome of the instructional design process is an instructional plan that serves as a guide for the instructors or facilitators of the learning activity being constructed (e.g., a class, a workshop, or an online program). Depending on the nature of the program, more than one instructional plan may be needed. In designing instruction, instructors and program planners complete the following tasks:

• Develop clear and understandable learning objectives for each instructional session and ensure they match the proposed learning outcomes (acquiring new knowledge, enhancing cognitive and psychomotor skills, problem-solving and -finding capabilities, and changing attitudes, beliefs, values, or feelings).

- Select and organize the content on what participants "must learn," which is based on the learning objectives. Content that supplements the essential material should be included only if time allows. Be cognizant that there is no best way to select and sequence the content.

- Choose instructional techniques (e.g., lectures, case studies, online formats, storytelling, games, or metaphor analysis) that match the focus of the proposed learning outcomes, that the instructor is capable of using, and that take into account the backgrounds and experiences of the learners and the learning context.

- Select instructional resources that enhance the learning effort (e.g., "real resources," printed materials, visual aids, online resources, or interactive technologies).

- Choose ways to evaluate instructional assessment data related to how the instruction was delivered and the resources used.

- Select appropriate assessment techniques for assessing the learning outcomes or results of the instructional activity.

- Use instructional assessment data in formative and summative ways for the instructional aspects of the program as well as the program as a whole.

- Prepare clear and concise instructional plans as guides that can assist instructors and learners to stay focused as they move through the instructional process.

- Make the instructional process work by ensuring that instructors know their content, are competent learning facilitators, care about learners, use instructional and assessment techniques appropriately and skillfully, and are well prepared for each instructional event.

This chapter has addressed the many elements and factors that influence the instructional design process. Addressed in the next chapter is devising transfer of learning plans that are a critical and yet, until very recently, an often overlooked component of program planning. These transfer of learning plans assist learners in applying what they have learned to their work, personal, or public lives.

Notes for Additional Online Resources

1. See Scenario 8.A: Planning Instruction for an Environmental Awareness Day.

2. See Exhibit 8.A: Sample Learning Objectives for examples of learning objectives that address each major category of learning outcomes.

3. See Exhibit 8.B: Examples of Action Words for Learning Outcomes.

4. See Exhibit 8.C: Guidelines for Organizing Content for a set of guidelines to help planners think about what sequence might work best (Tracey, 1992; Morrison et al., 2011; Wlodkowski, 2008).

5. See Scenario 8.B: Training for the Christmas Rush.

6. See Exhibit 8.D: Ten Major Factors to Consider When Choosing Instructional Techniques for further detail.

7. See Exhibit 8.E: Examples of Techniques by Learning Outcomes for a listing of numerous instructional techniques appropriate for each category of learning objective.

8. See Exhibit 8.F: Sample Instructional Resources by Category.

9. See Scenario 8.C: Frustrating Learners.

10. See Exhibit 8.G: Sample Questions to Guide Participant Assessment of Resources and Process.

11. See Exhibit 8.H: Example of a Survey for Assessing Transfer of Learning for a sample of a questionnaire for assessing learning transfer.

12. See Exhibit 8.I: Assessment Techniques by Learning Outcomes Category for some of the most widely used techniques for assessing what has been learned.

13. See Exhibit 8.J: Evaluation of a Workshop for a simple but very useful evaluation form that could be filled out in person right after the program, or completed online at a later time.

14. See Exhibit 8.K: Nine Indicators of Useful Assessment.

15. Sample forms for an instructional plan are given in Exhibits 8.L: Seminar for Program Planners and 8.M: Workshop for Cancer Volunteers.

 Application Exercises

The first application exercise helps you to develop learning objectives and the second gives you the opportunity to think through alternative instructional techniques that you could use for the same session. The third exercise focuses on choosing and evaluating assessment evaluation techniques, and the fourth on developing an instructional plan.

EXERCISE 8.1

Developing Learning Objectives

1. Describe briefly an educational program for which you will act as the instructor or be part of an instructional team.

_____

_____

_____

_____

2. Develop a set of learning objectives for your part of the program using the following format. Complete each part for each objective, as appropriate.

The Learner...	Action Verb	... Content	Conditions Under Which the Learning Is to Be Demonstrated*	Criteria for Acceptable Performance*

*These two elements of the learning objective are not applicable for learning objectives that cannot be stated in behavioral or performance terms.

EXERCISE 8.2

Selecting Instructional Techniques

1. For the same session you described in Exercise 8.1, develop two alternative ways the material could be taught. Keep in mind the focus of the learning outcomes, your expertise, the backgrounds and experiences of the learners, and the context for learning.

Alternative 1:

_____

_____

_____

_____

_____

_____

_____

_____

_____

_____

_____

_____

Alternative 2:

_____

_____

_____

_____

_____

_____

_____

_____

_____

_____

_____

_____

_____

EXERCISE 8.3

Creating an Instructional Assessment Process

1. For the same session you described in Exercises 8.1 and 8.2, describe the major reason or reasons for completing an instructional assessment.

    _____

    _____

2. Select and describe one or more techniques you will use to evaluate this instructional session.

    Technique:

    _____

    _____

    Description:

    _____

    _____

    Technique:

    _____

    _____

    Description:

    _____

    _____

3. Describe how you will ensure that the assessment process exhibits at least the following qualities (see Exhibit 8.K):

    Clear:

    Specific and Constructive:

    Timely:

    Useful:

    Ongoing and Frequent:

    Accessible:

    Affirming:

    Changeable:

    Justifiable:

    Personal and Differential:

    Stated with Care and Concern:

Preparing Instructional Plans

Using the material from Exercises 8.1, 8.2, and 8.3, develop an instructional plan, using either Exhibits 8.L or Exhibit 8.M as a guide, for a session in which you will serve as instructor.

Title:

Date and Time:

Learning Objectives	Content Heading	Key Points to Emphasize	Instructional Techniques	Estimated Time
The participants will be able to:				

Assessment Plan:

Instructional resources and equipment needed:

For instructor:

For participants:

Room Arrangement needed:

Chapter 9
Devising Transfer of Learning Plans

 SCENARIO 9.1: A NEW KIND OF TRAINING

Hector has been the director of training for Indosoro Refinery in Washington State for ten years and feels the quality of the training programs he has provided is very good. The program evaluations have always been reasonably positive, and thus Hector has continued using a program characterized by traditional lectures and tasty food. Because the Occupational Safety and Health Administration (OSHA) requires frequent training about safety procedures, Hector holds these training sessions once a year.

This year the OSHA training is very important because of new regulations and a prepared shutdown of operations for routine maintenance and inspections, known as a turnaround. It is a process that can be filled with danger as the tanks are emptied and there is high risk of explosion if the workers do not take care with their tasks. Glen, a company trainer, comes from the Texas refinery to assist with the important training session. Hector has a discussion with Glen about the training and Glen talks about involving the employees in the decisions for their learning. Glen also believes that the managers have a role in helping the learners incorporate their new ideas into the work in the refinery. He talks about shared learning and preparing the employees to immediately apply their learning in their work.

Hector is somewhat suspicious of the training Glen suggests because it surely will take more time and effort on his part, and he believes the workers should be able to learn information and then apply it on their own—they do not need to be "taken by the hand." Hector also knows that management does not want any more time than absolutely necessary used for this training; however, the pressure is on and the refinery has already received a few safety citations. Hector decides to take a gamble and listen to Glen's ideas. Over the next week Hector sees Glen out in the refinery unit talking with some of the workers and working with their superintendent to show them a new procedure he will be using in the programs. Hector wonders if these discussions are what Glen was talking about.

Six weeks after the program was presented, Hector sees all of the OSHA lessons being used by the workers and the superintendent involved in the implementation. Hector thinks back to the last workshop he presented where the supervisor was not even present and not too many of the workers tried out Hector's new ideas. What were some of the lessons that Hector, the workers, and their superintendent learned about successful transfer of learning from Glen? What made the difference in this training compared to the more traditional lecture and note taking that Hector had used for ten years?

The previous chapters have provided guidance for program planners to put together educational programs using the Interactive Model. Many program planners assume that if they follow the ideas and model, the program will be planned well, the educational event will be successful, and everyone will leave for the better because of the excellent planning. These assumptions are all certainly true; however adult educators need to ask two further questions: did the learners actually learn what was intended, and will they be able to apply the new information in their personal, work, or public lives?

In this chapter we first discuss how transfer of learning is defined, and then how the transfer of learning process is linked to other components of the Interactive Model of Program Planning. Next we explore why transfer of learning is an important component of the program planning process, and we examine models of learning transfer, with an emphasis on the Successful Transfer of Learning Model. We then review samples of key factors that are either barriers or enhancers to the transfer of learning process, followed by a section presenting a framework for planning transfer of learning, highlighting the people involved, the timing of when to use transfer, and a number of strategies to assist participants in applying what they have learned. The chapter closes with a discussion of specific techniques, including those for individuals and groups, followed by an exploration of the challenges that program planners face in the application process.

Defining Transfer of Learning

What does it mean to "transfer" learning? Why should program planners, like Hector in Scenario 9.1, be concerned with the issue of transfer or application of newly acquired information and skills to the job site or other areas of adult lives? Transfer of learning is the effective application by program participants of what they learned as a result of attending an education or training program (Baldwin & Ford, 1988; Broad & Newstrom, 1992; Daffron & North, 2011; Merriam & Leahy, 2005). It is often referred to as the "so what" or "now what" phase of the learning process. What do these phrases mean, and how can what was learned be applicable to the situations of the program participants? Transfer of learning (also termed *transfer of training* or *applications process*) is not a new component of the planning process (Baldwin & Ford, 1988; Cervero, 1985; Fox, 1984); rather, it is an element of the process that is receiving increased attention as participants and sponsors of education and training programs demand more concrete and useful results. In Merriam and Leahy's review (2005) of the transfer of learning research from 1990 to 2000, they report a continued need for adult educators to gain a clearer understanding of how learners transfer their learning into practice. Not all educational programs for adults need to have a plan for this part of the process, however. In fact, for some programs—such as a public lecture series or a weekend retreat for spiritual renewal—having a transfer of learning plan may not be appropriate or even needed. However, for many programs, such as skill-based programs, to be successful a plan for helping participants apply what they have learned is required.

Transfer of learning has most often been thought of in behavioral terms—that is, what is to be transferred can be clearly specified in terms of observable changes in knowledge, skills, and attitudes (Broad & Newstrom, 1992; Merriam & Leahy, 2005). Therefore, the assumption has been that as long as everyone knows ahead of time what is to be transferred and how this learning transfer will be accomplished, the transfer will happen without any additional interventions. Although this assumption is true in some situations, learning transfer is often more complex and multifaceted than just simply being clear about what learning needs to be applied and having a plan to do that (Austin, 2008; Holton, 2000; Daffron & North, 2006, 2011; Lim & Morris, 2006; Ottoson, 1995a; Yelon & Ford, 1999). As Ottoson (1995a) has so aptly observed: "Application is a complex, multidimensional process that takes more than just a good idea. It takes knowledge, skill, endurance, and artistry. Application requires multiple kinds of knowledge, including knowledge of the *thing*, the context, the practical, and the skill to put it all together" (p. 24; emphasis in the original). In addition, a number of other factors have been identified that affect learning transfer, such as learner characteristics, professional backgrounds, learner motivation, program design and delivery, and organizational strategies.

Viewing the transfer process from this point of view requires that program planners and others involved in the transfer process have the "skills of translation, negotiation, adaptation, and decision-making" (Ottoson, 1995a, p. 26).[1] Assisting people to make changes is the heart of what transfer of learning is all about—changes in themselves, other people, practices, organizations, or society. Some of these changes may be easy and even fun, like learning how to be a better gardener or skier. Other changes may be difficult and painful, such as learning to cope with a major illness or how to lay off large numbers of staff members due to budget or technological changes.

Although many education and training programs focus on individuals' learning, often some of what has been learned cannot be applied, as noted in the previous case, unless changes are also made in the context where the changes are expected (Austin, 2008; Bennett, Lehman, & Forst, 1999; Daley, 2002; Daffron, Cowdrey, & Doran, 2007; Daffron & North, 2011). These contextual factors, such as transfer climate, cultural differences, and structural issues, are especially important when what is learned is to be applied primarily in a work or other organizational setting, in a different cultural milieu, or when it depends on others having to agree to or also make those changes (see Chapter Four). For example, a frontline customer representative may want to use some alternative strategies of working with customer complaints as a result of attending a series of professional development seminars, but encounters a stumbling block when his departmental supervisor voices strong opposition. This supervisor claims that the new procedures will take too much time and thus will be less efficient. A more global example would be assuming that workers are highly self-directed in their transfer activities in a cultural context "where they are more accustomed to being told what to do and letting someone else take both the credit and the responsibility" (Latimer, 1999, p. 4). These contextual factors are one of the bases, among others, upon which transfer of learning plans are grounded.

Linking Transfer of Learning Component to Other Planning Components

There are a number of linkages between the planning factors that influence the transfer of learning component and the other components of the Interactive Program Planning Model, as demonstrated by Scenario 9.2.

SCENARIO 9.2:   THE COMPLEXITIES OF PLANNING FOR TRANSFER

Sheila is chairing a committee that is planning an outdoor adventure experience for recovering alcoholics. The members of this committee include recovering alcoholics, a person with experience in outdoor education, and the assistant director of the sponsoring organization, as well other key stakeholders. Sheila knows her population as well as she has worked in drug and alcohol programs for a number of years, and she is a recovering alcoholic herself. She is a bit worried as the potential participants are all from urban areas, and only a few of them have any experience with hiking in the mountains, rafting, or wilderness camping, but the recovering alcoholics on the committee and the outdoor educator convinced her this program would benefit this population. Also, she is wondering, as are other committee members, about how to "sell" the relevancy of this kind of program to her audience, despite the many committee members for whom these kinds of physical activities are foreign and who think trees only grow in parks. In addition, although she has funding for this program, a number of the other stakeholders in the planning process, including her own organization and the local Alcoholics Anonymous groups, have serious doubts about whether an outdoor experience program can have any positive impact on the people who will attend. She and her committee know the program must have clear outcomes, in terms of what it can offer to recovering alcoholics that fits the participants' needs. She also is aware that she must respond to the many questions she has received from sponsors and other stakeholders. Sheila's final decision after a great deal of examining the pros and cons of planning this program was to go ahead with the idea.

In addition to working with her local program committee, Sheila has contracted with a private outdoor adventure group, using grant funds, to plan and lead the actual activities for the program. Sheila and two of her committee members have met twice with this group and have asked them to draw up program and learning objectives and specific activity plans that fit with what she and her committee hope the program outcomes will be. Sheila and her committee members also discussed with this outdoor adventure group how the participants could apply what they learn from this experience to helping them stay on the road to recovery, especially as the learning context and activities will be novel to these participants. In addition, as this program is government-funded, Sheila needs to demonstrate that both the outdoor adventure experience itself and the transfer strategies and techniques they use to apply what has been learned actually produce the desired outcomes. Sheila's next step is to have the whole program committee meet with the outdoor adventure group and hammer out the various complexities of the program plan:

- Do the instructional and transfer plans meet the stated program and learning objectives?

- How will the participants demonstrate to Sheila's organization, the funding agency, and other stakeholders that they really met the program outcomes with these plans?

- How will the learning context and the participants' backgrounds, experiences, and needs affect what are selected as instructional and transfer techniques?

- How will the transfer of learning strategies and techniques fit into the whole picture, as these are central to the learning outcomes being met?

Sheila knows that planning and implementing the transfer of learning process will be challenging because as one part of the plan changes, so will others. Transfer of learning is intricately connected with many other components in the Interactive Model of Program Planning, and thus as other components change, the transfer of learning plan is greatly affected.

Although this scenario describes well the linkages among devising transfer plans and selected components of the Interactive Model of Program Planning, there are not always as many factors influencing transfer of learning as in this scenario. For example, in some planning endeavors the transfer process is connected only to instructional plans and, more specifically, as one means of meeting the learning objectives. As is seen from Sheila's planning endeavors, the transfer of learning strategies and techniques often hold the key to whether or not program outcomes can be achieved. Therefore, planning for learning transfer is a critical part of the planning process, as is further discussed in the next section.

The Importance of Planning for Learning Transfer

There are a number of reasons why planning for the transfer of learning is so important. First, as noted, both sponsoring organizations and participants are asking for outcomes that are applicable, practical, and make a difference. For example, billions of dollars are spent annually for continuing professional training and education.

The American Society for Training & Development's (ASTD) Trend Report of 2006 estimates that organizations spend $190 billion annually on workplace learning. "When all costs, direct and indirect, are combined, the range goes even higher. Management expectations from training and education programs are high" (Daffron, Metzgen-Ohlswager, Skinner, & Saarinen, 2012, p. 613).

Estimates of transfer of learning since the 1980s have generally been low. Recently, studies show estimates still remain low at about 10 percent (Awoniyi, Griego, & Morgan, 2002). Much of this expensive training and continuing education is wasted because of "continued low transfer. [Rather], practitioners have emphasized and developed sophisticated delivery devices at the expense of the critical connections between the training site and the work [and other environments]" (Brinkerhoff & Montesino, 1995, p. 264). Broad and Newstrom (1992) and Broad (2005) go on to assert that for organizations to remain competitive in the global marketplace and prepare highly skilled workers, improving transfer of learning must be a high priority. Although this reported low rate of transfer of learning pertains primarily to training and continuing professional education, there is reason to suspect that a low rate may be found in other programs for adults. Second, there are many issues and concerns related to the lives of adults that can be at least partially addressed through educational programs—health care reform, violence in our communities, restructuring of public education, world peace, and environmental concerns, to name a few. What is critical about so many of these issues and concerns is that solutions were needed yesterday. Therefore, it is no longer viable or ethical for educators to leave up to chance whether people, as a result of attending education and training programs, can apply what they have learned to solving these complex problems.

Third, many people need assistance in reflecting changes they must make in themselves, other people, organizations, or society before what they have learned can be translated into concrete results. For example, some people are predisposed to change, whereas others need support from a variety of sources (for example, work supervisors, family members, friends) to apply what they have learned. These and other factors, such as organizational climate and available funds, that enhance or block the transfer of learning process are discussed further in this chapter.

Models of Planning for Transfer of Learning

One of the earliest models for transfer of learning, by Baldwin and Ford (1988), has been the basis for many subsequent models that describe the process. In their model, Baldwin and Ford (1988) placed emphasis on the planning stage. One of their major conclusions was that if the program planning included the planner, the educator/trainer, the participants, and the managers of organizations, the program would surely be successful and the learner would transfer the new information. Both researchers continued their studies of transfer of learning but, like other researchers noted earlier, were disappointed to find that transfer only happened in small amounts, and concluded that an emphasis on planning was not enough to facilitate transfer. Broad and Newstrom (1992) and Broad (1997) used their own research in the field of training to create examples for program planners to use to make education and training productive. At the same time Cervero (1985) suggested methods of adult learning that would help professional program planners.

Reported in a number of studies over the years were that managers were the primary group responsible for lack of transfer in organizations (Brinkerhoff & Montesino,1995; Clarke, 2002; Kirwan, 2009), and that organizational environments were not conducive to making the transfer process happen (Bates & Khasawneh, 2005; Holton, Bates, Seyler, & Carvalho, 1997; Rouiller & Goldstein, 1993). Other researchers began to see that the problem was not just with each of the stakeholders mentioned here or with one setting or another, but that it was with multiple variables (Cervero, 1985; Cheetham & Chivers, 2000, 2001; Kirwan, 2009) or a link between organizational learning culture and innovation (Bates & Khasawneh, 2005). Still others discovered that the culture and climate of the particular profession affected the transfer process (Daffron & North, 2006; Daffron & Davis, 2005; Daffron, Cowdrey, & Doran, 2007; Daffron, Goulet, Gray, & Viada, 2008; Daley, 2001, 2002).

Despite new knowledge about learning transfer, researchers in recent studies continue to find that transfer is still not reaching the learner (Bates & Khasawneh, 2005; Cheetham & Chivers, 2000, 2001; Daffron et al., 2008; Daley, 2001). A new model for transfer of learning, the "Successful Transfer of Learning Model," has provided a unique picture of key factors that influence the transfer process and how these factors are interrelated to ensure that transfer is effective (see Figure 9.1). This model is a result of an in-depth study of the transfer of learning process that involved 498 interviews of professionals from seventeen professional groups (e.g., state court judges, ESL and K–12 teachers, physicians, attorneys, and firefighters), all of whom

FIGURE 9.1

Successful Transfer of Learning Model

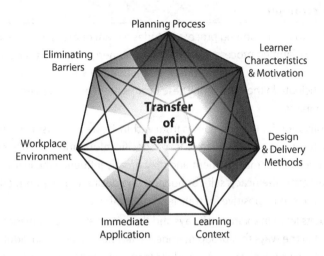

Daffron, S. R., & North, M. W. (2011). *Successful transfer of learning*. Malabar, FL: Krieger. Used with permission.

had taken part in a number of professional development programs. The interview questions were grouped into four parts: the program-planning process, the delivery of the program, the post-program phase, and suggestions to help with transfer of learning to practice. Although the results and conclusions of this study are appropriate for program planners who conduct training and continuing professional education, they can also easily be adapted to other less formal programming.

Seven factors identified as a result of this research are critical for the process of transfer to successfully occur, including: the planning process, learner characteristics and motivation, design and delivery methods, learning context, immediate application, workplace environment, and eliminating barriers to transfer. Although some of these factors have been stressed in earlier studies, the graphic of the model, shown in Figure 9.1, exemplifies the intertwining aspects of all the factors that contribute to learning transfer. Similar to the Interactive Model of Program Planning, this transfer model is multifaceted, nonlinear, and interactive in nature. Transfer of learning is indeed a complex and enigmatic process, often neglected by the stakeholders because of difficulty in understanding how the process works. The ideas included in each factor facilitate translating theories and models developed about transfer of learning and how to use them in actual practice. The factors from the model are summarized in Exhibit 9.1.

EXHIBIT 9.1

Description of Factors

Factors	Description
Planning Process	The program planning process includes a team or group of representatives involved in the planning process (e.g., program planners, potential trainers or instructors, content experts, organizational management or supervisors, and learners who plan to participate in the program). These groups meet as often as necessary to plan specific programs.
Learner Characteristics and Motivation	Motivation for learners comes from within. However, outside motivation, such as directions or instruction to learn specific information or skills, can come from supervisors or management and may greatly influence the learners' motivation. The learners' self-efficacy, self-confidence. and desire to gain information create a mind-set that has to be positive for transfer to take effect.
Design and Delivery Methods	Adults learn in a variety of ways and thus an array of delivery methods are prepared to match the ways that group members learn best. In addition, adult education principles and assumptions about how adults learn are used to design the program.
Learning Context	An effective context for learning is used to engage the group in the learning process. Program planners, designers, and trainers consider the specific groups of learners that will be attending the programs and their personal contexts for learning. Planners also think about the preferred learning style for the groups with whom they are working.
Immediate Application	Immediate application of the new information given in a program is very important for the transfer of learning process to take place. The amount of time for "immediate" application can vary according to the situation of learners. However, if new information or skills are not used within 60–90 days, it probably will not be applied or transferred in the learners' settings.
Workplace Environment	When learners return to their jobs or other life roles, many factors will come into play to prevent the transfer of learning (see Eliminating Barriers). One solution is to plan for the transfer process before attending the program and have a plan for how to implement on the job or in other situations immediately. It is helpful to have supportive supervisors, management, peers, and others in ensuring that the learning transfer will be successful.
Eliminating Barriers	Barriers of time constraints, lack of applicability, personal challenges, workplace issues, and other life issues are realities that stop transfer to practice. There are also policies in place that prohibit transfer—supervisors and other people in learners' lives who are too busy or disinterested to hear about the new information and skills acquired, and the learners' need to "catch up" with their daily activities while being away at a program.

Barriers to transfer come from a lack of sufficient planning; great ideas but no solutions for implementation; poorly designed training; disinterest on the part of learners, management, or other important people in the learners' lives; and a lack of follow-up by program planners, presenters, management, or others involved in the program planning process. |

Adapted from *Successful Transfer of Learning*, Daffron & North (2011) and Daffron, S., Metzgen-Ohlswager, I., Skinner, S., & Saarinen, L. (2012). Acquiring knowledge, skills, and abilities across a lifetime by transferring to one's own practice. In Aspin, D., Chapman, J., Evans, K, and Bagnall, R. (Eds), *Second International Handbook of Lifelong Learning,* Vol. I & II, pp. 613 – 625. London: Springer.

Recent events such as tough economic times, cuts in budgets for education and training, and a need to be accountable for education and training have led to discussions about return on investment (ROI) and a whole team effort to overcome barriers to ROI. Where possible, anticipating and eliminating the barriers to learning transfer in the beginning of the planning process is more important than ever for consideration by all stakeholders (Daffron & North, 2011). In addition, it is also important for stakeholders to take into account actions that can enhance the transfer process throughout the program presentation itself.

Barriers and Enhancers to Learning Transfer

In thinking through the many factors that are discussed about why people do or do not apply what they have learned, it is useful to categorize these ideas into a clear and manageable number of key influencing factors (Daffron & North, 2011, Hall & Hord, 2011; Holton, 2000; Holton & Baldwin, 2003; Kirkpatrick & Kirkpatrick, 2005; Kirwan, 2009; Ottoson, 1997; Yamnill & McLean, 2001). These key factors include: participants; design and execution; content; changes required to apply learning; organizational content; and community and societal forces. These factors were chosen from a larger group, as they illustrate program features and characteristics that frequently serve as barriers or enhancers to transfer of learning.[2] Which outcome is experienced—successful transfer of learning or no change in practice—depends on the unique context and needs of each program.

Rarely does any one of these factors affect a program in isolation. Rather, it is the interaction among a number of the factors that makes a difference in whether learners can apply what they have learned outside the formal learning situation (Daffron & North, 2011; Hall & Hord, 2011; Holton & Baldwin, 2003; Kirwan, 2009; Ottoson, 1995b; Leberman, McDonald, & Doyle, 2006; Phillips & Broad, 1997). Nevertheless, not all the major factors that influence learning transfer come into play for every education and training program.[3] Therefore, the more complex the program's scope and goals, the larger the number of people affected, and the greater the magnitude of the changes; the less control over organizational and societal forces, the more difficult it is to successfully complete the transfer of learning process.

A Framework for Planning Learning Transfer

In planning for the transfer of learning three key elements are addressed: when the transfer strategies are employed, the variety of strategies used to help in applying what has been learned, and the key people involved (Baldwin & Ford, 1988; Broad, 2000, 2005; Holton & Baldwin, 2003; Kirkpatrick & Kirkpatrick, 2005; Kirwan, 2009; Silberman, 2006; Yamnill & McLean, 2001).

In terms of timing, transfer strategies are used before the program begins, while the program is in progress, and after the program is completed. Transfer strategies employed after the program is completed are usually the most difficult for program planners to influence, for a number of reasons, including a potential mismatch between the content of the program and what the learners need to know and do; lack of support from coworkers, peers, or family and friends; resistance by learners to change; or specifics of the settings where these changes need to happen. Although they are the most difficult to achieve, transfer strategies used after the program is completed are often the most effective. Daffron and North (2011) recommend that follow-up strategies be planned with the participants and appropriate organizational personnel before the program is presented, which makes it is easier to apply what has been learned after the program.

The second element that is considered in planning for learning transfer is to determine what strategies and techniques are the most useful in assisting learners to apply what they have learned to their personal, work, and other roles they play as adults. Samples of these strategies and techniques include: involving key people in the planning process, being aware of how contextual and cultural differences influence applying what has been learned, and using specific techniques that learners prefer. To allow learners and others to be a part of this selection process, planning staff, including instructors, participants, supervisors, or other stakeholders need to be informed about learning strategies and techniques. Providing this information to learners and other stakeholders permits them to make informed choices about which of these strategies and techniques are most appropriate and likely to help learners apply what has been learned in their own settings. If working with a professional group, program planners find each professional group has their own best way of learning and that this "learning context" can be ascertained by talking with the learners and their organizational sponsors before putting the strategies and techniques together (Broad, 1997; Daffron & North, 2011; Daley, 2001).

Key people—the final element to be addressed—are those who need to be involved so that transfer of learning actually happens. Program planners themselves have a number of roles and functions, such as taking into consideration the learners, instructors and facilitators, and other stakeholders in preparing transfer plans. The other key players to include in the planning of learning transfer may be any of the following: instructors or trainers; representatives of sponsoring organizations including supervisors and managers; and when addressing personal issues, members of the community or family and friends. For example, in work situations, senior managers may be critical players; in community action programs, city council members, other community leaders, and "grassroots" constituents may need to be included; and in personal situations, a close friend, partner, or professional or peer counselor may be important to the process.

Exhibit 9.2 shows examples of specific activities these players take to enhance the transfer process before, during, and after education and training programs.

It is essential in developing a framework for the transfer of learning process that all parties involved be aware of the techniques that are useful for learners in applying what they have learned during the education and training program.

Transfer of Learning Techniques

Program planners have a repertoire of specific techniques that are used to facilitate learning transfer. These techniques are grouped into three categories: techniques for individual learners, group techniques, and techniques that can be used either by individuals or in groups. Although a few of these techniques involve direct instructional activities (for example, refresher sessions, online tutorials or sessions), the majority are designed to be used within the context in which the learning transfer is taking place.[4]

More in-depth descriptions of these and other techniques that are used in learning transfer can be found in Baldwin, Ford, and Naquin (2000); Biech (2005); Bonk and Zhang (2008); Holton and Baldwin (2003); Garrison and Vaughan (2008); Kirkpatrick and Kirkpatrick (2007); Kirwan (2009); Palloff and Pratt (2011); Silberman (2006); and Ukens (2001). In employing these techniques, careful thought should be given to matching transfer techniques to the preferences and capabilities of the learners, resource availability (e.g., facilitator skills, time, technology, and money), the nature of what is to be transferred, and the context in which the transfer is to happen. For example, peer coaching and support groups may be very effective for people who are self-motivated and like to work with others, but may not work for people who need a supervisor to intervene before they will change the way they behave or practice.

Challenges Program Planners Face in Organizational Settings

"There is no question that transfer of learning is a formidable challenge to organizations" (Holton, Baldwin, & Naquin, 2000, p. 1) and to learners,

EXHIBIT 9.2

Framework for Transfer of Learning: People, Timing, and Strategies

Before

Program Planners	Instructors and Facilitators	Learners	Other Key Players
Identify clearly what is to be transferred: knowledge, skills, attitudes, and beliefs.	Obtain a clear picture of what learning is to be transferred as a result of the activities for which they are responsible.	Clarify how the expectations for what they are learning is to be to be applied into their life situations (e.g., work role, volunteer work, personal issues).	Provide clear information on what information and skills are to be applied by serving on planning committees, responding surveys, and individual discussions with planners.
Ascertain the contextual aspects of where the learning is to be applied (e.g., learner and sponsor expectations, organizational climate, political environment, cultural differences between and among learners, planners, and program sponsors).	Ask specific questions of program planners or learners about the contextual aspects of where the learning is to be applied.	Select specific "things" they believe they can change related to the expectations for learning transfer.	Arrange for incentives for program participants for positive changes they make related to the objectives of the program (e.g., recognition luncheons, pay increases or bonuses, and celebrations).
Set the guidelines for what constitutes successful transfer of learning, and make provisions for a negotiation process for changes in what determines this success.	Ask learners to select projects or other activities to complete that encompass what learning is expected to be transferred (e.g., request that learners think about who or what in their environments would help them successfully complete these projects or activities).	Discuss with key people who could assist them with how what they are learning is to be applied, and how this learning should or might affect their current situations.	Discuss with potential participants what they believe the barriers and enhancers might be to ensure a successful transfer process, and work through with them alternative ways the barriers could be addressed and how those positive forces for learning transfer might be enriched.
			Ensure, for those groups and organizations that are assisting in funding the program, that there are adequate monies included for learning transfer.

During

Involve people who are key to the learning transfer in implementing the program (e.g., as instructors, site coordinators). Monitor the program to ensure instructors are incorporating instructional techniques that address transfer issues. Use formative evaluation techniques to assist instructors who are not adequately addressing the transfer aspects of the program to change what or how they are teaching while the program is still in progress. Provide ideas for alternative techniques to assist learners with transfer of learning so they can incorporate into their own action plans (e.g., support groups, peer coaching, online computer formats). Provide a plan for instructors and give learners different transfer strategies and techniques so they can better select which of these strategies and techniques might work better for them in applying what they have learned within their own settings.	Use active learning techniques (e.g., case studies, live or computer simulations, applications exercises) that enhance learning transfer. Incorporate the learning context as part of the learning environment (e.g., learners try out new skills in similar or their own settings). Suggest transfer resources (e.g., online formats, creating transfer groups). Provide learners opportunities to develop specific action plans and assist them in assessing barriers and enhancers to learning transfer in their own environments. Teach learners about different transfer strategies and techniques so they can better select or assist in selecting which of these strategies and techniques might work better for them in applying what they have learned within their own settings.	Actively prepare for and participate in each of the learning activities. During the learning activities link what they are learning to their own situations. Try out, where possible (e.g., in multiday activities) what they are learning in the settings in which this learning will be used to explore the potential for transfer. Use the learning resources provided and give feedback to the instructors on whether they are useful. Ask the instructors about additional resources that might be helpful. Select, with assistance of instructors or planners, learning strategies and techniques that will help them most in applying what they have learned in their own settings. Develop specific action plans that include strategies and techniques that can assist them with the learning transfer and anticipate barriers and enhancers they might find in the transfer process.	Support participants while they are active in the program (e.g., do not interrupt participants with calls or text messages during the actual training activities; provide funding, have other family members or friends ensure that child-care needs are covered). Provide ways to assist individuals or groups of participants who are in programs that last more than one day in developing action plans focused on the application of what they are learning (e.g., through individual coaching; facilitating group meetings). Ensure that critical tasks or responsibilities at work are covered for participants, such as having other employees complete a report that is due while these participants are at the program or making sure that there are people who can cover if a child or older parent gets sick. Make sure staff members or volunteers, if needed, are available to assist with program registration, taking care of room arrangements, and other details that are required for programs to be successful.

(Continued)

EXHIBIT 9.2 (*Continued*)

Program Planners	Instructors and Facilitators	Learners	Other Key Players
After			
Initiate and support people involved in the transfer process to help ensure that the outcomes that are expected can be achieved.	Provide follow-up assistance through a variety of techniques (e.g., coaching, follow-up sessions, refresher courses, mentoring).	Implement their application plans and be willing to change those plans. Use the transfer resources and seek additional support when needed.	Encourage participants to use a variety of transfer of learning techniques that will assist them in the applications process (e.g., mentoring, job aides, transfer teams, support groups, attending follow-up sessions, networking, and using online resources).
Develop different transfer techniques that emerge from the needs of the learners, instructors involved in follow-up activities, or the sponsors of the program.	Facilitate the process of initiating these different application techniques and provide support for these efforts.	Initiate different transfer techniques that facilitate learning transfer within their particular context.	Become actively involved in the transfer of learning process with individuals or groups of participants. This involvement could take a number of forms (e.g., assisting in carrying through action plans, coaching, mentoring, helping in finding needed resources, letting them know that it is OK to make mistakes as they go through the transfer process).
Negotiate and change, as needed, what the outcomes of the transfer of learning process should be with all interested parties.	Provide feedback to program planners, learners, and other key players on what the participants have learned that can realistically be transferred based on their knowledge of the participants and the situations in which they will apply this learning.	Provide feedback to program planners, instructors, and other key players on what learning can realistically be applied based on their own experiences in the transfer process and their specific situations.	Negotiate and change, as needed, what the outcomes of the transfer of learning process should be with all interested parties (e.g., program planners, learners, other stakeholders).
			Change policies or practices to embrace the changes gained from the educational experience.
			Set up networks on the Web to engage the learners with others who were also learners or those who were unable to participate but would like to learn more about the experience.

planning staff, instructors, and other stakeholders who are responsible for ensuring transfer happens. In planning for the transfer of learning as part of the design and execution of education and training programs, program planners take into account the previously described six factors that influence the transfer of learning (program participants, program content, changes required to apply learning, organizational context, and community and societal forces). One useful tool for improving the learning transfer process is the Learning Transfer Systems Inventory (LTSI) (Holton, 2000, 2003; Holton, Bates, & Ruona, 2000; Velada, Caetano, Bates, & Holton, 2009). The LTSI is an 89-item instrument used to measure the factors influencing learning transfer of the learner and within an organization. Holton and Bates (2002) created this diagnostic instrument so that program planners "can access potential factor problems, investigate known transfer problems, target interventions designed to enhance transfer and incorporate evaluation of transfer as part of regular employee assessments" (Holton, 2000, p. 8). When measuring the learning transfer climate, Bates and Khasawneh (2005) found a different measurement was needed, and created a "training-in-general" measurement of the task support element, individual cognitive states, and measurement of performance coaching (p. 516). They called the three measurements performance self-efficacy (PSE), transfer effort-performance expectations (TEPE), and performance-outcome expectations (POE) (p. 516).

Broad (2005) acknowledges the increased attention stakeholders and organizational decision makers have on measuring outcomes, in particular, Return on Investment (ROI). Broad finds five stages of measurement of transfer of learning or improved performance. She begins with the Human Performance Technology (HPT) process, or "The knowledge of human performance technology (HTP) and abilities to identify and analyze performance problems and opportunities and to design, implement, and evaluate interventions to resolve them" (p. 53); this stage 1 sets up the intervention and measurement in the organization before the training begins. In stage 2, the results of HPT are identified and significant gaps identified. Stages 3 and 4 take the gaps and examine actual performance, and Stage 5 uses specific metrics to measure each desired performance and results (p. 113). Phillips and Stone (2002) use examples of the five stages with large organizational performance measurement.

Another helpful mechanism for responding to the challenges of the learning transfer process is the Stages of Concerns (SOC) model proposed by Hall and Hord (2011). As people go through a change process, which is, as noted earlier, the heart of learning transfer, "there is a developmental pattern to how [people's] feelings and perceptions evolve as the change process unfolds" (Hall & Hord, 2011, p. 57). Within their model, Hall and Hord (2011) have identified and confirmed seven specific categories of concerns that people move through as they confront change; these seven categories are further organized into three levels: self, task, and impact concerns. Most people go from self concerns (e.g., "How will using this new idea affect me?") to task concerns (e.g., "I seem to be spending all of my time getting materials ready") to impact concerns (e.g., "I am concerned about relating what I am doing with what my coworkers are doing") (Hall & Hord, 2011, p. 61).

There are three major techniques for assessing the levels of concern for people involved in the change process: one-legged interviews, open-ended concerns statements, and SOC questionnaires. These techniques are fully described in Chapter Four of Hall and Hord's book *Implementing Change: Patterns, Principles and Potholes.* What is useful to learners as they journey through the transfer process is knowing which stage(s) they are in so that they can use choose appropriate transfer techniques, in concert with program planners and other stakeholders. Learners in the self-concerns category may benefit more from techniques that allow them to further explore the impact of implementing a new practice or making a life change (for example networking, support groups, and reflective practice). Those in the task-concerns stage look more to techniques that give them hands-on assistance, such as job aids and follow-up training sessions. And finally, learners who are in the impact-concerns arena usually seek techniques that permit them to work with others (e.g., coaching, mentoring, transfer teams, and online social networks).

Implementing measures for transfer of learning is complicated and there are many details to be handled and many people involved in the process. For too long, program planners have believed they did not have a role in the transfer process once the programs were over. In addition, in some cases planners have viewed themselves as having little or no control over the transfer process, and thus have ignored this aspect of the program planning. As one of the shifts of emphasis related to program planning is on evidence-based planning, more planners are paying attention to the transfer process because they are expected to document the specific changes that have resulted from the programs they put together (Calley, 2011). Program planners have also become more skilled in negotiating changes that need to be made related to barriers that block learning transfer. They have requested that instructors incorporate more active learning methods, including techniques that give participants a chance to address the changes they need to make during the education and training sessions. Planners are also working hand-in-hand with supervisors, managers, and chief executive officers to ensure their support for the transfer process (e.g., time for learners to make the changes required of them, providing tangible awards for learners who excel at making changes, and adopting policies that support learning transfer). However, there are barriers that may be beyond the control of program planners; they must accept this and move on. What Ottoson (1995a) observed a number of years ago still holds true today: "Application means getting one's hands dirty, it means having the heart to persevere in the face of obstacles, it means having the touch to apply with sensitivity, it means having the guts to make tough choices, and it means having one's feet firmly grounded in practical reality" (p. 25).

Chapter Highlights

Devising transfer of learning plans means helping learners, instructors, and program sponsors to systematically think through how program participants can apply what they have learned back at work, or in their personal lives. But even though transfer to practice is considered to be an important part of the planning process, this component continues to be neglected. Rather, it is often assumed that the application of what was learned at an education or training program somehow just happens and any resultant changes are the worry of someone other than those responsible for planning the program. Transfer plans are based on and linked primarily to five components of the planning process—the context, program ideas and needs, program objectives, instructional plans, and program evaluation. Planners, especially those who are unfamiliar with the process, find it useful to have models for planning transfer of learning.

It is important that program planners consider planning for the transfer of learning to be an integral part of their responsibilities. In preparing transfer of learning plans, program planners concentrate on the following six tasks:

- Be knowledgeable about the major barriers and enhancers that influence transfer of learning (e.g., learners' backgrounds, experiences, and motivation; climate of organizations related to changes in practice).

- Decide when the transfer of learning strategies should be employed (before, during, and after the formal program).

- Determine the key players who should be a part of the transfer of learning process (e.g., participants, program planning staff, instructors, work supervisors, and other stakeholders such as funders, community leaders, and family and friends).

- Provide information to learners, supervisors, and other stakeholders about transfer of learning strategies and techniques so they know what strategies and techniques are available and can choose or assist in choosing appropriate ones for the transfer process.

- Choose and select, with the assistance of learners, instructors, and others, transfer strategies (e.g. involving learners, supervisors, and other stakeholders in planning the transfer process; taking into account contextual and cultural differences; ascertaining the contextual aspects of where the learning is to be applied); and techniques (e.g., mentoring, peer coaching, support groups, online discussions, reflective practice, transfer teams) that are the most useful in assisting participants to apply what they have learned.

- Negotiate and change, where possible, the content, skills, or beliefs that are to be transferred, based on barriers and enhancers to learning transfer in the application site.

As noted in this chapter, developing transfer of learning plans is tied directly to the program evaluation component of the planning process, which is described in the next chapter. Without clear and doable transfer plans, it is often difficult to trace how program activities are related to program outcomes and to provide justification for the judgments made on the worth and value of a program.

Notes for Additional Online Resources

1. Also see Scenario 9.A: Helping Teachers Transfer Learning to Practice.

2. See Figure 9.A: Examples of Barriers and Enhancers to Transfer of Learning.

3. See Scenarios 9.B: Reach for Recovery Program and 9.C: Workplace Diversity.

4. See Exhibit 9.A: Sample Techniques to Facilitate Learning Transfer for examples of some of the most popular techniques.

 Application Exercises

The two application exercises presented here are designed to help you facilitate the transfer of learning. Exercise 9.1 assists you in identifying those factors that enhance or inhibit the learning transfer, and Exercise 9.2 helps you to incorporate transfer of learning into the design and execution of your chosen program.

EXERCISE 9.1

Identifying Elements That Enhance or Inhibit Transfer of Learning

1. Describe briefly a program for which you planned or need to plan for the transfer of learning.

_____

_____

_____

_____

_____

2. Using the following chart, first list specific things (related to one or more of the six factors from Figure 9.A that did or can enhance or inhibit the learning transfer; see web site). Next, indicate what span of decision-making control you had or have for each enhancer or inhibitor you listed. Finally, for those items for which you have indicated only some or little or no influence, list who did or could assist you in the transfer process.

Factor	Things That Enhanced or Inhibited	Span of Decision-Making Control	People Who Did or Can Assist in Transfer
Program Participants			
Program Design and Execution			
Program Content			
Changes Required to Apply Learning			
Organizational Context			
Community and Societal Forces			

3. Discuss with your planning group or some colleagues your responses and ask them to provide feedback on the choices you made and to share other strategies they might suggest.

EXERCISE 9.2

Choosing Strategies and Techniques to Use in Transfer of Learning

1. Using the same program that you described in Exercise 9.1 describe three or four transfer strategies that you did use or could use for each group listed in the chart below (refer to Exhibit 9.1).

_____

_____

_____

_____

_____

People Involved	Strategy for Before Program	Strategy for During Program	Strategy for After Program
Program Planners			
Instructors or Facilitators			
Learners			
Work Supervisors			
Other Stakeholders (specify each of those stakeholders)			

2. For each of the strategies that you listed do one of the following:

   2a. For the previous program you planned, indicate whether this strategy worked or did not work and why.

   _____

   _____

   _____

   2b. For the program you are currently planning, explain why you chose this strategy.

   _____

   _____

   _____

3. Using Exhibit 9.A outline in the following chart what transfer techniques were or should have been incorporated in a previous program (or will be incorporated into a current program you are planning). Provide a justification for why each technique was or could be useful in enhancing the applications process of a current program you are planning.

	Technique	**Reason for Using**
A.	_____	_____
B.	_____	_____
C.	_____	_____
D.	_____	_____
E.	_____	_____
F.	_____	_____

4. Review these materials with your planning group or colleagues and discuss whether they agree or disagree with your choices and why.

Chapter 10

Formulating Program Evaluation Plans

JUANITA, A NEW coordinator for a safety training program, is not alone in inheriting an education or training program that has had, at best, haphazard evaluation.[1] Although systematic evaluation has in theory been touted as an essential part of the planning process for decades (e.g., Houle, 1972; Kirkpatrick, 1976), until fairly recently many planners have not felt the need to go beyond asking for participants' reactions or perhaps trying to gauge what knowledge has been acquired. However, with the call for greater accountability from many sectors, more planners are experimenting with practical ways of ensuring that evaluation becomes an integral part of their planning and delivery processes.

In this chapter, we first address how program evaluation is defined, and then describe how evaluation connects with other components of the Interactive Model of Program Planning. We outline a twelve-element process for conducting a systematic program evaluation, which is followed by a description of developmental evaluation and how unplanned or informal evaluation opportunities can be used. We then review sample types of program evaluation, and provide descriptions of techniques used to collect and analyze evaluation data. The chapter concludes with a discussion of ways judgments are made about programs on the basis of the data presented. Although the chapter emphasizes formal evaluation approaches, in practice program planners may not have the skills to carry through these kinds of evaluations, especially those who are new to the program planning process. In addition, resources are often either not available or are inadequate to carry through with effective formal evaluation, except in the case of comprehensive programs with funding from external sources, or when program evaluation is required as a part of accreditation or legislative mandate. Even if not performing a formal evaluation, program planners can still use the material provided in this chapter to guide their actions to determine how programs can be improved or whether they should be continued.

Program Evaluation Defined

Program evaluation is most often defined as a process used to determine whether the design and delivery of a program were effective and whether the proposed outcomes were met. Although systematic or strategically planned evaluations are important, so are developmental evaluations and more informal and unplanned evaluation activities.

Systematic evaluation, the approach most often discussed in the literature, is a structured process with a number of elements that need to be addressed (for example, determining the purpose of the evaluation, the major evaluation questions, and the techniques and analysis procedures). For example, systematic evaluations related to governmental rehabilitation programs for veterans with post-traumatic stress disorder can track program outcomes over time to see whether participants received appropriate and helpful treatment, whether they have been able to find meaningful employment, and whether being a part of the program has made a positive difference in the quality of their lives. There are two types of systematic evaluation, both of which ideally are included in the evaluation plans. Formative evaluations focus on what should be done to improve or change a program while it is in progress, while summative evaluations address the results or outcomes of a program. Developmental evaluations have "the purpose of helping develop innovations, interventions, or programs ... with the evaluator typically becoming a part of the design team" (Methison, 2005, as cited by Patton, 2011, p. 20). This approach to evaluation is a relatively new way of viewing one of the roles of evaluators and is especially useful "under conditions of complexity with a focus on adaption to the local context" (Patton, 2011, p. 20), such as providing assistance in developing countries, or when sudden changes, like destruction from tsunamis or earthquakes, call for immediate action. Informal evaluations are often spontaneous in nature. offering insights into what is happening in the "here and now." This approach to evaluation is most often used to revise the content, delivery, or administrative tasks of program coordination while it is still in progress. Whichever approach or combination of approaches of evaluation are used, evaluation is a continuous process that begins in the initial planning phase and continues throughout the life of the program (Knox, 2002; Newcomer, Hatry, & Wholey, 2010; Patton, 2011; Sork, 2000). In essence, good program evaluation provides useful feedback throughout the life of the program to planners, participants, instructors, organizational sponsors, community groups, funders, and other stakeholders.

The central purposes that drive evaluation processes are gathering and analyzing data for decision making and accountability. Displayed in Exhibit 10.1 is a sampling of the kinds of decisions that planners and other

---

EXHIBIT 10.1

Kinds of Decisions Made Using Evaluation Data

Outcomes of Evaluation

- Changing the design, delivery, management, and evaluation processes of program activities while in progress
- Determining whether program goals and objectives have been successfully achieved
- Establishing whether a program was conducted in a cost-effective way
- Justifying resource allocations
- Negotiating outcomes as participants apply their learning in their work or personal lives
- Assessing how the program context (e.g., political, economic, organizational) affects program processes and outcomes
- Revising current programs
- Deciding whether programs should be continued
- Cancelling programs either before they start or while in progress
- Investigating reasons for program failures
- Responding to needs and ideas identified for future programs (e.g., feasibility, cost-effectiveness, timeliness)

---

stakeholders make as a result of conducting program evaluations (Gboku & Lekoko, 2007; Kirkpatrick & Kirkpatrick, 2006, 2007; Knox, 2002; Newcomer et al., 2010; Mertens & Wilson, 2012; Patton, 2011; Ottoson, 2000).

Whereas decisions about program planning may be done internally or with other stakeholders, accountability often involves more than just those engaged with the program in some direct way. Although program planners have traditionally wanted to demonstrate to their immediate constituents and stakeholders that their programs are producing the desired results or outcomes, the external pressure for program accountability is on the rise from such sources as regulatory agencies, professional associations, government officials (e.g., legislative bodies), and the general public (Knox, 2002; Linn, 2000; Schuh & Associates, 2009; Wholey, 2010). This external pressure for accountability can be a positive force for enhancing and expanding programs for adults, but also can have negative and even disastrous consequences for participants and the groups and organizations that sponsor these programs.

Connecting Evaluation to Other Components of the Interactive Model

Evaluation intersects and overlaps with most other components in the Interactive Model of Program Planning, a characteristic shared by the transfer of learning component (Bryson & Patton, 2010; Daffron & North, 2011; Newcomer et al., 2010; Knox, 2002; Ottoson, 2000; Smith & Ragan, 2005; Sork, 2000). This junction of components stems primarily from the data being generated and analyzed throughout the program planning and delivery process. More specifically, data gathered about the program context (see Chapter Four), the ideas and needs for programs (see Chapter Six), the information used in developing program goals and objectives (see Chapter Seven), and the results of transfer strategies and instructional assessments (see Chapters Eight and Nine) are often used as baseline, formative, or outcomes information for program evaluations. In addition, in this age of uncertainty and fast-paced change in many parts of the world, the interweaving of the evaluation component with these other components becomes even more of a necessity as continuous revisions of education and training programs become a given (Morell, 2010; Patton, 2011; Piskurich, 2006).

For example, in evaluating a program with multiple sponsors it is first important to understand the people and organizational contexts in which the programs are planned and delivered (Newcomer et al., 2010; Sork, 2000). Program planners should ask themselves: Was the planning process collaborative or more contentious, in that one of the partners dominated the others for the purpose of advancing their own organizational agenda? Were all voices that should have been heard included in the planning process, or were some intentionally excluded and others overly represented? How was the program structured in terms of decision-making authority, and was it planned so that the cultures of each of the organizations were somehow acknowledged in the final product? These and other contextual factors often affect program outcomes regardless of whether the program was well designed and the participants appropriately chosen. Using contextual data, as stressed in planning for transfer, may mean that program processes and even outcomes may need to be negotiated throughout the program, which in turn makes the evaluation process more complex, and yet more realistic.

Data for program needs and ideas assessment, collected from program participants and the organizations that would most likely employ graduates of the program, are used as baseline data in a number of different ways (Daffron & North, 2011; Ottoson, 2000). Participants' knowledge and skill levels when they entered the program could be used in a formative way to see if there were changes occurring as they went through the program. If not, how might the program be modified to better enable participant learning? Also, contextual data about these participants—for example, current job situations, language differences, and cultural ways of learning—are also helpful in the initial design and in making needed program modifications.

Are the participants able to hold down full-time jobs and complete the program in the time frame and mode that are provided? Does the program need to be offered in languages other than English? And what cultural norms might inhibit or enhance these participants' chances of completing the program? These same data could then be used in a summative way at the end of the program. Were there actual gains in skills and knowledge as a result of completing the program? Did the design of the program, related to contextual factors, make a difference in whether students actually completed the program? Were the participants able to find employment in their field and was what they learned in the program applicable to their jobs?

The organizational data are also used in a formative way by reflecting throughout the program on whether the needs and ideas as expressed by these employers were (1) being addressed in the program and (2) what these graduates needed to know and do once they entered the workforce. This type of evaluation is done by instructors and organizational representatives through review of course material and observations.

Program goals and objectives, as seen later in this chapter, often form the foundation for program evaluation (e.g., in the levels of evaluation, and objectives-based approaches). In these approaches, the evaluation is done to determine whether the stated program objectives have been adequately addressed. For example, if the program objectives state that there will be a change in the knowledge and skills needed to perform well as computer technicians, were the participants able to demonstrate those outcomes through performance and other types of tests? If the program objectives state that participants will be able to apply their new knowledge and skills in a work situation, were these participants able to do this? If the program objectives establish that as a result of this certificate program 70 percent of participants will be employed, within a month of program completion, in jobs that require the knowledge and skills they learned, were in fact 70 percent of the participants employed?

Information gathered as a result of transfer of learning strategies and instructional assessments, like the needs assessment data, is also used in formative and summative ways (Daffron & North, 2011; Piskurich, 2006; Smith & Ragan, 2005). Are students adequately learning the content? If so, are they able to transfer what they are learning, perhaps through formal internships or other types of experiential learning, into work situations? If not, how could courses and the overall program be changed so that content knowledge is adequate and applications of what has been learned are enhanced?

In summary, when formulating evaluation plans, it is critical to think about how evaluation strategies can be woven into the planning process in general, and more specifically into at least five key components of that process: discerning the context, identifying program ideas and needs, developing program goals and objectives, designing instructional assessments, and devising learning transfer plans. One way to envision this integration is to see it as a layered process where one set of data links to another and is used for one or multiple purposes. Thinking about evaluation as a layered activity is important for each of the major approaches to evaluation—systematic, developmental, and informal or unplanned evaluations.

Systematic Program Evaluation

There is no one acceptable systematic process for conducting a program evaluation. The ideal time for this process to begin is when the program is being planned, so that the data obtained can be used to make changes while the program is functioning and to analyze the outcomes or results of the program. However, in practice, designing these types of evaluations may not even be thought of during the hectic development and implementation of the program. Rather, program planners either scramble to collect any type of data that will demonstrate their program is effective or may even choose not to complete any evaluation of their programs. A number of descriptions of the systematic program evaluation process have been developed (e.g., Gboku & Lekoko, 2007; Knox, 2002; Newcomer et al., 2010; Ottoson, 2000; Sork, 2000).[2]

It is important to remember, as noted earlier, that planning for systematic evaluations should not happen as an afterthought once the whole program has been planned. Ideally, evaluation is a process that occurs throughout the planning cycle and is often linked to a number of other components of the model, such as contextual scans, developing program objectives, and learning transfer. As Vella, Berardinelli, and Burrow (1998) have noted: "Evaluation may be ignored if planned separately. Given the real time and resource pressures of delivering many educational programs, they must be implemented quickly (or even before) the planning is finished. Despite good intentions, the result is often that evaluation procedures are never developed or that evaluation is done on the spur of the moment, usually as the program is ending" (p. 19).

In addition, although this approach to the evaluation process may occur in logical order, in a step-by-step fashion, the various elements of the process may overlap, need to be revisited, or have already been addressed through other planning activities. For example, planners may be analyzing

EXHIBIT 10.2

Problems in Systematic Evaluation

Time Frame	Examples of Problems
Before Evaluation Begins	Failing to ensure that an evaluation can be completed in time to be useful even though there are adequate resources (e.g., funding, staff)
	Ensuring that the "right things" are evaluated
	Not paying attention to the concerns of those who are planning and implementing the program as they may be leery of what might come out of the evaluation and how those results will be used
During the Evaluation	Failing to take into account the inevitable changes that often need to be modified in the data collection and analysis phase
	"Collecting too many data and not allowing adequate time for analysis of the data collected" (Harty & Newcomer, 2010, p. 567)
	Not taking into account key contextual factors that affect the evaluation process, such as major layoffs of staff when studying whether a training program was effective or not
After the Evaluation	Failing to do a reality check with key program staff, both as a courtesy to provide them an idea of the results and also as a way to receive their findings that appear out of line with actual practice
	Presenting conclusions without really having the data to support them
	(1) Failing to report evaluation results in such a way that the material is clear, concise, and intelligible to the different audiences (e.g., program planners, stakeholder groups, and funders)

one set of data while collecting another. During this same time period they may also need to revise the original purpose, questions, and criteria as the program unfolds and as participants attempt to incorporate what they have learned into their work or personal roles.

In conducting systematic program evaluations planners need to pay attention to five major potential pitfalls (Bernhardt, 2000; Hatry & Newcomer, 2010; Vella et al., 1998). First, there are a number of problems that arise before, during, and after the data collection and analysis phases of the evaluation process (Hatry and Newcomer, 2010). Examples of these problems are provided in Exhibit 10.2.

Those involved in doing program evaluations need to anticipate the problems they may face as they move through the process, and generate alternative ways to address them.

Second, "program effects are often unclear, are often ill-defined, and can be quite messy to measure" (Hatry & Newcomer, 2010, p. 557). Program outcomes may be too complicated and the number of variables affecting those outcomes too numerous to allow planners to demonstrate that a given program actually produced the desired ratings. For example, it appeared that one three-week (two hours per day, twice a week) training program increased the proficiency of staff in the use of a new computer networking system. This conclusion was reached by comparing pretest and posttest scores of all workshop participants on the use of the system once the program was completed. Yet, when the participants were asked what key element had helped them to increase their proficiency, 95 percent cited on-the-job trial and error. They said that the training program had, in fact, hindered their progress more than it helped, because the instructor often gave poor and incomplete descriptions of how to use the new system and there were not enough work stations to go around.

The third pitfall is that current evaluation procedures, however scientifically rigorous, may not be able to provide hard evidence that the more subtle, and at times the most important, aspects of the education and training programs have been achieved. For example, education and training programs whose major objectives are to foster changes in personal, organizational, or societal values and beliefs are especially difficult to evaluate.

Fourth, conducting systematic program evaluations costs time and money. Some organizations and groups are not able, as mentioned before, or willing to provide these resources. For example in a tough budget year what may happen is that funds for evaluation are either cut back or eliminated.

The fifth pitfall is when planners continue to collect evaluation data even though they know that no action will or can be taken on the basis of evaluation findings. Rather, it would be better not to collect the data at all, because the evaluation process raises expectations on the part of participants and sponsors that changes will be forthcoming.

Developmental Evaluation

Unlike systematic evaluations, which focus on making judgments on the outcomes of programs, developmental evaluation centers on supporting the development of innovative programs. The programs most likely to benefit from this kind of evaluation take place in "highly dynamic environments where those involved are engaged in ongoing trial and error experimentation to find out what works, learning lessons, adapting to changing circumstances, [and] working with new participants" (Patton, 2008, p. 278).

Although developmental evaluation is currently not widely used, the basic tenets of this form of evaluation makes sense for: (1) addressing problems with no real answers, such as alleviating poverty; (2) taking programs that worked in one context and trying them out in an entirely different setting, or with participants who have dissimilar backgrounds and experiences; and (3) developing programs that need a rapid response (Patton, 2011). Examples are given in Exhibit 10.3 that demonstrate situations in which program planners find developmental evaluation to be useful.

Patton (2011) provides throughout his book very useful descriptions of programs in which developmental evaluation has been used. Among these examples is a major innovative program that was initiated through the McKnight Foundation for a statewide program in Minnesota centering on anti-poverty work. As Patton observes: "The best thinkers about these issues took their best shot. They planned carefully and brought enormous in-the-trenches experiences to these programs. And *not one of them unfolded as planned*" (p. 31; italics in original). The resulting programs were not even close to what was originally planned in most cases. What those planners learned was that "they

---

EXHIBIT 10.3

Examples of Situations Where the Developmental Evaluation Approach Is Useful

Reason for Using	Examples of Situations
Problems with No Real Answers	Developing a statewide program for people who have defaulted on their mortgages primarily due to a long-term recession and unemployment, and who need to have information on their options are for housing and other needs.
Transferring Programs into a Different Context	Piloting an existing program on providing nutritious meals on a low budget, which has been highly successful with primarily low-income, urban, Caucasian women, with Latina migrant workers in a rural area.
Rapid-Response Needed	Coordinating with local, national, and international relief organizations a program to provide food, shelter, and other basic needs to thousands of refugees from a country where a bloody civil war has just broken out. With few resources, these refugees had to flee to a low-income country whose border was still open to them.

had to adapt their plans to the realities of who entered their programs and complex dynamics within which they worked, for example reforms in welfare policies, a revised federal definition of poverty, souring of the political climate, and the depressed state of the job market" (p. 31). It must be said that planners for this program were fortunate in that the grant they received was for multiyear funding and the foundation was open to the innovations that were proposed. In addition, Patton also provides stories throughout the book in the form of vignettes from experienced developmental evaluators that focus on such topics as lessons learned, challenges encountered, potential for making major changes, and pitfalls in the process that they have faced.

In conducting developmental evaluations, engaging program planners with the intended users is central to the process. This approach does not depend on any particular techniques for collecting data, nor the types of data that are gathered, which are described later in this chapter. However, as noted earlier, this approach does emphasize that this process is continuous throughout the project. The techniques used emerge throughout the process, which calls for flexibility to be a hallmark of those involved with the planning process. As few program planners are well versed in using a wide range of techniques and analysis strategies, they accept learning as a given when using developmental evaluation, and often seek the support of outside experts to assist in the process.

Informal Evaluation Opportunities

Although most models of program planning advocate a systematic or strategic process of evaluating programs, informal and often unplanned evaluation opportunities are also very useful. In some cases, they are a critical part of a program planner's responsibilities (Knox, 2002; Champion, 2000; Hall & Hord, 2011). As with systematic and developmental evaluations, these informal evaluation strategies are used prior to the start of the program, during the program, or after a program has been completed. Because informal evaluations are by nature difficult to describe, Scenarios 10.1–10.3. illustrate this type of evaluation and demonstrate when and the how such evaluations are used.

 SCENARIO 10.1: PRIOR TO THE PROGRAM—A POSSIBLE FAILURE IN THE MAKING

Wen-Hauer Li, the director of the English as a Second Language (ESL) program, has been overseeing, with the help of an outside consultant, the planning of a two-day professional development program for all teaching staff. He has a feeling that what has been proposed—even though it seems to address the problems that have been identified with the delivery of services by his department—is not really what the instructors need to know or do to be able to carry out their jobs more effectively. He decides to talk with three staff members, people he knows will give him direct and honest feedback about the format and content of the proposed program. If their reactions are similar to his, he has enough time and the authority to either ask for changes in the program or, if needed, cancel the consultant's contract.

SCENARIO 10.2: DURING THE PROGRAM—A LOOK FROM THE TOP

Diego, the vice president for human resource development, decides to attend part of the new training program for nonexempt personnel. He is interested in finding out how receptive the employees are to the training events. Diego randomly chooses three sessions that fit into his schedule. He times his arrival and departure around the coffee break so that he can hear what the trainees are saying informally about the program. In addition, so the participants do not wonder who this "stranger" is walking into their program in the middle of it, he has asked the program coordinator to let them know that a trainer she knows from another organization will be sitting in for part of the program.

SCENARIO 10.3: AFTER THE PROGRAM—IT'S NOT TAKING

Dave, the principal of Shelly High School, has heard both directly and through the teacher grapevine that a recent two-day district-wide conference on how to initiate a new literacy program was perceived by his teachers as worse than even he thought it was. The content was a jumbled mess of unclear information and how-to tips that were unrealistic for a district of this size. The major outcome of this program appears to be that some teachers are even more opposed to the new initiative, and even those who supported it before are having major doubts. Dave knows that the superintendent and the board are committed to implementing the new literacy program within the next year. He decides to check with three or four other principals to see if they and their teachers reacted the same way to the program. If these principals and their staff had the same reaction, he will ask one or two of these colleagues to join him at an informal breakfast meeting with the assistant superintendent and the superintendent, who happen to be golfing buddies of his. At the breakfast, he plans to provide them with his informal feedback about the program and offer to help in planning further informational and action agendas around this new initiative.

A common theme among these scenarios is that people were willing to observe what was happening, listen to feedback about programs, and then take action on what they learned.[3]

Whether program evaluations are systematic, developmental, or informal, it is useful for staff members involved with the program planning process to have a working knowledge of the following elements of the evaluation process: evaluation approaches, data collection techniques, data analysis procedures, and making judgments about the program. These elements, which are discussed in the remainder of this chapter, are the nuts and bolts of the evaluation process.

Types of Program Evaluation

There are numerous ways to evaluate education and training programs (Kirkpatrick & Kirkpatrick, 2006; Knox, 2002; Mertens & Wilson, 2012; Ottoson, 2000; Wholey, 2010, Wholey et al., 2010; Worthen & Sanders, 1987). These ways consist of a framework with relatively explicit perspectives and procedural methods for conducting evaluation.[4] Because evaluation is often a multifaceted endeavor, more than one type may be employed in combination in the evaluation process. As is evident from the descriptions, there are overlaps and commonalities of focus and techniques between and among the types. The broadest overlaps are between the "levels of evaluation" and the "objectives-based" approaches, because both types focus on similar areas. In addition, some of the types (e.g., levels of evaluation review and participatory action research) are sometimes used as part of the data collection and analysis process for other types.

The "levels of evaluation" type—more specifically, the participant level of that approach—is one of the most commonly used forms of evaluation, especially in programs of short duration, such as on-site or web-based workshops and conferences (Kirkpatrick & Kirkpatrick, 2006). Participants are usually asked to complete some form of questionnaire indicating their reactions on such items as content, instructors, instructional techniques, facilities, and food service.[5] Two sources of practical evaluation forms are Piskurich (2006) and Dick, Carey, and Carey (2009).

Participants are also sometimes asked to more generally list the strengths and weaknesses of the program, what they perceive they have learned, and recommendations for future activities. Soliciting these participant reactions is most often done at the end of the formal program activities, either on site or via the Internet once they return home. In addition, some program planners also like to request participant feedback for individual sessions within longer programs. For example, at workshops or conferences where there are numerous instructional events, from small-group sessions to large-group presentations, evaluation data are collected at the end of each session. When evaluation data are generated for individual sessions, these data are used in two ways. The first is to provide feedback to individual instructors and presenters. The second is to contribute to a larger data set focused on evaluating the program as a whole (see Chapter Eight).

A second approach that is also frequently used for program evaluation is the goals- and objectives-based approach. In this approach, the purpose, design, and criteria for the evaluation are all drawn from program goals and objectives. This focus does not mean that other aspects of the program (such as facilities or on-site coordination) are excluded from the evaluation; rather, the program goals and objectives serve as the primary guidepost for the evaluation process. Within this approach, the goals and objectives may address changes in individual participants; in the procedures and practices of the education or training unit or the program itself (e.g., program formats, instructor competence, and program coordination); in the organization; or in the community or society. If these goals and objectives need to change as the program evolves, so too will the evaluation purpose, approach, data collection and analysis tools, and criteria need to be revised. It is also important, as noted in Chapter Nine and previously in this chapter, that evaluation data be collected both during and after these activities have been completed.[6]

Similar to the processes used for the short programs, data are also collected on site or via the Internet. Some evaluators have also found in-person interviews, observations, and phone interviews to be useful data collection techniques.

Collecting Evaluation Data

There are a number of techniques for collecting evaluation data, whether in systematic, developmental, or informal ways. Selecting data collection techniques depends on the purpose, the evaluation approach, and the type of information needed. Other important variables to take into consideration are the types of people administering and responding to the evaluation and the cost of using a given technique. Twelve of the most widely used techniques for collecting evaluation data are described in Exhibit 10.4 along with a list of operational guidelines.

EXHIBIT 10.4

Techniques for Collecting Evaluation Data

Technique	Description	Operational Guidelines
Observations	Watching participants at actual or simulated tasks and recording the knowledge, skills, problem-finding and problem-solving capabilities, or values and attitudes participants display.	Determine whether these should be open-ended or formally structured rating scales. Observers must have a clear picture of what they want to know, whom they will observe, and how and what they are monitoring.
Interviews	Individual and group sessions with people (for example, learners, program planners, supervisors, program partners, and funders). Those conducting the interviews should be excellent listeners, and trained in interviewing techniques. Sessions may be done in person, by phone, or online.	Determine whether these should be open-ended or formally structured (with specific questions to ask). For formally structured interviews, the interview schedule should be pilot-tested. Interviewers must listen to responses without judgment.
Surveys	Gathering opinions, perceptions, or beliefs about program planning, delivery, or results using a valid and reliable questionnaire. The purpose for conducting the survey and the questions that need to be answered should be clear, the respondents carefully chosen, and the data collection and analysis procedures well designed prior to administering any survey. Questionnaires can be administered by mail, online, or given to individuals or groups to complete.	Craft a good set of questions, meaning "they need to be clear to the respondents and answerable by them" (Newcomer & Triplett, 2010, p. 278). Select from among a variety of question formats: ranking, checklists, scales, forced choices, or open-ended. Plan to administer the survey when reaching your participants is most likely, choose sponsors that participants respect, and provide incentives (e.g., money, in-kind rewards) to increase response rates. Ensure that your data collection and analysis procedures are well executed.

(Continued)

EXHIBIT 10.4 (*Continued*)

Technique	Description	Operational Guidelines
Pre-and/or Post-Tests	Paper-and-pencil or computer-generated tests used to measure participants' knowledge, skills, problem finding or problem-solving, or values and attitudes.	Know what the test measures (knowledge, skills, problem finding or problem-solving, or attitudes and values) and use it as an evaluation tool for only those areas. In addition, make sure the test is both reliable and valid. Choose a test carefully. Check to see whether what it measures is important and relevant.
Product Reviews	Tangible items that participants produce as a result of the program (e.g., written materials, portfolios, clay pots, rebuilt engines, flower arrangements, videotapes, web sites, computer simulations, and multimedia presentations).	Clearly and precisely define the nature of the project and the criteria on which it will be judged. Participants, whenever possible, should be able to use the products.
Performance Reviews	Demonstration of a specific skill or procedure (e.g., team building, responding to customer complaints, and speaking a new language) in either simulated or real-life situations.	Identify specifically what the elements and criteria are for the performance to be evaluated. Determine what tools will be used in the process (such as checklists, rating scales, and experts' judgment) and ensure consistency.
Organizational and Community Records and Documents	These materials are most often found in computerized database systems, developed by organizations and communities, although some of these materials are provided in paper form (e.g., annual reports).	Systematically collect and record data so that the information is easy to retrieve and sort. Examples include performance appraisals, financial reports, annual reports, committee and board minutes, employment data, and reports on hours of training time and numbers of participants involved.
Portfolios	Purposeful collections of learners' work assembled over time that documents events, activities, products, or achievements.	Include items produced by the learners and attestations from others (for example, honors and awards' certificates). Portfolios may take the form of notebooks or web-based e-portfolios. They are used in a number of different ways (e.g., for active reflection by learners while the program is in progress, as summative evaluative tools).

Technique	Description	Operational Guidelines
Cost-Benefit Analysis	A method for assessing the relationship between the outcomes of an educational program and the costs required to produce them.	Develop the cost side of the equation. Include both direct and indirect costs. Calculate the benefit side by focusing on either increasing revenues or decreasing expenses. Evaluators must have quantitatively measurable outcomes to use this technique.
Focus Groups	Group interviews of no more than five to twelve people, guided by an experienced facilitator, related to a specific topic or issue designed to obtain in-depth qualitative data. These groups are homogenous in nature, meaning participants all have something in common (e.g., have all attended the same program or share the same demographic factors).	Facilitators pose no more than three or four questions, one at a time, with participants building on the responses of other group members. The discussion is among the participants; the facilitator provides a comfortable environment, encourages open and honest exchanges, and ensures all participants have a voice. Group discussions are audio- or videotaped to use during the analysis phase.
Self-Assessment	Individually or in groups, learners appraise what they have learned and whether they have been able to apply that learning in their own contexts. Program planners, instructors, and other stakeholders can also use this process, but these people usually focus on the program structure, processes, and organizational or community-wide impact of the program.	Identify methods for doing self-assessments (e.g., personal journals and diaries, videotaping, using portfolio materials, and online systems). Specify the time frame, what is to be recorded or discussed, and whether the process will be done individually, with one or two other people, or in groups. Guarantee confidentiality for sensitive areas, especially related to learners' personal lives and feelings.
Storytelling	A narrative account of participants' or staff members' experiences that provide planners with insights related to specific aspects of the program (e.g., the presentations, program arrangements).	Stories can be gathered individually or in groups guided by questions that elicit observations about "something that happened, what was meaningful, what didn't work" (Krueger, 2010, p. 413) or what worked well. Once analyzed, these stories provide rich material to illustrate common themes and patterns and, in addition, insights that are related to specific aspects of the program.

Helpful resources that include more detailed descriptions of specific evaluation techniques include: Cellini and Kee (2010); Gboko and Lekoko (2007); Krueger (2010); Krueger and Casey (2010); Marienau (1999); McMillan and Schumacher (2010); Mitchell (1998); Newcomer and Triplett (2010); Patton (2002, 2008); and Wholey, Hatry, and Newcomer (2010).

Data Analysis

At whatever point the evaluation data are collected, it is important to have set procedures for analyzing the data, because one of the most frequent flaws in the evaluation process, especially among those who have little or no experience with evaluating programs, is inadequate preparation. In addition, as noted earlier, program planners may become frustrated when they find they have collected too much data and have not allotted "adequate time for the analysis of the data collected" (Hatry & Newcomer, 2010, p. 567).[7]

There are three major ways to analyze data—quantitative, qualitative, and multiple methods—each of which gathers different types of data to be analyzed. Quantitative data, which are gathered through such mechanisms as surveys, tests, and secondary data sources, give precise numerical measures. Analyses of this kind of data require that those interpreting the data be well versed in statistical analysis procedures. Qualitative data provide rich descriptive materials as well as visual representations (for examples, photographs and videos) (Merriam, 2009; Patton, 2002, 2008; Rogers & Goodrick, 2010). Those analyzing this type of data need to make sense from a variety of sources (e.g., verbatim transcripts and field notes). In essence, making sense out of qualitative data means "moving back and forth between the content bits of data and the abstract concepts, between inductive and deductive reasoning, [and] between description and interpretation" (Merriam, 2009, p. 176).

Using multiple methods analysis, meaning that that both quantitative and qualitative data are used, requires planners to be familiar with analyzing both of these forms of data (Green, 2007). One of the most prominent benefits of the multiple methods approach is that it allows for greater flexibility in how the evaluation is structured, and "is well-suited for situations where unexpected outcomes emerge and new questions are raised" (Schutz, Nichols, & Rodgers, 2009, p. 251). However, using a multiple methods approach to data analysis is quite tricky and rarely used by program planners, except in large well-funded evaluations.

Examples of the types of data that are analyzed addressing three different issues often evaluated in education and training programs are displayed in Exhibit 10.5.

EXHIBIT 10.5

Types of Data Collected

Focus of Evaluation	Types of Data Generated
What have participants learned as a result of attending a specific training program?	**Quantitative** Prior to the start of the program, participants take tests that measure their knowledge, skills, beliefs, attitudes, values, and feelings. These same tests, termed posttests, are then given after the program is completed. If a transfer of learning component is included as part of the program, the posttest is given after the transfer of learning phase. The test scores are then analyzed to determine whether any significant changes have occurred as a result of attending the training program. **Qualitative** Observations are made by selected individuals, such as instructors, work supervisors, program planners or external consultants, on the extent of change in participants' knowledge, skill levels, beliefs, attitudes, values, and feelings after the program has been completed. The data collected consist of field notes and brief stories that illustrate what the program participants have learned related to the evaluation questions that were posed or those that emerged during the analysis phase.
What are the strengths and where are improvements needed in the operations of the training unit?	**Quantitative** Using a five-point Likert Scale, members of the training staff, advisory committee members, and key stakeholders provide feedback on specific procedures and practices of the education and training unit such as adequacy of the physical facilities, quality of support offered for online programs, and professional development opportunities for staff. The numerical ratings that are gathered indicate strengths and weaknesses of the areas that were evaluated. **Qualitative** Department heads and staff are interviewed, using semistructured questions about their perceptions of the effectiveness of specific aspects of the education and training unit. The interviewers' notes are then transcribed and the transcriptions are used as the primary data source for the analysis.

(Continued)

EXHIBIT 10.5 (*Continued*)

Focus of Evaluation	Types of Data Generated
Are volunteers able to increase their skill levels through participating in the current training programs that are offered?	**Quantitative** Volunteers who have completed three two-hour training programs are asked to demonstrate the new skills they have learned at the end of the formal program, and then again three months after the training program has been completed. The scores each volunteer receives based on the competency level they have achieved at each of these time intervals are recorded and analyzed to determine whether the volunteers have mastered these skills. **Qualitative** After completing three two-hour training programs, a group of volunteers was asked to keep a weekly reflective journal for a two-month period on changes they had made in providing services to the clients that related to what they had learned in the training program. The director of volunteers and staff members who work directly with these volunteers also made observations of any specific changes they perceived these volunteers made during that two-month period. The material in the reflective journals and the observational logs are the data used for the analysis phase.

In choosing data analysis procedures, the evaluation questions, evaluation approaches and types, data collection techniques, and kinds of data collected are considered. Content and thematic analysis is one of the most often used methods for reviewing qualitative data. More detailed descriptions of specific quantitative, qualitative, and multiple methods procedures can be found in many resources (Berg, 2010; McMillan & Schumacher, 2010; Merriam, 2009; Newcomer & Conger, 2010; Rogers & Goodrick, 2010).

Making Judgments About the Program

Program planners make judgments on the worth and value of the program as they interpret the data compiled during the analysis phase. This judgment process involves bringing together various pieces of the information gathered and supplying answers to the evaluation questions (Gboku & Lekoko, 2007; Knox, 2002; Newcomer et al., 2010; Sork, 2000). Was what the participants learned in the program worthwhile? Were the goals and objectives of the program addressed in an effective and efficient manner? Were the learners able to apply what they learned back into their work or other life situations? Do management and administrative personnel and policymakers believe the education and training programs provided vital assistance in fulfilling the mission and goals of the organization? Does the program address compelling community and societal concerns? These judgments provide the basis for making final conclusions and recommendations or suggestions for both the program being evaluated as well as future programs (Grob, 2010).

Judgments about programs using measurable data are based primarily on criteria related to the program processes or outcomes and are reached by comparing results of the data analysis with the criteria that were set for each evaluation question or objective.[8] For types of criteria that are measurable, the judgments may appear quite simple; that is, the changes produced as a result of the program either meet the criteria or they do not. However, nothing is ever simple in the evaluation process. Often what happens is that the criteria or the processes for analysis may not be reliable, and therefore neither are the conclusions. If, for example a group of new volunteers were not asked why they had chosen to volunteer at this time, program planners would really have no idea if the recruitment plan they had devised had anything to do with the volunteers stepping forward. In order words, the planners really would not know why the increase in the number of volunteers had happened. In addition, planners need to be careful in making cause-and-effect statements about the results of education and training programs, without either taking into account or acknowledging other factors that also might have resulted in either the success or failure of their programs.

Developing clear criteria upon which judgments can be made is difficult to do, especially for program outcomes that are not quantifiable, are unclear at the onset of the program, or need to be changed as the program evolves. This difficulty does not mean that criteria for program success should or cannot be developed, but program planners have to think differently about the evaluation processes they use, the type of data they will collect, and who is involved in making these judgments. Scenario 10.4 illustrates a program that will extend throughout the academic year for which criteria are difficult to develop, because the program planners are not really able to describe up front exactly what the tangible outcomes will be.

 ### SCENARIO 10.4:   A COMMUNITY COLLEGE IN TURMOIL

The major professional development goal adopted by administrators and instructors of Mountain Plains Community College is to have all staff use open and honest communication styles and to work on rebuilding trust between and among staff members. Those who have been working at the college for the last two years know that communication has been a problem; little trust exists between the instructors and administrators and between and among some of the instructional staff. It is a tough agenda, but one that a majority of staff are committed to, even those who have been the most angry and disillusioned. The catalyst for this commitment has been twofold: the hiring of a new president and public statements by respected instructors that students are being negatively affected by the actions of instructors and administrators. The initial activity for addressing this problem will be a one-day retreat held at an off-campus site.

An effective method planners could choose in evaluating this program is qualitative data collection and analysis procedures. Data could be collected through focus groups during the retreat and individual interviews after the retreat. In this way, using the data from the program participants could generate an initial direction about where the program should go next and what might be the focus of the criteria for program success. Therefore, rather than having the criteria for the whole program set in advance, criteria would emerge as the program progressed, starting with perceptions of what participants believed was of value to them as a result of the initial retreat. For example, central themes that might emerge from this retreat could include that participants believed:

- They were able to share their major concerns during the retreat in such a way that they felt they were heard by at least some staff members.

- Legitimate concerns were identified related to improving the communication processes, many of which could be addressed via future face-to-face and online educational programs and activities.

- Valid concerns that focused on issues of organizational changes were acknowledged by those responsible for implementing those changes, and they agreed to follow through with further deliberations and actions related to the changes.

- These themes would be used to both develop the program further, as well as to develop possible important areas for which criteria to demonstrate program success could be constructed. In other words, the criteria would emerge as the program progressed over time, and come from different sources.

For other programs, such as support or self-help groups, the criteria often remain highly personalized for each program participant. Allowing participants the freedom to form their own criteria for judging program quality and success, whether these criteria remain personalized or become a collective statement, means that program planners accept multiple ways of saying programs are worthwhile. Ways in which these kinds of judgments are made include self-reflection, reflective group procedures, and reviews of participants' journals.

Chapter Highlights

Program evaluation is a process used to determine whether the design and delivery of a program are effective and whether program outcomes are achieved, including anticipated outcomes and those that emerge as a program progresses. The heart of program evaluation lies in judging the value and worth of a program, which is not an easy assignment. The program design and delivery are usually easier to evaluate than program outcomes; outcome criteria are often elusive, and using them in judging whether a specific program is worthwhile can be problematic. As in transfer of learning, evaluation overlaps and converges with many of the components of the Interactive Model of Program Planning.

Program planners take advantage of informal and unplanned evaluation opportunities that take place throughout a program as well as systematic program and developmental evaluation approaches. In formulating evaluation plans, program planners consider both formal and informal evaluation processes as valid sources of evaluation data. In preparing evaluation plans, planners concentrate on six major tasks:

- Develop, as warranted, systematic program evaluation or developmental evaluation approaches.

- Use informal and unplanned evaluation opportunities to collect formative and summative evaluation data (e.g., observing participant behavior during a program, listening to learners' comments during break times).

- Specify the evaluation type or types to be used (e.g., goals- and objectives-based, levels of evaluation, and professional or expert review).

- Determine the techniques for how evaluation data are to be collected (e.g., observations, surveys, and product reviews), keeping in mind that some evaluation data may already exist.

- Think through how the data are to be analyzed, including how to integrate the data that are collected through any informal evaluation processes.

- Describe how judgments are made about the program, using predetermined or emergent evaluation criteria for program success.

Beginning with the next chapter, we move our focus to the administrative components of the program planning process. The next chapter discusses determining formats, schedules, and staff.

Notes for Additional Online Resources

1. See Scenario 10.A: Demonstrating a Program That Worked.

2. See Exhibit 10.A: Elements of a Systematic Evaluation for a composite description of how to design a systematic evaluation consisting of twelve elements, with operational guidelines and an example from practice for each element.

3. See Scenario 10.B: During the Program—Instructor Problems and 10.C: During the Program—Will They Ever Be Able to Apply This Stuff? for additional examples.

4. See Exhibit 10.B: Various Types of Program Evaluation for salient examples of these evaluation types and sample questions and data collection techniques appropriate for each type.

5. See Exhibit 10.C: Sample Participant Questionnaire.

6. See Exhibit 10.D: Sample Participant Questionnaire for Transfer Activities for a sample transfer of learning evaluation form.

7. See Scenario 10.D: Chaotic Data.

8. See Exhibit 10.E: Examples of Judgments Made on Education and Training Programs Using Quantitative Evaluation Criteria for sample criteria for measurable data.

Application Exercises

Application Exercise 10.1 assists you in planning a systematic program evaluation, while Exercise 10.2 provides you an opportunity to reflect on how you have used information you gleaned from informal or unplanned evaluations either during or after a program has been completed. The third exercise focuses on making judgments about program outcomes using measurable data.

EXERCISE 10.1

Planning a Systematic Program Evaluation

1. Briefly describe an education or training program for which you have or need to develop a systematic program evaluation.

    _____

    _____

    _____

    _____

    _____

2. Using the program situation you described above, apply the twelve-element model (see Exhibit 10.A) to either analyze the evaluation process you conducted or in developing further the evaluation you are currently planning. Draw on Exhibits 10.4, 10.5, and 10.A (see web site) as guides for completing this exercise.

Elements	Your Evaluation Plans
Secure support for the evaluation effort from those who have a stake in the results of the evaluation.	
Identify the individuals to be involved in planning and overseeing the evaluation process. Define precisely the purpose of the evaluation and how the results are to be used.	
Specify what is judged and formulate the evaluation questions.	
Determine who supplies the needed evidence, or whether some of that evidence is already available.	

Elements	Your Evaluation Plans
Delineate the evaluation type. Choose the data collection techniques to use, when the data will be collected, or how already available data can be put into usable forms. Indicate the analysis procedure(s).	
Stipulate what criteria to use in making judgments about the program or what process to apply in determining the criteria. Determine the specific time line, budget, and other necessary resources.	
Monitor and complete the evaluation, make judgments about the value and worth of the program, and think through ways the evaluation data can be effectively used.	

3. For those who are developing new evaluation plans, ask a colleague or your planning group to review the evaluation plan you have analyzed or proposed. Revise your plan based on the feedback you receive.

EXERCISE 10.2

Informal and Unplanned Evaluation Opportunities

List at least three ways that you have used an informal or unplanned evaluation approach in evaluating education and training programs. Indicate next to each whether what you did was helpful, and describe briefly why or why not.

Informal or Unplanned Ways to Evaluate Education and Training Programs	Helpful? (Why or Why Not)
1.	
2.	
3.	

EXERCISE 10.3

Making Judgments About Programs

1. Using information from a program evaluation where measurable data were used, complete the following chart. Use Exhibit 10.E as a resource in completing this activity (see web site).

Evaluation Question or Area Judged			
Way Data Were Collected and Analyzed			
Criteria Used			
Interpretations and Conclusions			

2. Were any of the processes or procedures used unclear? Are there blank spaces on your chart? If the answer to either question is yes, how might you have made this evaluation a more complete process? More specifically, what might you have done differently?

Chapter 11

Selecting Formats, Scheduling, and Staffing Programs

 SCENARIO 11.1:   SELECTING THE RIGHT FORMAT

Yana is the lead member of a planning team responsible for putting together a three-year training grant for faculty members and staff working in innovative technology programs for the Department of Education, Moscow State University, Russia. Yana questions whether she can use the same format (a two-week long summer workshop) and staffing pattern, which primarily included external experts, that she has used in the past. Yana's questions come from two different sources: the funders of the grant, and the mix of participants for this year's program. She has learned from the funders she will receive less money for this summer's training program and that she also needs to incorporate a number of new technological tools into the program, very few of which are currently being used on campus. In addition, the participants vary greatly this year in age, previous work experience, and aptitude with current technology, most particularly the technical tools required for distance education. Yana wonders how she will be able to manage this summer's program with less funding, and what this might mean for the format or formats she might choose and whether or not she will be able to afford the cost of the external staff she used last year. She decides the best strategy in restructuring the training program is to ask the current faculty members and staff about their preferences for learning formats. She will also determine their expertise in using the technical tools listed in the grant in order to ascertain which faculty may be able to serve as trainers in addition to their roles as participants during the training session, which is one way that she can lower costs. Yana learned from the faculty

259

and staff who would be attending this year's training that they did not like the two-week intensive workshop, but would rather break up the training time over the summer. She also found that none of the older staff have expertise in using the technical tools listed in the grant, and thus the knowledgeable younger faculty members who had actually used many of these newer technological tools could serve as trainers as well as program participants. However, there is an additional problem that may arise about who should serve as trainers of the technical tools. It has been a tradition in Russia for the senior faculty, who are usually older, to teach the younger generation. This custom, which is age-old, is based on the belief that those in the younger generation have little to offer the older generation. What is clear to Yana is that she has some key decisions about what formats she should use, staffing issues, and how she should schedule the program.

With the increasing alternatives for how education and training programs are structured and delivered, dilemmas around the "right" choice or choices for learning formats, scheduling, and staffing are not uncommon for program planners. In making these decisions about what will work best for each of these aspects of the program, planners keep up to date on newly developed formats and alternative schedules and staffing patterns that could be used.

In this chapter we first describe five major formats for learning, with specific examples given for each. We then look at which formats have the best promise for building learning communities among participants and staff members. Next, we outline samples of program schedules, which demonstrate both single and combined uses of program formats, and give examples of how complicated developing a schedule for a program can become. The chapter concludes with a discussion of staffing issues, including the different roles staff members play, the use of external staff, and the importance of obtaining effective instructional staff members.

Determining Program Formats

"Program format" refers to how education and training activities are structured and organized. Five kinds of formats are used in these programs: individual learning, small-group (face-to-face) learning, large-group (face-to-face) learning, distance learning, and community-based learning. These are not discrete categories; indeed, some formats easily fit into more than one category. For example, although a workshop is usually viewed as a small-group activity, it can also be used for a large group of people (with the large group divided into smaller workgroups so that the "flavor" of the intensive interaction and product orientation is not lost). In addition, program formats are often used in combination. A video conference, for example, might be integrated into a locally sponsored program at which participants also become involved in face-to-face small- or large-group interactions, or individualized learning formats. Live chats delivered through a Course Management System (CMS) can include large groups listening to a lecture and smaller groups working through a problem, followed by a self-directed assignment.

In the past, education and training programs for adults have been equated primarily with face-to-face learning in groups, such as lectures for the whole group with the usual questions and answers (Q&A) at the end. However, as technology is increasingly used in newer and more innovative ways, and as individualized learning programs have become recognized as another method adults seek to further their learning, program planners are incorporating more of these formats into their programs. In addition, the use of technology has allowed for more creative formatting and can include a larger and more diverse audience, if desired. Brief descriptions of a variety of options within each of the five categories of learning formats are given in Exhibit 11.1.

Program planners are very creative in choosing and designing their own formats and activities. Carr-Hill, Roberts, and Currie (2010) brainstormed various approaches to deliver cost-effective adult literacy programs in Africa through a discussion with professionals in the adult literacy field in Africa. Although they learned that a number of formats are currently being used, such as formal classes and peer-to peer learning guided by a tutor, the exact modality for delivering these programs varies from country to country. Therefore, when choosing formats it is important to make sure they fit into the local context (see Chapter Five). For example, in the field of science Massa, Donnelly, Bell, Vallieres, & Hanes (2005) describe a review of web-based professional development for science teachers. The formats that were used were interesting, creative, and innovative and they included a range of activities, from face-to-face small-group activities to online science labs.

More detailed information about these formats can be found in: Bates and Sangrà (2011); Chang (2010); Galbraith (2004); Garrison and Vaughan (2008); Joosten (2012); Lakey (2010); Lenning (2013); Littleman, Campell, & Liteman (2006); Oitsephile, Ntsean, Osborn, and Preece (2012); Palloff and Pratt (2007); and Weissner, Sheared, Lari, Kucharczyk, and Flowers (2010).

EXHIBIT 11.1

Descriptions of Program Formats

Individual Formats

Apprenticeship. A formal relationship between an employer and an employee where the employee is trained for a craft or skill through practical experience under the supervision of experienced workers.

Coaching. One-on-one learning by demonstration and practice, with immediate feedback given by peers, supervisors, or experts in the field.

Computer-Based Education (CBE). In this highly structured format, individuals work at their own pace and address problems that are designed to teach knowledge, skills, and applications. Learners are assessed by the quality of their products or test scores.

Interactive Tutorials. Face-to-face or online instruction in which an individual works with an assigned tutor or an instructor who is a content expert in the subject area.

Internet Search. Through the Web, learners can access unlimited sources of information from databases, libraries, and organizations across the globe.

Writing. Learners share their knowledge, observations, insights, and feelings using different forms of written expression (e.g., reflective journals, articles, books, poetry wikis, blogs, and via various social media sites).

Mentoring. An intense, caring relationship in which someone with experience works with a less experienced person to promote both professional and personal growth. Mentors model expected behavior and values, provide support, and are willing to serve as a sounding board for the person being mentored.

On-the-Job Training (OJT)/Job-Embedded Training. Instruction is provided by experienced individuals, groups of workers, supervisors, or external consultants either face-to-face, online, or a combination thereof, for new employees, interns, or volunteers while they are on the job and engaged in productive work. These experienced instructional staff members demonstrate and discuss their knowledge and skills with the learners, then give opportunities for practice and provide feedback throughout and after the process is completed.

E-learning. A type of distance learning that is provided online where instructional staff members and participants are in different places and a wide variety of technological tools are used in the learning process. The instructor manages the learning with a Course Management System (CMS) (also called a Learning Management System [LMS]).

Small-Group Formats (Primarily Face-to-Face)

Courses or Classes. Groups with a definite enrollment that meet at predetermined times for the purpose of learning a specified content area under the direction of an instructor. These classes are held at educational institutions, workplaces and other organizational sites (e.g., a military base), or in community settings. They may also be part of a distance-learning program, where instructor and students may be in various locations, or a combination of face-to-face and online instruction.

Clinics. Sessions that focus on a single problem or skill as participants present case illustrations of practice problems to an expert or panel of experts who serve as consultants to assist them in finding alternative solutions to these problems.

Field Visits. A group visits a work site or other situation that is similar to theirs for on-site observation and learning, usually of a short duration (one or two days). Field visits provide the opportunity for further experiences with people, places, and situations that cannot be found in a formal classroom setting.

Workshops. Intensive group activities that emphasize the development of skills and competencies in a defined content area. An emphasis is placed on participants being able to use what they have learned in different situations such as in their workplaces or various life roles they play, for example, parents or volunteers.

Action Learning. This process is aimed at helping organizations solve real problems, while at the same time developing individuals and groups within the organization. Most often occurring in team situations, groups of learners pinpoint the cause of problems, work to solve the problems, and formulate goals for how to proceed.

Social Networks. Online loosely configured groups of people with similar experiences, interests, problems, or ideas who come together to give and receive information and to provide support.

Support Groups. Groups in which people work together on shared problems or practices. Usually participation is voluntary, and sharing and equal status among group members is the norm. In some cases, a trained facilitator works with this type of learning group.

Communities of Practice. Groups of learners share their expertise and provide problems and solutions for teaching and learning.

Cohort Groups. Groups of learners take a series of courses, workshops, or other learning experiences together over an extended time period. In addition to the content or skills being learned, instructional staff members stress team building and mutual participant support.

Large-Group Formats (Primarily Face-to-Face)

Conferences and Conventions. One or more days of meetings where one of the primary purposes is education to present information, exchange experiences, improve skills, learn new skills, engage in problem-solving activities, or establish learning networks. Sessions include large- and small-group meetings, networking, and a variety of formal and informal instructional strategies. Virtual conferences are becoming commonplace.

Clubs and Other Types of Organized Groups. Groups that frequently engage in activities that foster learning as part of their agenda (e.g., hobby, environmental, or investment groups). These groups can also be a small-group format, depending on the size of the club or group and are both formal and informal in nature.

Institutes. Intensive sessions, usually over several days, emphasizing the acquisition of knowledge and skill in a specialized area of practice.

Exhibits. A display of ideas, products, or processes. Resource people may be available face-to-face or on a virtual connection to respond to questions about the content of the exhibit or exhibits.

Theater. Use of formal and informal acting situations for a variety of learning purposes. For example, theater serves as a way to dramatize a specific issue, problem, and major event with the objective of helping the audience to become familiar with a topic, or encouraging learners to become involved with action programs related to the topic under discussion.

Educational Tours. A program in which participants travel for a period of time (e.g., one week to a month) for the express purpose of learning about educational systems and programs, often in cultural settings different from their own situations. Activities include visits to different types of programs, sessions with educational leaders and teachers, conversations with learners, and tours of cultural sites.

Residential Learning. Participants live and learn together, 24 hours a day, as they complete a common program. The residential experience could be a stand-alone event or part of a larger program which also includes other formats. Residential programs are hosted in a variety of venues, such as retreat centers, university conference centers, and outdoor settings.

Lecture Series. A series of presentations by one or more speakers who offer material on a given topic over a specified period of time.

(Continued)

EXHIBIT 11.1 (*Continued*)
Descriptions of Program Formats

Online Formats

Distance Learning. Education and training programs presented through a variety of online tools. In most cases this is used with classes, groups, or employees and the presenters are located at another site; it is also possible to have learners scattered at various sites.

Correspondence Study. Prepared instructional materials (e.g., course syllabi, manuals, texts, worksheets) that are delivered online to homes or offices. Participants engage in reading or other learning activities, send assignments to instructors to evaluate, and take examinations that can lead to college degrees or certification in specific fields.

Audio and Video Conferencing. The linking of one or more sites using only audio, or audio and video, to provide live and interactive exchanges of information between and among program participants or instructional staff members. Examples of tools used are conference phones, video conference equipment, such as a large television or monitor, a computer, a computer camera, a computer microphone, and video conference software, such as Skype or Google Chat.

Cyber Conferences. Use of the Internet to share information and promote interactive communication among participants. These conferences are usually no more than two days and can be a mix of live cyber presentations and panel discussions. The conference may be recorded for use indefinitely.

Social Media and Networks. Individuals who interact or meet online to share information—professional, personal, or political—with each other. They form support groups and groups for social, personal, or professional interaction. In addition, this type of communication can lead to political action, or other undetermined kinds of activities.

3D Avatar-Based Digital. A newer model using the 3D online social environment of Second Life where users can create online avatars and interact with other users in real time; courses can be taught using this digitally based tool.

Combinations of Formats. Classes and conferences can use combinations of face-to-face audiences with videostreaming for live chats and groups that respond by tweeting their thoughts about the class or program. Advances in technology will incorporate live productions delivered to cyber audiences and incorporate their responses.

Community-Based Learning Formats

Community Resource Centers. These centers provide learning opportunities to individuals and groups within the community. Examples of these types of centers include museums, libraries, community schools, and learning exchanges.

Community Development. Educators serve as instructional staff members, facilitators, or consultants for action-oriented groups focusing on community change. One of the basic requirements for this format is that the project or activity has been identified by community members as something that is important to them.

Community Action Groups. Groups formed for the primary purpose of social action (e.g., churches groups, human rights groups, and civic organizations). Although their primary purpose may not be learning, many of these groups organize activities that foster learning and development.

Virtual Communities. A group of people who interact online to share common goals, ideas, or values. These communities can provide a rich source for personal, professional, and community growth and development across geographic boundaries.

Popular Theater. Participants identify, interpret, and act out their own social, political, and cultural beliefs with the purpose of spawning collective action aimed at changing these conditions in their own communities. This form of theater allows learners to develop and reflect on their own aims and objectives and gives facilitators an opportunity to build on the social and cultural backgrounds of the participants.

Action-Based Brainstorming Sessions. Selected participants engage in thinking together as a catalyst for innovative solutions to a range of public policy and other types of community and organizational issues.

Learning Cities or Communities. A geographic entity, like a town, city, region, or even a village, that forms economic, political, educational, social, cultural, and environmental structures that support the development of talent and human potential among all its citizens. The glue that holds these communities together is a focus on learning for the common good, and the ability to reach out to other communities and establish linkages among these entities.

Again, as stressed earlier and noted in some of the format descriptions, this categorization of format examples is only one of the illustrative categories that are used. What is key is that program planners think in terms of alternative formats for learning, recognizing that there is no one right (and sometimes no one best) way to structure a specific program.

In choosing a format or formats for learning, seven factors, which are similar to those needed for choosing instructional techniques (see Chapter Eight), are considered: the background and experience of the participants, availability and expertise of staff, cost, types of facilities and equipment, program content, program outcomes, and the context in which the learning is to take place. Especially for more comprehensive programs, planners are advised to include more than one format so that a wide range of styles and conditions for learning can be accommodated. "Besides, a variety of formats adds to the aesthetic quality of a program by giving it a sense of liveliness and rhythm, and a richer texture" (Knowles, 1980, p. 130). In addition, educational planners have also been interested in using a combination of different formats to build communities of learners.

Building Learning Communities

 SCENARIO 11.2:   A GRADUATE CLASS BECOMES A LEARNING COMMUNITY

Participants in a graduate class in international training and development were excited by what had happened in their class but also saddened that the class had come to an end. These feelings came from a sense that they had built a learning community, one that had evolved over time. As one student commented, "I truly believed it was an open, honest, and safe environment in which to ask questions and offer my ideas."

Both students and the instructor observed that the different formats used for learning—small- and large-group interactions (both in terms of time and intensity), lively listserv "chats," a retreat weekend, and learning in partnerships—helped create this learning community. The norms that the class set for themselves also contributed to the sense of community (e.g., actively listening to each other; respecting one another; being truly interested in learning about each other; providing positive and useful feedback; being willing to challenge each other; and addressing any problems or concerns of the class, or among class members and the instructional staff members). And as observed by a second student, there was also a sense that participants had fun learning and that "no one person had to 'carry' the total load of leadership for the community. Obviously, you [meaning the instructor] had ultimate responsibility for the class, but everyone seemed willing to help."

Among the forces mentioned here, those with the biggest impact and drive in the formation of learning communities around the globe are: learning as a collaborative process, the globalization of learning, learning in cyberspace, and the purposeful goal of establishing learning organizations (Cooperrider, Sorensen, Yaeger, & Whitney, 2001; Horton, 2003; Lakey, 2010; Palloff & Pratt, 2005; Teemant, Smith, Pinnegar, & Egan, 2005; Vella, 2008; Weissner, et al., 2010). What these four forces have in common is that the learning environment has expanded from individual formats and self-contained classrooms to organizational learning and virtual communities, with diversity among learners, and acknowledgment of political and ethical questions about which learners should be served and why. The program planner has many more options in building a learning community to support the learning experience because of the global audiences made possible due to contact through the Web. As with individual, group, online, and community-based formats, there are numerous designs that lend themselves to building learning communities.[1]

Just using different formats will not create learning communities. Program planners, instructional staff members, and learners work together to create a climate that engenders respect, collaborative interaction, trust, caring, and openness to diversity of both people and ideas (Ginsberg & Wlodkowski, 2009; Lakey, 2010; Silberman, 2006). Being willing and able to challenge conventional ways of thinking and knowing is also critical to this process. More specific techniques for allowing a learning community to develop and grow are included in Chapters Four and Eight in this book, as well as in the final section of this chapter.

Scheduling the Program

Once the format is chosen, program planners identify the appropriate length and breakdown of the program and set specific dates and program schedules. See Exhibit 11.2 for three examples of program schedules. One is for a three-day conference; the second for a field site visit; and the third a distance learning format combined with small face-to-face support groups.

In addition, there are a number of other considerations that planners take into account when formulating schedules. In finalizing the dates for the program, planners take care that the dates and times chosen fit into the participants' personal or job schedules, and they understand the consequences for expecting participants to take off work. Education and training programs should not be scheduled around times when the target audiences have other commitments, such as a seasonally heavy workload, family responsibilities, or religious celebrations. For example, programs should not be planned on or near major holidays or vacation times unless a vacation package option is a part of the marketing strategy (including, for example, sightseeing tours and special hotel rates). Likewise, to hold education and training programs for managers or their administrative assistants during budget preparation time is not advisable.

There is the added problem for planners who have to depend on the decisions of others in order to even know when their participants are able to attend. For instance, judicial educators have to work through court administrators to arrange for substitute judges or for the courts to close for the day of the program. Also, some participants must meet for specified time periods in order to maintain certification requirements for their jobs, such as the number of clock hours of instruction that are required. In addition, in planning programs that include participants from many countries, the schedules become even more complicated when attempting to meet the scheduling needs of various time zones and cultures. For example, Western countries use Saturday and Sunday as days off whereas most Middle Eastern countries only have Fridays off but work on Saturday and

EXHIBIT 11.2
Sample Program Schedules

Sample 1: Individual-, Large-, and Small-Group Formats: Three-Day Conference

Day 1

9:00 a.m.–Noon	Registration
Noon–1:45 p.m.	Opening luncheon with speaker
2:00–4:00 p.m.	Individual and team time to develop learning plans for the conference and transfer of learning strategies with conference staff support
4:00–5:30 p.m.	Break and time to network
6:00–7:00 p.m.	**Session 1:** *Participant choice of small-group sessions*
7:00–9:00 p.m.	Reception Dinner with entertainment

Day 2

8:30–10:00 a.m.	General session
10:00–10:30 a.m.	Break and time for networking
10:30–Noon	**Session 2:** *Participant choice of small-group session*
12:45–1:45 p.m.	Conference luncheon
2:00–5:00 p.m.	**Session 3:** *Participant choice of workshops*
5:00–7:00 p.m.	Networking and free time
7:00–9:00 p.m.	Awards Banquet

Day 3

9:00–10:30 a.m.	**Session 4:** *Participant choice of small-group session*
10:30–11:00 a.m.	Break and time for networking
11:00–Noon	Time for group and team planning for learning transfer with conference staff support
12:15–2:00 PM	Lunch with closing session and evaluation

Sample 2: Field Site Visit, Combined with Large- and Small-Group Interactions

8:00 a.m.	Departure from home organization
9:30 a.m.	Arrival at destination for site visit
9:30–10:00 a.m.	Refreshment and stretch break to prepare for day
10:00–11:00 a.m.	Introductory session with whole group to organization and programs
11:00 a.m.–12:30 p.m.	Tour of facilities with whole group
12:30–1:45 p.m.	Lunch in organization's cafeteria and break time
1:45–3:45 p.m.	Choice of one of three seminar groups related to different operating divisions of the organization
3:45–4:15 p.m.	Refreshment break and time for networking
4:15–5:15 p.m.	Choice of small-group sessions to form e-mail and/or face-to-face interest groups as a transfer of learning strategy

Sample 2: Field Site Visit, Combined with Large- and Small-Group Interactions	
5:15–6:00 p.m.	Wrap-up session and evaluation with whole group
6:00 p.m.	Departure (trip includes dinner at restaurant in the area)
10:00 p.m.	Arrival at home organizations

Sample 3: Distance-Learning Formats Combined with Multiple On-Site Small-Group Support Groups: Four-Week Training Program with Transfer of Learning Support

Week One

Monday	9:00–Noon	On-site small groups meet with facilitator and technical support staff to introduce training program and ensure participants know how to use the learning management system (LMS).
Tuesday–Friday		Individuals, using the interactive LMS, are required to review materials online and participate in at least two chat room discussions. They participate at a time most convenient to their schedule.

Week Two

Tuesday	9:00–Noon	On-site small groups meet with facilitator to review and discuss what they have learned thus far and to plan for learning transfer both during and after the training program.
Wednesday–Friday		Same format as previous week, except that participants are required to also take part in two live-chat sessions (synchronous) with group discussions (Wednesday, 1:00–3:00, and Friday, 9:00–11:00).

Week Three

Tuesday	9:00–11:00	On-site small groups meet for purpose of peer support.
Tuesday–Thursday		Same online format as Week One.
Friday	9:00–Noon	On-site small groups meet with facilitator to review and discuss applications of what they have learned from the training experience.

Week Four

Monday–Thursday		Same online format as Week Two.
Friday	9:00–2:00	On-site small groups meet with facilitator to review and discuss applications of what they have learned. Ensure transfer plans are in place, complete program evaluation.
		Host a group celebration.

Transfer of Learning Component After the Training: Six-Month Period
On-site small groups meet biweekly either by themselves or with a facilitator.
Online support discussion groups continue.
Two formal full-day sessions are held on-site, which include online live chat with whole group and small-group interactions.
Other transfer techniques used by individual program participants (e.g., supervisor support for transfer, mentor, online assistance).

Sunday. Overall, planners need to keep in mind that choosing formats, formulating the schedule, and selecting and training staff, which is discussed next, is just one among many of the other details they need to address to ensure a successful program (see Chapter Fourteen).

Identifying the Roles of the Program Staff

Program planning staff members design, conduct, evaluate, manage, and coordinate education and training programs. In addition, often there is a need for specialists, whether full or part time, to assist with the technical aspects of the program. One person may take on all of these tasks or the tasks may be divided among a number of people, depending on the size and complexity of the program being planned. However the tasks are divided, program planners and others assume the following five major roles (Rothwell & Cookson, 1997; Morrison, Ross, Kalman, & Kemp, 2011; Smith & Ragan, 2005):

- **Program Planner's Role**

  This role entails such tasks as gathering ideas for programs, conducting needs assessments, setting program priorities, developing program objectives, planning transfer of learning activities, seeking funding, and preparing budgets and marketing plans. Program planners are responsible for all aspects of the planning process.

- **Instructional Staff Member's Role**

  This role entails designing or delivering the instructional portions of the program, and includes people such as teachers, presenters, speakers, and facilitators. These staff members are responsible for assisting participants to achieve the learning objectives using a variety of instructional techniques, ranging from lectures to highly interactive activities. In addition, they use different kinds of resources (e.g., handouts, PowerPoint presentations, and video clips) and online tools (e.g., web sites and Facebook) to enhance participant learning. When instructional staff need assistance and technological tools for instruction, technicians may be needed to assist in using these tools.

- **Program Evaluator's Role**

  This role includes choosing or designing techniques for evaluating programs (e.g., questionnaires, interviews, or observations) and analyzing the data that are collected. In addition, evaluators make observations about the program strengths and weaknesses; whether the program is of value and worthwhile (after specifying who judges what, how, and on what criteria); and makes recommendations for future programs.

- **Program Coordinator's or Manager's Role**

  This role involves coordinating specific program events and ensuring that all logistical details are taken care of, which if not done well can make or break a program. Some of the tasks these persons are responsible for include arranging facilities; registering participants; handling all problems that arise before, during, and after the program; and monitoring on-site or online programs. In carrying out this role, these people can also act as information givers, brokers, negotiators, and resource specialists.

- **Technical Support Staff Member's Role**

  This role consists of assisting the other staff with ideas and suggestions related to which online tools could be used, including how to make programs interactive. In addition, they also train other staff members in how to use the tools effectively, by updating these tools periodically and by offering support during the programs to ensure a smooth flow to the program. This latter role has become more important in the last decade as more online programs are offered.

Some of the program planner's specific tasks (such as identifying needs and ideas for programs, determining program goals and objectives, and planning transfer of learning activities) are discussed in Chapters Six, Seven, and Nine. A more detailed description of the coordinator or manager role is given in Chapter Fourteen, while the roles of instructor and evaluator are discussed in Chapters Eight and Ten, respectively. The various tasks of these six roles are not necessarily independent of each other. For example, although program coordinators or managers usually arrange the facilities and equipment, program planners may choose to do this task because of specific program requirements that program coordinator or managers may not understand. For smaller programs, and even for larger programs in tough economic times, the roles of program planner, instructional staff, evaluator, coordinator, and manager may all be handled by one or two people.

Deciding to Use External Staff

Program staff, whether paid or volunteer, may be internal to the organization. However, there are a number of situations where external staff members are needed. Paid staff members include temporary full- or part-time staff and consultants, and often are not recruited for these positions through any formal process. Volunteer staff members offer their services because they are committed to a specific cause, are expected to assist because of roles they play in organizations (such as president or board members of a professional association), or are recruited through special sessions targeted just for this purpose. Sometimes a mix of organizational personnel and external staff are used. For example, in large comprehensive programs, while internal staff members coordinate, design, and deliver an education or training program, consultants may be responsible for the evaluation of that program. In this same situation, though it is possible for internal staff to analyze the data and prepare evaluation reports, a better choice is often to hire someone outside the organization to complete this part of the evaluation; external evaluators offer a report detached from personal relationships with the programs being reviewed. In addition, many funding agencies actually require the use of outside evaluators to keep the program planners honest and to provide unbiased feedback about the program and recommendations for program changes or whether a program should continue to be funded. However, planners must keep in mind the cost of using external evaluators, especially for programs that are long term in nature and complex in their focus, for the evaluation is often an expensive process.

There are seven good reasons for hiring staff external to the organization:

1. *Expertise*. While program planners can handle the processes of planning, content experts are often needed to present the program.

2. *Short-term expansion of staff*. An organization's staff may be working on other projects and do not have the time to direct a program, hold an advisory meeting, or take care of any of the many responsibilities in program planning. Therefore, part-time program planners can be hired.

3. *Specific programs*. Certain kinds of programs, such as large conferences or one-of-a-kind special events, need extra hands or different kinds of expertise in order for these programs to be successful.

4. *Political leverage*. Those with political clout might be speakers for a program or serve as advisors to the planning group or program presenters. In addition, professional lobbyists may be useful to obtain funding for a program or to advocate for a position (e.g., for governmental training programs or professional associations).

5. *Cost-effectiveness*. It is often cost-effective to either use volunteers or hire those with skills in marketing, design, technology, journalism, and printing, as needed, instead of keeping people with this expertise as regular staff.

6. *Staff development.* Opportunities for internal staff to learn new skills and competencies are sometimes provided by outside consultants, trainers, and even volunteers. Even though there may be personnel on staff with the same expertise, it is sometimes wise to bring in external staff to work in cooperation with internal staff in program preparation or delivery.

7. *Organizational planning.* Educational organizations, like other organizations, need a strategic plan and may need someone with expertise in directing discussions about the future to help set the goals of the organization; it is useful to have external assistance with this activity (Hesselbein & Goldsmith, 2006; George & Sims, 2007; Wilbur, Smith, Bucklin, & Associates, 2000).

Selecting External Staff Members

Guidelines and questions to judge external staff quality and performance and assist in external staff hiring decisions are provided in Exhibit 11.3 (Hesselbein & Goldsmith, 2006; Mitchell, 1998; Parry, 1996; Wilbur et al., 2000). Types of external staff, as noted earlier, are consultants, full and part time temporary staff, and volunteers.

EXHIBIT 11.3

Guidelines and Questions for Selecting External Staff Members

- *Caliber and Credibility.* Are the individuals competent and capable? Are they credible to your organization and the participants?
- *Quality of Their Resources.* Are the resources the outside consultants use or develop (e.g., online instructional materials, training manuals, videos, simulations) of good educational quality? Are these resources useful to the participants? Are they up to date and created with current resources and technical tools?
- *Problem-Solving Capabilities.* Do the external staff have a solid understanding of the problem(s) being tackled? Does what they are proposing lead to positive changes?
- *Adaptability.* Are the external staff willing to tailor their work (e.g., presentations, resources) to meet the requirements of the organization, versus using prepackaged materials or materials obviously designed for other groups?
- *Scope and Depth of Available Resources.* Do the outside consultants add to the scope and depth of the present educational resources of the organization?
- *Context Knowledge.* Do the outside consultants know something about the organization and the business of that organization (e.g., banking, communications, or agriculture)?
- *Technology Capability.* Do external staff have experience with the technological tools they are expected to use for the job (e.g., PowerPoint, Course Management Systems, online systems for learning, equipment for recording audio and video)?
- *Cost.* Do the external staff cost more than internal staff for the same activity? If so, is this additional cost justifiable?

When trying to locate external staff, there are several good sources: direct references from colleagues, suggestions from other organizations, a search on the Web, private consulting firms, or as noted previously in the discussion of volunteers, a recruitment event to gather assistance with specific program tasks. Once it is decided to hire paid external staff, a common practice is to gather recommendations from colleagues or to create a bidding process in which external staff submit a Request for Proposal (RFP) through a competitive process. "There is no one universally applicable model for a good RFP. You must spell out what you want [an external staff member] to accomplish and ask for specific recommendations as to how the [this person or if employed by a] consulting firm will execute the project" (Wilbur et al., 2000, p. 353). No matter which process is used to hire paid external staff, it is critical that program planners review the past work history and credentials carefully prior to signing a formal contract. This process of checking references and the background of paid consultants or temporary staff to gather information about them can be done by talking with knowledgeable colleagues, current clients of the external staff, or others in their workplaces. Because reference checks today, by law, can be very limited, planners should go further than having regular face-to-face or online (for those candidates not in the immediate area) interviews and discussions in assessing a candidate's qualifications and dispositions for a position. It is important to review materials prepared by the interviewee, and, when possible, it is enlightening to sit in on a session the person or consulting group is conducting. If using university faculty as consultants, planners can also find it helpful to ask the opinion of current or former students and faculty colleagues. If the consultants and temporary staff are not using professional networking social media tools, it may be a warning sign that they are not up to date with technological tools that may be used in the program planning process.

External Staff Fees, Contract, and Agreements

Rules and regulations for hiring paid external personnel vary from organization to organization, with all organizations having strict rules and regulations that have been prepared by legally trained people. Program planners look at an "employee handbook" for guidance on hiring these temporary personnel and consultants. All government-based organizations—public colleges and universities; national, state, and local governmental agencies; and the military—have protocols for hiring these types of staff. As mentioned previously, these agencies often use a bidding process to hire potential external staff. The stricter the rules and regulations for hiring external staff, the easier it is for program planners to manage the hiring task. If required to use a bidding process, program planners provide a description of the job to be done, the amount of time it is expected to take, the activities that are expected, and the qualifications needed for the person who will be hired. If program planners work for an organization that is civic, community, private, or corporate, but not government regulated, they still ought to include in the job description the same information that is required for government agencies. In the case of government-regulated or nongovernmental hiring, the fees are either set by the organization or negotiated with the consultant or temporary personnel that are selected for the job.

Paid external staff are usually compensated in one of three different ways: time plus expenses, a fixed fee, or by a percentage of the income generated by a specific program. The fees for temporary staff are usually figured by an hourly or daily rate. The rate is often higher than staff working for the organization because those working temporarily do so only on a limited basis. For consultants, the organization can pay a percentage of the first weeks or quarter of the contract with the remainder due when the work is completed. No matter how consultants are paid, it is important that the hiring organization have a written contract for services. A contract avoids confusion and problems between the organization and the external staff members.

The following checklist indicates what the negotiation process and the contract or letter of agreement includes (Cagney, 2010; Parry, 1996; Wilbur et al., 2000).

- A brief description of the program, project, or service
- A list of the responsibilities (e.g., developing instructional modules, serving as the instructor, developing and conducting the program evaluation)
- Time requirements and schedule for which services will be provided; a more specific schedule is better
- Costs for external staff members' wages or fees, expenses to be paid related to the work such as per diem expenses, supplies, and direct expenses such as technical tools, books, shipping charges, printing or copying
- On-site support services that are needed for the job, such as administrative assistance, copying, office space
- Project or service start and completion dates
- Conditions and terms for contract extension or termination
- Internal staff contact information (e.g., project manager, principal, director of training, manager of human resource division, executive director, division director)

- Billing dates, forms for billing, process for submitting fees for services and expenses, and deadlines or dates related to billing

- Rights to use any copyrighted material to be distributed or used after the contract is completed

- Rules of protection of the employing organization's intellectual property and overall confidentiality (e.g., a statement promising nondisclosure of proprietary information)

- The appeal process should the organization find the external staff member's work inadequate

- Web sites, Internet access, and social media options of the organization that can be accessed and used by the external staff members

Although negotiating a written contract or letter of agreement does not guarantee a good working relationship between external and internal staff members, this contract helps set the stage for making the process work and ensuring the desired results.

Selecting Effective Instructional Staff Members

Instructional staff members include, as noted earlier, instructors, presenters, speakers, and group facilitators. These staff members play a key role in making education and training events a success, and come from a variety of sources, both internal and external to the sponsoring organization(s). Because these staff members, whether they are paid or volunteer, are responsible for assisting participants to learn, it is important that they be successful in their role (see Chapter Eight). But how do program planners determine who will be effective instructional staff? Displayed in Exhibit 11.4 are criteria that can assist planners in the selection of top-notch instructional staff (Apps, 1996; Palmer, 1998; Pratt & Associates, 1998; Ginsberg & Wlodkowski, 2009).

Instructional staff members come from a variety of sources, again both internal and external to the sponsoring organization. Although adult educators, trainers, and staff developers are the main sources, there are many people without this specialized background who, through experience or training, are competent. For example, technical employees often provide instruction for other technical staff, and volunteers serve as instructors and peer coaches for other volunteers. No matter what background or training instructional staff members have, program planners are best served when they discuss the presentation with each of these people and suggest, where needed, adult education practices and principles they could use. Program planners also may want to provide guidelines to group facilitators who are often left on their own to figure how to process these groups.

EXHIBIT 11.4

Ten Criteria to Consider When Selecting Instructional Staff Members

1. *Content Knowledge.* Instructional staff members are knowledgeable about their content areas and, where applicable, are successful practitioners of their knowledge or skills.

2. *Competence in the Processes of Instruction.* Instructional staff members are competent in a number of instructional techniques and processes and match those techniques to their subject matter and the learners. These staff are able to use a variety of methods. They also know how to provide helpful feedback and evaluate what the participants have learned.

3. *Ability to Respond Effectively to the Background and Experience of the Participants.* Instructional staff members work well with specific groups of participants (e.g., culturally diverse groups, low-income participants, people of color, women and men, individuals with differing educational levels and various levels of job responsibility) and demonstrate capability to tap into their participants' varied and diverse experiences and backgrounds.

4. *Belief That Caring for Learners Matters.* Instructional staff members care about learners and provide an environment where respect, trust, and cultural richness are key norms. Giving "space" to participants to negotiate when and how they will learn when "adult life" gets in the way of their learning is important in demonstrating a caring attitude.

5. *Credibility.* Instructional staff members demonstrate credibility based on their position, background, experiences, or personal impact. High credibility predisposes participants to accept more readily the material presented.

6. *Enthusiasm and Commitment.* Instructional staff members are enthusiastic, even passionate about their subject and committed to teaching it to others.

7. *Personal Effectiveness.* Instructional staff members are organized and prepared. They use humor effectively and have a genuine interest in whether or not the participants learn. They also adjust their presentation to the needs of the audience and model the behaviors or attitudes they are teaching.

8. *Enterprise Knowledge.* Instructional staff members have basic information about the organizations or groups from which the participants come (e.g., products, services, culture).

9. *Ability to Teach from the Heart and Spirit, as Well as the Mind.* Instructional staff members know and share who they are—that is, they are authentic in what they do and say. They also acknowledge the "personhood" of each learner and recognize that participants search for personal and communal meanings for their lives through learning experiences.

10. *Skills in Using Technology Effectively.* Instructional staff members know how to use appropriate technical tools at the level of the participants and in keeping with the culture and context of the setting or organization.

By paying attention to the instructional staff members, program planners play a major role in producing an effective program.

Chapter Highlights

Making decisions related to formats, schedules, and staffing is an important part of the program planning process. This process is complex, as it involves making decisions about what type(s) of formats to use, the schedules, and the staffing patterns, all of which have greatly expanded over the years. For example, the trend of adopting online formats calls for different kinds of schedules as well as instructional staff members who have the capability of presenting online using a variety of tools, and also the addition of technical staff members.

- Choose the most appropriate format or combination of formats for the learning activity (e.g., individual, small-group, large-group, distance learning, or community-learning formats).

- Take into account, where appropriate, the building of learning communities as part of the goals and objectives of programs.

- Devise a program schedule that fits the formats chosen, the specific activities planned, and the participants' personal or job commitments.

- Identify the staff roles that are needed for the program, which include program planners, instructional staff members, program evaluators, program coordinators or managers, and technical support staff members.

- Determine whether internal staff (paid or volunteer) will plan and conduct the program, or whether external consultants are required.

- Make careful choices about speakers and instructional staff members for the various activities to ensure that they possess content expertise, competence in teaching adults, and the ability to respond effectively to the background and experiences of the learners.

Selection of formats, schedules, and staff needs are often guided by the financial resources available to the program planner. How to link these financial resources to the planning process is discussed in the next chapter.

Notes for Additional Online Resources

1. See Exhibit 11.A: Sample Formats for Building Learning Communities.
2. See Scenario 11.A: Something Is Rotten in This Picture.

 Application Exercises

The first application exercise assists you in determining program formats and identifying what roles each staff member for an education and training program will or has played. The second exercise focuses on scheduling the program, while the third focuses on selecting effective instructional staff.

EXERCISE 11.1

Determining the Program Format and Staff Members' Roles

1. Identify an education or training program that you are in the process of developing or have developed, and give a short description of that program.

   _____

   _____

   _____

   _____

   _____

2. Identify at least two alternative formats (or combinations of formats) that are or were appropriate for this program, and outline the reasons why you chose them.

   Alternative One

   _____

   _____

   _____

   Alternative Two

   _____

   _____

   _____

   Which of these formats would or did you use and why?

   _____

   _____

   _____

3. If one of the objectives of this program is/was to build a learning community, does or did the format(s) you have or had chosen enable the participants and instructional staff members to accomplish this goal? If yes, how does or did that format(s) address building learning communities? If no, what format(s) might be more applicable?

   _____

   _____

   _____

   _____

4. Using the following chart, identify the specific staff members that are or did plan and carry out the program.

Staff Role	Specific Person or Persons Who Are Carrying or Will Carry Out Each Role	Internal or External to the Organization	Paid or Volunteer Staff Members
Program Planners			
Instructional Staff Members			
Program Evaluators			
Program Coordinators or Managers			
Technical Support Staff Members			

EXERCISE 11.2

Scheduling the Program

Using the same example you gave in Exercise 11.1, lay out a program schedule that takes or took into account the participants' personal or job situations, and when, where, and how the program will be held or was located. Use Exhibit 11. 2 to guide you in developing this schedule.

EXERCISE 11.3

Selecting Effective Instructional Staff Members

Using the same example you gave in Exercise 11.1 choose one of the two following options. Utilize Exhibit 11.4 to guide you through this exercise.

1.a. For a program you are in the process of developing, use the chart given below in selecting key instructional staff for the program in one or more roles that are appropriate.

1.b. For a program you have already given, use the same chart to evaluate whether the key instructional staff met the criteria outlined in one or more roles that person took on for the program.

Criteria	Name and Role of Instructional Staff Members	(Use for 1.a.) Why do you believe the staff members chosen will meet the criteria appropriate for their role(s)	(Use for 1.b.) Why do you believe the staff members chosen either did not meet or met the criteria appropriate for their role(s)
Content Knowledge			
Competence in the Process of Instruction			
Ability to Respond Effectively to the Background and Experiences of the Participants			
Belief That Caring for Learners Matters			
Credibility			
Enthusiasm and Commitment			
Personal Effectiveness			
Enterprise Knowledge			
Ability to Teach from the Heart and Spirit, as Well as the Mind			
Skills in Using Technology Effectively			

Chapter 12
Preparing and Managing Budgets

 SCENARIO 12.1: SARAH'S TINY MISTAKE

Sarah is a new program planner and is learning program planning skills as she plans a conference for eight hundred basic skills teachers and their program directors. Sarah has only three months to plan this conference, but is successful in her efforts. The conference evaluations were quite positive and post-conference feedback from program directors assured Sarah she did a good job in her planning. As she was reading the evaluations a third time, she opened the financial statement about the conference that came from the university. Sarah had calculated that enough income would be generated at the conference to present several future workshops. She was shocked to see there was only a small amount of surplus. Once Sarah checked with the sales director of the hotel and the university financial officer, she found each meal had a 17 percent gratuity added and a 7 percent sales tax. This "tiny mistake" was a costly budget omission. Fortunately, the conference broke even and Sarah did not lose her job. However, she was very disappointed that the amount left over was so little that the extra workshops for teachers could not be held.

Program planners are responsible for their program budgets, no matter the size of the program or the budget. Even simple budgetary errors can make the difference between a program's success or its failure (see Scenario 12.1). Most programs cannot be considered successful if the program loses money, but there are exceptions to this norm (e.g., putting together selected new programs that an organization is exploring, and is willing to take a loss to determine the potential for this type of content or format). Unfortunately in times of a tough economy, organizations may not be able or willing to risk these kinds of investments, so being prudent in managing program budgeting matters.

Every organization, no matter the size or status, has a fiduciary responsibility to manage its income and expenses. This responsibility of the organizational or group governing body (e.g., a board of directors or an executive committee) is a legal obligation in which they are responsible for overseeing the spending and protection of the assets (see Chapter Five). This governing board generally reads and approves the financial reports on a quarterly basis while the chief executive officer manages the finances. It would be extremely rare for program planners or chief executive officers to be fired for making money for their organizations. However, the opposite is certainly true: if these staff members lose money for an organization, their days may be numbered.

For those managing governmental programs, the origin of the funds necessitates additional fiduciary obligations and responsibilities. The Core Finance Data Task Force and National Forum on Education Statistics (2003) web page advises that: "In most cases, for governmental entities, the budget represents the legal authority to spend money. Adoption of a budget in the public sector implies that a set of decisions has been made by the governing board and administrators that culminate in matching the government's resources with the entity's needs. As such, the budget is a product of the planning process." Program planners for governmental programs sign contracts with the government pledging to make quarterly financial reports and to adhere to the budget or face losing the grant or program.

In this chapter we first discuss the critical details of budgeting, followed by the definitions of key terms used in preparing and managing budgets. We then describe several budgeting models that can be used for budgeting program income and expenses. Next, we illustrate how to estimate costs and prepare budgets, including the worksheets program planners use in calculating the expenses for specific programs. We explore the management of program budgets and discuss developing contingency plans as a part of this management process. The chapter concludes with an exploration of ways to finance programs and increase program income through fund raising.

Gaining a Clear Picture of the Budgeting Process

 SCENARIO 12.2:   SUE'S BIG PLAN

Sue is director of one of the adult basic education and high school completion programs in the region that Sarah's project serves. She returned from the conference excited about some of the ideas she heard in sessions. Sue wanted to expand her program currently focused on General Educational Development (GED) and Adult Basic

Education (ABE) to include English as a Second Language (ESL). To add to the ESL component of her program she had to follow a protocol established by the federal government through the state board of education and write a proposal for funding the new addition. Sue conducted a needs assessment of her community, determined there was a need for ESL classes, consulted her advisory council, and developed an initial proposal for this program. Among the questions she asked herself as she put together this proposal were:

- How large a program could be developed?

- How many students might attend the program?

- Where would these students come from?

- How would they pay the fees?

- How would she work the new program into a night class in the high school she used for the other programs?

Once Sue had these and the many other details worked out, she had to put together a budget for three years. The form for the proposal was standard and included estimates of income versus direct expenses. She was able to put together the budget, but was not sure how much the school district wanted to charge for the "indirect or the overhead costs." Sue was very surprised to find the school district wanted 15 percent indirect costs and that charge when added in, put her budget over the amount the state was willing to fund. The district financial officer pointed out that Sue also needed to charge more for the fringe benefits of the employees (30 percent) due to the increase in health care costs.

Sue knows that planning programs requires a whole range of activities that go beyond thinking through the educational components of the plan. She recognizes that budget planning and management is an integral component of the planning process and serves as one of the major driving force behind their program development efforts (Calley, 2011; Rothwell & Kazanas, 2008). In other words, program planners understand financial planning and budgeting because it is part of their job responsibilities. Examples of various tasks they will handle include:

- Making changes or adjustments in the financial and budgeting structure

- "Balancing the books" throughout the program year

- Reporting the fiscal health of their organization to the governing board of the organization or group or other stakeholders

- Making sound decisions related to personnel issues such as hiring or cutting staff, and giving raises based on the fiscal health of the organization or group

- Making purchasing decisions or investments based on the funds available

- Generating money through fundraising efforts, including the writing of grants and contracts

- Even the smallest program costs money and program planners' duties are clear—to budget income and expenses carefully to ensure the program or project will not lose money.

Preparing a program budget is essentially translating intended program goals and activities into monetary terms (Finkler, 2010; Pawlak & Vinter, 2004; Rothwell & Kazanas, 2008). As Allison and Kaye (2005) have observed: "A budget simply stated, is a plan expressed in dollars. To estimate further expenses, . . . staff will have to review goals and objectives with an eye to identifying what major resources are going to be needed to achieve those end results. This [process] can be an extremely difficult task" (p. 242). Some program planners work in education and training units that are funded as budget centers, and therefore have organizational funding in addition to whatever funding they generate (e.g., nongovernmental organizations, training departments in business and industry). Other planners are employed by units, such as distance-learning programs in colleges and universities, which operate on a cost recovery basis. In this type of system planners have to generate the funding to cover all of the expenses that are incurred in all phases of the planning process. In addition, there are planners who are located in profit centers, such as private consultancy firms, where they are expected to demonstrate their programs are good "money-making operations" for their organizations (Birkenholz, 1999; Tracey, 1992).

To gain a clear picture of the budgeting process it is necessary for program planners to understand general budgetary terminology in order to effectively prepare and manage their program budgets (Core Finance Data Task Force, 2003; Kettner, Moroney, & Martin, 2008; Meisinger & Dubeck, 1984; Woodard & von Destinon, 2000). Budgeting is a process and a best guess of how much revenue is projected by an organization compared to the expenses resulting from the work of the organization. Wilbur, Smith, Bucklin, and Associates (2000) advise nonprofit managers that "there should be a direct relationship between projected revenue and the expenses that will be incurred to carry out the nonprofit's mission" (p. 296).

EXHIBIT 12.1

Examples of the Six Most Often Used Budget Models

Types of Budget Models	Descriptions
Incremental Budgeting	Program budgets are carried over from one year to the next and sometimes increased or decreased by a specific percentage figure.
Zero-Based Budgeting	Program budgets start over each year with a new budget.
Planning, Programming, and Budget Systems (PPBS)	Tied to the direction of a strategic plan, the PPBS budget items include funding for special projects and programs in addition to the basic operations of the organization.
Formula Model	Program funds are appropriated on workload information.
Cost-Centered	Each department handles its own budget/income/expenses. This type of budget is also often called self-sustaining, off line, or other terms meaning the program pays for itself or it does not move forward. A cost-centered model is advantageous to program planners because all income and expenses are known, charted on the monthly report, and adjustments can be made more easily than in the four previous models, which often do not have the monthly updates or all of the information.
Responsibility-Centered	Program budgets are handled within the center, and they are continued each year with deficit or profit carried over.

Adapted with permission from Woodard, D.B.J., & von Destinon, M. (2000). Budgeting and fiscal management. In M. J. Barr & M. K. Desler (Eds.), *The handbook of student affairs administration*, 2nd Ed. (pp. 332–336). San Francisco: Jossey-Bass.

Whether programs are privately or publicly funded, program planners benefit by understanding the processes and terms of budgeting. A quick search of "budgetary terminology" leads to many sources giving slightly different definitions of these terms that fit the range of organizational settings (e.g., state and national governments, nonprofit organizations, for-profit corporations). Despite the varied terminology that is used and no matter whether the budget is small or large, there are some key words and phrases that are usually considered universal. As program planners need to share the budget information with others with whom they work, it is a good idea to use terms that are considered universal and easily understood by all. Examples of these key terms are income and expenses; direct and indirect costs; fixed and variable expenses; profit; return on investment; and cost-benefit analysis.[1]

Using Budgeting Models

Program planners never assume someone else will worry about or handle their budgets, or that it is not necessary to understand the budgeting process. All institutions have a budgeting process, no matter the size or type of organization. Program planners examine budgeting models to help them form a basis for understanding the budgeting language and process in their own organization, each of which is briefly described in Exhibit 12.1 (Woodard & von Destinon, 2000). When planners inquire about which one of these models is used in their organizations, they should not be surprised if the financial officer, accountant, or treasurer, or others who work with the budgets report that they have a hybrid model for the organization.

Program planners are at an advantage when they fully understand the model or hybrid model used by their organization, no matter the size of the program or project. Sources for further information are: Bernstein and Wild (2000); Bolton (2011); Finkler (2010); Schmidt (2011); Strauss and Curry (2002); and White, Sondhi, and Fried (1997).

Estimating Costs and Preparing Budgets

 SCENARIO 12.3:   TO APPLY OR NOT TO APPLY, THAT IS THE QUESTION

Terri, the director of continuing education at a small private college, has proposed her division increase its revenues by 10 percent for each calendar year for the next three years. She would use this additional money for two primary purposes: to provide faculty incentive funds for developing new programs for adults and additional distance-learning programs. Prior to making this proposal Terri discussed with her staff members whether this operational program objective is doable and, if so, what strategies could be used to accomplish the objective. Her staff was very positive—they viewed the idea as a proactive way to respond to the needs of adult students and the faculty simultaneously. They were able to come up with at least three strategies for making this objective a reality. These strategies include marketing their student portfolio development guide nationally to other small colleges, increasing the offerings for five current high-demand, high-revenue-generating programs, and charging fees for certain services that were formerly offered without charge. Terri also conferred with a number of faculty leaders over lunch to see whether they believed their colleagues would be responsive to such an incentive plan for program development. In addition, she had two preliminary planning sessions with chairs and faculty who expressed interest in offering part or all of their programs via distance learning. Again, Terri received positive feedback on her proposal. The faculty members were especially responsive to the idea of being able to apply for incentive funds for planning. This procedure breaks with the current campus norms, whereby the faculty members are paid only for what they actually deliver, not for the time and effort of developing innovative programs.

Terri has reached the point of preparing the budget for her program proposal. She knows there are three basic kinds of costs or expenses associated with each program offered: the cost to develop the program, to deliver it, and to have it evaluated or assessed for its value. Expense items to budget include direct costs and indirect costs (see Exhibit 12.A; see also Allison & Kaye, 2005; Pawlak & Vinter, 2004; and Piskurich, 2006).

In the three scenarios given so far in this chapter, the program planners had to go through slightly different budgetary processes specific to their own programs and organizations. They each prepared their budgets to fit the regulatory guidelines of their institutions or funders. In addition, Sarah developed a budget for a conference—a specific event. This budget had to be approved by the university and the state board of education, and pass the federal regulations governing the project. Sarah had to work with a financial officer from the university. In the second scenario, Sue was preparing a budget to develop a new educational program in her school district that would be a long-term program. Her budget needed to be approved by the superintendent of the school district and the school financial officer and fit the state and federal regulations governing programs for adults. In the third scenario, even though Terri also worked in the academic arena and was preparing a budget to develop a new program, her budget had to fit the requirements of the private sector as it was a private college. She had to prepare the budget for approval by her supervisor and the provost, who would then send her plan to the financial officer of the college. Nonacademic organizations in the private sector would have similar budgetary requirements with supervisors and financial officers to give approval to their budgets.

Although program planners work in a variety of institutions and settings, each institution has its own regulations, and program planners identify what those regulations are and the way a budget is to be developed for the institution. Sometimes program planners develop and manage a grant for their institution. For grant budgetary management, the program planner uses the "Indirect" or "Overhead" percentage rate set by their institution. The rate is calculated by the accountants of the institution, in accordance with federal regulations, and determined with federal approval. In some cases this percentage can be negotiated by both parties and sometimes the funding agency will determine what budgetary items can be covered by "Direct Costs" and those that can be used to calculate the "Indirect Costs" For more information on these terms, good resources are: Financial Services of University of Toronto (2006); Flood and Phelps (2003); and U.S. Department of Education (2009).

For the speculative items in a budget, the program planner can speculate on the high side or more on target in determining the costs. Birkenholz (1999) suggests, "It is best to estimate expenses on the high side" (p. 129), especially when the sources of funding are fixed or depend primarily on participant fees. One item that is good to estimate expenses on the high side is travel.[3] See Exercise 12.1 for a worksheet for estimating the program costs, which is a helpful tool in the budget preparation process (Allison & Kaye, 2005; Birkenholtz, 1999; Calley, 2011; Pawlak & Vinter, 2004; Piskurich, 2006). This tool can be useful for building: (1) program budgets for specific events, such workshops or conferences; (2) project budgets such as initiating a new program through grant funding in an existing organization; and (3) annual operating budgets in organizations or units of organizations that offer multiple programs, such as continuing education professional organizations and training units in private businesses or government agencies (Calley, 2011).

Explanations of budget items can be helpful when calculating specific line items when preparing a worksheet for estimating program expenses. For example, in estimating costs planners may have to account for staff members' time, and travel for attendees. Examples of other costs that are part of planning program budgets are those for materials, printing, and copying; equipment; and supplies, postage, telephone, and miscellaneous expenses.[4]

Once the budgets are in place, program planners also manage those budgets in such a way that the costs of various programs and activities do not exceed the amount budgeted, or in the case of profit-making organizations, that they bring monies into the organization which are usually predetermined in advance.

Managing Program Budgets

 SCENARIO 12.4:   THE CAREFUL PLANNER

Gail is the director of a work training program funded by government grants. She has a staff of ten trainers, a part-time accountant, and a program planner. Her training program lives or dies by the ever-changing political scene of the government's interest in helping those without adequate knowledge and skills to be productive in the workforce. Gail has to worry about managing her budgets for five different training programs, and also has to plan ahead to write enough grants to keep the current programs funded and her staff employed. Gail's lease is ending in three months and she has to make a decision to either stay in the building where they are, which is really too small for the size of program she has now, or to move to a larger space with the anticipation that her program will expand. To add to her difficulty in making a decision about the space, there may be a potential change in the government in late fall. Gail's program has strong support from liberal government sponsors, but if a conservative government takes over she may have difficulty obtaining grant funding for her next program.

Managing a budget does not mean just counting the dollars left in the budget. Program planners have many issues to face in managing a budget that involves each of the components of the budget described in the previous section. A budget is a well-educated guess at how the money will be spent (Allison & Kaye, 2005). The longer program planners are in business, the better they get at "guessing" how the budget will work out. The management of the budget is a three-part process: looking at past budgets to see how closely they met the anticipated budget; managing the current expenses; and looking toward the future to stretch the budget out or to cut back on expenses so the budget estimates are correct. Program planners have several guidelines to follow:

1. Set financial goals based on a close estimate of necessary expenses and of possible income.

2. Develop a detailed plan for producing whatever income is required.

3. Prepare a budget to serve as a guide and a basis for making responsible financial planning decisions, financial control, and financial strategies.

4. Make expenditures only with proper authority and within the budget allowance.

5. Have adequate records of all financial transactions that are clear, accurate, measurable, and complete.

6. Notify outside funding agencies when budget shortfalls seem inevitable and gather advice and support for decisions to either avoid the shortfall or handle it.

7. Do not make financial information about programs widely known and most especially do not give out information to those who should not have the information.

8. Develop a working relationship with fiscal officers and keep asking questions about the financial status of programs, projects, or the organization.

9. Do not make annual reports before receiving the year-end statement, no matter the circumstances, as one bill or one donation can turn the annual report around.

10. Do not commingle funds of various projects and programs and never commingle these funds and personal funds.

11. Look for any type of discrepancy in the accounts, and question whoever is responsible for them (e.g., the business office, an accountant), and when not satisfied, contact the legal department and ask for an outside auditor to check the issue.

12. Use an outside agency, even if the organization has an internal auditing process to complete an annual audit and make yearly reports to all external funding agencies, as these agencies (especially governmental organizations) often require that annual audits of the projects they fund be conducted by an outside auditing firm.

13. Be aware that these "year-end" reports may fall at different times of the year depending on the fiscal year of the funding organization.

Gail, introduced earlier in this section, was very careful in expanding her space only when she had her contracts in hand. On the other hand,

Pete, another program director, chose to expand his for-profit continuing professional education (CPE) organization based on a personal dream for this organization and a less than promising opportunity, with the result being the loss of his job.[5] There are several lessons for program planners to consider from Scenarios 12.4 and 12.A. First, when trying to decide future program budgets, be conservative rather than optimistic. It is always much better to be surprised with a surplus of funds than to have a loss. Gail waited until she had the next contract in her hand before moving to a larger and more desirable space. Pete not only let his enthusiasm for realizing his dream get in the way of common sense but he took a big risk on happenings that were not under his control. The owners of the office space would have given Pete six months' notice before tearing down the building, plenty of time to line up a move. Pete believed rumors rather than facts. Pete also paid for a needs assessment of his clients but then ignored their responses to the questions. Worst of all, Pete violated ethical practices when he lied to his board of directors about the whole situation. Planners always have to be honest with their boards, their supervisors, and management. The last lesson would be to keep on top of the budget at all times. One or two slips with the expenses can spell catastrophe. When in a tough situation with the budget, it is much better to ask for help than to try to hide the problem.

Managing the income side of the equation is also vital. For some sources of income, the amounts are fixed for a given time period, like organizational subsidies, grants and contracts, and government funds. Although these sources are usually fixed, planners still pay attention to which sources fund each program and ensure the monies are appropriately used. In addition, as noted in the previous section, programmers build in "safety systems" or margins within these fixed sources of funds to cover unexpected costs, program changes, and program cancellations.

For revenue that is customarily variable, such as sponsorship funds and participant fees, it can be tricky to know how much to ask sponsors to donate and what to charge participants. For example, establishing participant fees depends on a number of factors, such as what the market will bear, competitors' prices, other sources of available income, perceived need for the program, and knowing the target audience. Establishing minimum enrollment figures, especially for nonprofit organizations, is often "one of the most arbitrary and subjective decisions [that] educators make in the planning process. However, the decision to establish a minimum enrollment may significantly affect participant fees and, ultimately, whether programs have to be canceled due to insufficient enrollments" (Birkenholz, 1999, p. 128). Even organizations that use extensive historical data, marketing surveys, and established policies and procedures may rely heavily on "hunches" and "intuitive guesses" to project enrollment numbers. In addition, for programs that rely primarily on participant fees, establishing the final registration fee is critical to the overall success of the program. If potential participants perceive the cost as too high, they may not sign up. At the same time, if the fee is too low, they may wonder about the program quality and therefore choose not to enroll.

Using Cost Contingency Plans

"In today's complex and multi-layered world, contingency planning is no longer a luxury; it has become a necessity" (Landry, 2006, p. 1). Organizations and businesses most likely have contingency plans in place when problems arise, often related to finances, but sometimes to problems that become devastating to the organization or business. Various contingency plans can be found. Landry's (2006) three phrases of a contingency planning process can easily be adapted to the program planning process as illustrated in Exhibit 12.2.

Though the Landry (2006) contingency plan can be used broadly for management of serious problems within an organization or business, it can easily be understood and used by program planners. Program planners often need to build in contingency plans for handling costs since the budgeting process is not an exact "science." Several situations often become problematic in handling the costs of program planning: (1) costs exceed the projected budget, (2) revenue is lower than expected, (3) programs are cancelled, or (4) extreme circumstances call for adjustments immediately prior to or at the time of the program. The best solution, of course, is to build in a cushion in the program/project budget with the realization that often projects cost more than anticipated or at least there will be unexpected expenses. In these cases, program costs have to come down if there is no cushion to rely upon. Exhibit 12.3 contains a list of strategies for cost contingency planning for educational programs.

When preprogram revenue is low, a program is canceled, or extreme circumstances occur after a program has been developed, skilled program planners can still save a program. Often, revenues do not materialize due to participation being down or when funds from other sources are less than expected. In response, program planners take a hard look at the program and cut out activities, services, or alter food choices. These items can be scaled back or not provided at all. If participation is low planners also can save by reducing the funds being spent on instructors and facilitators, instructional materials, travel, food, meeting rooms and equipment. Some of these items are difficult to alter if these services are already contracted

EXHIBIT 12.2

Phases of Developing and Managing a Contingency Plan

Phases	Description
Phase One: Notification	Evaluate the damage
	Recover any usable assets
	Give notification to the stakeholders and personnel involved about the damage
	Make a decision about activating a contingency plan
	Develop strategies for recovery
Phase Two: Recovery	Implement recovery strategies
	Establish temporary systems to stabilize
	Repair the damage
	Move forward with rest of the contingency plans
Phase Three: Reconstitution	Implement activities needed to get back to a normal operation
	State lessons learned about the cost of the contingency

without an escape clause. Program planners are careful with contracts and know exactly what is optional or not and what the "drop-dead" deadlines are (see Chapter Fourteen). Cost contingency plans can be incorporated during various stages of the planning process.[6] For example, if hotel reservations are not meeting the count anticipated, planners can cut the room reservations in agreement with the hotel contract without penalty, usually thirty to sixty days prior to the event. If registration numbers are low two weeks before a program, it may be possible to cancel the program for the lack of adequate projected revenue. If there are unforeseen emergencies like a snowstorm, the meal count and room count can be adjusted, but with penalties stipulated by the event contract. Adjustments on food counts can be made no less than 24 hours before the event; some hotels or catering businesses use a 48-hour cancellation clause. Airline tickets, in today's market, usually cannot be cancelled, and presenters' honorariums or fees may still need to be paid when a program is cancelled.

Planners must absorb the already expended or encumbered costs within other revenue streams. The most often used contingency plan for covering these costs is to set aside a certain percentage of the total operating budget for this purpose, reallocate funds, and build into other programs the costs expended for cancelled programs. Another way that costs are recovered is to take the instructional materials that were developed for the cancelled program and sell them.

EXHIBIT 12.3

Cost Contingency Planning Strategies for Educational Programs

Budgeting Stage

- Use less staff to plan, deliver, and evaluate the program and use outside consultants as they may be less expensive than hiring staff.
- Budget for a smaller number of participants.
- Budget for less expensive teaching/training techniques.
- Use either a less expensive facility or one that does not cost direct dollars.
- Hold the program at a facility close to where participants live or work so that they do not have to pay for overnight accommodations; this will attract additional participants.
- Budget for electronic marketing and materials delivered on CDs or web sites.
- Have participants pay for their own meals rather than including meals.

Planning Stage

- Substitute less expensive instructional materials or eliminate certain materials altogether.
- Cut down on the number of participants.
- Choose less expensive meals and breaks.
- Require presenters who are compensated for their expenses find the cheapest mode of travel to and from the program.
- Change the program to a date when the prices for the facilities, meals, and so forth are lower (e.g., an off-season time or days of week that are normally not filled).
- Make promotional material for the program less elaborate and send by email and put on web site.
- Shorten the program and tighten the design.
- Post all materials for the program on the Web or put them on a CD, saving printing costs.
- Deliver the program online or through a video conferencing system if the costs are less.
- Consider subcontracting some of the tasks if the costs are lower.

Determining How Programs Are Financed

The income or revenue sources for education and training programs vary depending on the type of organization (that is, for-profit versus nonprofit); the purpose, content, and format of the program; and whether or not fees are charged for the program. The primary income sources for educational programs are parent organizational subsidy; donor and sponsorship funds; participant fees and tuition; auxiliary enterprises and sales; grants and contracts; government funds; profits from the education or training unit itself; and miscellaneous income. Brief descriptions of these income sources are listed in Exhibit 12.4, with examples of each.

EXHIBIT 12.4

Sample Income Sources

Income Source	Description	Example
Organizational Subsidy	The educational program or event receives operating funds from the parent or partnership organization as part of the internal budgeting mechanism.	The Division of Correctional Education (DCE) receives an expense budget of $200,000 annually for salaries, materials and equipment, travel, general office supplies, and printing. In addition, a collaborative partnership of which the DCE is a part of also provides $100,000 in additional revenues for new technology-based programs.
Donations and Other Sponsorship Funds	Other organizations (e.g., business, philanthropic, professional, and trade groups) and individuals give financial support to a specific program or series of programs.	Two local businesses, one philanthropic organization, and three individual donors have agreed to underwrite some of the costs for a series of outdoor adventure programs for a group of adults who are disabled. These organizations and individuals will sponsor the program in conjunction with a community-based program that provides services for adults with disabilities and the local university.
Participant Fees	Participants are charged a fee or tuition for attending a program.	Eighty percent of all adult literacy and GED programs sponsored by the local community college must break even. Thus the participants' fees must cover a large amount of the expenses of those programs.
Auxiliary Enterprises and Sales	Revenue is earned from the sale of materials, publications, technology-based programs, and services provided by the educational unit to other organizations and individuals.	A nationally prominent accounting firm has developed an excellent online program and is now selling it to other organizations for profit.

(Continued)

EXHIBIT 12.4 (*Continued*)

Sample Income Sources

Income Source	Description	Example
Grants and Contracts from Foundations and Other Organizations	Foundations, businesses, trade and professional organizations, labor unions, special interest groups, and other organizations award funds to an educational unit to develop a specific program. Usually these awards go to nonprofit organizations.	Funding is given to a community action agency that serves low-income people in the community to increase their participation in local, state, and national elections.
Government Funding (Federal, State, and Local)	Government funds are awarded or given to an education or training unit to develop a specific program. These funds may be given to for-profit or nonprofit agencies (depending on the regulations governing the funds).	A local community college, in partnership with a workplace learning program, is awarded a grant to initiate a job-training program for unemployed workers.
Profit from Educational Unit	The educational unit produces a profit from the operation, which in turn can be used for future programs.	The extended and summer programs division of the university supports continuing education programs for teachers through distance education with the profit they make from their summer programs.
Miscellaneous Income	This category covers all other sources of funding that are not listed above. A sampling of these sources includes endowments, royalty income, fundraising events, investments, and in-kind contributions.	The miscellaneous income for the mentoring program for new principals is used to host luncheons for the mentors and their protégés.

Funding for programs is often pieced together and thus it is important that program planners have a clear understanding of their funding sources; an up-to-date knowledge of the policies and regulations that govern each revenue stream; and a realistic approach to working with these sources (Calley, 2011). In essence, it is best to estimate "revenues on the conservative side" (Birkenholz, 1999, p. 129).

Increasing Income

It is often wise and necessary in some organizations to have a fundraising campaign to support programs. Before taking action, the organization should ask the "why and what" questions: Why raise funds? What is the purpose for the funds? What will the funds be used for first, second, and third? Wilbur et al. (2000) stress the importance of having a purpose and a clear identifiable and quantifiable need for the fundraising activity. They suggest building a "case for support" (p. 99), or a justification for fundraising efforts. To build this "case for support" within several paragraphs, planners think about the statement as being of interest to prospective donors. The case informs, challenges, and leads to ways to involve these donors in fundraising. Elements for building the "case for support" statement for fundraising campaigns are provided in Exhibit 12.5 (DeWitt, 2011).

Jackson (2000) suggests answering several additional questions to make sure the strategy for fundraising is sound. For example, will program

---

EXHIBIT 12.5

Elements of the Case for Support

1. Describe the organization with these statements and answers to the questions:
   a. Name, mission, and current status: What is the general information on the organization?
   b. Purpose/objectives/function: Why does the organization exist?
   c. Services: What activities does your organization perform?
   d. Targeted population: Whom does this organization currently serve and how does serving this specific clientele affect the programs being offered and the organization's focus?
   e. Geographic reach: Where are programs currently offered? Is where these programs are offered limited by geographical boundaries?
   f. Philosophy: What are the core principles, values, and ideas that are fundamental to the organization?
2. What is the need, problem, or challenge that you address that requires funding?
3. What strengths qualify the organization to address this need/problem/challenge?
4. What new challenges does the organization have in carrying out this mission?
5. How does the organization plan to address those challenges?
6. What resources are needed; cost, time, and personnel?
7. What opportunities and options are there to raise money for the activities?
8. What will be the benefits for the organization, community, or society as a whole as a result of raising these funds?
9. What kind of supportive materials are needed (e.g., kinds of gifts, opportunities to name physical facilities, summary of financial information over the past five years, and examples of achievement)?

Adapted with permission from Wilbur, Smith, Bucklin, & Associates (2000). *The complete guide to nonprofit management* (2nd ed.). New York: Wiley, p. 100.

planners "seek funds consistent with missions of the institution [and program]?" (p. 601). By asking this question, the organization does not get into difficulty by having a generous donor try to take the organization in another direction. Jackson continues with eight other questions about the process, staff capability to carry out the fundraising, institutional fiduciary responsibilities, and involvement in the fundraising process. Jackson also warns that an organization should "whenever possible seek funds for programs that do not compete with [other] priorities" (p. 601). To make sure the case for support for fundraising is on target, planners can check with the board and stakeholders to see if they will agree to join in the effort, and ask external supporters to see if they approve of the fundraising effort.

Jackson concludes by suggesting sound principles of fundraising that need to be used. For example, the executive director of a continuing medical education (CME) program housed in the medical school was approached by a pharmaceutical company representative with an offer to earn $25,000 during the year. The CME director could use the money to hire a part-time assistant. All the director had to do is hand out a new diabetes medication and information flyers being promoted by the pharmaceutical company to each physician as they came to all of the CME programs that the medical school provided during the year. The director believed this was a pretty easy way to get $25,000 for hiring staff but he wondered if this would fit with the ethical guidelines of the university in which the medical school was housed. After a check, he found the answer was *"no, absolutely no!"*

Fundraising can bring an organization and its members many unexpected outcomes, illustrated in the following example.

> Thirty years ago the Mothers Club at Lakeside School in Seattle, Washington, held a rummage sale. There was nothing unusual about that—volunteers have excelled at fundraising events in the New World since the Pilgrims raffled off the first turkey. What was unusual was that these moms used the proceeds to buy a computer terminal and rent time on a big computer somewhere else. Two of Lakeside's students, Bill Gates and Paul Allen, used their lunch hour to teach the cumbersome computer how to play tic-tac-toe. You probably know the rest of this story. A few years later, Bill dropped out of college, Paul quit his day job, together they created the Microsoft Corporation, and together they designed the software which helped launch consumer demand of household computers around the world. (Flanagan, 2002, p. 1)

Once the decision is made to raise funds, then approval is sought, the fundraising goals and objectives are determined, and further decisions are made about the kind of fundraising efforts that fit best for the program or organization (e.g., direct mail, special events, e-mails including social media) (Andresen & Higman, 2011; Calley, 2011; Jackson, 2000; Nobel, 2011; Wilbur et al., 2000). Flanagan (2002) says there are more good ways to raise funds in the present day than ever before. However, in tough economic times program planners put their efforts on what they already know how to do before launching into untried fundraising events. A solid rule in fundraising is to ask people you already know who support your organization or program for donations. "This is the most basic, and the most successful, strategy for fundraising for any cause" (Flanagan, 2002, p. 2). Flanagan provides three basic principles of fundraising commonly found in literature on how to raise funds. She observes that successful fundraising must be:

- Built on the widest possible base of donors and members

- Focused on creating long-term relationships with your best donors

- Driven by donor choice

Novice fundraisers often believe they can walk up to people who would be likely donors and ask for a donation (McManus, 2011). This plan usually fails because a relationship with the donor has not been established. It often takes a year or two to build these relationships with potential donors before planners can expect sizable gifts.

 ### SCENARIO 12.5:   A STORY WITH A GREAT ENDING

A judicial reform organization wanted to establish a center for judicial independence. The organization was used to writing grants, had many government and private grants for their programs, and a solid membership who contributed to their organization. But the board of directors felt this would be a special center and believed they could set up the center with a donation from one of their long-time members. Much discussion and planning went into the effort and the executive director and the president of the organization had breakfast with a member the board they knew had an interest in funding the center. The president and executive director developed the plans, budget, and approach they would use at the breakfast meeting. In addition, the president was a former college roommate of the potential donor and therefore had interacted with him in a number of ways over the years. As the donor was quite wealthy, the president said in the invitation for breakfast that he and the executive director of the organization wanted to present an idea to him. The meeting was held, the president and executive director presented their idea and left the breakfast with a check for $150,000 for the center.

Although this scenario is an exciting success story, the plan for this meeting took months to develop. The organization followed the principles of fundraising and worked through the questions and issues raised by Wilbur et al. (2000) and ideas from other sources. The organization also sent the executive director to a two-week fundraising school to learn how to properly ask for donations and then put together a year's plan to raise funds, which included approaching this board member. However, experienced program planners know that this type of outcome does not happen every day and that it takes a lot of preparation, as just described, to make any large donation of this nature to happen.

There are numerous strategies to raise funds for training and development programs (Allen, 2009; Andresen & Higman, 2011; Flanagan, 2002; Grace, 2005; McManus, 2011).[7] Strategizing for fundraising begins with choices planners make regarding which programs they believe will "bear the most fruit" or gain the most in funds and resources. Because funds are raised from people and organizations, the pyramid presented in Figure 12.1 helps with the planning.

At the bottom of the pyramid is the biggest amount of donors—but they give the least amount. The top of the pyramid has the smallest number of donors, but they give the most, and the rest of the donors fall between these two groups. Information gained from the donor pyramid helps to chart the plans for the activities of fundraising. Most organizations already do some type of fundraising so it is helpful to record the past activities and results, and then the goals for the next five years.[8] The information from the pyramid and strategy planning worksheet provides a quick glance and important information for the program planner, the board, the advisory groups and those leading the fundraising efforts.

A program does not have to be large or even located in urban areas to do fundraising. Technology has made the art of raising funds for a program much easier to do. The use of e-mails, web sites, and promotional materials that can be created without cost and used as attachments have become the norm in fundraising in many parts of the world. "Smaller charities are mastering the art of endowments, rural communities are running efficient community foundations, and the largest institutions keep leap-frogging

FIGURE 12.1

Donor Pyramid

Planned-Gift Donors - Bequests, insurance, and life income plans

Major Donors - Person-to-person requests, clubs, memorials, and honorary gifts

Pledgers and Frequent Donors - Credit card and payroll deduction

Annual Donors and Members - Direct mail, E-mail, the Internet, phone calls, door-to-door

Guests - Special events

Customers - Product sales

Clients - Fees for service

Individual Prospects - Potential donations

Commitment to Mission

Amount of Money

With permission from Flanagan, J. (2002). *Successful fundraising: A complete handbook for volunteers and professionals* (2nd ed.). Lincolnwood, IL: Contemporary Books, p. 14.

over each other's multibillion-dollar capital campaigns" (Flanagan, 2002, p. 2). It is not unusual to get requests for donations from other parts of the world to fight hunger, to buy a sewing machine so a woman can start a business, or to buy a cow for a small village to have milk. Each of these organizations started its fundraising in many of the basic ways mentioned above.

Materials on fundraising that program planners find are very useful include Allison and Kaye, 2005: Flanagan, 2002; Hall and Howlett, 2003; Heyman, 2011; and Wilbur et al., 2000. In addition, fundraising workshops can be helpful in developing and enhancing skills, although planners should carefully check the parameters of the fundraising workshops before signing up. Once planners are conversant on the tasks required for fundraising, and before discussing the issue with the advisory committee or board of directors, planners consider the following:

1. Have firm and established relationships with the community [from which] they are seeking funds, allies and networks in place, common interests and projects with their audiences;

2. Know how the upper management members of their organizations feel about fundraising activities and make sure that they have permission from management to launch a campaign.

3. Work closely with stakeholders to get their support and help, and to understand their positions on projects and programs of the organization (Jackson, 2000, p. 599)

As can be seen in this last section, increasing income for programs is an important responsibility that program planners undertake.

 ## Chapter Highlights

Preparing and managing program budgets is one of the key components of the planning process. No matter what the organizational setting is, program planners are responsible for understanding all financial responsibilities and are ethically and sometimes legally responsible for managing the budget and reporting the finances accurately. Whether the expectations for planners are to break even, have a surplus, or be profit-making ventures, there are six important tasks that they pay attention to when planning and managing budgets.

- Gain a clear understanding of the budgeting process used by the organization in which they work, and the terminology and budget model used in this process.

- Estimate the costs for the program and, based on these estimated costs, prepare program budgets.

- Manage the program budgets and maintain accurate financial records.

- Develop financial contingency plans for specific programs and activities as it is not unusual for costs or income plans to change.

- Determine how the program is financed (e.g., by participant fees, organizational subsidy, government and foundation funding, dues, fundraising activities), and estimate the program income.

- Generate funding for the program (e.g., through fundraising campaigns, obtaining major gifts, grant writing).

Successful fundraising and planning and managing program budgets effectively are two of the key aspects that help program planners meet their financial commitments. The next chapter, which focuses on organizing marketing campaigns, is linked closely to the fundraising efforts of organizations and groups. For example, the messages developed and some of the materials and tools used in marketing campaigns are often also used in fundraising activities. Marketing educational programs can increase participation in educational programs, help to develop and maintain the credibility of programs and the organization, and place the program or organization into the market niche, all of which are critical to bringing funding into the organization.

Notes for Additional Online Resources

1. See Exhibit 12.A: Descriptions of Key Budgetary Terms for a clear description of each of these terms.

2. Further explanations about some of the differences among these six models are given in Exhibit 12.B: Differences Among Budgeting Models.

3. See Exhibit 12.C: Worksheet for Estimating Program Expenses.

4. See Exhibit 12.D: Estimating Costs for Personnel and Travel for a Three-Day Conference and Exhibit 12.E: Examples of Other Costs When Planning Programs.

5. See Scenario 12.A: The Passionate But Dishonest Planner.

6. See Scenario 12.B: Saving the Conference.

7. See Exhibit 12.F: Fundraising Strategy Planning Worksheet.

8. See Exhibit 12.F: Fundraising Strategy Planning Worksheet.

 ## Application Exercises

Exercise 12.1 provides you the opportunity to prepare a program budget through estimating program expenses and identifying the sources of income you will need for this program, including how much funding will come from each source. Exercises 12.2 and 12.3 focus on reducing the costs for the program, and learning more about strategies for fundraising.

EXERCISE 12.1

Preparing Program Budgets for Estimating Expenses and Income

1. Choose an educational program that you are presently or will be planning and prepare an estimated expense budget for that program using the following chart. Put an *X* in the space provided if no costs are incurred for that item.

Budget Items	Expenses

Personnel

Program Director _____

Instructors/facilitators _____

Support Staff _____

Other Staff _____

Fringe Benefits

Program Director _____

Instructors/facilitators _____

Support Staff _____

Other Staff _____

External Staff

Program Consultants _____

Instructors/facilitators _____

Honorariums _____

Sub-Contractors _____

Others _____

Materials

Copying _____

Design _____

Printing _____

CDs _____

Technical Support

Website Costs _____

Internet Fees _____

Learning Management System _____

Other _____

Equipment

Computers _____

Printers _____

Projectors _____

Budget Items	Expenses
Screens	_____
Microphones	_____
Other	_____
Travel	
Airfare	_____
Ground Transportation	_____
Mileage	_____
Rental Car	_____
Parking Fees	_____
Facilities	
Overnight Rooms	_____
Meeting Rooms	_____
Food	_____
Hospitality	_____
Receptions	_____
Special Activities	_____
AV Rental	_____
Supplies, Telephone, Postage	
Supplies	_____
Telephone	_____
Postage	_____
Special Services for Participants (e.g., sign language experts, note takers, interpreters)	_____
Miscellaneous	_____
Total Direct Expenses	_____
Indirect Costs—Capitalize Direct	_____
Total Expenses	_____

2. To cover all or part of these program costs, identify on the following chart what sources of income you will use and estimate how much funding will come from each source (use Exhibit 12.4 for further descriptions of each income source).

Income Source	Amount of Income/Subsidy
Parent organizational subsidy	$ _____
Sponsorship funds or donations	$ _____
Participant fees (fee × # of estimated participants)	$ _____

(Continued)

Income Source	Amount of Income/Subsidy
Auxiliary enterprises and sales (item or service to be sold × # of estimated customers)	$ _____
Grants and contracts (List each source of funding with amount)	
1.	$ _____
2.	$ _____
3.	$ _____
Government funds (List each source of funding with amount)	
1.	$ _____
2.	$ _____
3.	$ _____
Profit from any educational units	
Miscellaneous income	$_____
Total Income	$ _____

3. If your expense and income sources are not in line, describe how you would adjust either one or both in order to achieve your budget objective (for example, breaking even on expenses, earning 10 percent over cost).

4. Review your budget plan with other members of your planning team or with people from your organization or sponsoring group. Revise your expense and income estimates and your ideas on how to meet your budget objectives.

EXERCISE 12.2

Reducing Program Costs

1. Describe a specific conference or workshop that you are currently planning or have planned in the past. As part of that description estimate the funds that will be spent or were spent for that event.

    _____
    _____
    _____
    _____
    _____

2. Image that two months before the event you described in question 1 you were required to reduce the costs for that program by 10 percent, due to a reduction in the budget of your program unit. Using Exhibit 12.3, choose which strategies you would employ to make this 10 percent cut in your program budget using the following guide to record your response.

Strategies	Reasons for Choosing This Strategy

3. Discuss the strategies and the reasons you chose these strategies with one or two of your colleagues from your organization or other program planners who have experience with reducing program budgets.

    3a. If you chose a program that you are currently planning ask these colleagues to provide feedback on your choices and reasons for those choices. Sample questions you may want to ask them are: Do the choices I would use make sense? Can these choices be implemented in the remaining timeframe? What other choices might you have made and why?

    _____
    _____
    _____
    _____
    _____

    3b. If you chose a program that you have planned in the past, ask these colleagues to evaluate these choices in terms of whether they would have worked, using similar questions as shown in item 3.a.

EXERCISE 12.3

Learning about Specific Strategies for Fundraising

1. Approach someone who is knowledgeable about fundraising in the organization where you are currently employed or someone in the community where you work that offers education or training programs. Ask this person to describe to you at least three strategies that the organization uses in fundraising that you are unfamiliar with or that you have not used yourself. Request copies of specific materials for fundraising strategies that were used by this organization.

2. Discuss these strategies with one or two other colleagues, from a different organization to assist you in evaluating the strengths and weakness of these materials as fundraising tools. This conversation would need to be within a confidential framework and only with the permission of the organization that you visited.

Chapter 13

Organizing Marketing Campaigns

A CRUCIAL TASK of the Interactive Model of Program Planning is to target the right audience for the program being planned. The targeting or marketing process is an essential component of the program planning process but one that most program planners have not been trained for or know how to do. With increased competition for education and training programs for adults in many sectors, this need for program planners to develop and conduct marketing campaigns, whether online, in print, or by word-of-mouth, is vital in situations where participation is voluntary, funds are limited in terms, and potential participants have little or no affiliations with the sponsoring organization. Program planners know that if the marketing strategies they use are not eye-catching or appropriate for their intended audience, the program they have so carefully planned may have to be cancelled, which does not bode well for marketing future programs to this same audience.[1]

In this chapter we first address how marketing is defined, and follow with an overview of what goes into creating a marketing campaign, and in-depth descriptions of each of the elements of the marketing campaign, starting with conducting a target and contextual analysis. Next we explore the need to consider the competition in marketing programs, and the concept and use of organizational branding. After reviewing the importance of selecting and developing clear and concise marketing messages, we examine the various promotional materials and tools that are used to ensure the messages are packaged well. We look at the more traditional materials, such as brochures and posters, and tools that are used in online promotion, such as web sites and social media. The chapter closes with a brief discussion of implementing marketing campaigns.

Defining Marketing

Kotler (1987) defines marketing as "the function of . . . [an organization] whose goal is to plan, price, promote, and distribute the organization's programs and products by keeping in constant touch with the organization's various constituencies, uncovering their needs and expectations for the organization and themselves, and building a program of communication to not only express the organization's purpose and goals but also their mutually beneficial . . . products" (p. 5). These tasks—to find out who our constituents are, what their needs are, and how to market to them—are not easily understood or carried out (McLeish, 2011). Communicating a message that programs are useful and meaningful to potential participants is critical in ensuring participation. In addition, marketing also has two other purposes: to communicate the mission of the organization and its programs, and to convince others of the value of the organization's work to the community and the funding or sponsoring organizations (Birkenholz, 1999; DiAddezzio, 2012).

The framework for marketing that has been most often used over the years to describe the major components of what marketing is all about is the 4 P's of marketing—product, price, place, and promotion (Chandrasekar, 2010; Rogers, Finley, & Galloway, 2001; Tate, 2010; Yudelson, 1999). These four areas are interconnected and thus program planners consider how each of these components affects the others as they work through the planning and implementation of a marketing campaign.[2]

It is essential for program planners to become aware of the best way to sell or "package" the product.[3] Whether the product is marketed through traditional methods, such as brochures, flyers, notices, or ads, or through electronic tools such as social media, web sites, or e-mail, the content is the same and the packaging of the product has to be complete. It is important to produce marketing pieces for the product that are attractive, appear professionally prepared, and are packaged with the brand of the organization so it is instantly recognized. The packaging of the product will be seen by the potential consumer and appraised in less than 30 seconds; if the first impression of the product does not connect with the consumer in those 30 seconds, the opportunity is lost and the "product" is not sold to the consumer.

In determining the price for education and training program planners triangulate their decisions using three considerations: (1) what the targeted audiences will bear (get as close to this amount as possible); (2) what the competition charges for similar programs (get below this price); and (3) what it costs to produce (get above this cost when needed) (DiAddezzio, 2012;

McLeish, 2011; Tate, 2010).[4] The price charged for programs should either exceed the cost of the program or at least pay for itself, meaning that the program cost is covered by the program fees. When program planners choose to offer the program at a higher cost it is usually for three major reasons:

- To ensure that programs that go over their budgets will not affect the overall bottom line for the organizations who are offering them.

- To support the organization's operational cost or assist in the funding of new programs.

- To make sure in profit-making organizations that the fees charged for the programs offered allow these organizations to stay in business or expand their operations.

There are occasional exceptions to this premise that programs should either generate funds for the organization or break even, such as investing in new programs that planners believe will become "best sellers" in the future. Programs of this nature usually recover these lost revenues by offering the same program again in the future to new groups of people. Therefore the up-front cost is an investment in expanding program offerings. Sometimes a nonprofit organization will ask donors to cover the cost of programs (e.g., training programs for the unemployed and family literacy education programs; McLeish, 2011).

Places where education and training programs are offered have expanded tremendously with the number of available online programs. Therefore, when thinking about venues, program planners are skilled in coordinating program activities and events that require specific locations and facilities as well as what specifications, if any, they need to arrange when offering programs in cyberspace.[5] For face-to-face programs, the location must be consistent with the program design, audience, and budget. For example, hosting a three-day national conference for a professional association in a place that planners believed would be attractive to participants, but is relatively inaccessible by air (which usually means higher airfares), is generally not a good decision, especially if the participants have to obtain low airfares to attend the conference.

Online programs involve different issues, as participants may take part in these programs totally online or meet face-to-face individually or in small or large groups for a live chat. For those meeting in groups, program planners may need to arrange spaces for them to meet, or work with someone at each site to ensure the facilities used are appropriate to the design of the program. For example, if breakout groups are a major part of the program design and the facilities chosen are ones in which discussions among the participants are just not suitable for these types of interaction, then other facilities must be chosen.

Program planners consider the details and costs to reach the intended audience. In other words, what does it take to notify the intended audience of the program? This step requires knowing everything about the intended audience to make the promotional materials and tools as targeted as possible. As observed by DiAddezzio (in a personal communication), promotion "is the most visible and well-known stage of the marketing method. Many people mistakenly believe this stage is all of what marketing is about." Though marketing campaigns consist of a number of elements, promotion is tremendously important in ensuring that the marketing campaigns are successful. Promotion is a form of communication that has the ultimate purpose of getting people to attend education and training programs or convincing them to invest their resources into specific programs or projects. This "selling" of programs is done through personal contacts, public relations, and materials and tools, such as printed brochures, e-mail, and web sites. Even though some educational programs are required, program planners still promote their programs to their audiences. Promoting these programs usually does not cost as much as active marketing campaigns, and program planners do not let an opportunity pass by them when promotion of the "product" is possible.

The 4 Ps of marketing—product, price, place, and promotion—all help to define the major elements that need to be taken into consideration in developing comprehensive and organized marketing campaigns. Program planners, by taking into account each of the 4 Ps, are better able to create workable marketing campaigns.

Creating Marketing Campaigns

Successful marketing is defined by Simerly as "a process for ensuring that an organization reaches its goals and objectives by exchanging its products, services and knowledge for program registrations" (1989a, p. 445). Communicating messages that education and training programs are useful and meaningful to potential participants is critical to ensuring program participation. In addition, it is important to share these messages with other publics, such as sponsoring organizations, funding agencies, and the general community, in order to increase awareness of the program's purpose and its subsequent value and importance to the wider community (Blomberg, 1989; DiAddezzio, 2012). Program planners create realistic and workable marketing plans to guarantee that audiences are effectively reached. In developing these marketing plans, there are three key tenets that are important for planners to consider (Craven & DuHamel, 2000; Mitchell, 1998).

- *Develop and maintain program credibility.* Acquire a track record of well-run, high-quality programs that build respect and trust with your regular participants and convey to potential audiences they will get their money's worth.

- *Build on successes.* Listen to former participants, colleagues, sponsoring organization, funding groups, and others in the wider community in terms of suggestions on how to change current programs and practices and what future programs they might find useful and why.

- *Find a market niche.* Although overlap in services by organizations in similar market areas is not unusual, groups and organizations should find unique content areas and ways of offering programs that are theirs alone, or form collaborative partnerships where there are overlaps (see Chapter Five).

Craven and DuHamel (2000), DeWitt (2011), DiAddezzio, (2012), McLeish, (2011), Miller, (2010), Mitchell (1998), and Winton and Hochstadt (2011) have all contributed helpful ideas related to the various elements that planners address in creating marketing plans, which include: a target audience analysis, a context analysis, the competition, organizational branding, powerful messages, and promotional materials and tools.[6] More in-depth explanations of each of these elements are provided in subsequent sections.

Prior to initiating this process, program planners need to know who will be responsible for addressing each part of the process. For example, in some organizations planners may be responsible for conducting target and context analysis, while marketing specialists actually develop the slogans and marketing materials, and choose and implement the best promotional strategies for the target audience. Marketing specialists are more likely to be found in large organizations, whereas in smaller ones, planners may actually be responsible for carrying out the entire marketing plan.

Conducting a Target Audience Analysis

Completing a target audience analysis is one way to gather information on characteristics of potential participants. This process assumes that the staff knows which individuals or groups of people are or might be interested in attending the program to be offered. McLeish (2011) notes that "for most institutions, it is no longer business as usual. Rather than continuing to send marketing . . . messages to an increasingly unsympathetic and sometimes resentful audience, many organizations are trying to engineer a different sort of social engagement with their stakeholders" (p. xviii). With the high cost of time and resources to produce programs, the planner cannot afford to misunderstand the audience. A target audience analysis is useful for open enrollment programs and programs that have eligibility requirements (e.g., specific types of jobs or educational backgrounds). These data can assist in determining whether audiences for both types of programs exist in the designated market area and, for programs with eligibility requirements, the data can serve as a screening device for potential participants (Sternthal & Tybout, 2001). The target audience analysis entails having potential audience members answer a series of questions, which planners choose depending on the potential participants (Lee & Owens, 2000; Smith & Ragan, 2005; Sternthal & Tybout, 2001).[7]

There are two common ways in which planners fail to understand the needs and characteristics of the audience in designing marketing plans: (1) they believe all learners are alike, and (2) they believe what appeals to them will appeal to learners (Smith & Ragan, 2005). When marketing plans are designed for "general learners" or according to what appeals to program planners (see Chapter Six), planners are less likely to reach their desired audience. A target analysis, which can be done in a number of ways, helps planners to better understand who their target audience is and how to reach them. One primary method for gathering these data is to use information collected at other points in the program planning process. Although often incomplete, these data are often readily available through previous efforts for identifying program ideas or preparing instructional and transfer of learning plans. The terms *market analysis, needs assessment,* and *target audience analysis* mean different things to different professions and industries, thus it is wise to clarify what a target analysis means and for whom the results are intended. When additional or all new information is required, program planners may use other existing databases, conduct interviews, do observations, have participants fill out assessment instruments, examine job descriptions, conduct surveys, or review texts and materials that pertain to the potential participants to collect the necessary information (Cervero & Wilson, 2006; Daffron & North, 2011; Hall & Hord, 2011; Kumar, 2004; Smith & Ragan, 2005).

One note of caution regarding using a target audience analysis to assess the characteristics and needs of the potential audience for education and training programs is that potential program participants and the program audience may or may not be one and the same. For example, in planning an educational program for entry-level managers, planners might assume that those entry-level managers are their prime audience. This assumption may be true, but there may be other possible audiences depending on the organization and setting. The impetus for that particular program may have come from upper-level management, and thus a dual audience may exist: the entry-level managers and upper-level managers. In this instance, upper-level management may in fact be the primary audience. Therefore, program planners may need to go beyond a target audience analysis (perhaps by conducting interviews with selected upper-level managers) in order to get a complete picture of their audience.

Completing a Contextual Analysis

Having a clear picture of the potential audience is not enough for program planners to develop solid marketing plans. The planner needs a sense of the people, organizational, and environmental contexts from which their potential participants or customers are drawn. Although a more complete description of each of these contextual elements and how to obtain information about them may already be known, the following questions are especially useful in preparing marketing plans.

- In addition to the potential participants, who else in the participants' public or private sphere might need "to be sold" on the value and worth of the program (e.g., supervisors, senior management, colleagues) (see Chapter Five)?

- For the people who have been identified, what types of promotional materials would most likely capture their attention? Would different copy or pictures make a difference in reaching this wider audience? How do these people usually find out about programs (e.g., online, print materials)?

- What organizational factors should be highlighted to attract potential participants into the program? For example, for organizations that are team-based, describing how the program is designed for teams of participants is a good marketing strategy.

- Are there wider environmental factors related to the program content that might influence potential participants to attend? If so, how could attention be drawn to these factors in the promotional materials?

- Is there a particular context or climate for the learning that has to be incorporated to ensure transfer of the information to practice? Have the discussions with the potential audience, the trainers, and the management been held about transfer of learning and if so, what information ought to go into the marketing materials and plan (see Chapter Nine)?

Much of this information gathered for the marketing plan discussed this far may have already been gathered through earlier efforts to discern the context (see Chapter Four). If programs have been previously planned for the same or similar organizations or groups of people, and if the environments in which programs are held or will be held remain relatively stable, there is even a greater chance that these data are available.

Considering the Competition

An important issue to consider at this point is the competition. An analysis of the competition may have already been completed for other purposes in the program planning process. If not, a SWOT analysis is a good tool to use to evaluate the **S**trengths, **W**eaknesses, **O**pportunities, and **T**hreats of an organization or program. When conducting a SWOT analysis, all factors affecting the organization or program, the internal as well as external factors, are analyzed, no matter if they are favorable or unfavorable. A SWOT analysis defines a desired end or objective and continues with an assessment of these factors (Daehn, 2005).[8]

For marketing planning purposes, it is critical to have the collected data from the SWOT analysis. These data are added to other information about the organization. When putting all the data and information together, program planners need to consider the following issues (DiAddezzio, 2012).

- Who else has presented this program; does most of the target market participate in this program or is there room for another program of this nature too?

- Where have similar programs been offered? Are the programs on this topic identified with the site (e.g., the Pediatrics Annual Conference is always held at a resort)? Does it matter where the program is held?

- Have the competing programs been successful from the participants' and sponsors' perspectives?

- Who are the big names in similar program types? Is this a short list, or does it need to be cut down to the top two or three? Would a big-name person consider participating in your program?

- What provider has "top of mind awareness" among your target audiences in this arena? For example, does the American Medical Association have the advantage in presenting a program on heart disease over your organization?

- Is the most important consideration that the program is unique, or is it essentially similar? If the answer to the latter is that the program is similar to others, would a particular program or speaker help to raise the status of the organization or program?

Find out everything possible about the competition for one reason only—so that your program can be different in an advantageous way. Straight up copying cannot prevail in what can be a very competitive environment. It may be possible to collaborate with the competition to check dates and topics that are presented in the same city or region to avoid duplication. Caution is advised when collaborating with the competition; ideas are often stolen and used by the competition.[9] A good example of what happens in a competitive market is seen in Scenario 13.1.

SCENARIO 13.1:   THE QUEEN MARY AND TUG BOAT ORGANIZATIONS

The director of a continuing professional education organization once advised his new assistant program director to attend meetings with other program directors who were in direct competition with the organization to "keep an eye on the competition." The new assistant director cheerfully attended the meetings month after month, kept a log of the competing programs and their dates, and faithfully reported them back to the director. The director waved off the importance of the information and told the new assistant program director that their organization was like a ship—he called it "The Queen Mary"—and these other competitors were like tug boats that sometimes glanced off the side of "The Queen Mary" organization but were not important enough competition to make a dent. The director ignored the information raised by the assistant director on competing dates and competing programs. After several "collisions" of the smaller "tug boat" organizations hosting programs on the same date or month as "The Queen Mary" organization, the assistant director began to worry about declining attendance at her programs and again brought the issue to the attention of the director. The director again waved off the competition as insignificant and said the declining program participation was due to other factors. The "tug boat" competitors of "The Queen Mary" organization were embolden by their successes and presented even more programs at a cheaper price, and at more convenient times than "The Queen Mary" organization. The audiences soon abandoned "The Queen Mary" organization for less expensive and more convenient programs. Within a year, "The Queen Mary" organization sank and the problem was blamed directly on the competition. Meanwhile the "tug boat" organizations that did pay attention to the problems of "The Queen Mary" organization moved into the same waters as a direct competitor.

Lesson learned? Even "The Queen Mary" type organizations have to study the competition and be aware of the strategies and activities of the "tug boats" circling around in the same waters.

Using Organization Branding

"When [organizations are] trying to be visible in multiple places and to communicate with participants, [other organizations, stakeholders, and the wider community] in various ways, it's easy to end up with a mishmash of ways [education and training programs are] represented, both in print and online" (Miller, 2010, p. 109). This mishmash of ways could result in mixed messages, inconsistent information, and a lack of consistent program or organization recognition across marketing outlets. Developing creative and positive "brands" or "images" that reflect the value of an organization and their programs and "all of the assets and capabilities that are linked to them" (McLeish, 2011, p. 209) is therefore an important aspect of any marketing strategy. When this strategy is used regularly it enhances the chances that organizations will attract more people to their programs. Having a "brand" that captures the attention of the various audiences that have been targeted by organizations allows these organizations to differentiate themselves from the pack and their competitors (McLeish, 2011).

"To be effective, [organizational] brands and branding [strategies have] to create value for [their] internal and external stakeholders" (McLeish, 2011, p. 209). McLeish also stresses that these brands should include one or more key attributes (see box).

- Through their branded images, organizations need "to educate or inform their supportive publics and constituents regarding their goals, objectives, and the role in the communities . . . in which" [they operate].
- Organizational brands are designed to build up the types of programs, and possibly other services, offered to garner favorable opinions about their work; in doing so, they differentiate themselves from others that have similar goals and offer comparable programs.
- Brands should reflect confidence in how organizations address the needs of their various audiences, ensuring that they use their funds and other resources well in addressing those needs.
- Brands of organizations should suggest that they are strategic, visionary, and willing to be long term in their orientation and principled in their pursuit of their goals.

Adapted with permission from McLeish, B. (2011). *Successful marketing strategies of nonprofit organizations* (2nd ed.). Hoboken, NJ: Wiley, p. 209.

Organizational brands consist of both graphic and narrative "that when used consistently ensure the [organizations] are "quickly recognized and understood by key audiences" (Miller, 2010, p. 109). It is critical, for example, to use the same logo and colors on all marketing materials and tools, as illustrated by Scenario 13.2.

SCENARIO 13.2:   UNPLEASANT SURPRISE

An external team was asked to examine the various materials and tools used for donor development, marketing, promoting their programs, and informing the general public about an organiza-tion. What they thought they primarily would find would be incon-sistent messages, text that had not been proofed, pictures that did not portray the essence of the organization's programs, and the like. Although they did find a number of problems related to these areas, what really surprised members of the team was that the logo for the organization was different in terms of color and even the type of lettering that was used. For example, the logo displayed on the web page was purple and pink, while in other places it was black and red. As a result the team recommended that the project's immediate task was to agree on the colors and typeface that would best represent their primary focus as well as attract the audiences they were trying to reach. Although they also suggested that these changes be made as soon as possible, they also counseled that those who would be doing this task be very thoughtful in this process, and that final selections of the "branding" or graphic be approved by the major stakeholders in the organization.

As this scenario attests, a process should be put in place to review these materials and tools on a regular basis.

Although the focus in this section is on organizational branding, this same process is also used for major projects or programs that are part of an organization. For example, a community college has just received a major grant from a foundation to initiate a multifaceted vocational training pro-gram that will involve a number of units and departments across campus as well as businesses and other types of organizations in the area. The tar-get audience is different from the majority of students enrolled in other programs on the campus, both credit and noncredit programs. In order to highlight this project, the foundation that provided the funding encour-aged the new project director to use a branding strategy to differentiate it from the other programs offered by the college; the administration readily supported this idea, as their hope was that the training programs offered through this funding would eventually become a part of the college's regular offerings.

Selecting and Developing the Messages

In selecting and developing marketing messages, whether these messages are in written, verbal, or visual form, make sure the messages are clear, concise, important, and framed in a way that convinces the various publics, such as past, current, and potential participants, partners, and other stakeholders, that the programs being offered are timely and worthwhile. These messages usually include logos, slogans, and other ways that express the brand of the organization. In ensuring that the messages being used in program or organization marketing fulfill these requirements, programmers need to:

- Listen and respond to the needs of their target audiences and other stakeholders.

- Keep the intended audiences' interests, experiences, backgrounds, and contexts in which they live and work at the forefront.

- Ensure that messages fit within the mission, goals, and values of the organization.

- Portray the message in a way that readers can understand the goals, objectives, and outcomes of programs, whether you are trying to reach just potential participants or multiple audiences.

- Make it easy for potential participants to register, and so on.

- Convince the target audiences that either they or others will learn and benefit from the program (e.g., obtain useful job skills, be better parents, spouses, or partners, lose weight), and be able to actually use what they learn (see Chapter Nine).

- Appeal to the target audiences' emotions as well as giving them the facts.

Useful resources related to selecting the message are: Miller (2010); Mitchell (1998); Simerly (1989b); and Winton and Hochstadt (2011).

The messages need to be eye-catching and capture the interest of the intended audience(s). No matter how these messages will be conveyed, in developing these kinds of messages planners need to choose the right words, phrases, and sentences that meet the criteria as stated above.

Handley and Chapman (2012), Miller (2010), Mitchell (1998), and Simerly (1989b) provide useful pointers for packaging messages into words.[10]

Developing a fact sheet before preparing the actual copy is helpful. The questions on the fact sheet are the same ones that program planners answer when preparing the actual program: who, what, when, where, why, and how.

In addition to the important program information that needs to be included in messages that are created, there are two specific kinds of written messages that planners use that can be powerful in conveying the benefits of attending the program to potential participants and other targeted audiences: (1) testimonials from past participants; and (2) storytelling. In testimonials, former participants convey the message that the programs they attended were both useful and worthwhile learning experiences (Handley & Chapman, 2012). Examples of these types of statements are as follows:

> "The skills that I learned as a result of attending this program have been invaluable in doing my job more effectively. I recommend it highly for all mid-level managers who are finding that their supervisors are expecting them to be able to use social media tools as a way to stay connected to their clients."

• • •

> "Attending this program has provided me with critical information, such as where I can find resources and services available in my area on caring for my elderly mother. This program proved invaluable to me, especially as a week after the program I found that I needed a home health nurse to assist with her care and knew exactly who to call for this service."

As can been seen in these examples, testimonials are brief and to the point, usually either a sentence or two.

Storytelling can also be brief, but stories often are longer, and can be very useful in some promotional materials and tools, such as newspaper articles and web sites. As Miller (2010) has observed: "one of the most effective yet underused . . . marketing techniques is storytelling" (p. 77). Miller goes on to add that storytelling usually adds a different dimension to the written message in that it allows planners "to use more emotion in sharing their messages" (Miller, 2010, p. 64). Storytelling not only assists in marketing current programs, but also in supporting the initiation and future marketing of new programs. Scenario 13.3 illustrates this point.

SCENARIO 13.3:   A STORY FROM THE HEART

"I'm very happy to be here. The journey is not all tears and sadness and actually being paralyzed is not that bad. People rush to help you and you don't always get this treatment when you're standing. I'm like Cleopatra who has men carry a lady up to her throne and when I was lifted up it was a beautiful sunny day and I enjoyed the moment. Even though it is frightening, God is great. You need silliness, a good sense of humor, and you need to communicate."

The whole audience was spellbound as Aida, a cancer survivor, told this story to other survivors, physicians, policymakers, and other health care providers at a cancer survivorship workshop hosted by a major education and resource center in Malaysia. As a nine-year survivor she has provided a number of services as a volunteer over the years, including serving as the coordinator of a breast cancer support group, visiting newly diagnosed patients in hospitals and their homes, and planning educational, spiritual, and other types of programs. Although Aida has been back in treatment a number of times over the past nine years, after each course of treatment she continued with her volunteer work until very recently. Aida made a special effort to attend the current workshop as the purpose was to initiate a new program for survivors, which would include such activities as support groups, and new policy initiatives.

There was no doubt that her story left everyone who attended with the sense that this new program would be a very important addition to the center's current offerings.

When using these written or oral messages to market programs, planners also use graphics or pictures of what will occur to attract participants. "Photography and graphics—both stills and video—can be incredibly powerful in conveying [these written and oral] messages" (Miller, 2010, p. 65).[11] What is important is that these images enhance any written or oral messages or, when used alone, clearly portray what the programs and activities are all about.

There are a number of sources from which program planners can obtain images that are appropriate to the messages they want to communicate. The best images are original photos, videos, and graphics that are produced by the planner's own organizational or program staff. However, if these are not available or prove too costly, there are stock photography and images that can easily be found online. Usually the use of these types of images are low cost, but program planners "must always be aware of the copyrights attached to [them], which determine what anyone other than the original creator can or cannot do with the [images] and under what terms" (Miller, 2010, p. 65). Miller also recommends getting into "the habit of taking photos [or making videos] all of the time . . . , using stock photography or photo-sharing sites to fill the gaps, and visual images in all of your communications offline and online" (p. 67).

Choosing Promotional Materials and Tools

Promotion, as described earlier in this chapter, involves developing materials and using tools aimed at generating or increasing enrollments for education and training programs. Even for participants in programs that are mandatory, at least some of information conveyed will show that the programs will be useful and of value. In general, if the promotional materials and tools are of poor quality or have targeted the wrong audience, the end result is "people just never heard about them [the programs] or did not realize how good they were" (Knowles, 1980, p. 176). There are myriad promotional materials and tools for planners to choose from, especially as planners move toward promoting their programs online. Planners choose carefully what materials and tools are most often used by their targeted audiences, and get the messages across in a way that encourages people to come to the programs and promotes those sponsoring the programs in a positive way.

Traditional Promotional Materials

The most often used "traditional" materials for promoting education and training programs for adults include such items as brochures, posters, and written publicity.[12] Many of these materials are not used as often as they were before the advent of online marketing. However, there are still situations where some of them are used as one of the major ways to promote specific kinds of programs. For example, in Malaysia, although both traditional and online promotional techniques are employed, program planners frequently use phone calls or text messages to encourage potential participants to attend programs. These calls or text messages take place usually after people have received information in other ways, but it appears they work very successfully in increasing program attendance. Perhaps one of the reasons is that the process of building relationships in program development as well as promotion fits well with the cultural ways of doing things in the Malaysian context. However, no matter how useful these traditional ways of promoting programs have been, the big explosion in marketing has been the use of online formats.

Online Promotional Tools

Since the mid-1990s, the Internet has played an increasingly important role in marketing efforts. In 2011, The Pew Research Center found that 78 percent of individuals over the age of 18 went online at least occasionally; and a third of these individuals regularly went online for no particular reason, just for fun, or to pass time (Rainie, 2011). The Internet has quickly become a means to reach and influence growing numbers of adults (Handley & Chapman, 2012).

The tactics and tools used for online marketing efforts vary considerably according to the resources available to planners and their organizations. Some organizations have sufficient funds to hire full-time staff devoted to online marketing efforts, whereas others include these tasks as a small part of one job. No matter how much time, money, and manpower are available to the organization, there are many options. The first place to start in the world of online marketing is by creating an online presence—a web site. Most organizations today have their own web site. But if the planner is creating a new program within a new organization, creating a web site is the first order of business. After that, planners may want to delve into the world of social media and explore the various forms of online personalized communication.

Creating and Using Web Sites

Web sites providing information about education and training programs and organizations are essential to begin marketing a program online. Web sites serve a similar function to the nearly obsolete yellow page ads—if the program cannot be found on the Internet, then it simply does not exist. Visually attractive web pages that provide descriptive information about organizations and programs can serve to recruit potential participants or volunteers and to advertise the program to fundraising organizations, partnering organizations, and clients.

There are many options available to create web sites—from simple and cheap to complex and sophisticated. Larger organizations with more staff and funds frequently hire an outside organization or create an internal department responsible for developing and maintaining a comprehensive web site. They may also hire an organization to develop a site using a content management system, allowing any individual to log in to the site to update content without needing to know any specific web development code. If numerous daily updates are not required, this option will likely be cheaper as development of the site is contracted out and maintenance is done by current employees when needed.

Smaller organizations with less time and funds may choose to create their own website using free or inexpensive applications available online. One site is www.web.com/WebBuilder. Sites like this one are designed to allow users to create and edit web sites similar to the way in which they would create and edit a Word document or PowerPoint presentation—and no knowledge of HTML is required. Google Sites is one such application that is free, easy to use, and does not display ads on the pages created. Although the majority of service providers give a URL address/domain name (e.g., www.myaddress.com/name-of-site), planners may also purchase a unique "domain name," such as www.Name-of-my-Site.com, from any one of a number of domain registrars. Some of these registrars, such as www.godaddy.com, also provide inexpensive hosting services to make it easy for the customer to manage everything in one place. In other words, planners can often buy a domain name such as www.Name-of-my-Site .com that goes directly to the site. This option is ideal for smaller organizations that have limited funds.

Quality web sites that are most helpful to users provide guidelines concerning structure, organization, and content. They are organized in a fashion that permits users to easily find information and pages through the main navigation categories as well as return to the main pages of the site once immersed in the site. Levinson, Adkins, and Forbes (2010) caution individuals to assume site visitors will not read a web site in a linear fashion, but they will instead jump around the site in random ways. They encourage site designers to use "breadcrumb" navigation links on each page (e.g., Home ➢ About Us ➢ History) and to provide an overall navigation system that helps visitors to stay focused on the message of the site.[13]

Once organizations or programs establish their web sites, it is important to maintain the sites. The most essential component of site maintenance is keeping the content up to date. Outside of this task, there are a few additional things organizations or programs can continually do to make sure their sites are visited and are useful to their desired audience.

There are many tools and applications which can help planners stay in touch with their audience and make sure they are meeting their audiences' needs. "Google Analytics" is a free application that provides information about how many people visit a site, which pages they visit, how long they stay on the site, and more. This information can help organizations determine which pages or programs are frequently viewed, and they can then make decisions about which programs to keep and which programs might need to be altered or promoted in a different manner. Organizations can also include forms on a web page or create a pop-up box which displays such facts as the number of visits to the site and time spent on the site, for use by the organization, or prompts for users for feedback, to sign up for a newsletter, or for any other information desired by users. This information can help to better understand visitors' backgrounds, improve the site or programs, and to form a more personal and regular connection with visitors. It is good to occasionally use such tools to help assess whether or not an organization is reaching its desired audience.

There are also tools that can help to further promote traffic to web sites. Search engine optimization (SEO) is currently very popular and involves a host of tactics that help a web site to show higher search results. For more information about this topic, please refer to Grappone and Couzin (2011), Kent (2010), Jones (2010), or current, reliable web site services.

Organizations may also invest in online ads. There are two different kinds of ads; "pay-per-click" ads are charged only when someone clicks on the link displayed, and "pay-per-view" ads are charged each time the ad is displayed. Program planners "can set a maximum amount of money to spend on ads so that this does not exceed whatever amount that has been budgeted" (Mirchandani, 2005, p. 36). Social media is another means by which to direct traffic to a site. Social media involves promoting sites, organizations, and programs through alternative online means, such as Facebook, blogs, or Twitter. This approach to marketing is discussed in greater depth in the next section.

Utilizing Social Media for Promotion

Social media is a rapidly growing method of communicating with people and organizations about ideas, plans, and beliefs. In May 2011, 66 percent of Internet users (18 years of age and above) said they use social networking sites like MySpace, Facebook, or LinkedIn (Smith, 2011). These social media outlets are becoming a place to meet, organize, promote, and plan actions and events surrounding business, policy issues, social justice concerns, and educational initiatives. Social media has been successfully used to help an individual with leukemia find the one-in-twenty-thousand chance of a matching bone marrow donor, to create a movement begun by a former nightclub promoter to bring clean water to 800,000 people, and to assist two students beginning a fashion business for men to break even and actually profit after their first year in business (Aaker, Smith, & Adler, 2010). Program planners use social media tools so that they can better reach and communicate with their target audience; if they do not currently use these tools, they need to learn to harness the benefits they have brought to marketing education and training programs.

Effectively utilizing social media requires a planned and strategic attack. Program planners critically think about who they want to reach, how much time and resources they can devote to social media, and what they would like to accomplish (Miller, 2010). It can be easy to get "lost" in social media, and thus planners set specific time limits and goals. Although there are many potential social media outlets, planners focus on a few that they believe will be most useful to their organization in reaching their desired audience and accomplishing their goals; in this way they will effectively utilize a few key sources instead of spreading themselves too thin (Mansfield, 2012). "The era of 'winging' it in social media is over. Supporters and donors now expect well-executed, integrated social media campaigns" (Mansfield, 2012, p. 54). See Exhibit 13.1 for examples of the most commonly used social media tools.

There are many more social media tools available. For more information about these additional tools or more in-depth information about the tools presented in Exhibit 13.1, please refer to Handley and Chapman (2012), Mansfield (2012), Levinson et al. (2010), Mathos and Norman (2012), and Orsburn (2012). There are also many free applications online (e.g., www .hootsuite.com or http://dlvr.it/) that can help program planners manage multiple social media tools in one location, allowing them to control a few days of tweets or status updates at one time, update multiple social media tools with the same information, and even analyze user traffic.

Personalized Communications and Staying Connected

The Internet also provides the means by which program planners engage in more personalized and timely communications with a larger audience. Online newsletters, event reminders, and personalized thank-you notes can be sent via e-mail to build and maintain quality relationships at a low cost. Questions and concerns can be received and addressed in a timely manner, conveying the idea to interested parties that organizations are responsive and caring. However, it is important to remember not to abuse the privilege of e-mail. Individuals are inclined to ignore frequent e-mails from the same sources and may even mark them as spam, effectively cutting off future communication. Thus organizations must always walk the fine line between informative, personalized communications and overcommunication. It is best to err on the side of caution and send fewer e-mails if possible. It is also good practice to add links at the bottom of mass e-mails, such as newsletters and event reminders, that allow the users to be removed

EXHIBIT 13.1

Commonly Used Social Media Tools

Site	Description	Examples of Common Use
Facebook	A social networking tool where individuals create profiles, upload pictures, add friends, like pages, comment on other people's walls and photos, and oversee all of their network's interactions.	*Facebook Pages.* Planners create a Facebook page for their organizations that serve as their Facebook portals. These pages convey information about their organizations, notify followers who have linked to their page of updates, allow them to invite people to events, and provide an interface for discussions and exchanges. *Causes.* Planners use the Facebook applications to help raise funds for their organizations or programs.
Twitter	A micro-blogging tool to carry on conversations and send updates in 140 characters or less.	*Make Connections.* Program planners follow other organizations and professionals in the field to begin to build professional networks and gain important resources. Staff from these other organizations are likely to follow you back. Planners also comment on their tweets and converse to promote their organizations and issues. *Tweet.* Planners post information about upcoming events, organizational successes, and relevant issues. Tweets can occur during programs when attendees comment to each other; these communications can lead to rich interactions.
YouTube	A video-sharing web site that allows users to create accounts, upload videos, and share them with others online through links or embedding them in web pages. Users can comment on videos and post video responses.	*Broadcast Events.* Videos or picture slideshows of organizations' events or media releases can be uploaded and shared to help demonstrate the organizations' missions, goals, and actions. *Favorite Channel.* Even if organizations do not have original videos to upload, they can post other "favorite" videos related to their mission or goals to build channels and create a YouTube presence.

Site	Description	Examples of Common Use
Flickr	A photo-sharing web site that allows users to create accounts, upload photos to albums online, and share them with other users on the Web. Viewers can also comment on photos and albums.	*Catalog Events.* Photos of organizational events and projects can be taken and posted to help demonstrate the organizations' missions, goals, and actions. *Raise Awareness.* A picture can often convey an idea better than words. Photos capturing issues relevant to organizations can be posted to raise awareness.
LinkedIn	A professional networking web site in which users create profiles which function as online résumés. Employers can connect with qualified candidates looking for jobs.	*Company Pages.* These pages serve as company web sites on LinkedIn, providing information about these companies and the people that work there. According to LinkedIn, Company Pages "reveal the human side of these organizations." *LinkedIn Groups.* Smaller networks that individuals can create or join. Organizations can create their own groups to discuss relevant topics or actively participate in other group discussions.
Blog	Web sites created by individuals containing posts or entries displayed in chronological order. They commonly allow readers to provide comments or feedback which are posted at the bottom of the entry.	*Awareness Blogs.* Through a blog and all of their subsequent posts, planners can relate to a specific issue to promote awareness around a topic. *Organization Blogs.* These blogs can provide information about upcoming events for organizations, display pictures, and present relevant news pertaining to the organization's goals and mission.
Webinars	Interactive web-based seminars individuals use to listen, learn, and interact with specific messages (e.g., videos, spoken word, PowerPoint slides).	*Inform and Educate.* Videos or live lectures and discussions can be uploaded and shared with any interested parties. *Collaborate and Brainstorm.* Webinars can be interactive and promote discussion. This interface can be used as a portal for focused debate and discussion on topics among colleagues—known and unknown.

from future mailings. These kind of links help ensure that users feel in control of their level of participation with the organizations from whom they are receiving these e-mails.

Throughout all of the organization's online marketing efforts, it is important to stay connected. Organizations should not completely contract these online marketing tasks out or assign them only to younger staff members more experienced with the Internet and social media but less familiar with organizational missions and goals. Levinson et al. (2010, p. 185), for example, caution planners to "beware of yielding all control of [their websites] to technical support (IT) people; these people rarely understand marketing. Numerous . . . organizations are hamstrung with pointless websites run by people who know all about the latest software and programming tricks but have no clue about marketing." These actions may also promote a disconnect between the organizational or program goals and the online marketing priorities, as individuals making decisions about the organization and program will be less familiar with the realities of online marketing.

Funding and Keeping Track of Marketing Campaigns

Prior to implementing marketing campaigns it is essential that program planners know the costs and ensure they have the resources to meet them. Questions planners consider in implementing a marketing campaign are shown in the following box.

- What financial resources are required?
- Where will these resources come from?
- What staffing resources are required?
- Do the current staff members have the skills and time?
- Is there a need to hire consultants or, for some organizations, find volunteers who can assist?
- What elements of the plan will be scaled back first if adequate resources are not available?

Adapted with permission from Miller, K. L. (2010). *The nonprofit marketing guide: High-impact, low-cost ways to build support for your good causes.* San Francisco: Jossey-Bass, p. 17.

Answering these questions when beginning to put together marketing campaigns saves program planners the potential embarrassment of going over budget prior to programs even starting. In addition, it is very helpful for planners to keep track of the important aspects of marketing campaigns to ensure that all bases are covered: knowing that the right audiences have been chosen; the promotional materials and tools have been selected wisely; the time schedule for getting the message out is workable; and a record is made of the proposed plans and the costs.[14]

Chapter Highlights

Organizing marketing campaigns is a key component of the planning process and, depending on the nature of the organization or program, inadequate marketing can be disastrous. Because programs are usually expected to either break even or make a profit or surplus, knowing how to develop and use high-quality marketing materials and tools within a well-planned marketing scheme is essential for success. In addition, with increased competition for education and training programs for adults in many sectors, program participation is often voluntary, and funds are limited for participants to attend these programs. Therefore, it is vital for program planners to pay attention to this administrative responsibility throughout the planning process. The following tasks are central to developing and managing marketing campaigns:

- As one of the starting places for the marketing campaign, conduct a target audience analysis to help determine the background and experiences of the potential audience.

- Use already existing contextual information or complete a contextual analysis to help frame the marketing campaign.

- Choose tactics that will assist in achieving a competitive edge with other organizations who serve a similar population, or are located in the same geographic area, and that either have or could develop comparable programs.

- Utilize or develop a well-designed "brand" that reflects the value of organizations and their programs and "all of the assets and capabilities that are linked to them" (McLeish, 2011, p. 209) as a way to capture the attention of the various targeted audiences.

- Select or develop marketing messages, whether they are written, oral, or visual, that are clear, concise, important, and framed in such a way that convinces their various publics that the programs being offered are timely and worthwhile.

- Choose promotional materials and tools that are most often used by the targeted audiences and get the messages across in a way that encourages people to come to the programs and promotes those sponsoring the programs in a positive way (e.g., brochures, posters, web sites, Facebook, LinkedIn, and Twitter).

• Implement a lively marketing campaign, paying careful attention to the target audiences, types of promotional materials and tools to use, target times for when these tools and materials will be used, and campaign costs.

In summary, this chapter demonstrates the importance of a successful marketing campaign. As noted, one of the things that is essential in developing the marketing message and choosing the promotional tools is that the details, such as where and when the education and training program will be held, the cost of the program, and how to register, need to be clear to potential participants. These details are just a few of the many details that program planners must address, which is the focus of the next chapter.

Notes for Additional Online Resources

1. See Scenario 13.A: The Challenging World of Marketing.

2. See Figure 13.A: The Four Ps of Marketing.

3. See Scenario 13.B: How to Attract the Residents?

4. See Scenario 13.C: To Market or Not to Market, That Is the Question.

5. See Scenario 13.D: Face-to-Face or Online Program?

6. See Exhibit 13.A: Elements of a Marketing Plan.

7. See Exhibit 13.B: Questions for Target Audience Analysis.

8. See Exhibit 13.C: Examples of Factors Reviewed in a SWOT Analysis.

9. See Exhibit 13.D: Tactics for Achieving Competitive Advantage for suggested tactics for achieving a competitive advantage for organizations (McLeish, 2011).

10. See Exhibit 13.E: Pointers for Packing Messages into Words.

11. See Exhibit 13.F: Examples of Images Often Used for Marketing.

12. See Exhibit 13.G: Examples of Promotional Materials and Ways to Use Them for a more complete list, description, and ways these materials are used (DeWitt, 2011; Havercamp, 1998; Miller, 2010; Simerly & Associates, 1989).

13. See Exhibit 13.H: Qualities of Good Web Sites for a more comprehensive list of qualities of good web sites (Levinson, Adkins, & Forbes, 2010; Mirchandani, 2005).

14. See Exhibit 13.I: Sample Marketing Campaign Plans for a sample of a simple form to assist planners to keep track of these details for two specific programs.

15. Also see Exercise 13.A: Conducting a Target Audience Analysis and Exercise 13.B: Keeping a Record of a Marketing Campaign to ensure that all bases are covered.

 Application Exercises

This chapter's Application Exercises address the marketing of education and training programs. The first exercise is designed to help you choose promotional materials and tools, and the second is an exercise in evaluating the qualities of a web site of your choice (see web site).[15]

EXERCISE 13.1

Choosing Promotional Materials and Tools

1. Choose promotional materials or tools, using Exhibits 13.G (see web site) and 13.9, that are appropriate for the audiences described in the following situations and give reasons why you would choose these materials and tools.

Planning Situation	Appropriate Promotional Materials or Tools	Reasons for Choosing
Ann is planning an event to raise funds for the homeless shelter in her local community. She is volunteering her time and the shelter has no extra funds to market the event.		
Boyd has a group of tutors who are teaching basic skills for adults of the Nooksack Tribe. It will soon be summer and many of the tutors are college students who leave for the summer. Boyd needs to recruit 20 tutors for the summer.		
Emma is offering classes on preparing nutritious meals made from native grasses and berries for women in Swaziland.		
Jean is expanding her master's program in adult education to a distance-learning program and wants to reach a whole new market, perhaps international students, but certainly those who live outside of driving distance to her university.		

2. Discuss your responses with one or two other program planners or interested parties in terms of whether one or more of your choices are appropriate or not, and what other materials and tools might also work.

EXERCISE 13.2

Evaluating the Qualities of a Good Web Site

1. Evaluate your own education and training organization's or program's web site, or another site you are familiar with, and evaluate the features that are provided in this exercise (use Exhibit 13.H for descriptions of each of the features (see web site)).

2. Using this same chart, evaluate a web site for an education or training program or organization that you are unfamiliar with, again using the features provided. Please note that if the first web site you evaluated was of high quality, choose one that is not well put together or, if the first one needed a number of improvements, evaluate one that you judge to be of higher quality.

Feature	Qualities	Analysis of Those Qualities
URL	Short and memorable.	
Website Name	Conveys organization name or program mission. Short to medium length. Large and at the top of each page.	
Navigation	Clear and consistent.	
Design, Color Scheme, Etc.	Readable font. Consistent with print materials.	
Content	Up-to-date. Precise and direct. Provides contact information. Includes date last updated.	

3. Discuss your evaluation with one or two other program planners or interested parties, after they have evaluated the same sites, in terms of the similarities and differences in your evaluations.

Chapter 14
Details, Details, Details

PAYING ATTENTION TO the many logistical details that program planners must address, whether the programs are face-to-face, in cyberspace, or a combination, is an essential component of planning programs. There is nothing more frustrating to participants and presenters than discovering that some of the program logistics have been overlooked and the program isn't running smoothly. Being detail-oriented is what separates good planners from those who should find another vocation—the good planners focus on the "details, details, and more details!" Unfortunately, there is no end to stories where planning has gone terribly wrong because of planners' failure to take care of details, as illustrated by Scenarios 14.1 and 14.2.[1]

 SCENARIO 14.1: IGNORING THE SCHEDULE OF EVENTS

The program participants are beginning to get restless. According to the schedule, this session should have finished over fifteen minutes ago. A number of people have already walked out of the session, while new arrivals looking for their next session keep opening and closing the door. Still, Julie, who is the presenter, goes on and on, seemingly oblivious to the time. Finally someone who has just entered the room—Jim, who is the next presenter—tries in a very diplomatic way to let Julie know that his session is scheduled in this room next. Julie's response to this interruption is to tell him to wait his turn because she still has some important material to cover.

 SCENARIO 14.2: THE SOGGY POTATO CHIP THEORY

Iris is new to conference planning and wants to learn as much as she can about the previous conference, conducted a year ago for the same eight hundred people she serves, Adult Basic Education (ABE), General Education Diploma (GED), and Teachers of English as a Second Language (TESOL) directors and teachers. She visits programs across her territory to ask some of these people about the previous conference. She hears time after time that the conference was "terrible" and they hope she does a better planning job. When asked for details, people say the speakers were good, the hotel was great, and other elements of the conference were given good ratings. Why then did so many complain about the conference? "Soggy potato chips!" She finally gets the answer! The Saturday luncheon speaker went overtime by thirty minutes and the staff put the tuna salad into the refrigerator, with the potato chips on the same plate! "Soggy potato chips!" Iris decides right then and there to never serve potato chips at conferences she plans.

How could such things as long-winded speakers and soggy potato chips ruin a program? Very easily! These are a few of the many logistical details of education and training programs that program planners must tackle and handle before they become problems. These types of logistical problems arise whether the program is a single event of a half day or less (e.g., a workshop), one with multiple sessions for a number of days (e.g., a conference), or a program that is conducted over a longer period time (e.g., a continuing education course offered by a university or literacy classes for adults). No matter the kind of program, one of the hallmarks of top-notch planners who have the responsibility for logistics is a detail-oriented disposition and the ability to keep track of numerous tasks in a timely manner. The larger the program, the more important it is to spend the time and effort before, during, and after the program to make sure it runs as smoothly as possible.

In this chapter we first address choosing dates and sites that work for education and training programs for both the participants and the sponsors of these programs. Next we look at the importance of obtaining suitable program facilities, and explore negotiating contracts for locations that charge for the use of space. The chapter concludes with a discussion of special issues that relate specifically to one type of program, that of managing conferences.

Choosing Dates and Locations

All educational and training event planning starts in the same way, with three tasks to complete: choosing the date, the location, and planning the budget for the program (see Chapter Twelve for details on budgeting). There are no shortcuts in making decisions about these tasks and until they are set, the program does not move forward.

Program history and organizational history can provide invaluable information to assist in setting a date for an educational event. Previous program planners, advisory committees, or other individuals working with the organization may be consulted as a resource for this information. Data to collect that help in selecting the date are:

- Prior choices of dates (e.g., particular months, days of the week, daytime or evening)

- Reasons why these dates have been chosen before

- Participants' expectations about spending a smaller amount of time on their learning or spending a weekend at the site to attend meetings

- The educational program's traditional ties to family or personal vacation times

- Traditional connection with holidays

- Dates to avoid due to religious holidays, local, or countrywide holidays

It is never a good idea to start off a new program with a bold departure from tradition; thus, the dates and location selected should follow previous customs and expectations. If the program being planned is a new program or the group planning the program is new, the planner can gain information about participant expectations and customs from similar groups or groups in the same location and same profession. The dates for the program or event should be nearly set before program planners look for a site to present the program.

In choosing the venue for an event, as with selecting the dates, program planners consult past traditions of the group. Where have they previously met for educational programs? Again, data can be gathered from previous program planners, advisory committees, or other individuals working with the organization to help the planner reach a decision agreeable to all.[2]

Though there can be some flexibility, novice program planners ought to be wary of securing a space during a time no one else wants it or when the space is offered at a significantly reduced price, a discount likely driven by lack of other bids (e.g., Labor Day weekend in the United States, Hanukkah, Boxing Day in Canada, Christmas, or Eid holiday in a Muslim country).

Investigating and Obtaining Suitable Facilities

Program planners must also face a series of choices when determining the actual facilities to use for a program. The only way planners may avoid this task is when they hold their programs primarily within their own facilities (e.g., programs for adults sponsored by colleges and universities, professional organizations, and training centers). However, the majority of planners will still have to make decisions at some point in their career about where programs may be held off site. Even those who plan distance-learning programs may need to reserve physical facilities to offer speakers or participants a place to use equipment. Whether programs are delivered face-to-face or via distance learning, learners need to feel comfortable in the chosen facilities, which should also allow for the different formats, equipment, and techniques that program planners intend to use (see Chapters Eight and Eleven).

Investigating Facilities

There are five types of facilities commonly used for face-to-face or online education and training activities for groups of people: in-house organizational facilities, hotel facilities, conference and retreat centers, college and university facilities, and public buildings (e.g., community centers and libraries). Each type has advantages and disadvantages, depending on the goals and objectives of the educational event, the instructional techniques to be used, the participants, the program presenters and facilitators, the cost, the accessibility, and the type of services the facility provides (Allen, 2009; Munson, 1992). For example, for an organization's three-hour workshop for in-house personnel, the organization's seminar room is probably the best choice. If that same workshop is offered to people from a wide geographic area, however, a central meeting place in a local hotel or community college may work better.

If outside facilities are used, such as conference centers and hotels, program planners must check them out thoroughly. A checklist for selecting facilities can help program planners with this task (see Exercise 14.1) (Allen, 2009; Hartwig, 2000).[3] Depending on the kind of program that is being held, planners may use all or only parts of this checklist to ensure all is in order.

In investigating facilities, three other areas are important: choosing meeting rooms, estimating costs, and negotiating contracts. Chapter Twelve contains a sample worksheet for budgeting expenses for facilities as well as other items. This cost estimation is completed prior to negotiating any contract with the rental facilities. Negotiating contracts is discussed in a later section of this chapter.

Choosing Suitable Meeting Rooms

Different learning activities require different types of meeting rooms and seating arrangements—from large auditoriums and fixed chairs to small seminar rooms and movable chairs. For example, instructors who foster group interaction and team building do not want a huge room with chairs arranged in rows or fixed seats, preventing participants from seeing each other. They prefer chairs placed around tables or in circles in rooms that are appropriate for the number of participants. Such room arrangements provide much better learning environments for these kinds of activities. In addition, some kinds of learning activities require special facilities, such as space for prototype machinery or equipment.

In choosing meeting rooms, the planner has to consider a number of details (Cohen, Rogelberg, Allen, & Luong, 2011; Leach, Rogelberg, Warr, & Burnfield, 2009; MacKeracher, 2004). Attendees expect the seats to be comfortable, to be able to hear the speaker, and to not be distracted by physical factors such as heat, cold, dim lighting, smells, and sounds from outside the room. In addition, instructors, facilitators, and coordinators must present, communicate, and handle the program logistics to ensure optimum productivity.[4]

Program planners may have meeting room requirements that cannot be met by the facility available to them. For example, they may have to use the space available in their organization even though it is not the best environment for learning. In situations like these, it is important to think how the available space can be used to its best advantage. If the lighting is poor, can extra lights be obtained for the session? If the placement of outlets is inconvenient, are extension cords available and can they be placed so that people are not tripping over them? If the room is too warm, could quiet fans be used to cool it down? Could more comfortable chairs be borrowed from another room just for this session? If speakers require Wi-Fi connections, a computer, projector, and screen, can they be placed in the room and is the Wi-Fi connection reliable?

Arranging Meeting Rooms

The following question is often asked of program planners, "How do you want the meeting rooms arranged?" Sometimes, planners provide detailed drawings or names of the requested room arrangement to those setting up the facilities; at other times, they stumble in trying to describe the room setup and produce a quickly scribbled picture on a napkin or other scrap of paper. A lack of knowledge of language to describe meeting room arrangements reveals a novice program planner. This lack of detail or uncertainty could lead others to treat the planner as a newcomer to program planning and indirectly decrease their negotiating power. Experienced program planners usually know the names of the room arrangement to give to whoever is setting up the space. Smaller meeting rooms may be desired to foster greater interaction between and among participants.[5]

By giving the standard room arrangement names such as *classroom style, theater style, U-shape,* and *fan shape,* most people who arrange the room will understand the arrangement desired. They will ask if there is a need for a "head table" for speakers. They will also want to know if risers are needed to lift the head table up for all to see and if podiums are needed, on the riser or off to one side. The next question will be about the number of chairs to have at the head table and then the types of microphones desired and AV setup for the head table. Program planners know these requirements before meeting with those responsible for the room arrangements. For larger programs room arrangements are made well in advance and then checked a few weeks before the program and again the day of the program.

Arranging for Instructional Equipment

In arranging facilities, program planners know whether the necessary instructional equipment (commonly called Audio Visual or AV Equipment) is available at whatever facility the program is to be held. This equipment is likely to be screens, computers, projectors, video players, special microphones, camera, televisions, and a way to connect to Wi-Fi. Some groups may require outlets to hook up laptops for the attendees. For education and training programs held at the host organization, this checking usually only involves scheduling the equipment, but equipment may also have to be borrowed or leased if the host organization does not own what is required. Sometimes an outside facility allows an organization to bring its own AV equipment, but this has to be approved in advance. If planning a multiday program, the organization needs to arrange with the facility where the program is located for a secure, locked room to keep its equipment for the second day. Equipment is expensive and can easily be stolen when rooms are empty during breaks or meals. If necessary, be sure to include any AV rental in the budget (see Chapter Twelve). In addition, some programs presenters need to bring their own equipment, which in most cases is a laptop computer.

Whether planners are arranging for in-house or rental equipment, several considerations must be taken into account: Will the equipment be in good working order on the day of the program? Are there proper cords, and compatible mobile equipment? Will the equipment be available at the times requested? If several sessions are presented at the same time and they need the same equipment, is there enough to cover all sessions? Who will be responsible for setting up and checking the equipment prior to presentation times? Are these people knowledgeable in troubleshooting technical problems or do they really not know the equipment that well and cannot figure out how to make it work? Presenters expect that if equipment does not work that there is someone either in the room or close by to help them. Problems with any type of AV equipment can ruin a speaker's presentation and the experience for the attendees. It is a good idea to have an assigned staff member or volunteer to coordinate the handling of all of the AV equipment set-ups and to be available throughout the program to address all potential AV problems. In some locations there are actually in-house staff members that ensure all of the equipment is in working order throughout the program. It is good practice to ask these questions of the facility representative to make sure these details are in order, and to check again early in the day, before the program begins.

Negotiating Contracts for Rental Facilities

Negotiating contracts for rental facilities is another important task that program planners manage in finalizing arrangements for facilities for education and training programs. However, there are also spaces, as mentioned in the previous sections, where this task is not needed, such as in-house facilities, libraries, and community centers. Scenario 14.3 illustrates the need for giving careful attention to selecting a facility.

 SCENARIO 14.3:   A RETREAT IN THE WOODS

Deb needed a facility to hold a retreat for thirty judges for a weekend. She wanted to hold the retreat in the northeastern part of the United States where most of the judges lived and so it could easily be reached by car, train, or a short plane ride. However, Deb was frustrated by the costs for hotels in the Northeastern corridor. Most of them offered reduced government rates, for which the judges qualified, but the government rates were still beyond her budget. She mentioned this to the chair of her board who worked as general counsel for a prominent company. He was able to arrange use of their company retreat at a much better rate per person. Not only did the rate cover the room, but meals were also included. He assured Deb the facility was a favorite of his company employees and it was also in a beautiful wooded setting. Deb looked at photos online of the facility and decided that if the chair/general counsel and his fellow employees went to the retreat site, it would be perfect

for the judges. Deb broke her own rule about always visiting a
site before booking it for a meeting and handled all negotiations
for the contract over the phone. She had another program planner start the meeting with the judges and arrived on the second
day. As soon as she arrived, everyone started complaining to her
at once. The facility was in a beautiful setting, but the rooms were
shared with baths down the hall, the facility was very stark and
labyrinthine, and everyone, including Deb, got lost each time they
left their rooms. The judges spent most of the weekend complaining to her about the facility instead of working on the program set
for them.

As with "soggy potato chips," the facility choice can make or break a
program. The first part of this chapter has discussed the locality, the setting, the meeting rooms, the arrangement of the rooms, and the needs of
the participants. Even handling all of these details still does not assure the
site is a good fit without a close on-site inspection and a face-to-face discussion with the sales staff. Meeting planners today may have to depend
upon someone else to assure them the facility fits the group and may need
to negotiate the rental contract by phone. But if it is at all possible, the
program planner ought to visit the facility and sit with the sales staff to
negotiate the rental contract.

The Negotiation Process
Negotiating with the rental facility takes a certain amount of skill and
knowledge of the information required by the sales staff and caterer.
Program planners should enter the negotiation process armed with the
required information, the confidence to negotiate skillfully, and the ability
to make decisions about the contract. If planners are not experienced in
negotiating with a rental facility, they should find a planner to help with
negotiations and learn how it is done.[6]

Program planners think through carefully each of the steps as they
move through this negotiation process. They pay attention to the details,
gather the necessary information from the facility staff, and are aware of
the goals and objectives of the facility staff they are working with, so they
will not be misled.

Facility Contracts Are Legally Binding
Novice program planners have been known to think facility contracts can
be negotiated after they are signed if they find they will not have as many

attendees as planned or if the event needs to be cancelled. Nothing could be further from the truth. These documents should never be taken lightly. These contracts are legal documents that if abused can cost an organization a great deal of money. Facility contracts are as sound as a contract to buy a house. In addition, these contracts are fairly standardized documents that have been honed through decades of business dealings. Program planners and sales and catering staff all expect things to go well and the program to go forward, but things happen and a solid contract can support and protect the facility or the program planners.

The first and very important segment to examine in any facility contract is the cancellation clause because things happen and sometimes cancellations are needed. The cancellation clause in facility contracts are written to protect the facility, but also to help organizations to scale down their obligation to the facility if the conditions in the contract cannot be met. Cancellation clauses have strict deadlines and if the need for the facility has changed, within the deadline, the organization can cancel the contract with no penalties or, in some cases, with lesser penalties.

Facilities set a request for a monetary deposit to hold the property for a designated date. The deposit is expected when the facility contract is signed, and the amount is determined by the facility based on a percentage of the income they expect to make on the business under contract. The larger the business, the bigger the required deposit. If facilities did not have this request for a contract and a deposit, anyone could walk into their facility and arrange to use the facility and not have to meet the obligation.

A Checklist for a Facility Contract

Program planners do not sign contracts without legal advice and without checking these contracts several times for the following items:

- Desired meeting dates are stated
- Number and size of meeting rooms are agreed upon
- Correct number of overnight rooms are secured for the accurate dates
- Complimentary rooms for so many overnight rooms are listed
- Deposit requirements are outlined and dates for payment stipulated
- Cancellation clauses are stated and penalties are given for cutting room numbers with dates; sliding scales are spelled out
- Liabilities are clearly articulated

- Schedules of events are listed with meals, breaks, receptions, and special events

- All costs, gratuities, and taxes are identified and fixed

- Conditions that might trigger price increases are clear; rates can be guaranteed for one year, possibly more, and this needs to be stated in the contract or the facilities can raise them without notice

- Master accounts and direct billing are arranged

- Agreements on late fees and charges are complete

- Mediation is agreed upon for disputes

Facility staff members, especially their sales directors and caterers, want to help program planners be successful with the event booked in their facilities. Novice program planners or instructors teaching program planning can ask the sales director and caterer from the local area to sit with them to explain the details of negotiating facility contracts. Staff members are usually very happy to provide this service to encourage future business. All information provided in this subsection can be points of discussion with program staff members as well as points of discussion with facility staff while touring the facility.

The negotiating of contracts with outside facilities is especially important for an organization if planning for large groups, such as conferences. Details in planning conferences multiply as conference size increases. The next section guides program planners in actually managing a conference before, during, and after the event.

Managing Education and Training Programs

All program planners, no matter what their program's venue, number of participants, or format, need to handle the logistics involved in managing education and training programs. In programs with a large number of participants, such as two- or three-day conferences or overseas educational travel trips, handling these details is usually shared among a number of people. However, for program events that are one day or less, planners may or may not have assistance tackling details, and some even have to deal with everything by themselves. This section explores the many kinds of details that program planners have to take care of through the example of planning large conferences.

Most personnel who coordinate education and training programs agree that carrying out a conference is very hectic. Juggling many unknown details can be a "nightmare," as shown in Scenario 14.4.

SCENARIO 14.4: THE NIGHTMARE

It is several nights before the opening of the Standing Conference on University Teaching and Research (SCUTREA) international conference in Cambridge, Great Britain, and Mary Ellen, who is an experienced program planner, had a nightmare that seemed quite real. It was the day of the conference and one problem after another occurred in her dream as the conference unfolded. Mary Ellen serves as the president of SCUTREA and as part of that role she is responsible for planning and managing the annual conference, a conference primarily planned and staffed by volunteers. When she arrives at her office the next morning, she busily checks all the last-minute program arrangements for the three-day conference. The conference is being held at the university, with some registrants staying in the dorm rooms and others scattered in three hotels surrounding the university campus. It is the first time Mary Ellen has used these campus facilities, so she has double-checked all the dorm room arrangements, the menus, and AV equipment orders. Mary Ellen had several volunteers from higher education institutions in London meet with her the day before in Cambridge to review the plans for the conference. They met with the catering director, Susan, at the campus, to make sure all was in order there. They had lunch in one of the hotels and met with Peter, the catering director for the hotel, to check a dinner to be held there. Mary Ellen recalled some of her bad dream as they went over the details and double-checked everything again. One of Mary Ellen's worries concerns a potential rail strike that is scheduled later in the week. She calls the office of transportation but cannot get any good information on the strike. She discusses this issue with the volunteers planning the conference and comes up with a contingency plan to get the attendees to the airport by bus after the conference ends. The luncheon meeting included generating problems that each person feels may happen, followed by a group discussion to outline another set of contingency plans to handle each problem. Mary Ellen returned home that evening and slept much better. She believes that her team is ready for just about anything that will happen at the conference.

Conferences are often planned by volunteers such as Mary Ellen and her team (Holmgren, 2011). As illustrated in the scenario, even as a volunteer

Mary Ellen was expected to oversee all arrangements and to work primarily with a group of volunteers. Using volunteers to manage conferences sounds like a good idea, but in reality, it can be a nightmare and more than one conference has been ruined by the volunteers who meant well but were consumed by all the details. Other organizations, such as corporate training centers, professional organizations, and university continuing education units, have professional staff members, internal or external, who serve as the conference planners and managers.

Although some organizations may have guidelines to plan "the annual conference," most do not. Instead, they assume that whoever manages the conference will know what to do. The first and perhaps most important job for conference managers or designated program planners is to figure out what are the behind-the-scenes tasks that go into making a conference successful and the time needed to handle these tasks (Holmgren, 2011). Usually conference managers establish a number of groups to handle these tasks, each of which is charged with handling myriad details related to specific areas. These tasks include marketing; technology and products; hospitality and special events; program and assessment; and administration and housing.[7]

Most conferences are at least two to three days in length, so the details for the planning process multiply by the number of days. Conferences, except perhaps one-day events, always include overnight rooms for participants and facilities for the meeting (e.g., small and medium-size rooms for breakout sessions, large spaces for keynote speakers and social functions, such as conference-wide receptions); thus, they have to be planned well in advance to ensure that all of the arrangements for the conference are made in a timely manner. A two-day conference where participants spend one or two nights in town usually requires program planners to have at least one year in advance to set up the planning process, secure the dates, and book the hotel or conference site. For each additional day of the conference, planners can usually add another six months of preparation. Therefore, a three-day conference is best planned a year and a half in advance. The time needed to plan a conference is also affected by the number of people who are expected to attend the conference. The larger the conference, the more time it will take for the planning. To have less time for planning usually means that details are often overlooked, forgotten, or deemed unimportant. Time is especially important for programs that are managed by volunteers.

A time line of tasks for a conference that is completed by program planners, staff, or committee members is provided in Exhibit 14.1.

EXHIBIT 14.1

Conference Planning Time Line

This time line is a list of all tasks to be completed in the preparation of a conference or program, in approximately six months. The time frames suggested may be altered to conform to particular institutional experiences or specific program needs. Those responsible for the planning process complete the tasks by a date listed and check off the task when completed. Tasks and lead time requirements vary depending on the size of the conference and the capability of those completing the task.

Task	Time Period	Date to Be Completed	Completed
1. Develop budget	6 months		
2. Submit budget for approval	6 months		
3. Select hotel or site	6 months		
4. Meet with site staff to give specifications	6 months		
5. Sign contracts with site	6 months		
6. Prepare program proposal for sponsors	6 months		
7. Issue general press release	6 months		
8. Contact VIPs and send letter of invitation	5 months		
9. Draft and refine brochure or flyer; set up web site	5 months		
10. Compile final list for mail/e-mail	5 months		
11. Meet with advisory group; decide on speakers, topics, and moderators	4 months		
12. Complete brochure/flyer and get any printing estimates	4 months		
13. Hold second meeting and confirm all speakers and moderators	3 months		
14. Develop marketing plan; carry out	3 months		
15. Record all disbursements; keep records	3 months		
16. Write more detailed press release	3 months		
17. Review room arrangements with site	3 months		
18. Confirm the program schedule and meeting rooms with site	3 months		
19. Mail/e-mail brochure or flyer; post on web	8 weeks		
20. Request biographies from speakers	6 weeks		
21. Arrange for speakers' rooms and travel requirements	6 weeks		
22. Compile and copy handout material; prepare the CD	6 weeks		
23. Arrange audiovisual (AV) equipment for all sites	6 weeks		

24. Post notices in social media sites	5 weeks
25. Hire or find a volunteer photographer	4 weeks
26. Arrange for press room at conference	4 weeks
27. Send list of attendees to speakers	3 weeks
28. Send detailed press release to media and conferees; post on web site	3 weeks
29. Send final confirmation letter to speakers and have conference call or meeting	3 weeks
30. Assemble registration materials and packets	2 weeks
31. Make name cards for moderators and speakers	2 weeks
32. Prepare and copy roster of attendees and speakers	2 weeks
33. Assign registration staff	2 weeks
34. Print name badges	2 weeks
35. Contact appropriate committees regarding speakers' travel arrangements	2 weeks
36. Confirm AV equipment and special items, including directional signs	2 weeks
37. Print alphabetical list of attendees	1 week
38. Arrange news conference	1 week
39. Check hotel site	Day before conference
40. Check hotel registrations and arrangements	Day before conference
41. Pick up speakers on arrival at airport	Day before conference
42. Arrange dinner or breakfast meeting for speakers and key committee chairs	Day before conference
43. Arrange to get speakers to conference	Conference day
44. Staff the registration desk	Conference day
45. Check meeting room setups and AV equipment	Conference day
46. Keep track of number of registrants; greet speakers	Conference day
47. Provide secretarial services as needed	Conference day
48. Approve and sign all bills; be available at registration desk	Conference day
49. Hold news conference	Conference day
50. Send thank-you letters	2 weeks after
51. Finish conference proceedings and mail/post on web	Post-conference
52. Pay all bills; close books	Post-conference
53. Evaluate and issue post-conference releases	Post-conference

This time line can be adjusted according to the unexpected complexity of completing a task or tasks. In addition, the time line should be revisited on a regular basis to make sure none of the tasks are overlooked.

Managing Volunteer Conference Committees

One of the real secrets of success with planning a conference with volunteers is to make sure each volunteer knows exactly what they are to do, the limits of their duties, and when to notify the conference manager with problems (Holmgren, 2011). Problems can easily arise if the volunteers are not carefully supervised or, in the case of experienced volunteers, they assume too much responsibility.[8]

All volunteers try to do a good job in conference planning or they would not volunteer in the first place. Unfortunately, not all volunteers are good planners and can get into difficulties. The chair of the conference planning can be successful if there are periodic meetings held with the volunteers, the expectations of the roles for each volunteer are written down and given to the volunteer, committee responsibilities are made very clear, and time lines are established and checked periodically. All of the materials in this chapter can help a conference chair manage a group of volunteers and their committees.

Provided in the following subsections are examples of problems that might occur before, during, or after conferences and offer sample solutions to those problems, all of which relate to the details of conference management. The illustrations provided are not unusual, whether conference managers are volunteers or paid staff. It is important for conference managers to think about potential problems ahead of time and have solutions ready in case problems arise and need to be addressed immediately.

Handling Details Before the Conference

Displayed in Exhibit 14.2 are possible problems and sample solutions that night happen before the conference actually begins.

Many of these problems may seem daunting when they first occur, but can be corrected to ensure that the "the show will go on."

Handling Details During the Conference

There are many more details that can be challenging during the actual conference as shown in Exhibit 14.3. Program planners can anticipate some of these challenges and prepare the staff for them just in case; others might be a surprise, but either situation does not mean the conference will fail. Program planners can have contingency plans for many of these details.

EXHIBIT 14.2

Examples of Problems and Solutions That Might Occur Before the Conference

Problems	Solutions
The press releases go out too late to have the program covered by the media.	Create media announcements by calling key people who can contact people to welcome them to the conference.
The brochures are sent out and did not include the date.	Start making calls to target key people and sending out e-mails to the same group.
	Make a big, bright, splashy announcement of the date.
The keynote speaker's name has been misspelled on all the publicity materials; the wrong first name was used; the keynote speaker's name was not included.	Follow the same plan as explained above but start by calling the keynote speaker (call, do not e-mail) and apologize!
There are not enough registrants to make the program a go.	Check the budget to see what can be cut and what will still cost money.
	Try to redeem travel money: work with the rental facility to cancel overnight rooms.
	Cancel everything else that is possible to cancel.
	Move forward with a slimmed-down program at a lower cost and invite those who would not have been able to attend due to the cost, such as government workers or graduate students.
The keynote speaker cancels the day before the program.	Change the order of the speakers to fill the keynote address.
	Ask the keynote if either he can recommend someone else to give his presentation or if he can send his material so that someone else familiar with the material can give his keynote. Or see if one of his staff members who is working with the conference staff and actually prepared his presentation can give the speech, which sometimes is the case.
An emergency has occurred right before the program and affects attendance.	Start contacting people who are registered to see if they are still coming to the program.
	Determine your loss of attendees and either go ahead with a smaller group or reschedule.
The hotel renovations are not complete and the other hotels in the city are booked for a big conference.	Go to the facility manager and see what can be done to accommodate the group.
	Look for other sites rather than hotels for your event.
	Keep in mind that this situation would not have happened if the planner had kept in touch with the hotel staff.
The hotel lets go of your room block earlier than you planned and there are not enough rooms for your program attendees. This situation is not unusual if the hotel was able to sell these rooms to another group.	Notify your potential participants the rate has gone up; offer good room rates at other hotels close by.

EXHIBIT 14.3

Examples of Problems and Solutions That Might Occur During the Conference

Problems	Solutions
The sound system goes out while one of the keynote speakers is presenting, and you have several hundred people in attendance.	Stop the program, move to the podium with a handheld mike, apologize, hand the mike to the speaker, and then move back to the AV manager/coordinator to find out how long the situation will last.
	Have the AV operators get more handheld mikes for the presenters.
The meeting rooms are too big or too small; too hot or too cold.	Call the facility contact person (at a hotel, this will be the caterer; in another facility this will be the person the planner has worked with during the planning process) and get the situation corrected.
	Do not approach the person emptying the trash or delivering the food—they cannot help you. Go to the top person for faster service.
One of the presenters is locked out of the meeting room.	Follow the solution to the second problem and wait unless there is someone in the area with a room key.
	Know where the house phones are and carry a cell phone at all times.
The printer sends too few program agendas and instructional materials.	Hold the materials back and initially do not give them to anyone but the speakers if there is a significant amount missing.
	Put the agenda on computer screens or Smart Boards, or project the agenda on the screen in each room until the session starts, and then pull up again when the speaker ends.
	Find a place as soon as possible that can print up or duplicate a simple agenda, which includes at least the name of the presentation and the presenters, the times, and the rooms where sessions will be held.
	Reprint those instructional materials that are a "must" for presenters to have for their sessions.
	E-mail or put on the conference web site the full set of instructional materials to all participants immediately after the program is over, with a note apologizing.
All the speakers show but there are very few attendees.	Put several speakers in one room for a panel presentation, even if their topics are not similar, and move participants to those rooms.
	Have a list on the doors of who the speakers are so the attendees can make a choice.

Problems	Solutions
Some workshop presenters do not have any attendees in their sessions.	Check each conference session to look for this problem once the sessions have started (have staff do this task).
	Ask participants in overcrowded rooms if some attendees will move to hear the other presenters with little or no attendees.
	Ask those presenters who had an overflow crowd if they can repeat their session at another time, then make the announcement and move the speaker without a crowd into a room with another speaker and ask them to share the time.
Presenters find themselves in a room with a divider that is not soundproof and participants can hear the presenter and whatever is going on in the next room (e.g., the speaker's presentation, the laughter of the audience, and video clips given as part of the presentation).	Call the contact person in charge of the facility and request that one of the groups be moved immediately.
	Cancel the session and offer it at another time during the conference and make sure attendees are aware of this change.
	Make a note that for future conferences that conference managers must complete inspections of the site up front, including all of the meeting spaces, so that this situation will not happen again.
The bagels donated for breakfast are frozen.	An ingenious program planner started up his truck and thawed the bagels on the hood of the truck! (Believe it or not, this solution, which actually happened, worked and the participants were never aware.)

Although this list could go on indefinitely, and strange things do happen, prepared conference managers may be able to handle each of these problems and still have a successful conference. As illustrated by the opening scenario, one of the ways to prevent panic among paid staff or volunteers helping with the conference is to prepare them for these unexpected events by discussing the possibilities ahead of time and having a plan of how to move forward to make the changes needed. The frozen bagel story makes a good point and gets a laugh, but it also helps to convey the importance of being creative in attending to even the most unexpected details.

In one conference, for example, graduate students in adult education who planned and managed a regional conference took great pride spending many hours outside of class coming up with creative ideas that added value to the conference. In thinking ahead about even the "smallest details" prior to conference, the students ensured there would be as few problems as possible during the conference, and in the end their efforts added value to the conference for both presenters and speakers. A sampling of these details is provided below.

- Keynote speakers were given the VIP suites at the hotel and had a basket of fruit waiting. The fruit was a welcome treat, as some of the speakers had arrived after a long plane trip.

- A student was assigned to host the keynote speaker, which included taking her to the hotel when her shuttle from the airport arrived, helping her set up before the presentation, getting a sandwich and snack before the presentation, and setting up the PowerPoint presentation in the meeting room.

- Students also hosted various presenters by picking them up from the airport or the shuttle and taking them to the hotel, sitting with them at the banquet table, and inviting other students, alumni, and guests to join them for meals.

- Students planned local recreational and cultural events, such as a boat trip into the islands located in the bay with a meal featuring local food and a historian to answer questions—and they even arranged for the boat to pause as the sun was setting so everyone could enjoy the beautiful sight.

- Students collected flowers from gardens, locally grown apples, pumpkins, and other decorations and special treats for room decorations and "goodie bags" for the attendees.

- Students and alumni drove attendees to their favorite local restaurants for dinner and to the conference site for a keynote speech and reception, and then delivered the attendees back to their hotel rooms.

There are many other "small touches" that make a conference enjoyable and memorable, but the main purpose of all of these details is to ensure a positive experience and to make the participants and the presenters feel at home and welcome.

Handling Details After the Conference

There are some details that can be problems after a conference is complete, but again, these can be anticipated and may be prevented. Examples of such problems and solutions are shown in Exhibit 14.4.

Most of the problems listed here should not be a surprise; program managers who are aware and involved in the conference should expect and be prepared for such issues. For each of these problems, further discussion might resolve the problems. It is possible that the hotel bill is incorrect and can be changed. You might want to have a discussion with some of the speakers to see what the problems have been, but it will not help to be defensive and argue. It is never a good idea to give money back to participants unless they have a very good reason. In one particular program, the hotel hot water

EXHIBIT 14.4

Examples of Problems and Solutions That Might Occur After the Conference

Problems	Solutions
The hotel bill is much larger than you expect.	Go immediately to the main office of the facility and request to see the caterer or facility manager. Always go back to the person you worked with in person because the accountants will not provide the answers you need.
	Ask this facility manager to come with you to see the accountant as she will not discuss this issue unless the facility manager is there.
	Be aware that there could be a few added charges, but there should not be any big surprises unless mistakes were made by either conference managers or planners who misunderstood the charges to be made; answers lie somewhere in the billing process.
The major speaker was not happy because the technical arrangements were disruptive to his session (e.g., the session did not start on time, the sound system was poor, the person in charge of ensuring the AV equipment was working properly did not know how to do her job).	Avoid this problem by making sure that all of the possible technical problems are taken care of prior to the session.
	Seek out the speaker immediately after the session and apologize profusely.
	Provide the speaker with a time elsewhere at the event when she can hold a discussion session for interested participants who would like to get a better idea of the major messages she was delivering.
	Be aware that no matter what is done that this speaker may contact the organization's executive director and complain anyway; come up with ideas for how to response to the speaker's frustration.
Problems surfaced during the program that could be traced back to either the facility staff or to the conference manager.	Have an "exit" meeting with the caterer or facility manager and start this meeting by complimenting him and his staff on the good services that were provided and noting how pleased the attendees were.
	Discuss issues that arose during the conference and how they were handled; ask whether the facility has a plan to remedy these problems in the future (e.g., the poor service of the wait staff at the banquet or the lack of a timely response to meeting room issues).
Several registrants complain about the poor quality of the program and want their money back.	If at all possible, avoid refunding registration fees and instead provide them with something that might "keep them happy," like a gift coupon to cover registration fees for the next conference.
	Apologize and keep in mind that at least some of the issues these registrants noted might not have arisen if they had been thought through prior to the conference (e.g., if planners had carefully screened keynote speakers, asked for copies of other presenters' materials so they could provide feedback if the materials were of poor quality).
	Walk around during the program and talk with participants and if complaints are voiced, remedy them immediately, where possible.

(Continued)

EXHIBIT 14.4 (*Continued*)

Problems	Solutions
Program evaluations are not good.	Review the evaluation results carefully and challenge those issues for which you have contradictory data (such as comments made during the conference that present a different point of view) and put these in writing.
	Use the results as a learning tool and think about how to make the conference better the next time; focus on making improvements.
Funding agencies are expecting a full report on the conference and reports received from the evaluators were negative in tone.	Be truthful about the evaluation but begin with the positive points and then list the problems encountered and what was done to handle the problems.
	If you disagree with the evaluations have counterpoints ready; ask others to help in developing these responses.
	List the problems at the end of the report and suggest solutions to make the next program much better.

heater went out after midnight and all registrants woke up to face cold showers. The hotel sales director appeared at the first session and assured everyone they would get the problem fixed and they subtracted the first night's charge from everyone's bill. No one had further complaints. However, if the problems listed here could not be addressed when they occur, program managers need to address them immediately after the program.

No matter how tired program planners, conference managers, and staff members are at the end of a conference, they cannot simply walk out the door of the conference site and not finish up the work. The following tasks are the minimum of what should be done:

- Go through facilities and where necessary put meeting rooms and other spaces back in order.

- Pick up and store extra materials (e.g. handouts, conference programs, and proceedings).

- Make sure any equipment and other types of resources brought to the site (e.g., banners, brochures related to future conferences) are accounted for and returned or stored properly.

- Give tips to facility staff who were particularly helpful and ask for their names so you can write letters commending them, which takes very little time but can mean a raise or promotion for them.

- Stop by the facilities sales staff or catering office or even the front desk and compliment workers on a good job and thank them for their help; even if there were problems, you can usually assume everyone involved in the facility tried their best to make the program successful.

Once program planners are back at the office, there are a few more things to attend to:

- Complete all administrative forms

- Reconcile and pay bills

- Conduct a staff debriefing

- Write letters of appreciation to presenters and other resource people, including notes to the hotel or conference site personnel

- Jot down suggestions for program improvements

- Read evaluations and compile the data

- Make reports to funding agencies and other organizational sponsors

As noted in the introduction to this section, no matter the venue, number of participants, or format chosen, all program planners attend to the details of managing education and training programs. This handling of details may appear trivial to novice planners, but they quickly learn— most often as a result of a failed program—that paying close attention to logistics is well worth the time. There are also program planners who are just not good at this kind of detail work. These planners need to realize that the only way they will be successful as program planners is to make sure they have people to work with who are willing and good at detail work (e.g., administrative assistants, another colleague, or trained volunteers).

 # Chapter Highlights

Handling the logistical end of the program often feels like a thankless task; yet if these chores are not done well they can negatively affect all aspects of education and training programs. One of the hallmarks of program planners who handle these types of arrangements is a thorough understanding of the importance of organizing and paying attention to the countless details that continually pop up throughout the program planning process. Eight specific tasks complete this component:

- Be aware of the challenges that may come into play when juggling all of the program details.

- Choose dates and locations that work.

- Investigate and obtain suitable facilities.

- Negotiate, when needed, contracts for rental facilities.

- Ensure all program logistics are addressed (e.g., a time line is in place for what details need to be done, where and by whom, and confirm that each of these details has been completed).

- Make sure all necessary staff, whether paid or volunteer, are in place to assist in managing the program details so that they will be handled well (e.g., registration, room setups, AV equipment, evaluations).

- Know how to work well with each of the individuals or committees who assist in taking care of program details.

- Anticipate any problems that might arise before, during, and after the program and have possible solutions in mind if any of them do occur; discuss these plans with those who are assisting with the program details.

This chapter on taking care of program details completes the discussion of each of the eleven components of the Interactive Model of Program Planning. In the final chapter, a review is provided of the Interactive Model and its key components and tasks, along with a brief glimpse at what program planning may look like in the future.

Notes for Additional Online Resources

1. See also Scenario 14.A: Workshop Woes and 14.B: Can You Hear Me?

2. See Exhibit 14.A: Examples of Data That Can Assist with Choosing Dates and Locations.

3. See Exhibit 14.B: Checklist for Selecting Facilities.

4. See Exhibit 14.C: Paying Attention to Meeting Room Details for a list of important details that planners check when arranging for meeting room space.

5. Figure 14.A: Layouts for Setting Up Meeting Rooms shows there are many room arrangements that can be used, depending on the size of the room, and how the program is to be presented.

6. See Exhibit 14.D: The Negotiation Process for a Rental Agreement for a Facility.

7. See Exhibit 14.E: Organization of Task Groups.

8. See also Scenario 14.C: The Fight; Scenario 14.D: Missing in Action; and Scenario 14.E: The Big Registration Mistake.

 Application Exercises

The first two application exercises assist you in selecting program facilities and meeting rooms. The third exercise allows you to reflect on program arrangements that were made at a recent event that you either planned or attended. The fourth exercise focuses on how to handle problems before, during, and after the education or training programs.

EXERCISE 14.1

Selecting Program Facilities

1. Choose a program you are currently planning or work with someone who is currently planning a program. Using the following checklist, visit at least one possible program facility and evaluate its suitability for the program being planned.

Checklist for Selecting Facilities

Availability of program dates

_____   1st choice   _____

_____   2nd choice   _____

_____   Other   _____

Location

_____   Good transportation access (plane, car,   _____
ground transportation)

_____   Participant appeal   _____

_____   Safe and secure (lighting, security staff)   _____

_____   Ease of parking   _____

_____   Affordable for the program budget and/or   _____
for participants

Meeting rooms: General sessions, breakout rooms, social and entertainment areas (see Exhibit 14.B for a description of each of these features; see web site)

_____   Size   _____

_____   Appearance   _____

_____   Lighting   _____

_____   Decor   _____

_____   Furnishings   _____

_____   Ventilation, heating, and cooling   _____

_____   Sound projection   _____

_____   Electrical outlets   _____

_____   Wi-Fi connection   _____

Support services (at same or different facility from where the program will be held)

_____   On-site meals (catered by same or   _____
different group)

_____   Accommodations   _____

_____   Restaurants   _____

_____   Recreation, fitness facilities   _____

(Continued)

_____   Phones, Wi-Fi access   _____

_____   Business center   _____

_____   Equipment services   _____

On-site transportation (frequency, convenience, cost)

_____   Public   _____

_____   Private   _____

Accessibility requirements under Americans with Disabilities Act (ADA)

_____   Accessible parking spaces   _____

_____   Ramps, lifts   _____

_____   Elevators   _____

_____   Accessible sleeping rooms   _____

_____   Accessible public restrooms   _____

_____   Doorway and corridor width for wheelchairs   _____

_____   Floor surfaces smooth and firm   _____

_____   Lowered public telephones   _____

_____   Telecommunications device for deaf (TDD),   _____
              readable signs with large lettering, Braille, or
              raised symbols

_____   Sufficient lighting in rooms and corridors   _____

_____   Emergency warnings in multiple delivery methods   _____

General factors

_____   Attractions and entertainment in area   _____

_____   Experience in hosting educational programs   _____

_____   Site personnel   _____

_____   Safety issues   _____

_____   Medical and emergency services   _____

2.   Discuss your evaluation with others involved in this program planning process, or other colleagues who are program planners.

EXERCISE 14.2

Choosing Meeting Rooms

1. No meeting room is perfect. Knowing that, choose from the chart your top seven requirements for a room that is adequate for the education or training program you described in Exercise 14.1. (See Exhibits 14.B and 14.C for descriptions of each item; see web site.)

_____ The room has barrier-free access.

_____ The room is a good size for the number of participants.

_____ The room structure, if possible, is square.

_____ Window placements and views are not distracting to participants, or there are no windows.

_____ The chairs are comfortable with good back support, and there is adequate work space available for every participant and instructor.

_____ The color of the room is cheerful.

_____ The room is clean and well maintained.

_____ The floors are tastefully carpeted.

_____ The lighting is good.

_____ There are no sources of glare in the room.

_____ The temperature of the room can be controlled.

_____ There is good air circulation.

_____ There is no background noise that might distract participants.

_____ The acoustics of the room are good and if movable doors separate the next room, there are no sound problems.

_____ There are plenty of electrical outlets spaced adequately around the room.

_____ There is a Wi-Fi connection.

_____ AV equipment is provided or can easily be used in the room.

_____ The room is close to restrooms, vending machines, and other needed conveniences.

_____ The furniture can be arranged according to specifications.

2. Compare with two or three others what you checked. Discuss first your areas of difference and then those that were similar. Examine what factors you think entered into the decisions that you each made.

EXERCISE 14.3

Overseeing the Program Arrangements

1.   Describe an education or training program you recently attended or coordinated.

_____

_____

_____

_____

2.   Using the following chart, reflect on this program you described in item 1, critiquing the program arrangements that were made. Write "NA" (not applicable) next to those items for which program arrangements were not needed.

Categories of Items	What Was Good About the Arrangements	What Problems Were There with the Arrangements?	How Could the Arrangements Have Been Improved?
Meeting Rooms			
Meals, Breaks, and Social Functions			
Sleep Accommodations			
ADA Requirements Met			
Roles of Instructors and Program Staff			
Equipment			
Materials			
Transportation			
Program Schedule			
On-Site Registration			
Message and Information Center			
Other (Please Specify)			

EXERCISE 14.4

Handing Problems Before, During, and After Programs

1. Briefly describe a program planning situation you are currently or have been involved in planning.

_____

_____

_____

_____

2. Related to this planning situation, using the chart provided, complete option either 2a or 2b related to the details planners handle in planning education and training programs.

2a. List a sampling of the problems you anticipate encountering before, during, and after the program and solutions you could use to handle these problems.

_____

_____

_____

2b. List a sampling of the problems you had to take care of before, during, and after the program and solutions used to handle these problems.

_____

_____

_____

Examples of Problems and Solutions

Examples	Solutions
Before	
During	
After	

3. Discuss your responses with others involved in this program planning process, or other colleagues who are program planners.

Chapter 15

Revisiting the Model and Looking to the Future

SWIMMING IN THE ocean—yes, it's a lot like planning programs for adults. Sometimes planners are swimming with the sharks, at other times with the dolphins. Swimming with either sharks or dolphins has challenges and surprises, some that fit their images and others that do not. For example, although sharks may appear scary, they are often quite harmless and may even offer swimmers protection. In other cases they are "deadly" and literally out to get whoever crosses their path. So, too, is it with dolphins: they often frolic with swimmers near the beach, but at other times beckon swimmers to travel with them to deeper and sometimes dangerous waters.

Although swimming or just playing in the ocean is fun, there also are times when even the most ardent water lovers just want to lie on the beach, and relax or perhaps read. They are soothed by the lapping waves and warmed by the sun. Beach lovers also like to walk along the surf and find interesting items that wash up on shore. They are excited when they come across colorful shells, crabs darting here and there, or see schools of fish that just happen by. So, too, is it with program planners. They also need to get out of the water, no matter how calm or rough, take time to listen to and feel what is around them, and discover new things, no matter how small, about their practice as planners and the environments in which they work. The authors hope that this book has presented an opportunity for those new to program planning, as well as those more experienced, to be on the beach, taking the opportunity to reflect on their practice, reinforce or gain new knowledge and skills, and refine or try out these ideas and skills.

In revisiting the Interactive Model of Program Planning, we first highlight how the model has changed since its first introduction in 1994, and the major factors that make this model a useful and viable resource for practitioners with varied backgrounds, experiences, and fields. We next describe the major tasks that make up each component of the Interactive Model, followed with a brief overview of how technology has made a major impact

FIGURE 15.1

Interactive Model of Program Planning Figures: 1994 and 2002

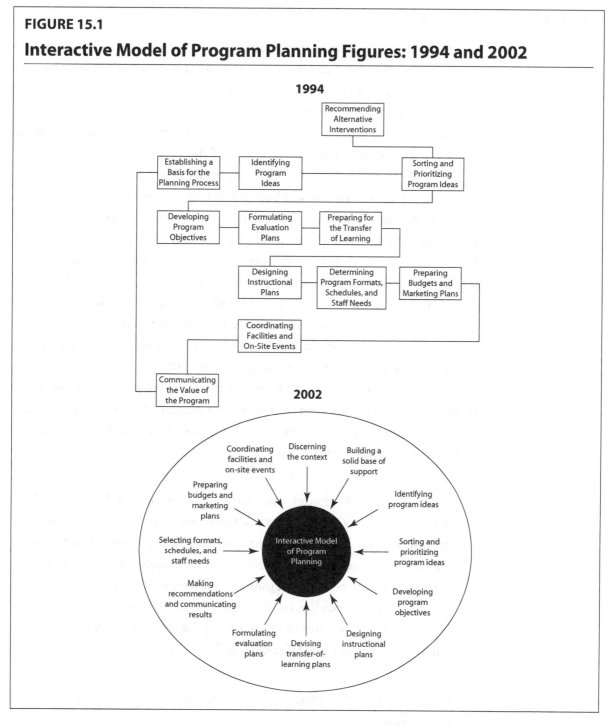

on how planners develop and implement programs. We then offer a snap-shot of what the future might hold for program planners, related to three specific areas: ways of planning; how technology will influence the plan-ning and administration of education and training; and global changes. We conclude the chapter with a brief personal reflection on the writing of this third edition of *Planning Programs for Adult Learners: A Practical Guide.*

Revisiting the Model

Over the years, the Interactive Model of Program Planning has provided a practical description of the types of activities and tasks that planners engage in during the process of planning and implementing education and training programs for adults. In studying and comparing each iteration of the model over the last nineteen years, the difficulty of creating a visual representation of the interactive nature of the process becomes apparent. In the first edition in 1994, the figure was displayed in a linear form (see Figure 15.1), and only the text belied the more interactive characteristics of the process: "Many experienced program planners have found [that] planning programs is not a step-by-step process" (Caffarella, 1994, p. 17). In addition, although the word "interactive" was in the title of the model, an initial definition of the word never appeared. Rather, the model stressed that program planners work "with a number of planning components and tasks at the same time and not necessarily in any standard order" (p. 17).

The 2002 rendition of the model, also shown in Figure 15.1, looked very different. It was pictured in a circular form with each component of the model located inside of the circle and with arrows all pointed to the center of the circle, which contained "Interactive Model of Program Planning." The word "interactive" was the major emphasis in the introduction of the model as illustrated by the text:

> What makes this model interactive is that first it has no real beginning or ending. Rather, persons responsible for planning programs for adults are encouraged to use the relevant parts of the model in any order and combination based on the program planning situation . . . [What planners] have found is the interactive nature of the model actually mirrors how they practice, and therefore confirmed [for many of them] that they actually do know what they are doing. (Caffarella, 2002, p. 22)

In this edition, the image of the model again looks very different, as shown in Figure 15.2.

Rather than have each component of the model displayed as separate, nine of the components are now linked together, representing the parts of the model that address specifically what program planners do in building the learning experiences that will make up the program—context, support, needs assessment, goals and objectives, instruction, learning transfer, and evaluation. As with the 2002 model, planners use those components that

FIGURE 15.2

The Interactive Model of Program Planning

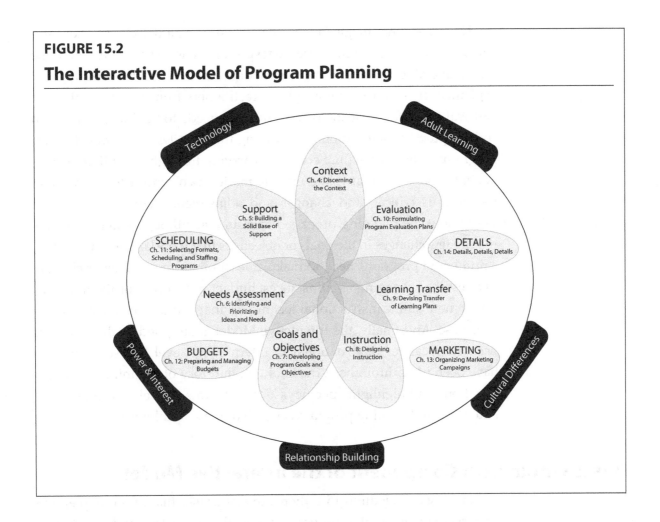

need to be addressed in this part of the planning process, and again in no particular order. They may find all of these components are applicable, or only a few, depending the particular planning situation. For example, in initiating a new program, planners often find that they need to take into account all the components. However, when offering a similar program, but to a very different audience in a new location, planners need to examine the context, the needs of potential participants, and learning transfer. The other four components—scheduling, budgets, marketing, and details—are focused on the "administrative" aspects of program planning. Thus, in actuality, planners are educators and administrators, both roles that are important in ensuring that education and training programs are of value and successful. Depicted also in this figure are the five areas of foundational knowledge—adult learning, cultural differences, power and interests, relationship building, and technology—that are especially important for program planners to understand when designing and carrying through training and educational programs.

There are three major factors that make this model useful and valuable for practitioners with varied backgrounds and experiences. First, the Interactive Model is one of the few models that is research-based, and yet explained in such a way that gives practitioners from a variety of fields and walks of life a realistic picture of what needs to be done, along with specific practical suggestions for tackling the countless tasks they face for programs to be successful. Second, in carrying through the different components and tasks that make up this model, two central tenets are that flexibility is critical, and changes and adjustments will often be made throughout the planning process. For example, although some programs require few changes in the goals or objectives that were laid out in advance, a number of programs need to make at least minor or even major changes as a result of changing circumstances, budget reductions, or the introduction of new online instructional techniques that could reach a larger audience base. And finally, the Interactive Model is designed so that it can be used at a local, regional, national, or international level. The scenarios that have been used throughout the book tell the story of planning in real-life situations and highlight specific issues and strategies related to planning education and training programs at each of these four levels.

Tasks Within Each Component of the Interactive Model

As can be seen in Exhibit 15.1, there are many tasks that program planners undertake to ensure that programs are well put together and lead to successful outcomes for all parties involved—program participants, organizational sponsors, and other stakeholders.

Some of these tasks have been changed or deleted since they appeared in the second edition; however most have remained relatively similar. What has changed are the options for how program planners carry out these tasks, which have greatly expanded, primarily through the use of technology. Many program planning tasks take place online and all types of programs are offered on the Web (e.g., international conferences, degrees from colleges and universities targeting adults who are returning to school, and professional and continuing education programs and updates). The Internet has become a major source for gathering information about the program context, funding sources that are available, and competing educational organizations and programs. In addition, online resources are available for conducting needs assessment and program evaluations, and there are tools that allow participants to complete these assessments online. E-mail, web sites, and social media also serve to further complement more

EXHIBIT 15.1

A Checklist for Planning Programs

Discerning the Context

❑ Become knowledgeable about the human, organizational, and wider environmental contextual facets that affect decisions made throughout the planning process.

❑ Know and be able to access sources of information about the context of the planning situation.

❑ Be well informed about the issue of power that is present in most planning situations and the influences that power relationships have in the planning process.

❑ Cultivate or enhance negotiation skills required to navigate situations in which power is a central issue.

Building a Solid Base of Support

❑ Ensure support from key constituent groups including current and potential participants, all levels of organizational personnel, and other stakeholders through such mechanisms as participating in planning and conducting education and training activities, supporting transfer of learning strategies, and serving on advisory committees or legally constituted boards.

❑ Cultivate continuous organizational support by establishing appropriate structural mechanisms, the choice of which depends primarily on the centrality of the education or training function.

❑ Promote an organizational culture in which continuous learning and education and training programs for all staff are valued.

❑ Obtain and maintain support from the wider community through formal and ad hoc groups and boards, with key underlying assumptions that ideas and observations from members are heard and used, democratic planning is fostered, and collaborative interaction is the operative norm.

❑ Build and sustain collaborative partnerships with other organizations and groups that provide different vehicles for program planning and delivery that are in the best interests of all involved parties.

❑ Connect to people, build relationships, and lead groups to support all aspects of the planning process through a variety of online tools.

Identifying and Prioritizing Ideas and Needs

❑ Decide what sources to use in identifying needs and ideas for education and training programs.

❑ Generate ideas through a variety of techniques.

❑ Be aware that structured needs assessments are not the only way to identify ideas and needs for education and training programs.

❑ Ensure that a structured needs assessment is warranted, and choose or develop a model for conducting this assessment that is appropriate to the situation.

❑ Consider contextual issues that might affect how ideas for programs are generated.

❑ Select people for the prioritizing process.

❑ Develop criteria on which the priorities will be judged, and that will also serve as the justification for the eventual choices.

❑ Select an approach, quantitative, qualitative or a combination of both, for how the program priorities, grounded in the criteria chosen, will be determined.

❑ Determine as part of the prioritizing process whether the needs and ideas that have been identified are appropriate for an education or training program, or whether alternative interventions are needed.

(Continued)

Constructing Program Goals and Objectives

❑ Have a clear picture to follow when developing the program goals of the changes that will be made as a result of this program, and why this program is worth doing.

❑ Choose the process or processes to be used in developing the program goals.

❑ Write program objectives that reflect what participants will learn, the resulting changes from that learning, and the operational aspects of the program.

❑ Ensure that both measurable and nonmeasurable program outcomes, as appropriate, are included.

❑ Check to see whether the program objectives are written clearly enough to be understood by all parties involved.

❑ Use the program objectives as an internal consistency and achievability checkpoint.

❑ Negotiate changes in program objectives, as appropriate, among the parties involved with the planning process.

Designing Instructional Plans

❑ Develop clear and understandable learning objectives for each instructional session and ensure they match the proposed learning outcomes.

❑ Select and organize the content on what participants "must learn," which is based on the learning objectives.

❑ Choose instructional techniques that match the focus of the proposed learning outcomes, that the instructor is capable of using, and that take into account the backgrounds and experiences of the learners and the learning context.

❑ Select instructional resources that enhance the learning effort.

❑ Choose ways that instructional assessment data related to how the instruction was delivered and the resources used can be evaluated.

❑ Select appropriate assessment techniques for assessing the learning outcomes or results of the instructional activity.

❑ Use instructional assessment data in formative and summative ways for the instructional aspects of the program as well as the program as a whole.

❑ Prepare clear and concise instructional plans as guides that can assist instructors and learners to stay focused as they move through the instructional process.

❑ Make the instructional process work by ensuring instructors know their content, are competent learning facilitators, care about learners, use instructional and assessment techniques appropriately and skillfully, and are well prepared for each instructional event.

Devising Transfer of Learning Plans

❑ Be knowledgeable about the major barriers and enhancers that influence transfer of learning.

❑ Decide when the transfer of learning strategies should be employed.

❑ Determine the key players who should be a part of the transfer of learning process.

❑ Provide information to learners, supervisors, and other stakeholders about transfer of learning strategies and techniques so they know what strategies and techniques are available and can select or assist in selecting appropriate ones to use in the transfer process.

❑ Select, with the assistance of learners, instructors, and others, transfer strategies and techniques that are the most useful in assisting participants to apply what they have learned.

❑ Negotiate and change, where possible, the content, skills, or beliefs that are to be transferred, based on barriers and enhancers to learning transfer in the application site.

Formulating Program Evaluation Plans

❑ Develop, as warranted, systematic program evaluation or developmental evaluation approaches.

❑ Use informal and unplanned evaluation opportunities to collect formative and summative evaluation data.

❑ Specify the evaluation type or types to be used.

❑ Determine the techniques for how evaluation data are to be collected, or whether some evaluation data already exists.

❑ Think through how the data are to be analyzed, including how to integrate data that are collected through any informal evaluation processes.

❑ Describe how judgments are made about the program, using predetermined or emergent evaluation criteria for program success.

Determining Formats, Schedules, and Staff

❑ Choose the most appropriate format or combination of formats for the learning activity.

❑ Take into account, where appropriate, the building of learning communities as part of the goals and objectives of programs.

❑ Devise a program schedule that fits the formats chosen, the specific activities planned, and the participants' personal or work commitments.

❑ Identify the staff roles that are needed for the program, including program planners, instructional staff members, program evaluators, program coordinators or managers, and technical support staff members.

❑ Determine whether internal staff will plan and conduct the program or whether external consultants are required.

❑ Make careful choices about speakers and instructional staff members for the various activities to ensure that content expertise, competence in teaching adults, and the ability to respond effectively to the background and experiences of the learners are evident.

Preparing and Managing Budgets

❑ Gain a clear understanding of the budgeting process used by the organization in which they work, and ensure the terminology and budget model used follows this process.

❑ Estimate the costs for the program and, based on these estimated costs, prepare program budgets.

❑ Manage the program budgets and maintain accurate financial records.

❑ Develop financial contingency plans for specific programs and activities as it is not unusual for the cost or income plans to change.

❑ Determine how the program is financed and estimate the program income.

❑ Generate funding for the program.

Organizing Marketing

❑ Conduct a target audience analysis to help determine the background and experiences of the potential audience as one of the starting places for the marketing campaign.

❑ Use already existing contextual information or complete a contextual analysis to help frame the marketing campaign.

❑ Choose tactics that will assist in achieving a competitive edge with other organizations who serve a similar population, or are located in the same geographic area, that either have or could develop comparable programs.

(Continued)

❑ Utilize or develop a well-designed "brand" that reflects the value of organizations and their programs and "all of the assets and capabilities that are linked to them" (McLeish, 2011, p. 209) as a way to capture the attention of the various targeted audiences.

❑ Select or develop marketing messages, whether they are written, oral, or visual, that are clear, concise, important, and framed in such a way that convinces their various publics that the programs being offered are timely and worthwhile.

❑ Choose promotional materials and tools that are most often used by the targeted audiences, get the messages across in a way that encourages people to come to the programs, and promotes those sponsoring the programs in a positive way.

❑ Implement a lively marketing campaign, paying careful attention to the target audiences, types of promotional materials and tools to use, target times for when these tools and materials will be used, and campaign costs.

Details, Details, Details

❑ Be aware of the challenges that may come into play when juggling all of the program details.

❑ Choose dates and locations that work.

❑ Investigate and obtain suitable facilities.

❑ Negotiate, when needed, contracts for rental facilities.

❑ Ensure that all program logistics are addressed.

❑ Make sure all necessary staff, whether paid or volunteer, are in place to assist in managing the program details so that they will be handled well.

❑ Know how to work well with each of the individuals or committees who assist in taking care of program details.

❑ Anticipate any problems that might arise before, during, and after the program and have possible solutions in mind if any of them do occur; discuss these solutions with those assisting with the program details.

traditional marketing strategies. Overall, the list of useful technological advances goes on and on. In today's world, many of the details that need to be addressed for programs to run smoothly are handled online.

Looking to the Future of Program Planning

 SCENARIO 15.1:   SAYING GOOD-BYE

Diane had given her notice of her retirement plans to human resources and was packing up her office. After thirty years as a program planner for three very different kinds of organizations (a continuing education professional association, an international relief agency, and a local community development group) she was ready to change her life and begin traveling the world. Her replacement had been hired, a recent graduate from the local university with little program planning experience. She pulled out an old name card from the big conference she had planned in 1985 for six hundred people. That conference had brought in about $15,000 in registration fees and caused a big headache because the hotel housing the conference was still working on renovations when the conference began. She found the program from the workshop she planned in 1997 for volunteers who were being trained for relief efforts they would be offering as a result of the massive flooding in India. The workshops had been well planned with great presenters and hands-on experiences; she was proud of how that worked out in spite of some last-minute changes that were needed as a result of an overrun of costs. What else was in her bottom drawer—a colorful flyer left from a 2007 fundraiser held in Boston. Wow! That event had almost cost her the very job she was leaving because the food for the event turned out to be much more expensive than her budget, but the crowd was larger than expected, so at the last minute, everything worked out well. Diane put the photos on the wall in her box and remembered fondly the staff she had seen come and go, some great and others who were not as well suited to handling the endless details of program planning. She wondered how the new program planner would work out.

As Diane was getting ready to head out the door with her boxes of memories, Zina, the new program planner replacing Diane, came rushing into the office. She was excited about her new job and wanted to meet Diane and get any advice Diane was willing to share at the last minute. Then Zina asked the magic question, "Are there any program planning models I could study to know about program planning?" It did not take Diane a minute to think back to her first year, thirty years ago, when she wondered the same thing. She had been handed several fairly simple, yet rigid models of program planning to help her organize all of the tasks for her first program. Diane found her file of program planning models and handed them to Zina, saying that she hoped these materials would be useful as she began her new job. Diane also thought about the many changes the field of program planning had gone through in thirty years and knew that Zina would be planning and administering education and training programs in ways that she was not aware of or are yet to be invented. Program planning had really changed in the last thirty years. Diane was certain that Zina was going to have a great ride into the future!

As Diane observed, program planners today are well aware that the program planning process will change and those changes will be coming at them at a faster and faster pace as alternative ways of planning programs are recognized and widely used; the unknown is the influence that technological advances and global changes will have on the planning and administration of programs.

From Linear to Interactive Planning

 ### SCENARIO 15.2:   BEING LEFT BEHIND

Jake, who has been a program planner for over twenty-five years, finds himself uncertain for the first time in a while about what he is hearing in some of the sessions he has been attending at a conference for program planners who plan programs in a wide variety of settings. What perplexes him the most are the sessions that focus on alternative models for planning programs. During Jake's career as a planner he has carefully developed education and training programs "by the book" (at least with planning models he used in his master's program in Adult Education years ago). He does thorough needs assessments, and based on the results of these needs assessments, develops his goals and objectives, instructional plans, and evaluation strategies. This talk about alternative planning models, all of which are interactive in nature, seemed to him just a jumble of crazy ideas.

However, two years later, the ideas begin to make sense when Jake takes a new job with the government, where he is responsible for developing education and training programs for varied audiences, ranging from technicians to career professionals. Jake knows he has continued to run successful programs for the technical staff, which were his primary audience in his old position, but he has not done as well with the programs for other types of staff members. Some of them have even complained that his new programs are already out of date, and therefore virtually useless. Jake wants to hold onto this job as he likes the people he is working with and at least at first he was enjoying the new challenges that this position presented him.

What Jake had missed along the way was that the type of linear planning that he was good at had pretty much been put aside, except in a few specific areas in the field of technical training, where he had spent most of his career. Jake has even missed out on the notion that program planning is really an interactive process, where planners no longer work in "straight lines," but rather between and among components of the process, which better match the reality of the planning process.

However, and not surprisingly, the reality of program planning will continue to progress to keep up with the fast-changing world in which planners will work. Although the interactive nature of the process will still hold true, the idea of separate components and tasks that fit within those components will not make sense in the same way they did before. Yes, there still will be tasks that program planners will do, such as handling details and making sure funds are managed well, but the planning process will become, for many, an ever-evolving process driven by complex realities. In this process, the norm will be that program goals and objectives are moving targets, depending on changing needs and situations, which then affect many other parts of the process, from designing instruction and evaluation to program outcomes. Program planners, participants, and other stakeholders will come to realize that following a predetermined plan no longer works. They will have learned through experience, by taking advantage of unforeseen opportunities and encountering the many and varied twists and turns of the planning process, that it makes more sense for planners to use these interactive models to ensure positive and useful outcomes.

Influence of Technology

 SCENARIO 15.3:   CONNECTED TO THE WORLD

Tami is flying to Uganda to the orphanage she supports for her job as a program planner for an organization that assists orphanages in countries that lack sufficient resources to adequately care for the children. Her nonprofit organization built the orphanage and has been adding resources to the orphanage over the last ten years. Tami's mission today is to conduct a training program for the caretakers on how to help the children with their grief resulting from losing their mothers and other family members, primarily from an AIDS epidemic. In addition to the training program, Tami has a surprise for the women and the two hundred children in the orphanage. She has a donation of twenty-five iPads for the women and children to share. The donation came at a good time because Tami just found another donor who is donating fifty cell phones for the children and the women caretakers. These generous donations would seem to be easy tools for the women and children to use except the orphanage still suffers "brownouts," or periodic outages of electricity. Tami also had to figure out how to use the iPads and the cell phones without any available server for this region. She has done a lot of searches on the Internet and talked to many technicians and has found a software program she can install on the iPads that can be used to connect to the cell phones, making them able to use the Internet, without a server. Tami graduated with a master's degree in adult education in the 1990s and has conducted many workshops and programs in her career. She never thought about the task of having to cross into the world of technology and learn how to use technical tools to bring a small group of Ugandan children and their caretakers into the global world, but she is excited by the task. She has also made sure to establish relationships with in-country technicians and academics to guarantee continued technological assistance and workshops. As the plane lands, Tami knows this aspect of program planning will bring more than connectivity to the children, that their lives will change as a result.

Tools provided by technology have changed the way program planners work. Being connected to the Internet and having access to web-based tools means that program planners work with more people who are not in the planners' offices, have access to broader audiences that were not available fifteen years ago, and generally work with less staff (Joosten, 2012). Technical tools have been found to help program planners carry out many of the tasks that are still considered important and listed in the Interactive Model of Program Planning, as well as new ones that have been added. Throughout this book, examples have been given about the role that technology plays during needs assessment (surveys through e-mail), conducting advisory committees (Skype calls), marketing (social media tools), instructional design and delivery (online learning), evaluation (course evaluations online), and delivery of materials (program materials posted on web sites after the program). Though there seems to be no limit to the technical tools available to today's program planners, the use of technology does not replace the need for these planners to think creatively about how they will address the various components of planning focused on putting together viable and exciting programs (e.g., discerning the context, identifying needs and ideas for programs, developing program goals and objectives, designing instruction, and devising transfer of learning plans). In addition, planners still need to pay attention to all of the administrative aspects of planning, including preparing and managing budgets, organizing marketing campaigns, and taking care of the many details that arise throughout the process. The technical tools are just that—tools for planners to use. Technology should never lead program planners away from the basic premise of meeting the needs of learners and establishing an environment that works for them. There still will be programs that will require face-to-face learning due to the nature of the goals and objectives and the content of these programs. In addition, not all learners are comfortable with programs delivered online, nor do all learners have access to the more advanced technologies, especially those who live in developing nations.

Mott (2009) discusses the evolution of adult education and, in particular, changes occurring in adult and continuing education within the last decade. She describes a number of potential trends which may be seen in the future of practice in the field. In her opinion, online learning will be the source of some of the most significant changes. Indeed, online learning is called the biggest "disruptive technology" of this decade (Christensen, Johnson, & Horn, 2008). According to Garrett and Vogt (2003), "Globalization, advances in technology, shifting demographics, economic change, and the ever-increasing need for skilled workers have cultivated an environment that is receptive to online learning" (p. 89). As Mott (2009) describes it, the need to be competitive and the increased "quickened obsolescence of knowledge . . . happens in virtually every field or discipline; the rate of that deterioration is often impacted by the degree of technicality embedded in that discipline—the more rooted and dependent on technology the field is, the quicker the rate of deterioration. Deterioration occurs when the knowledge ceases to be valuable, accurate, or sufficient for society's needs or progression" (p. 797). Because program planners need to understand the fields they work with, the context and culture for learning, and how they can anticipate future needs for their learners, they need to ask which technical tools will be most useful to them.

The Horizon Report, edited by Johnson, Smith, Willis, Levine, & Haywood (2011), is an annual report produced by educators and technicians on the use of technology in education. The group selected their pick of six emerging tools out of fifty that will catch the attention of program planners.

- **Electronic Books and Materials.** Learners will be using e-books for their programs and other types of online materials contributing to less use of paper materials in programs.

- **Mobiles.** Mobile devices such as iPads and cell phones will continue to evolve. Program planners will be using these with "cloud computing" instead of desktop computers or even laptops.

- **Augmented Reality.** The layering of the most recent information over a view of what is known or is a normal representation. Augmented reality brings a significant potential to add information via mobile devices to the printed book. For instance, instructors or program planners will ask participants to pull up on their mobile a YouTube video that just came out the week before. This YouTube video illustrates the latest model of program planning for the graduate students to view outside of their hardbound or electronic textbooks, which could be several years old.

- **Game-Based Learning.** Once thought of as a frivolous waste of time for youth, games now span all age groups, levels of skill, and interests. Educational games will become an alternate reality to integrate into programs or will be used to foster collaboration, problem solving, and procedural thinking. Program planners will find this tool to be an exciting alternative for instructional delivery.

- **Gesture-Based Computing.** Early models of this kind of computing use body movements to move actions on a screen. Program planners will use this gesture-based computing to illustrate, for example, how to do complicated surgery, assemble a digital motor, or learn ballet.

- **Learning Analytics.** Data-gathering tools and analytic techniques will help program planners conduct their needs assessments in real time and view their program immediately after. In addition, these learning analytics will mobilize the power of data-mining tools in the service of learning; actions of groups will be measured; participants' engagement will be analyzed; and instructors will know immediately how effective their presentations have been.

The process of teaching, learning, and demonstrating will become much more creative and effective with these six tools that program planners of the near future will use in their day-to-day planning. As the program planner uses the available technology, the world will appear to become smaller, with the planner experiencing greater access to educational resources, other program planners from around the world, and information and resources from multiple cultures.

Global Changes

SCENARIO 15.4:   A TRAINER'S CHALLENGE

Paul has been a trainer for a large multinational aerospace manufacturer in the Pacific Northwest for twenty years. His job has been to provide educational programs for the workers located in the United States. As the last decade has brought globalization and outsourcing of certain parts of the manufacturing process, Paul has learned to set up conference calls between management and supervisors in the United States and in India and China. But he is now faced with the challenge of having the latest airplane built by workers from ten factories around the world. There is a huge problem in the communication among the various supervisors and their workers. Not only is language a problem, but so is competition among the workers, with many trying to prove they are superior to those from the other nations involved. There is also a problem of lack of trust between three of the groups of workers. Paul is called into his supervisor's office and told he needs to figure out how to handle these various problems. The very balance of the production depends upon cooperation, collaboration, and trust among the supervisors and workers in the ten factories. Paul returned to his office and thought how much easier his job as trainer had been twenty years ago before globalization was such a reality.

Globalization is a word that will be used daily yet will mean different things to different people. For the program planner, globalization will be about communication and collaboration with people from other cultures, the convergence of several cultures, and the opportunity to meet and work together within a positive educational experience (Canton, 2006; Merriam, 2010). Global changes will continue to happen at blinding speed, with most of our leaders working without a script to follow. These lightning-fast changes will mean reinventing ideas and plans, sometimes each week or even each day. What do program planners need to know about globalization?

Some globalization trends that Canton (2006) has emphasized are displayed in Exhibit 15.2.

Although these dramatic shifts in globalization will signal disasters and conflicts over control of a dwindling supply of resources, there will be hope for a better world, a world that benefits from knowing more about

---

EXHIBIT 15.2

Examples of Future Trends in Globalization

- Of the 6.5 billion people on earth in 2006, relatively few were knowledgeable about the other cultures.
- Language barriers, differences in beliefs, religion, and customs will continue to lead to conflicts, skirmishes, and wars.
- Even with the conflicts and wars, there will be more peace and security than in the world today.
- People will live much longer due to access to essential services, better food, and medical care, yet the world will still be divided between the "haves" and "have-nots."
- The developing countries will continue to have much younger populations as at least half of their population will be under twenty-five. These young people will have lived in poverty all their lives, with uneven educational experiences, and yet will be anxious to obtain what many other young people across the world possess.
- Most of the "industrialized" nations will have a majority of the elderly population and will have fewer children per mother. In addition, they will be facing the need to support other less-developed nations that have much larger and younger populations living in poverty.
- The future of globalization will either be positive, hopeful, and peaceful, or controlled by terrorists, criminals, and tyrants keeping their people in poverty.
- Environmental problems will be a fact of life shared among all the nations of the world as well as economic, political, social, demographic and biomedical problems. What happens in one nation will be felt in the others.
- "Connectedness" will allow for collaboration across oceans; wireless networks; real-time video conferencing; and instant access and instant notification of events across the nation and the world.
- Supplies of natural resources will continue to dwindle and will often be one of the major reason for conflicts.

---

other cultures, even distribution of resources, and a well-educated youth in many regions. Program planners are hopeful and trust that they are playing a major role in bringing about changes that will create a better future for all peoples of the world through education and training.

Closing Reflections

In writing this third edition of *Planning Programs for Adult Learners: A Practical Guide*, we were challenged tremendously by taking into account the new knowledge we have about adult learners, the effect that culture has on the planning process, the role that power plays in what is planned and for whom, the importance of relationship building to planning, and the influence technology has on the planning and delivery of programs. These five areas caused us to think more deeply about the assumptions upon which the Interactive Model is grounded, and how we reframed the critical components and tasks of the planning process. In addition, we have placed more emphasis in areas that were either almost nonexistent or did not receive the attention they deserved, such as devising transfer of learning plans, preparing and managing budgets, organizing marketing plans, and using technology in the planning and implementation of programs.

We also were committed to making the material in the book more relevant to an international audience. We added numerous examples from different places around the world, stressed the ways of knowing, learning, and teaching of "non-Western" and Indigenous peoples as important knowledge for program planners to have, and incorporated as many scenarios, relevant studies, and references as we could from other countries. We chose to go in this direction for three reasons: our readership has increased to a wider audience in a number of countries; this edition of the book may be translated into other languages; and program planners need to be aware of the effect of globalization that brings other cultures and other parts of the world to their planning tables and audiences. We have travelled to and lived for a time in other countries, and worked with others from around the world. We know how much richer our lives have become thanks to working with many other cultures.

In closing, we hope that this third edition is as helpful to those who read and use it in planning education and training programs as it has been to us in reconceptualizing the planning process. In addition, we consider this rethinking of the Interactive Model of Program Planning successful only if practitioners and scholars, ourselves included, are actually able to use, critique, and mold the model into ways that are useful to them.

References

Aaker, J. L., Smith, A., & Adler, C. (2010). *The dragonfly effect: Quick, effective, and powerful ways to use social media to drive social change.* San Francisco: Jossey-Bass.

Abrokwaa, C. K. (1999). Indigenous music education in Africa. In L. Semali & J. L. Kincheloe (Eds.), *What is indigenous knowledge? Voices from the academy* (pp. 191–207). New York: Falmer Press.

Alessi, S. M., & Trollip, S. R. (2001). *Multimedia for learning: Methods and development* (3rd ed.). Boston: Allyn & Bacon.

Alinsky, S. D. (1969). *Reveille for radicals.* New York: Vintage Books.

Allen, J. (2009). *Event planning: The ultimate guide to successful meetings, corporate events, fundraising galas, conferences, conventions, incentives and other special events* (2nd ed.). Mississauga, Ont.: Wiley.

Allen, W. C. (2006). *ADDIE training systems revisited.* Thousand Oaks, CA: Sage.

Allison, M., & Kaye, J. (2005). *Strategic planning for nonprofit organizations: A practical guide and workbook* (2nd ed.). Hoboken, NJ: Wiley.

Altschuld, J. W., & Kumar, D. D. (2010). *Needs assessment: An overview.* Thousand Oaks, CA: Sage.

American Society of Training and Development. (2006). *2006 Trend Report.* Alexandria, VA: American Society for Training and Development.

Andresen, K., & Higman, R. R. (2011). Online fundraising. In D. R. Heyman (Ed.), *Nonprofit management 101: A complete and practical guide for leaders and professionals* (pp. 341–356). San Francisco: Jossey-Bass.

Apps, J. W. (1988). *Higher education in a learning society: Meeting new demands for education and training.* San Francisco: Jossey-Bass.

Apps, J. W. (1991). *Mastering the teaching of adults.* Malabar, FL: Krieger.

Apps, J. W. (1996). *Teaching from the heart*. Malabar, FL: Krieger.

Aragon, S. R., & Hatcher, T. (Eds.). (2001). *Ethics and integrity in HRD: Case studies in research and practice*. Thousand Oaks, CA: Sage.

Archer, W., & Garrison, R. D. (2010). Distance education in the age of the Internet. In C. E. Kasworm, A. D. Rose, & J. M. Ross-Gordon (Eds.), *Handbook of adult and continuing education* (pp. 317–326). Los Angeles: Sage.

Austin, M. J. (2008). Strategies for transforming human service organizations into learning organizations: Knowledge management and the transfer of learning. *Journal of Evidence-Based Social Work, 5*(3/4), 569–596. doi: 10.1080/15433710802084326

Awoniyi, E. A., Griego, O. V., & Morgan, G. A. (2002). Person-environment fit and transfer of training. *International Journal of Training & Development, 6*(1), 25. doi: 10.1111/1468–2419.00147

Baldwin, T. T., & Ford, J. K. (1988). Transfer of training: A review and directions for future research. *Personnel Psychology, 41*(1), 63–105. doi: 10.1111/j.1744–6570.1988.tb00632.x

Baldwin, T. T., Ford, J. K., & Naquin, S. S. (2000). Managing transfer before learning begins: Enhancing the motivation to improve work through learning. In E. F. Holton, T. T. Baldwin, & S. S. Naquin (Eds.), *Managing and changing learning transfer systems*. Baton Rouge, LA; San Francisco: Academy of Human Resource Development; Berrett-Koehler.

Barbazette, J. (2006). *Training needs assessment: Methods, tools, and techniques*. San Francisco: Pfeiffer.

Bates, R., & Khasawneh, S. (2005). Organizational learning culture, learning transfer climate and perceived innovation in Jordanian organizations. *International Journal of Training and Development, 9*(2), 96–109. doi: 10.1111/j.1468–2419.2005.00224.x

Bates, T., & Sangrà, A. (2011). *Managing technology in higher education: Strategies for transforming teaching and learning*. San Francisco: Jossey-Bass.

Beard, V. A. (2003). Learning radical planning: The power of collective action. *Planning Theory, 2*(1), 13–35. doi: 10.1177/1473095203002001004

Bennett, J. B., Lehman, W.E.K., & Forst, J. K. (1999). Change, transfer climate, and customer orientation. *Group & Organization Management, 24*(2), 188–216. doi: 10.1177/1059601199242004

Berg, B. L. (2010). *Qualitative research methods for the social sciences* (7th ed.). Boston: Allyn & Bacon.

Berger, N. O., Caffarella, R. S., & O'Donnell, J. M. (2004). Learning contracts. In M. W. Galbraith (Ed.), *Adult learning methods: A guide for effective instruction* (3rd ed., pp. 289–319). Malabar, FL: Krieger.

Bergsteiner, H., Avery, G. C., & Neumann, R. (2010). Kolb's experiential learning model: Critique from a modelling perspective. *Studies in Continuing Education, 32*(1), 29–46. doi: 10.1080/01580370903534355

Bernhardt, V. L. (2000). Intersections: New routes open when one type of data crosses another. *Journal of Staff Development, 21*(1), 33–36.

Bernstein, L. A., & Wild, J. J. (2000). *Analysis of financial statements* (5th ed.). New York: McGraw-Hill.

Biech, E. (Ed.). (2005). *The 2005 Pfeiffer annual: Training.* San Francisco: Wiley.

Birkenholz, R. J. (1999). *Effective adult learning.* Danville, IL: Interstate Publishers.

Blomberg, R. (1989). Cost-benefit analysis of employee training: A literature review. *Adult Education Quarterly, 39*(2), 89–98.

Bloom, B. S. (1956). *Taxonomy of educational objectives: The classification of educational goals.* New York: McKay.

BoardSource (2012). *The nonprofit board answer book: A practical guide for board members and chief executives* (3rd ed.). San Francisco: Jossey-Bass.

Bolman, L. G., & Deal, T. E. (2008). *Reframing organizations: Artistry, choice, and leadership* (4th ed.). San Francisco: Jossey-Bass.

Bolton, N. (January 11, 2011). What is a cost budget? *eHow Money.* Retrieved from http://www.ehow.com/info_7757683_cost-budget.html

Bonk, C. J., & Zhang, K. (2008). *Empowering online learning: 100+ activities for reading, reflecting, displaying, and doing.* San Francisco: Jossey-Bass.

Boone, E. J., Safrit, R. D., & Jones, J. (2002). *Developing programs in adult education: A conceptual programming model.* (2nd ed.). Prospect Heights, IL: Waveland Press.

Boucouvalas, M., & Lawrence, R. L. (2010). Adult learning. In C. E. Kasworm, A. D. Rose, & J. M. Ross-Gordon (Eds.), *Handbook of adult and continuing education* (pp. 35–48). Los Angeles: Sage.

Boud, D., Keogh, R., & Walker, D. (1996). Promoting reflection in learning. A model. In R. Edwards, A. Hanson, & P. Raggatt (Eds.), *Boundaries of adult learning* (pp. 32–56). New York: Routledge.

Bowl, M., & Tobias, R. (2012). Learning from the past, organizing for the future. *Adult Education Quarterly, 62*(3), 272–278. doi: 10.1177/074171361403830

Bowman, S. L. (2009). *Training from the back of the room! 65 ways to step aside and let them learn.* San Francisco: Pfeiffer.

Brabham, D. C. (2009). Crowdsourcing the public participation process for planning projects. *Planning Theory, 8*(3), 242–262. doi: 10.1177/1473095209104824

Bracken, S. J. (2011). Understanding program planning theory and practice in a feminist community-based organization. *Adult Education Quarterly, 61*(2), 121–138. doi: 10.1177/0741713610380446

Bradley, M. K., Kallick, B., & Regan, H. B. (1991). *The staff development manager: A guide to professional growth.* Boston: Allyn & Bacon.

Brinkerhoff, R. O., & Montesino, M. U. (1995). Partnerships for training transfer: Lessons from a corporate study. *Human Resource Development Quarterly, 6*(3), 263–274. doi: 10.1002/hrdq.3920060305

Broad, M. L. (1997). Transfer concepts and research overview. In M. L. Broad (Ed.), *Transferring learning to the workplace: Seventeen case studies from the real world of training* (pp. 1–18). Alexandria, VA: American Society for Training and Development.

Broad, M. L. (2000). Managing the organizational learning transfer system. In E. F. Holton, T. T. Baldwin, & S. S. Naquin (Eds.), *Managing and changing learning transfer systems.* Baton Rouge, LA; San Francisco: Academy of Human Resource Development; Berrett-Koehler.

Broad, M. L. (2005). *Beyond transfer of training: Engaging systems to improve performance.* San Francisco: Pfeiffer.

Broad, M. L., & Newstrom, J. W. (1992). *Transfer of training: Action-packed strategies to ensure high payoff from training investments.* Reading, MA: Addison-Wesley.

Brockett, R. G. (1988). *Ethical issues in adult education.* New York: Teachers College, Columbia University.

Brockett, R. G., & Hiemstra, R. (2004). *Toward ethical practice.* Malabar, FL: Krieger.

Brookfield, S. D. (1992). Giving helpful evaluations to learners. *Adult Learning, 3*(8), 22–24.

Brookfield, S. D. (2006). *The skillful teacher on technique, trust, and responsiveness in the classroom* (2nd ed.). San Francisco: Jossey-Bass.

Brookfield, S. D., & Holst, J. D. (2011). *Radicalizing learning: Adult education for a just world.* San Francisco: Wiley.

Brookfield, S. D., & Preskill, S. (2005). *Discussion as a way of teaching: Tools and techniques for democratic classrooms* (2nd ed.). San Francisco: Jossey-Bass.

Bryson, J. M., & Patton, M. Q. (2010). Analyzing and engaging stakeholders. In J. S. Wholey, H. P. Hatry & K. E. Newcomer (Eds.), *Handbook of practical program evaluation* (3rd ed., pp. 30–54). San Francisco: Jossey-Bass.

Buckley, F. J. (2000). *Team teaching: What, why, and how?* Thousand Oaks, CA: Sage.

Burge, E. J. (2009a). Doing "good work": Negotiating possibilities in ethical challenges. In E. J. Burge (Ed.), Negotiating ethical practice in adult education. *New Directions for Adult and Continuing Education, no. 123* (pp. 87–91). San Francisco: Jossey-Bass.

Burge, E. J. (2009b). Negotiating ethical practices in adult education. *New Directions for Adult and Continuing Education, no. 123.* San Francisco: Jossey-Bass.

Caffarella, R. S. (1994). *Planning programs for adults: A comprehensive guide for adult educators, trainers, and staff developers.* San Francisco: Jossey-Bass.

Caffarella, R. S. (2002). *Planning programs for adult learners: A practical guide for educators, trainers, and staff developers* (2nd ed.). San Francisco: Jossey-Bass.

Caffarella, R. S. (2009, October). Crossing borders: A conceptual framework. Paper presented at the Western Region Research Conference on the Education of Adults, Bellingham: Western Washington University.

Cagney, P. (2010). *Nonprofit consulting essentials: What nonprofits and consultants need to know.* San Francisco: Jossey-Bass.

Cain, J. H., Cummings, M., & Stanchfield, J. (2005). *A teachable moment: A facilitator's guide to activities for processing, debriefing, reviewing and reflection.* Dubuque, IA: Kendal/Hunt Pub.

Calley, N. G. (2011). *Program development in the 21st century: An evidence-based approach to design, implementation, and evaluation.* Los Angeles: Sage.

Canton, J. (2006). *The extreme future: The top trends that will reshape the world in the next 20 years.* New York: Plume.

Carr-Hill, R., Roberts, F., & Currie, E. (2010). Approaches to costing adult literacy programmes, especially in Africa. *International Journal of Educational Development, 30*(4), 428–437. doi: 10.1016/j.ijedudev.2010.01.00

Castellano, M. B. (2000). Updating Aboriginal traditions of knowledge. In G.J.S. Dei, B. L. Hall, & D. G. Rosenberg (Eds.), *Indigenous knowledge in global contexts: Multiple readings of our world* (pp. 21–36). Toronto: University of Toronto Press.

Cellini, S. R., & Kee, J. E. (2010). Cost-effective and cost benefit analysis. In J. S. Wholey, H. P. Hatry, & K. E. Newcomer (Eds.), *Handbook of practical program evaluation* (3rd ed., pp. 493–530). San Francisco: Jossey-Bass.

Cervero, R. M., & Wilson, A. L. (1994). *Planning responsibly for adult education: A guide to negotiating power and interests.* San Francisco: Jossey-Bass.

Cervero, R. M., & Wilson, A. L. (1996). Learning from practice: Learning to see what matters in program planning. *New Directions for Adult and Continuing Education,* (69), 91–99. doi: 10.1002/ace.36719966911

Cervero, R. M., & Wilson, A. L. (1998). Working the planning table: The political practice of adult education. *Studies in Continuing Education, 20*(1), 5–21.

Cervero, R. M., & Wilson, A. L. (1999). Beyond learner-centered practice: Adult education, power, and society. *Canadian Journal for the Study of Adult Education, 13*(2), 27–38.

Cervero, R. M., & Wilson, A. L. (2006). *Working the planning table: Negotiating democratically for adult, continuing, and workplace education.* San Francisco: Jossey-Bass.

Cervero, R. M., Wilson, A. L., & Associates. (2001). *Power in practice: Adult education and the struggle for knowledge and power in society.* San Francisco: Jossey-Bass.

Cervero, R. M. P. (1985). Continuing professional education and behavioral change: A model for research and evaluation. *The Journal of Continuing Education in Nursing, 16*(3), 85–88.

Champion, R. (2000). Got a minute? A stairwell talk can turn evaluation into everyday business. *Journal of Staff Development, 21*(3), 57–60.

Chan, J. F. (2010). *Training fundamentals.* San Francisco: Pfeiffer.

Chandrasekar, K. S. (2010). *Marketing management: Text and cases.* New Delhi; Singapore: Tata McGraw-Hill.

Chang, B. (2010). Culture as a tool: Facilitating knowledge construction in the text of a learning community. *International Journal of Lifelong Education, 29*(6), pp. 705–722. doi: 10.1080/026011370.2010.523947

Chang, W. W. (2007). Cultural competence of international humanitarian workers. *Adult Education Quarterly, 57*(3), 187–204. doi: 10.1177/0741713606296755

Charlez, P. A. (1997). *Rock mechanics.* Paris: Editions Technip.

Cheetham, G., & Chivers, G. (2000). A new look at competent professional practice. *Journal of European Industrial Training, 24*(7), 374–383. doi: 10.1108/03090590010349827

Cheetham, G., & Chivers, G. (2001). How professionals learn in practice: An investigation of informal learning amongst people working in professions. *Journal of European Industrial Training, 25*(5), 247–292.

Cheng, W., Chen, C.L.C., Huang, Y., & Yuan, Y. (2012). Exploring the unknown: International service and individual transformation. *Adult Education Quarterly, 62*(3), 230–251. doi: 10.1177/074171361402049

Claar, J., & Cuyjet, M. (2000). Program planning and implementation. In M. J. Barr & M. K. Desler (Eds.), *The handbook of student affairs administration* (2nd ed.). San Francisco: Jossey-Bass.

Clarke, A. (2011). *How to use technology effectively in post-compulsory education.* New York: Routledge.

Clarke, N. (2002). Job/work environment factors influencing training transfer within a human service agency: Some indicative support for Baldwin and Ford's transfer climate construct. *International Journal of Training and Development, 6*(3), 146–162. doi: 10.1111/1468-2419.00156

Cohen, M. A., Rogelberg, S. G., Allen, J. A., & Luong, A. (2011). Meeting design characteristics and attendee perceptions of staff/team meeting quality. *Group Dynamics, 15*(1), 90–104. doi: 10.1037/a0021549

Conrad, R., & Donaldson, J. A. (2011). *Engaging the online learner: Activities and resources for creative instruction.* San Francisco: Jossey-Bass.

Conrad, R., & Donaldson, J. A. (2012). *Continuing to engage the online learner. More activities and resources for creative instruction.* San Francisco: Jossey-Bass.

Conti, G. J., & Kolody, R. C. (2004). Guidelines for selecting methods and techniques. In M. W. Galbraith (Ed.), *Adult learning methods: A guide for effective instruction* (3rd ed., pp. 181–192). Malabar, FL: Krieger.

Cooper, T. R. (2012). *The responsible administrator: An approach to ethics for the administrative role* (6th ed.). San Francisco: Jossey-Bass.

Cooperrider, D. L., Sorensen, P. F., Yaeger, T. F., & Whitney, D. (Eds.). (2001). *Appreciative inquiry: An emerging direction for organization development.* Champaign, IL: Stipes Pub.

Core Finance Data Task Force & National Forum on Education Statistics. (2003). *Chapter 3: Budgeting Financial accounting for local and state school systems* (2003 ed.): National Center for Education Statistics (NCES). Retrieved from http://nces.ed.gov/pubs2004/h2r2/ch_3.asp.

Cranton, P. (2000). *Planning instruction for adult learners.* Toronto: Wall & Emerson.

Craven, R. F., and DuHamel, R. F. (2000). Marketing realities in continuing professional education. In V. W. Mott and B. J. Daley (Eds.), Charting a course for continuing professional education: Reframing our practice. *New Directions for Adult and Continuing Education, no. 86* (pp. 55–62). San Francisco: Jossey-Bass.

Daehn, M. (2005). *The seven keys to marketing genius: The complete guide to increasing your marketing IQ.* St. Louis, MO: Michael Daehn.

Daffron, S. R. (2005). Program planning in war-torn Palestine. *Adult Learning, 16,* 18–21.

Daffron, S. R., Cowdrey, D. T., & Doran, J. (2007). Transfer of learning for state court judges: Maximizing the context. *International Journal of Lifelong Education, 26*(6), 689–700.

Daffron, S., & Davis, W. (2005). Transfer of learning: Lessons learned from Palestinian law professors. *Journal of Legal Education, 55*(4), 571–582.

Daffron, S., Goulet, G., Gray, J., & Viada, J. (2008). Developing curriculum for police officers and firefighters: Tips to follow and pitfalls to avoid. In V.C.X. Wang (Ed.), *Curriculum development for adult learners in the global community. Volume I, Strategic approaches* (pp. 171–206). Malabar, FL: Krieger.

Daffron, S. R., Metzgen-Ohlswager, I., Skinner, S., & Saarinen, L. (2012). Acquiring knowledge, skills, and abilities across a lifetime by transferring to one's own practice. In D. N. Aspin, J. Chapman, K. Evans, & R. Bagnall (Eds.), *Second international handbook of lifelong learning* (Vol. 26, pp. 613–627). London: Springer.

Daffron, S., & North, M. (2006). Learning transfer: Tips from software company professionals. *PAACE Journal of Lifelong Learning, 15,* 51–67.

Daffron, S. R., & North, M. W. (2011). *Successful transfer of learning.* Malabar, FL: Krieger.

Daley, B. J. (2001). Learning and professional practice: A study of four professions. *Adult Education Quarterly, 52*(1), 39–54. doi: 10.1177/074171360105200104

Daley, B. J. (2002). Context: Implications for learning in professional practice. In M. V. Alfred (Ed.), Learning and sociocultural contexts: Implications for adults, community, and workplace education. *New Directions for Adult and Continuing Education, no. 96*(pp. 79–88). San Francisco: Jossey-Bass.

Daley, B. J., and Mott, V. W. (2000). Continuing professional education: From vision to reality. In V. W. Mott and B. J. Daley (Eds.), Charting a course for continuing professional education: Reframing our practice. *New Directions for Adult and Continuing Education, no. 86* (pp. 80–85). San Francisco: Jossey-Bass.

Davis, B. G. (2009). *Tools for teaching* (2nd ed.). San Francisco: Jossey-Bass.

Day, M. J., & Petrick, E. (2006). *Designing residential wilderness programs for adults.* Malabar, FL: Krieger.

Dei, G.J.S., Hall, B. L., & Rosenberg, D. G. (2000). *Indigenous knowledge in global contexts: Multiple readings of our world.* Toronto: University of Toronto Press.

Deshler, D. (1998). Measurement and appraisal of program success. In P. S. Cookson (Ed.), *Program planning for the training and continuing education of adults: North American perspectives* (pp. 301–329). Malabar, FL: Krieger.

Dewey, J. (1938). *Experience and education.* New York: Macmillan.

DeWitt, B.M. (2011). *The nonprofit development companion. A workbook for fundraising success.* Hoboken, NJ: Wiley.

DiAddezzio, F. (2012). *The crafty marketer.* Submitted for publication.

Diamond, R. M. (2008). *Designing and assessing courses and curricula: A practical guide* (3rd ed.). San Francisco: Jossey-Bass.

Dick, W., Carey, L., & Carey, J. O. (2009). *The systematic design of instruction* (7th ed.). Upper Saddle River, NJ: Merrill/Pearson.

Dirkx, J. M. (2008). The meaning and role of emotions in adult learning. In J. M. Dirkx (Ed.), Adult learning and the emotional self. *New Directions for Adult and Continuing Education, no. 120* (pp. 7–18). San Francisco: Jossey-Bass.

Donaldson, J. F., & Kozoll, C. E. (1999). *Collaborative program planning: Principles, practices, and strategies.* Malabar, FL: Krieger.

Dwyer, B. (2001). Successful training strategies for the twenty-first century: Using recent research on learning to provide effective training strategies. *International Journal of Educational Management, 15*(6), 312–318. doi: 10.1108/EUM0000000005910

Easton, P., Monkman, K., & Miles, R. (2009). Breaking out of the egg: Methods of transformative learning in rural west Africa. In J. Mezirow & E. W. Taylor

(Eds.), *Transformative learning in practice: Insights from community, workplace, and higher education* (pp. 227–239). San Francisco: Jossey-Bass.

English, L. M., & Peters, N. (2012). Transformative learning in nonprofit organizations. *Adult Education Quarterly, 62*(2), 103–119. doi: 10.1177/0741713610392771

Epstein, M. J., & McFarlan, F. W. (2011). *Joining a nonprofit board: What you need to know.* San Francisco: Jossey-Bass.

Ewert, D. M., & Grace, K. A. (2000). Adult education for community action. In A. L. Wilson & E. Hayes (Eds.), *Handbook of adult and continuing education* (pp. 327–343). San Francisco: Jossey-Bass.

Fenwick, T. J. (2003). *Learning through experience: Troubling orthodoxies and intersecting questions.* Malabar, FL: Krieger.

Financial Services of University of Toronto. (October 20, 2006). Financial services department: Indirect costs (overhead), from http://www.finance.utoronto.ca/gtfm/restricted/research/oh.htm

Finkler, S. A. (2010). *Financial management for public, health, and for not-for-profit organizations.* New York: Prentice Hall.

Fiskaa, H. (2005). Past and future for public participation in Norwegian physical planning. *European Planning Studies, 13*(1), 157–174. doi: 10.1080/0965431042000312451

Flanagan, J. (2002). *Successful fundraising: A complete handbook for volunteers and professionals* (2nd ed.). Lincolnwood, IL: Contemporary Books.

Flood, H., & Phelps, R. W. (2003). *Understanding indirect costs: They may be hard to figure and even harder to recover—but they should never be overlooked.* The Grantsmanship Center. Retrieved from http://www.tgci.com/magazine/Understanding%20Indirect%20Costs.pdf

Forester, J. (1989). *Planning in the face of power.* Berkeley: University of California Press.

Forester, J. (1999). *The deliberative practitioner: Encouraging participatory planning processes.* Cambridge, MA: MIT Press.

Forester, J. (2009). *Dealing with differences: Dramas of mediating public disputes.* Oxford, UK: Oxford University Press.

Fox, R. D. (1984). Fostering transfer of learning to work environments. In T. J. Sork (Ed.), *Designing and implementing effective workshops. New Directions for Adult and Continuing Education, no. 22* (pp. 25–38). San Francisco: Jossey-Bass.

Freire, P. (1970). *Pedagogy of the oppressed.* New York: Herder and Herder.

French, J.R.P., & Raven, B. (1959). The bases of social power. In D. Cartwright (Ed.), *Studies in social power.* Ann Arbor: Research Center for Group Dynamics, Institute for Social Research, University of Michigan.

Friedmann, J. (2008). The uses of planning theory. *Journal of Planning Education and Research, 28*(2), 247–257. doi: 10.1177/0739456x08325220

Galbraith, M. W. (2004). *Adult learning methods: A guide for effective instruction.* Malabar, FL: Krieger.

Garrett, L. A., & Vogt, C. L. (2003). Meeting the needs of consumers: Lessons from business and industry. In S. R. Aragon (Ed.), Facilitating learning in online environments. *New Directions for Adult and Continuing Education, no. 100* (pp. 89–101). San Francisco: Jossey-Bass.

Garrison, D. R., & Vaughan, N. D. (2008). *Blended learning in higher education: Framework, principles, and guidelines.* San Francisco: Jossey-Bass.

Gboku, M.L.S., & Lekoko, R. N. (2007). *Developing programmes for adult learners in Africa.* Hamburg, Germany: UNESCO Institute for Lifelong Learning; Pearson Education.

George, B., & Sims, P. (2007). *True north: Discover your authentic leadership.* San Francisco: Jossey-Bass.

Gettleman, J. (2011, July 8). South Sudan, the newest nation, is full of hope and problems, *New York Times,* p. A1.

Ginsberg, M. B., & Wlodkowski, R. J. (2009). *Diversity and motivation: Culturally responsive teaching in college* (2nd ed.). San Francisco: Jossey-Bass.

Gordon, W., & Sork, T. J. (2001). Ethical issues and codes of ethics: Views of adult education practitioners in Canada and the United States. *Adult Education Quarterly, 51*(3), 202–218.

Grace, K. S. (2011). Individual donor and major gift strategies: The 83% solution to fundraising. In D. R. Heyman (Ed.), *Nonprofit management 101: A complete and practical guide for leaders and professionals* (pp. 309–324). San Francisco: Jossey-Bass.

Grant, J. (2002). Learning needs assessment: Assessing the need. *British Medical Journal, 324*(7330), 156–159.

Grappone, J., & Couzin, G. (2011). *Search engine optimization: An hour a day* (3rd ed.). Indianapolis: Wiley.

Gravani, M. N. (2012). Adult learning principles in designing learning activities for teacher Development. *International Journal of Lifelong Education.* doi: 10.1080/12601370.2012.663804

Green, J. C. (2007). *Mixed methods in social inquiry.* San Francisco: Jossey-Bass.

Green, L. W., & Kreuter, M. W. (2005). *Health program planning: An educational and ecological approach* (4th ed.). Boston: McGraw-Hill.

Greene, R. (2000). The 48 laws of power. New York: Penguin Books.

Grenier, R. S. (2010). "Now this is what I call learning!" A case study of museum-initiated professional development for teachers. *Adult Education Quarterly, 60*(5), pp. 499–516. doi: 10.1177/0741713610363018

Grob, G. F. (2010). Providing recommendations, suggestions, and options for improvement. In J. S. Wholey, H. P. Hatry & K. E. Newcomer (Eds.), *Handbook of practical program evaluation* (3rd ed., pp. 581–593). San Francisco: Jossey-Bass.

Gupta, K., Sleezer, C., & Russ-Eft, D. F. (2007). *A practical guide to needs assessment* (2nd ed.). San Francisco: Pfeiffer.

Guskey, T. R. (2000). *Evaluating professional development.* Thousand Oaks, CA: Corwin Press.

Guy, T. C. (1999a). Culturally relevant adult education: Key themes and common purposes. In T. C. Guy (Ed.), Providing culturally relevant adult education: A challenge for the twenty-first century. *New Directions for Adult and Continuing Education, no. 82* (pp. 93–98). San Francisco: Jossey-Bass.

Guy, T. C. (1999b). Providing culturally relevant adult education: A challenge for the twenty-first century. *New Directions for Adult and Continuing Education, no. 82.* San Francisco: Jossey-Bass.

Hall, G. E., & Hord, S. M. (2001). *Implementing change: Patterns, principles, and potholes.* Boston: Allyn & Bacon.

Hall, G. E., & Hord, S. M. (2011). *Implementing change: Patterns, principles, and potholes* (3rd ed.). Boston: Pearson/Allyn & Bacon.

Handley, A., & Chapman, C. C. (2012). *Content rules. How to create killer blogs, podcasts, videos, ebooks, webinars (and more) that engage customers and ignite your business.* Hoboken, NJ: Wiley.

Hartwig, M. C. (2000). Programming: Nuts and bolts. *New Directions for Student Services* (Vol. 20, pp. 45–56). San Francisco: Jossey-Bass.

Hatry, H. P., & Newcomer, K. E. (2010). Pittfalls in evaluation. In J. S. Wholey, H. P. Hatry, & K. E. Newcomer (Eds.), *Handbook of practical program evaluation* (3rd ed., pp. 557–580). San Francisco: Jossey-Bass.

Havercamp, M. J. (1998). Program promotion and marketing. In P. S. Cookson (Ed.), *Program planning for the training and continuing education of adults: North American perspectives* (pp. 375–390). Malabar, FL: Krieger.

Hayes, E., Flannery, D. D., & Associates. (2000). *Women as learners: The significance of gender in adult learning.* San Francisco: Jossey-Bass.

Hendricks, S. M. (2001). Contextual and individual factors and the use of influencing tactics in adult education program planning. *Adult Education Quarterly, 51*(3), 219–235. doi: 10.1177/07417130122087250

Hensley, W. L. I. (2009). *Fifty miles from tomorrow: A memoir of Alaska and the real people.* New York: Sarah Crichton Books.

Herrmann, A., Fox, R., & Boyd, A. (2000). Unintended effects in using learning technologies. In E. J. Burge (Ed.), *New Directions for Adult and Continuing Education, no. 88* (pp. 39–48). San Francisco: Jossey-Bass.

Hesselbein, F., & Goldsmith, M. (Eds.). (2006). *The leader of the future 2: Visions, strategies, and practices for the new era.* San Francisco: Jossey-Bass.

Heyman, D. R. (Ed.). *Nonprofit management 101: A complete and practical guide for leaders and professionals.* San Francisco: Jossey-Bass.

Highum, A. C., & Lund, J. P. (2000). Partnerships in programming: Relationships that make a difference *New Directions for Student Services* (Vol. 20, pp. 35–44). San Francisco: Jossey-Bass.

Hoggan, C., Simpson, S., & Stuckey, H. (2009). *Creative expression in transformative learning: Tools and techniques for educators of adults.* Malabar, FL: Krieger.

Holmgren, M. (2011). Painless and effective event planning: Let's get this party started. In D. R. Heyman (Ed.), *Nonprofit management 101: A complete and practical guide for leaders and professionals* (pp. 459–477). San Francisco: Jossey-Bass.

Holst, J. D., & Brookfield, S. D. (2009). Program planning principles, goals, and evaluation criteria in the radical adult education tradition. Paper presented at the 50th Annual Adult Education Research Conference, National-Louis University, Chicago, Illinois.

Holton, E. E., III (2000). What's really wrong: Diagnosis for learning transfer. In E. F. Holton, T. T. Baldwin, & S. S. Naquin (Eds.), *Managing and changing learning transfer systems.* Baton Rouge, LA; San Francisco: Academy of Human Resource Development; Berrett-Koehler.

Holton, E. E., III, & Bates, R. A. (2002). *Learning transfer systems inventory.* Baton Rouge: Louisiana State Office of HRD Research.

Holton, E. E., III, Bates, R. A., & Ruona, W.E.A. (2000). Development of a generalized learning transfer system inventory. *Human Resource Development Quarterly, 11*(4), 333–360.

Holton, E. F., & Baldwin, T. T. (2003). *Improving learning transfer in organizations.* San Francisco: Jossey-Bass.

Holton, E. F., Bates, R. A., Seyler, D. L., & Carvalho, M. B. (1997). Toward construct validation of a transfer climate instrument. *Human Resource Development Quarterly, 8*(2), 95–113. doi: 10.1002/hrdq.3920080203

Horton, M. (2003). *The Myles Horton reader: Education for social change.* Dale Jacobs (Ed.). Knoxville: University of Tennessee Press.

Houle, C. O. (1972). *The design of education* (1st ed.). San Francisco: Jossey-Bass.

Houle, C. O. (1989). *Governing boards: Their nature and nurture.* San Francisco: Jossey-Bass.

Houle, C. O. (1996). *The design of education* (2nd ed.). San Francisco: Jossey-Bass.

Illeris, K. (2004). *The three dimensions of learning.* Malabar, FL: Krieger.

Indabawa, S. A., & Mpofu, S. (2006). *The social context of adult learning in Africa: African perspectives on adult learning.* Cape Town, South Africa; Hamburg, Germany: Pearson Education; UNESCO Institute for Education.

Ingram, R. T. (1999). *Ten basic responsibilities of nonprofit boards* (2nd ed.). Washington, D.C.: National Center for Nonprofit Boards.

Iseke, J. M. (2010). Importance of métis ways of knowing in healing communities. *Canadian Journal of Native Education, 33*(1), 83–87.

Jackson, M. L. (2000). Fundraising and development. In M. J. Barr & M. K. Desler (Eds.), *The handbook of student affairs administration* (2nd ed., pp. 597–611). San Francisco: Jossey-Bass.

Jarvis, P. (1987). *Adult learning in the social context.* London: Croom Helm.

Jarvis, P. (2006). *Towards a comprehensive theory of human learning.* London; New York: Routledge.

Jay, A. (2009). *How to run a meeting.* Cambridge, MA: Harvard Business School.

Jhurree, V. (2005). Technology integration in education in developing countries: Guidelines to policy makers. *International Education Journal, 6*(4), 467–483.

Johnson, L., Smith, R., Willis, H., Levine, A., & Haywood, K. (2011). The 2011 horizon report. Austin, TX: The New Media Consortium.

Johnson, W. B., & Ridley, C. R. (2008). *The elements of ethics: For professionals.* New York: Palgrave Macmillan.

Jonassen, D., Strobel, J., & Gottdenker, J. (2005). Model building for conceptual change. *Interactive Learning Environments, 13*(1/2), 15–37. doi: 10.1080/10494820500173292

Jones, K. B. (2010). *Search engine optimization: Your visual blueprint for effective Internet marketing* (2nd ed.). Indianapolis: Wiley.

Joosten, T. (2012). *Social media for educators: Strategies and best practices.* San Francisco: Jossey-Bass.

Kamis, M., & Muhammad, M. (2007). Islam's lifelong learning mandate. In S. B. Merriam (Ed.), *Non-Western perspectives on learning and knowing* (pp. 21–40). Malabar, FL: Krieger.

Kanter, B., & Fine, A. H. (2010). *The networked nonprofit: Connecting with social media to drive change.* San Francisco: Jossey-Bass.

Kasworm, C. E., Rose, A. D., & Ross-Gordon, J. M. (2010). *Handbook of adult and continuing education.* Los Angeles: Sage.

Kaufman, R. A., Rojas, A. M., & Mayer, H. (1993). *Needs assessment: A user's guide.* Englewood Cliffs, NJ: Educational Technology Publications.

Kent, P. (2010). Search engine optimization for dummies (4th ed.). Hoboken, NJ: Wiley.

Kettner, P. M., Moroney, R., & Martin, L. L. (2008). *Designing and managing programs: An effectiveness-based approach.* Los Angeles: Sage.

King, K. P. (2003). Learning the new technologies: Strategies for success. In K. P. King and P. A. Lawler (Eds.), New perspectives on designing and implementing professional development of teachers of adults. *New Directions for Adult and Continuing Education, no. 98* (pp. 49–58). San Francisco: Jossey-Bass.

King, K. P., & Lawler, P. A. (2003). Trends and issues in the professional development of teachers of adults. In K. P. King and P. A. Lawler (Eds.), New Perspectives on Designing and Implementing Professional Development of Teachers of Adults. *New Directions for Adult and Continuing Education, no. 98* (pp. 5–14). San Francisco: Jossey-Bass.

Kirkpatrick, D. L. (1976). Evaluation of training. In R. L. Craig (Ed.), *Training and development handbook: A guide to human resource development* (2nd ed., pp. 301–319). New York: McGraw-Hill.

Kirkpatrick, D. L., & Kirkpatrick, J. D. (2005). *Transferring learning to behavior: Using the four levels to improve performance.* San Francisco: Berrett-Koehler.

Kirkpatrick, D. L., & Kirkpatrick, J. D. (2006). *Evaluating training programs: The four levels* (3rd ed.). San Francisco: Berrett-Koehler.

Kirkpatrick, D. L., & Kirkpatrick, J. D. (2007). *Implementing the four levels: A practical guide for effective evaluation of training programs.* San Francisco: Berrett-Koehler.

Kirwan, C. (2009). *Improving learning transfer: A guide to getting more out of what you put into your training.* Farnham, England; Burlington, VT: Gower.

Knowles, M. S. (1970). *The modern practice of adult education: Andragogy versus pedagogy.* New York: Association Press.

Knowles, M. S. (1980). *Modern practice of adult education: From andragogy to pedagogy* (2nd ed.). Chicago: Follet.

Knox, A. B. (2002). *Evaluation for continuing education: A comprehensive guide to success.* San Francisco: Jossey-Bass.

Kolb, A. Y., & Kolb, D. A. (2008). Experiential learning theory: A dynamic, holistic approach to management learning, education & development. In S. J. Armstrong & C. V. Fukami (Eds.), *Handbook of management learning, education and development.* London: Sage.

Kolb, D. A. (1984). *Experiential learning: Experience as the source of learning and development.* Englewood Cliffs, NJ: Prentice-Hall.

Kotler, P. (1987). Strategies for introducing marketing into nonprofit organizations. In P. Kotler, O. C. Ferrell, & C. W. Lamb (Eds.), *Strategic marketing for nonprofit organizations: Cases and readings* (pp. 3–13). Englewood Cliffs, NJ: Prentice-Hall.

Kouzes, J. M., & Posner, B. Z. (2007). *The leadership challenge* (4th ed.). San Francisco: Jossey-Bass.

Krueger, R. A. (2010). Using stories in evaluation. In J. S. Wholey, H. P. Hatry & K. E. Newcomer (Eds.), *Handbook of practical program evaluation* (3rd ed., pp. 404–423). San Francisco: Jossey-Bass.

Krueger, R. A., & Casey, M. A. (2010). Focus group interviewing. In J. S. Wholey, H. P. Hatry, & K. E. Newcomer (Eds.), *Handbook of practical program evaluation* (3rd ed., pp. 378–403). San Francisco: Jossey-Bass.

Kumar, N. (2004). *Marketing as strategy: Understanding the CEO's agenda for driving growth and innovation.* Boston: Harvard Business School Press.

Kwak, H., Lee, C., Park, H., & Moon, S. (2010). What is Twitter, a social network or a news media? Paper presented at the Proceedings of the 19th international conference on World Wide Web, Raleigh, North Carolina, USA.

Lahiri, J. (2003). *The namesake.* Boston: Houghton Mifflin.

Lakey, G. (2010). *Facilitating group learning: Strategies for success with diverse adult learners.* San Francisco: Jossey-Bass.

Landry, M. (2006). Contingency planning: A process. *ISSA Journal* (July). Retrieved from http://www.issa.org/Library/Journals/2006/July/Landry%20-%20 Contingency%20Planning.pdf

Langdon, D. G., Whiteside, K. S., & McKenna, M. M. (Eds.). (1999). *Intervention resource guide: 50 performance improvement tools.* San Francisco: Jossey-Bass/ Pfeiffer.

Latimer, J. (1999). Cross-border knowledge transfer. *Technical Training, 10*(5), 49–53.

Lawler, P. A. (2000). Ethical Issues in Continuing and Professional Education. In V. W. Mott and B. J. Daley (Eds.), Charting a course for continuing professional education: Reframing practice. *New Directions for Adult and Continuing Education, no. 86* (pp. 63–70). San Francisco: Jossey-Bass.

Lawler, P. A., & King, K. P. (2003). Changes, challenges, and the future. In K. P. King and P. A. Lawler (Eds.), New perspectives on designing and implementing professional development of teachers of adults. *New Directions for Adult and Continuing Education, no. 98* (pp. 83–92). San Francisco: Jossey-Bass.

Lawson, K. (2009). *The trainer's handbook* (Updated ed.). San Francisco: Pfeiffer.

Leach, D., Rogelberg, S., Warr, P., & Burnfield, J. (2009). Perceived meeting effectiveness: The role of design characteristics. *Journal of Business and Psychology, 24*(1), 65–76. doi: 10.1007/s10869–009–9092–6

Leberman, S., McDonald, L., & Doyle, S. (2006). *The transfer of learning: Participants' perspectives of adult education and training.* Aldershot, England; Burlington, VT: Gower.

Lee, W. W., & Owens, D. L. (2000). *Multimedia-based instructional design: Computer-based training, web-based training, distance broadcast training.* San Francisco: Jossey-Bass/Pfeiffer.

Leigh, D., Watkins, R., Platt, W. A., & Kaufman, R. (2000). Alternate models of needs assessment: Selecting the right one for your organization. *Human Resource Development Quarterly, 11*(1), 87–93.

Lenning, O. T. (2013). *Powerful learning communities: A guide to developing students, faculty, and professional learning communities to improve student success and organizational effectiveness.* Sterling, VA: Stylus.

Levinson, J. C., Adkins, F., & Forbes, C. (2010). *Guerrilla marketing for nonprofits: 250 tactics to promote, recruit, motivate, and raise more money.* Irvine: Entrepreneur Press.

Lewis, C. W., & Gilman, S. (2005). *The ethics challenge in public service: A problem-solving guide* (2nd ed.). San Francisco: Jossey-Bass.

Lewis, C. W., & Gilman, S. C. (2012). *The ethics challenge in public service: A problem-solving guide* (3rd ed.). San Francisco: Jossey-Bass.

Lim, D. H., & Morris, M. L. (2006). Influence of trainee characteristics, instructional satisfaction, and organizational climate on perceived learning and training transfer. *Human Resource Development Quarterly, 17*(1), 85–115. doi: 10.1002/hrdq.1162

Linn, R. L. (2000). Assessments and accountability. *Educational Researcher, 26*(2), 4–15. doi: doi: 10.3102/0013189X029002004

Liteman, M., Campbell, S., & Liteman, J. (2006). *Retreats that work (Expanded Edition).* San Francisco: Jossey Bass.

MacKeracher, D. (2004). *Making sense of adult learning* (2nd ed.). Toronto: University of Toronto Press.

Mager, R. F. (1990). *Preparing instructional objectives* (2nd ed.). Belmont, CA: Kogan Page.

Mancuso, A. (2011). *Nonprofit meetings, minutes and records: How to run your nonprofit corporation so you don't run into trouble* (2nd ed.). Berkeley, CA: Nolo Press.

Mansfield, H. (2012). *Social media for social good: A how-to guide for nonprofits.* New York: McGraw-Hill.

Marienau, C. (1999). Self-assessment at work: Outcomes of adult learners' reflections on practice. *Adult Education Quarterly, 49*(3), 135–146.

Maruatona, T. (2005). Gender and minority issues in planning literacy education in Botswana. *International Journal of Lifelong Education, 24*(2), 149–164. doi: 10.1086/02601375000124116

Massa, N. M., Donnelly, J., Bell, A., Vallieres, K., & Hanes, F. (2005). The PHOTON2 web-based professional development model: A year in review. Paper presented at the Ninth International Topical Meeting on Education & Training in Optics and Photonics (ETOP), Marseilles, France.

Mathos, M., & Norman, C. (2012). *101 social media tactics for nonprofits: A field guide.* Hoboken, NJ: Wiley.

McCawley, P. F. (2009). *Methods for conducting an educational needs assessment: Guidelines for Cooperative Extension System professionals.* Moscow: University of Idaho Extension.

McCullum, P. C. (2000). 6 points of a partnership. *Journal of Staff Development, 21*(2).

McLeish, B. J. (2011). *Successful marketing strategies for nonprofit organizations: Winning in the age of the elusive donor* (2nd ed.). San Francisco: Wiley.

McManus, A. (2011). Fundraising: Knowing when to do what. In D. R. Heyman (Ed.), *Nonprofit management 101: A complete and practical guide for leaders and professionals* (pp. 291–308). San Francisco: Jossey-Bass.

McMillan, J. H. (2001). *Classroom assessment: Principles and practice for effective instruction* (2nd ed.). Boston: Allyn & Bacon.

McMillan, J. H. (2007). *Classroom assessment: Principles and practice for effective standards-based instruction* (4th ed.). Boston: Pearson/Allyn & Bacon.

McMillan, J. H. (2010). *Classroom assessment: Principles and practice for effective standards-based instruction* (5th ed.). Boston: Pearson.

McMillan, J. H., & Schumacher, S. (2010). *Research in education: Evidence-based inquiry* (7th ed.). Boston: Pearson.

Mehrens, W. A., & Lehmann, I. J. (1991). *Measurement and evaluation in education and psychology.* Fort Worth: Holt, Rinehart and Winston.

Meisinger, R. J., & Dubeck, L. W. (1984). *College and university budgeting: An introduction for faculty and academic administrators.* Washington, D.C.: National Association for College and University Business Officers.

Merriam, S. B. (2008). Third update on adult learning theory. *New Directions for Adult and Continuing Education, no. 119.* San Francisco: Jossey-Bass.

Merriam, S. B. (2009). *Qualitative research: A guide to design and implementation.* San Francisco: Jossey-Bass.

Merriam, S. B. (2010). Globalization and the roles of adult and continuing education. Challenges and opportunities. In C. E. Kasworm, A. D. Rose, & J. M. Ross-Gordon (Eds.), *Handbook of adult and continuing education* (pp. 401–410). Los Angeles: Sage.

Merriam, S. B., & Associates. (2007). *Non-Western perspectives on learning and knowing.* Malabar, FL: Krieger.

Merriam, S. B., Caffarella, R. S., & Baumgartner, L. (2007). *Learning in adulthood: A comprehensive guide.* San Francisco: Jossey-Bass.

Merriam, S. B., & Kim, Y. S. (2008). Non-Western perspectives on learning and knowing. Third update on adult learning theory, (119), 71–81. doi: 10.1002/ace.307

Merriam, S. B., & Leahy, B. (2005). Learning transfer: A review of the research in adult education and training. *PAACE Journal of Lifelong Learning, 14*, 1–24.

Merriam, S. B., & Mohamad, M. (2000). How cultural values shape learning in older adulthood: The case of Malaysia. *Adult Education Quarterly, 51*(1), 45–63. doi: 10.1177/074171360005100104

Merriam, S. B., & Ntseane, G. (2008). Transformational learning in Botswana: How culture shapes the process. *Adult Education Quarterly, 58*(3), 183–197. doi: 10.1177/0741713608314087

Mertens, D. M., & Wilson, A. T. (2012). *Program evaluation theory and practice: A comprehensive guide.* New York: The Guilford Press.

Mezirow, J. (1978). *Education for perspective transformation. Women's re-entry programs in community colleges.* New York: Teachers College, Columbia University.

Mezirow, J. (1991). *Transformative dimensions of adult learning.* San Francisco: Jossey-Bass.

Mezirow, J., Taylor, E. W., & Associates. (2009). *Transformative learning in practice: Insights from community, workplace, and higher education.* San Francisco: Jossey-Bass.

Michelson, E., Mandell, A., & Contributors. (2004). *Portfolio development and the assessment of prior learning: Perspectives, models, and practices.* Sterling, VA: Stylus.

Milano, M., & Ullius, D. (1998). *Designing powerful training: The sequential-iterative model.* San Francisco: Jossey-Bass/Pfeiffer.

Miller, K. L. (2010). *The nonprofit marketing guide: High-impact, low-cost ways to build support for your good cause.* San Francisco: Jossey-Bass.

Mills, D. P., Cervero, R. M., Langone, C. A., & Wilson, A. L. (1995). The impact of interests, power relationships, and organizational structure on program planning practice: A case study. *Adult Education Quarterly, 46*(1), 1–16. doi: 10.1177/0741713695046001001

Mirchandani, N. (2005). *Internet marketing 101: Strategies from a young web marketing guru.* San Francisco: Heliographica.

Mishan, E. J., & Quah, E. (2007). *Cost-benefit analysis* (5th ed.). New York: Routledge.

Mitchell, G. (1998). *The trainer's handbook: The AMA guide to effective training* (3rd ed.). New York: AMACOM.

Modise, O., Ntseane, P., & Preece, J. (2012). *Engagement in African universities: Perspectives, prospects, and challenges.* Leister, United Kingdom: National Institute of Health.

Moore, M. G. (Ed.). (2012). *Handbook of distance education* (3rd ed.). Mahwah, NJ: Erlbaum.

Moore, M. G., & Kearsley, G. (2012). *Distance instruction: A systems view of learning.* Belmont, CA: Wadsworth Cengage Learning.

Morell, J. A. (2010). *Evaluation in the face of uncertainty: Anticipating surprise and responding to the inevitable.* New York; London: Guilford Press.

Morrison, G. R., Ross, S. M., Kalman, H. K., & Kemp, J. E. (2011). *Designing effective instruction* (6th ed.). Danvers, MA: Wiley.

Mott, V. W. (2009). Evolution of adult education: Is our future in E-learning? In V.C.X. Wang (Ed.), *Handbook of research on E-learning applications for career and technical education: Technologies for vocational training* (Vol. 2, pp. 791–804). Hershey, PA: IGI Global.

Munson, L. S. (1992). *How to conduct training seminars* (2nd ed.). New York: McGraw-Hill.

Netting, F. E., O'Connor, M. K., & Fauri, D. P. (2008). *Comparative approaches to program planning.* New York: Wiley.

Newcomer, K. E., & Conger, D. (2010). Qualitative data analysis. In J. S. Wholey, H. P. Hatry, & K. E. Newcomer (Eds.), *Handbook of practical program evaluation* (3rd ed., pp. 454–492). San Francisco: Jossey-Bass.

Newcomer, K. E., Hatry, H. P., & Wholey, J. S. (2010). Planning and designing useful evaluations. In J. S. Wholey, H. P. Hatry, & K. E. Newcomer (Eds.), *Handbook of practical program evaluation* (3rd ed., pp. 5–29). San Francisco: Jossey-Bass.

Newcomer, K. E., & Triplett, T. (2010). Using surveys. In J. S. Wholey, H. P. Hatry, & K. E. Newcomer (Eds.), *Handbook of practical program evaluation* (3rd ed., pp. 262–297). San Francisco: Jossey-Bass.

Newman, M. (1995). *Defining the enemy: Adult education in social action.* Sydney: Stewart Victor.

Newman, M. (2006). *Teaching defiance: Stories and strategies for activist educators. A book written in wartime.* San Francisco: Jossey-Bass.

Newman, M. (2012). Calling transformative learning into question: Some mutinous thoughts. *Adult Education Quarterly, 62*(1), 36–55. doi: 10.1177/0741713610392768

Newstrom, J. W., & Lilyquist, J. M. (1979). Selecting needs analysis methods. *Training and Development Journal, 33*(10), 52–56.

Nobel, N. (2011). Online peer-to-peer fundraising. In D. R. Heyman (Ed.), *Nonprofit management 101: A complete and practical guide for leaders and professionals* (pp. 357–372). San Francisco: Jossey-Bass.

Ntseane, P. G. (2011). Culturally sensitive transformational learning. *Adult Education Quarterly, 61*(4), 307–323. doi: 10.1177/0741713610389781

Ntseane, P. G. (2012). Transformative learning theory: A perspective from Africa. In E.W. Taylor, P. Cranton, & Associates (Eds.), *The handbook of transformational learning: Theory, research, and practice* (pp. 274–288). San Francisco: Jossey-Bass.

Orsburn, E. M. (2012). *The social media business equation: Using online connections to grow your bottom line.* Boston: Course Technology/Cengage Learning.

Ottoson, J. M. (1995a). Reclaiming the concept of application: From social to technological process and back again. *Adult Education Quarterly, 46*(1), 17–30.

Ottoson, J. M. (1995b). Use of a conceptual framework to explore multiple influences on the application of learning following a continuing education program. *Canadian Journal for the Study of Adult Education, 9*(2), 1–18.

Ottoson, J. M. (1997). After the applause: Exploring multiple influences on application following an adult education program. *Adult Education Quarterly, 47*(2), 92–107. doi: 10.1177/074171369704700203

Ottoson, J. M. (2000). Evaluation of continuing professional education: Toward a theory of our own. In V. W. Mott and B. J. Daley (Eds.), Charting a course for continuing professional education. *New Directions for Adult and Continuing Education, no. 86* (pp. 43–53). San Francisco: Jossey-Bass.

Palloff, R. M., & Pratt, K. (2005). *Collaborating online: Learning together in community.* San Francisco: Jossey-Bass.

Palloff, R. M., & Pratt, K. (2007). *Building online learning communities: Effective strategies for the virtual classroom.* San Francisco: Jossey-Bass.

Palloff, R. M., & Pratt, K. (2009). *Assessing the online learner: Resources and strategies for faculty.* San Francisco: Jossey Bass.

Palloff, R. M., & Pratt, K. (2011). *The excellent online instructor: Strategies for professional development.* San Francisco: Jossey-Bass.

Palmer, P. J. (1998). *The courage to teach: Exploring the inner landscape of a teacher's life.* San Francisco: Jossey-Bass.

Parry, S. B. (1996). Consultants. In R. L. Craig (Ed.), *The ASTD training and development handbook: A guide to human resource development* (4th ed., pp. 1031–1046). New York: McGraw-Hill.

Patterson, K., Grenny, J., Maxfield, D., McMillan, R., & Switzler, A. (2008). *Influencer: The power to change anything.* New York: McGraw-Hill.

Patton, M. Q. (2002). *Qualitative research and evaluation methods* (3rd ed.). Thousand Oaks, CA: Sage.

Patton, M. Q. (2008). *Utilization-focused evaluation* (4th ed.). Thousand Oaks, CA: Sage.

Patton, M. Q. (2011). *Developmental evaluation: Applying complexity concepts to enhance innovation and use.* New York: Guilford Press.

Pawlak, E. J., & Vinter, R. D. (2004). *Designing and planning programs for nonprofit and government organizations.* San Francisco: Jossey-Bass.

Pearce, S. (1998). Determining program needs. In P. S. Cookson (Ed.), *Program planning for the training and continuing education of adults: North American perspectives* (pp. 249–273). Malabar, FL: Krieger.

Pennington, F., & Green, J. (1976). Comparative analysis of program development processes in six professions. *Adult Education Quarterly Adult Education Quarterly, 27*(1), 13–23.

Phillips, J. J., & Broad, M. L. (Eds.). (1997). *Transferring learning to the workplace.* Alexandria, VA: American Society for Training and Development.

Phillips, J. J., & Stone, R. D. (2002). *How to measure training results: A practical guide to tracking the six key indicators.* New York: McGraw-Hill.

Piskurich, G. M. (2006). *Rapid instructional design: Learning ID fast and right* (2nd ed.). San Francisco: Pfeiffer.

Pratt, D. D., & Associates. (1998). *Five perspectives on teaching in adult and higher education.* Malabar, FL: Krieger.

Pratt, D. D., Kelly, M., & Wong, W.S.S. (1999). Chinese conceptions of "effective teaching" in Hong Kong: Towards culturally sensitive evaluation of teaching. *International Journal of Lifelong Education, 18*(4), 241–258.

Rainie, L. (2011). The Internet as a diversion and destination. *Pew Internet & American Life Project.* Washington, D.C.: Pew Research Center.

Ray, N. M. (2010). Transforming teaching and learning: Teaching race. In V. Sheared, J. Johnson-Bailey, Colin, S.A.J., E. Peterson, S. D. Brookfield & Associates (Eds.), *The handbook of race and adult education: a resource for dialogue on racism* (pp. 71–82). San Francisco: Jossey-Bass.

Reagan, T. G. (2005). *Non-Western educational traditions indigenous approaches to educational thought and practice* (3rd ed.). Mahwah, NJ: Lawrence Erlbaum.

Rees, E. F., Cervero, R. M., Moshi, L., & Wilson, A. L. (1997). Language, power, and the construction of adult education programs. *Adult Education Quarterly, 47*(2), 63–77. doi: 10.1177/074171369704700201

Robert, H. M., III, Evans, W. J., Honemann, D. H., & Balch, T. J. (2004). *Robert's rules of order (11th ed.).* Bedford, MA: Applewood Books.

Rocco, S. (2007). Online assessment and evaluation. In S.C.O. Conceição (Ed.), *New Directions for Adult and Continuing Education, no. 113* (pp. 75–86). San Francisco: Jossey-Bass.

Rogers, E. M. (2003). *Diffusion of innovations* (5th ed.). New York: Free Press.

Rogers, G., Finley, D. S., & Galloway, J. R. (2001). *Strategic planning in social service organizations: A practical guide.* Toronto: Canadian Scholars' Press.

Rogers, J. R., & Goodrick, D. (2010). Qualitative data analysis. In J. S. Wholey, H. P. Hatry, & K. E. Newcomer (Eds.), *Handbook of practical program evaluation* (3rd ed., pp. 429–453). San Francisco: Jossey-Bass.

Rossett, A. (1998). *First things fast: A handbook for performance analysis.* San Francisco: Jossey-Bass.

Rothman, J. C. (2007). *Cultural competence in process and practice: Building bridges.* Boston: Pearson/Allyn & Bacon.

Rothwell, W. J., & Cookson, P. S. (1997). *Beyond instruction: Comprehensive program planning for business and education.* San Francisco: Jossey-Bass.

Rothwell, W. J., & Kazanas, H. C. (1998). *Mastering the instructional design process: A systematic approach* (2nd ed.). San Francisco: Jossey-Bass.

Rothwell, W. J., & Kazanas, H. C. (2008). *Mastering the instructional design process: A systematic approach* (4th ed.). San Francisco: Pfeiffer.

Rouiller, J. Z., & Goldstein, I. L. (1993). The relationship between organizational transfer climate and positive transfer of training. *Human Resource Development Quarterly, 4*(4), 377–390. doi: 10.1002/hrdq.3920040408

Rowson, R. (2006). *Working ethics: How to be fair in a culturally complex world.* Philadelphia: Jessica Kingsley.

Ryu, K., & Cervero, R. M. (2011). The role of Confucian cultural values and politics in planning educational programs for adults in Korea. *Adult Education Quarterly, 61*(2), 139–160. doi: 10.1177/0741713610380440

Schaefer, C. (2006). *Grandmothers counsel the world: Women elders offer their vision for our planet.* Boston: Trumpeter.

Schein, E. H. (1999). *The corporate culture survival guide: Sense and nonsense about culture change.* San Francisco: Jossey-Bass.

Schmidt, M. J. (2011). *Budget/budgeting. Encyclopedia of business terms and methods.* Boston: Solution Matrix. Retrieved from http://www.solutionmatrix.com/budget.html.

Schön, D. A. (1983). *The reflective practitioner: How professionals think in action.* New York: Basic Books.

Schuh, J. H., & Associates. (2009). *Assessment methods for student affairs.* San Francisco: Jossey-Bass.

Schutz, P. A., Nichols, S. L., & Rodgers, K. A. (2009). Using multiple methods approaches. In S. D. Lapan & M. T. Quartaroli (Eds.), *Research essentials: An introduction to designs and practices* (pp. 243–258). San Francisco: Jossey-Bass.

Scott, J. (2000). *Social network analysis: A handbook* (2nd ed.). London; Thousands Oaks, CA: Sage.

Semali, L., & Kincheloe, J. L. (Eds.). (1999). *What is indigenous knowledge? Voices from the academy.* New York: Falmer Press.

Sheared, V., Johnson-Bailey, J., Colin, S.A.J., Peterson, E., Brookfield, S. D., & Associates (Eds.). (2010). *The handbook of race and adult education: A resource for dialogue on racism.* San Francisco: Jossey-Bass.

Shepard, M. (2003). *Coming to consensus: Tips for cooperation and collaboration in decision making, or how to run meetings so everyone wins.* San Francisco: Shepard.

Shipp, T. (1998). The role of programmer. In P. S. Cookson (Ed.), *Program planning for the training and continuing education of adults: North American perspective*s (pp. 99–114). Malabar, FL: Krieger.

Silberman, M. L. (2005). *101 ways to make training active* (2nd ed.). San Francisco: Pfeiffer.

Silberman, M. L. (Ed.). (2007). *The handbook of experiential learning.* San Francisco: Pfeiffer.

Silberman, M. L. (2010). *Unforgettable experiential activities: An active training resource.* San Francisco: Pfeiffer.

Silberman, M. L., & Auerbach, C. (2006). *Active training: A handbook of techniques, designs, case examples, and tips* (3rd ed.). San Francisco: Pfeiffer.

Simerly, R. (1989a). A ten-step process to ensure success in marketing. In R. Simerly & Associates (Eds.), *Handbook of marketing for continuing education* (pp. 445–452). San Francisco: Jossey-Bass.

Simerly, R. (1989b). Writing effective advertising copy: Eight principles for success. In R. Simerly & Associates (Eds.), *Handbook of marketing for continuing education* (pp. 166–178). San Francisco: Jossey-Bass.

Simerly, R., & Associates. (Eds.). (1989). *Handbook of marketing for continuing education.* San Francisco: Jossey-Bass.

Sloane-Seale, A. (2001). Program planning in adult education. In D. H. Poonwassie & A. Poonwassie (Eds.), *Fundamentals of adult education: Issues and practices for lifelong learning* (pp. 118–132). Toronto: Thompson.

Smith, A. (2011). Why Americans use social media. *Pew Internet and American Life Project.* Washington, D.C.: Pew Research Center.

Smith, Bucklin, & Associates. (2000). *The complete guide to nonprofit management* (2nd ed.). New York: Wiley.

Smith, P. J., & Sadler-Smith, E. (2006). *Learning in organizations: Complexities and diversities.* London: Routledge.

Smith, P. L., & Ragan, T. J. (2005). *Instructional design* (3rd ed.). Danvers, MA: Wiley.

Sork, T. J. (1990). Theoretical foundations of educational program planning. *Journal of Continuing Education in the Health Professions, 10*(1), 73–83.

Sork, T. J. (1997). Workshop Planning. In J. A. Fleming (Ed.), Newer perspectives on designing and implementing effective workshops. *New Directions for Adult and Continuing Education, no. 76* (pp. 5–17). San Francisco: Jossey-Bass.

Sork, T. J. (1998). Program priorities, purposes, and objectives. In P. S. Cookson (Ed.), *Program planning for the training and continuing education of adults: North American perspectives* (pp. 273–300). Malabar, FL: Krieger.

Sork, T. J. (2000). Planning educational programs. In A. L. Wilson & E. Hayes (Eds.), *Handbook of adult and continuing education* (pp. 171–191). San Francisco: Jossey-Bass.

Sork, T. J. (2001). Needs assessment. In D. H. Poonwassie & A. Poonwassie (Eds.), *Fundamentals of adult education: Issues and practices for lifelong learning* (pp. 100–115). Toronto: Thompson.

Sork, T. (2009). Applied ethics in adult and continuing education literature. In E. J. Burge (Ed.), Negotiating ethical practice in adult education. *New Directions for Adult and Continuing Education, no. 123* (pp. 19–32). San Francisco: Jossey-Bass.

Sork, T., & Caffarella, R. S. (1989). Planning programs for adults. In S. B. Merriam & P. M. Cunningham (Eds.), *Handbook of adult and continuing education* (pp. 233–245). San Francisco: Jossey-Bass.

Sork, T. J. (2010). Planning and delivering programs. In C. E. Kasworm, A. D. Rose, & J. M. Ross-Gordon (Eds.), *Handbook of adult and continuing education* (pp. 157–167). Los Angeles: Sage.

Sparks, D. (2000). Partnerships need purposes. *Journal of Staff Development, 21*(2), 3.

Sternthal, B., & Tybout, A. M. (2001). Segmentation and targeting. In D. Iacobucci (Ed.), *Kellogg on marketing* (pp. 3–30). New York: Wiley.

Strauss, J. C., & Curry, J. R. (2002). *Responsibility center management: Lessons from 25 years of decentralized management.* Washington, DC: National Association of College and University Business Officials.

Sugrue, B., & Clark, R. E. (2000). Media selection for training. In S. Tobias & J. D. Fletcher (Eds.), *Training and retraining: A handbook for business, industry, government, and the military* (pp. 208–234). New York: Macmillan Reference USA.

Surowiecki, J. (2004). *The wisdom of crowds: Why the many are smarter than the few and how collective wisdom shapes business, economies, societies, and nations.* New York: Doubleday.

Tate, C. (2010). *Marketing your small business for dummies.* Hoboken, NJ: Wiley.

Taylor, E. W. (2007). An update of transformative learning theory: A critical review of the empirical research (1999–2005). *International Journal of Lifelong Education, 26*(2), 173–191. doi: 10.1080/02601370701219475

Taylor, E. W. (2009). Fostering transformative learning. In J. Mezirow & E. W. Taylor (Eds.), *Transformative learning in practice: Insights from community, workplace, and higher education* (pp. 3–16). San Francisco: Jossey-Bass.

Taylor, E. W., Cranton, P., & Associates (Eds.) (2012). *The handbook of transformational learning: Theory, research, and practice.* San Francisco: Jossey-Bass.

Teemant, A., Smith, M. E., Pinnegar, S., & Egan, M. W. (2005). Modeling sociocultural pedagogy in distance education. *Teachers College Record, 107*(8), 1675–1698. doi: 10.1111/j.1467-9620.2005.00538.x

Tennant, M. (2000). Adult learning for self-development and change. In A. L. Wilson & E. Hayes (Eds.), *Handbook of adult and continuing education* (pp. 87–100). San Francisco: Jossey-Bass.

Tennant, M. (2006). *Psychology and adult learning* (3rd ed.). London: Routledge.

Tennant, M. (2012). *The learning self: Understanding the potential for transformation.* San Francisco: Jossey-Bass.

Terry, M. (2006). The importance of interpersonal relations in adult literacy programs. *Educational Research Quarterly, 30*(2), 31–44.

Thaker, S., N. (2007). Hinduism and learning. In S. B. Merriam (Ed.), *Non-Western perspectives on learning and knowing* (pp. 57–73). Malabar, FL: Krieger.

Tisdell, E. J. (1995). *Creating inclusive adult learning environments: Insights from multicultural education and feminist pedagogy information Series* (Vol. 361). Columbus, OH: ERIC Clearinghouse on Adult, Career, and Vocational Education, Center on Education and Training for Employment, College of Education, the Ohio State University.

Tisdell, E. J. (2003). *Exploring spirituality and culture in adult and higher education.* San Francisco: Jossey-Bass.

Tracey, W. R. (1992). *Designing training and development systems* (3rd ed.). New York: AMACOM.

Tyler, R. W. (1949). *Basic principles of curriculum and instruction.* Chicago: University of Chicago Press.

Ukens, L. L. (2001). *What smart trainers know: The secrets of success from the world's foremost experts.* San Francisco: Jossey-Bass/Pfeiffer.

Umble, K. E., Cervero, R. M., & Langone, C. A. (2001). Negotiating about power, frames, and continuing education: A case study in public health. *Adult Education Quarterly, 51*(2), 128–145. doi: 10.1177/07417130122087188

U.S. Department of Education. (October 26, 2009). *Cost allocation guide for state and local governments,* from http://www2.ed.gov/about/offices/list/ocfo/fipao/bluebookqas.html

Van Kavelaar, E. K. (1998). *Conducting training workshops: A crash course for beginners.* San Francisco: Jossey-Bass/Pfeiffer.

Velada, R., Caetano, A., Bates, R., & Holton, E. (2009). Learning transfer: Validation of the learning transfer system inventory in Portugal. *Journal of European Industrial Training, 33*(7), 635–656. doi: 10.1108/03090590910985390

Vella, J. K. (2000). *Taking learning to task: Creative strategies for teaching adults.* San Francisco: Jossey-Bass.

Vella, J. K. (2008). *On teaching and learning: Putting the principles and practices of dialogue education into action.* San Francisco: Jossey-Bass.

Vella, J. K., Berardinelli, P., & Burrow, J. (1998). *How do they know they know? Evaluating adult learning.* San Francisco: Jossey-Bass.

Viergever, M. (1999). Indigenous knowledge: An interpretation of views from indigenous peoples. In L. Semali & J. L. Kincheloe (Eds.), *What is indigenous knowledge? Voices from the academy* (pp. 333–343). New York: Falmer Press.

Walker, V., & Heard, E. (2011). Board governance. In D. R. Heyman (Ed.), *Nonprofit management 101: A complete and practical guide for leaders and professionals* (pp. 501–518). San Francisco: Jossey-Bass.

Walter, P. (2007). Activist forest monks, adult learning and the Buddhist environmental movement in Thailand. *International Journal of Lifelong Education, 26*(3), 329–345.

Wang, V. C. X. (2010). *Integrating adult learning and technologies for effective education strategic approaches.* Hershey, PA: Information Science Reference.

Warschauer, M., & Liaw, M. (2010). *Emerging technologies in adult literacy and language education.* Washington, DC: National Institute for Literacy.

Weissner, C. A., Sheared, V., Lari, P., Kucharczyk, S. Z., & Flowers, D. (2010). Creating and re-creating community. In C. E. Kasworm, A. D. Rose, & J. M. Ross-Gordon (Eds.), *Handbook of adult and continuing education* (pp. 431–440). Los Angeles: Sage.

Whetten, D. A., & Cameron, K. S. (2007). *Developing management skills* (7th ed.). Upper Saddle River, NJ: Pearson, Prentice Hall.

White, G. I., Sondhi, A. C., & Fried, D. (1997). *The analysis and use of financial statements* (2nd ed.). New York; Toronto: Wiley.

Wholey, J. S. (2010). Exploratory evaluation. In J. S. Wholey, H. P. Hatry, & K. E. Newcomer (Eds.), *Handbook of practical program evaluation* (3rd ed., pp. 81–99). San Francisco: Jossey-Bass.

Wholey, J. S., Hatry, H. P., & Newcomer, K. E. (2010). *Handbook of practical program evaluation* (3rd ed.). San Francisco: Jossey-Bass.

Wiggenhorn, A. W. (1996). Organization and management of training. In R. L. Craig (Ed.), *The ASTD training and development handbook: A guide to human resource development* (4th ed., pp. 19–48). New York: McGraw-Hill.

Wiggins, G. P. (1998). *Educative assessment: Designing assessments to inform and improve student performance.* San Francisco: Jossey-Bass.

Wilson, A. L., & Cervero, R. M. (1996a). Learning from practice: Learning to see what matters in program planning. In R. M. Cervero & A. L. Wilson (Eds.), What really matters in adult education program planning: Lessons in negotiating power and interests. *New Directions for Adult and Continuing Education, no. 69.* San Francisco: Jossey-Bass.

Wilson, A. L., & Cervero, R. M. (1996b). Paying attention to the people work when planning educational programs. In R. M. Cervero and A. L. Wilson (Eds.), What really matters in adult education program planning: Lessons in negotiating power and interests. *New Directions for Adult and Continuing Education, no. 69.* San Francisco: Jossey-Bass.

Wilson, A. L., & Hayes, E. (2000). *Handbook of adult and continuing education.* San Francisco: Jossey-Bass.

Winston, J. E. R., & Creamer, E. D. (1998). Staff supervision and professional development: An integrated approach. *New Directions for Student Services, 1998*(84), 29–42. doi: 10.1002/ss.8403

Winton, J., & Hochstadt, Z. (2011). Nonprofit marketing. In D. R. Heyman (Ed.), *Nonprofit management 101: A complete and practical guide for leaders and professionals* (pp. 409–427). San Francisco: Jossey-Bass.

Wlodkowski, R. J. (2008). *Enhancing adult motivation to learn: A comprehensive guide for teaching all adults* (3rd ed.). San Francisco: Jossey-Bass.

Woodard, D.B.J., & Von Destinon, M. (2000). Budgeting and fiscal management. In M. J. Barr & M. K. Desler (Eds.), *The handbook of student affairs administration* (2nd ed., pp. 327–346). San Francisco: Jossey-Bass.

Worthen, B. R., & Sanders, J. R. (1987). *Educational evaluation: Alternative approaches and practical guidelines.* White Plains, NY: Longman.

Yamnill, S., & McLean, G. N. (2001). Theories supporting transfer of training. *Human Resource Development Quarterly, 12*(2), 195–208. doi: 10.1002/hrdq.7

Yang, B. (1999). How effectively do you use power and influence? In M. L. Silberman & P. Philips (Eds.), *The 1999 training and performance sourcebook.* New York: McGraw-Hill.

Yang, B., & Cervero, R. M. (2001). Power and influence styles in programme planning: Relationship with organizational political contexts. *International Journal of Lifelong Education, 20*(4), 289–296. doi: 10.1080/026013701100048827

Yang, B., Cervero, R. M., Valentine, T., & Benson, J. (1998). Development and validation of an instrument to measure adult educators' power and influence tactics in program planning practice. *Adult Education Quarterly, 48*(4), 227–244. doi: 10.1177/074171369804800403

Yelon, S. L., & Ford, J. K. (1999). Pursuing a multidimensional view of transfer. *Performance Improvement Quarterly, 12*(3), 58–78. doi: 10.1111/j.1937–8327.1999.tb00138.x

Yudelson, J. (1999). Adapting McCarthy's four P's for the twenty-first century. *Journal of Marketing Education, 21*(1), 60–67. doi: 10:1177/027345399211008

Ziegahn, L. (2000). Adult education, communication, and the global context. In A. L. Wilson & E. Hayes (Eds.), *Handbook of adult and continuing education* (pp. 312–326). San Francisco: Jossey-Bass.

Name Index

411

Subject Index

e represents exercise or exhibit; f represents figure.

A

AAACE. *See* American Association of Adult and Continuing Education

Acoustical adjustments, 154

Action learning process, 263e

Action plans, of learners, 202

Action, program support and, 113

Action-based brainstorming, 265e

Active Learning Credo, 188

Active learning methods, 226–227

Ad hoc committees, 115

Ads, online, 328

Adult learning: context for, 190–191; foundational knowledge in, 52–56; need for learning transfer in, 211; principles of, as assumption of Interactive Model of Program Planning, 33; trends in, 379

Adult life, 137

Advisory committees: conducting meetings of, 120–121; in constructing program objectives, 169; description of, 115; power of, 115; purpose of, 116; refocusing of, 116–117; roles and responsibilities of, 117–118; selecting members of, 118–120; support from, 115–121

African Americans, 66

African culture, 17

African model of program planning, 12–13

Agendas, meeting, 120–121, 354e

American Association of Adult and Continuing Education (AAACE), 116–117

American Society for Training & Development (ASTD), 215

Annual conferences. *See* Conferences

Anxiety, of learners, 197

Application: complex nature of, 211–212, 218e; requirements of, 227

Apprenticeship, 262e

Arguments, 93

Artifacts, 141e

Artistic nature, of program planning, 12

Attendance, in programs, 108–109

Audio Visual (AV) equipment, 343–344, 354e

Audioconferencing, 264e

Augmented reality, 380

Auxiliary enterprises/sales, 297e

B

Bargaining, as power tactic, 92f

Basic Principles of Curriculum and Instruction (Tyler), xxiv

Bias, 189

Bidding process, 274–275

Blocking programs, 110–111

Blogs, 331e

Board meetings: budget responsibilities of, 284; conducting, 120–121

Board members: roles and responsibilities of, 117–118; selecting, 118–120

BoardSource, 117, 119

Brainstorming: as learning format, 265e; in values-based disagreements, 98–99

Branding, 320–322

Budget cuts, 114, 309e

Budgets: definition of, 286; guidelines for, 291–292; institutional regulations regarding, 290; management of, 291–296; models of, 287e, 288; overview of, 286; preparation of, 284–291, 306–308e; responsibilities related to, 283–284, 304; terminology related to, 286–288

C

Cancellation clauses, 346

Case for support, 299

CBPP. *See* Contingency-Based Program Planning

Cell phones, 75, 380

Change: factors overlooked when planning for, 8; in laws of power, 93; learning transfer and, 225–226; as outcome of education/training programs, 5–8, 21, 33; time allotted for, 8; types of, 6. *See also specific types of change*

Chief executive officers (CEOs), 118, 120

Civil rights movement, 66

Classroom format, 262e

Clinic format, 262e

Clubs, 263e

Coaching, 262e

Coalition building, 85–86

Code of ethics, 41–42

Cohort groups, 263e

Collaboration, to benefit novice planners, 31

Collaborative partnerships, 122

College enrollment, 61

Peace keeping, 94
Performance, 126
Performance objectives. *See* Learning objectives
Performance reviews: for collecting data, 246e; to generate ideas for programs, 142e
Performance self-efficacy (PSE), 225
Performance-outcome expectations (POE), 225
Pew Research Center, 326
Photography, 324–325
Planning, Programming, and Budget Systems (PPBS), 287e
Planning Responsibly for Adult Education: A Guide to Negotiating Power and Interests (Cervero & Wilson), xxiv
Planning table, 15; power in, 68–69; purpose of, 116
POE. *See* Performance-outcome expectations
Political climate, 87, 272
Political factors, 85–86
Portfolios, 196; for collecting data, 246e
Positive power, 67–68
Post-tests, 246e
Power: of advisory committees, 115; centrality of, in program planning, 68–70, 90–91; in civil rights movement, 66; definition of, 66–67, 76; examples of, 67; exercise for learning about, 78e; importance of, as assumption of Interactive Model of Program Planning, 34; influence of, in program planning, 90–91, 93–94; keeping the peace and, 94; laws of, 93; learning game of, 90; measurement of, 91–94; needs assessment and, 144; negative and positive uses of, 67–68; program supporters and, 110–111, 112; as structural factor, 86; women accessing sources of, 89
Power and Influence Tactics Scale (POINTS), 91–92
Powerful people, as knowledge sources, 88–89
PPBS. *See* Planning, Programming, and Budget Systems
Practitioner profiles, 17
Press releases, 353e
Pressuring, as power tactic, 92f
Pre-tests, 246e
Priority needs/ideas, 149
Priority rating charts, 151
Private-sector materials, 192
Process reflection, 56
Product packaging, 312
Product reviews: for collecting data, 246e; to generate ideas for programs, 142e
Program coordinators, 271
Program Development and Evaluation Resource Book for Trainers (Caffarella), xix
Program evaluations: call for, 232; data analysis for, 248, 250; data collection for, 244–248, 249–250e; decisions made from, 234e; definition of, 233–234; developmental approach for, 239–241; by external staff, 272; informal approach to, 241–243, 257e; Interactive Model's link to, 234–237; making judgments from, 250–253, 258e; overview of, 253; pitfalls of, 238–239; program objectives and, 169–170, 171e, 179e; systemic process for, 237–239, 255–256e; tasks of, 253–254; timing of, 237, 238e; types of, 243–244
Program evaluators, 270–271
Program goals: definition of, 161–162; description of, 174; to learning objectives, 183e; process of setting, 162–165, 174–175, 176–177e; program evaluation and, 236
Program locations, 313

Program objectives: as checkpoints, 172–174; constructing, 162–165, 168–172, 174–175, 178e; defining, 165–168; evaluating, 179e; to learning objectives, 183e; versus learning objectives, 182; overview of, 161–162; program evaluation and, 236, 239; updating of, 172, 180e
Program planners: assumptions related to, 35–36; careful language use by, 91; ethical practice of, 43–46; expectations of, 3–4; experiences of, 17–20; from external sources, 271–276; formal education of, 27; foundational knowledge of, 52–56; knowledge of, regarding diversity, 19–20; as learners, 35–36; novice versus experienced, 31–32, 47–48; overview of, 8–9; pressures of, 40; roles of, 23e, 68, 270–271; selection of, 276–277; technology use of, 71; use of power by, 90; varied work methods of, 35
Program planning: approaches to, 10–16, 26e; challenges of, 27; checklist for, 371–374e; circular nature of, 30; ethical decisions in, 40–46; experience of, xxiii–xxiv, 1–2; flexibility in, 31; future of, 374–382; importance of diversity in, 30, 58–59, 64; learning transfer and, 218e; numerous tasks and details of, 27–28, 31–32; people as central to, 30; power in, 68–70; practitioners' experiences in, 16–20; seminal works in, xxiv
Program Planning for Adult Learners (Caffarella), xix
Promotion, of program: choosing materials and tools for, 325–332, 336e; description of, 314, 325
PSE. *See* Performance self-efficacy
Public-sector materials, 192

Q

Qualitative data, for program evaluation, 248, 249–250e, 252
Qualitative methods: definition of, 150; for prioritizing ideas/needs, 151–152
Quantitative data, for program evaluation, 248, 249–250e
Quantitative methods: definition of, 150; for prioritizing ideas/needs, 151
Questionnaires, 140e

R

Rankings, 151
Real-world constraints, 11
Reconstitution phase, of contingency plan, 295e
Recovery phase, of contingency plan, 295e
References, checking, 274
Reflection-in-action method, 54
Reflection-on-action method, 54
Reflective practice: elements of, 56; framework for, 54
Registration numbers, 295
Relationship building: cultural competence in, 65–66; culture's influence on, 64–65; description of, 61–62, 76; with diverse women, 64–65; importance of, as assumption of Interactive Model of Program Planning, 34; Internet communication for, 125; nature of relationships in, 62–64
Religion. *See* Spirituality/religion
Rental facilities, 344–347, 361–362e
Request for Proposal (RFP), 274
Residential learning, 263e
Responsibility-centered budgeting, 287e
Return on Investment (ROI), 225
Revenue. *See* Income
Revising objectives, 172, 180e
Revising programs, 36
Room arrangement, 342–343